The Life and Teaching of Tukaram

The Life and Teaching of Tukaram

BY THE LATE

J. NELSON FRASER, M.A.

AND THE

REV. J. F. EDWARDS

GYAN

Published by

GYAN

Gyan Publishing House
5, Ansari Road
Daryaganj, New Delhi-110002
Phone: 011-47034999, 9811692060
E-mail: books@gyanbooks.com

Distribution Network
gyanbooks.com
India, USA, Canada, UK, Australia

ISBN: 978-81-212-5701-5 (PB)
First Published, 1922

2nd Impression 2024

Printed at: Gyan Press, Delhi.

THE LIFE AND TEACHING OF TUKARAM
Author: J. NELSON FRASER AND J. F. EDWARDS

THE LIFE AND TEACHING OF TUKĀRĀM

The Life and Teaching of Tukārām

BY THE LATE

J. NELSON FRASER, M.A.

Indian Education Department, Joint-Author of *The Poems of Tukārām*

AND THE

REV. J. F. EDWARDS

Author of *The Holy Spirit, The Christian Dynamic* and the Article on 'Tukārām' in Hastings' *Encyclopædia of Religion and Ethics*

PROBSTHAIN & CO.,
ORIENTAL BOOKSELLERS AND PUBLISHERS,
41 GT. RUSSELL ST., LONDON, W.C.1.

CHRISTIAN LITERATURE SOCIETY FOR INDIA
MADRAS ALLAHABAD CALCUTTA RANGOON COLOMBO
1922

TO THE

STUDENTS AND PUNDITS

OF THE LANGUAGE SCHOOL,

MAHĀBALESHWAR,

PAST, PRESENT AND FUTURE

PREFACE

This book was promised many years ago by the late Professor James Nelson Fraser, Principal of the Training College in Bombay for Teachers in Secondary Schools, who passed away after but a few days' illness on March 12, 1918,[1] and some eighty pages may be regarded as coming from his pen. They are distributed among the first eight chapters as follows. six pages in chapter I, five in chapter II, six in III, twenty-three in IV, seven in V, five in IV, six in VII, twenty in VIII and two in appendix II. These pages I have carefully worked over and rewritten in the light of the latest findings, but whenever possible I have allowed his material to stand unchanged. e.g., page 28, the first half of page 32, and the third paragraph on page 123 are almost exactly as I found them. His one desire was 'to add a brick to the fabric of oriental learning', as he wrote in a letter three years before his untimely death.

For the remainder of the book, over two hundred pages, including the whole of the last two chapters and appendices I, III-V, as well as the footnotes throughout the work, I must accept full responsibility. Often has it seemed as if the many claims of work in a city like Bombay would preclude the completion of the task, but the preparation of a great part of the book for lectures to the Language School at Mahābaleshwar has helped to make it possible, and I have been sustained by the two-fold conviction that study of India's poet-saints is a sure road to unity between East and West, and is a master-key to unlock the treasures of religious aspiration in the soul of India.

Numerous and generous have been my helpers, their generosity being indicated by the fact that some prefer to remain anonymous. Some obligations must, however, be discharged. My first Marāṭhī pandit, Mr. Krishnarao Vitthal Kandhālkar, rendered much assistance to Mr. Fraser, as he has done also to myself; Dr. Macnicol has not only secured the loan from the Association Press of the

[1] Mr. Fraser's collaborator in the three volumes of English translations, *The Poems of Tukārām* (published by the C. L. S., Madras at Rs 2-8 per vol.), was the late Rao Bahadur Kashināth Bālkrishna Marāṭhe, passed away eight months later on November 13, 1918.

block of Viṭhobā but has given invaluable counsel at different stages; the *Bhārata Itihāsa Sanshodhak Mandala* of Poona has kindly lent three other blocks; Mr. Vināyak Laxman Bhāve of Thana gave me a photograph of Santājī Telī Jaganāḍe's manuscript and rendered much other priceless help besides: Mr. W. H. Warren, formerly of the Cambridge University Press and now of the C. L. S., has carried through a difficult piece of work with unfailing courtesy; and last but not least, the Honourable Dr. Sir Nārāyan G. Chandāvarkar, after reading through the book in page-proof, has most generously found time to write a *Foreword* which in itself is a worthy contribution to English-Marāṭhī literature.

Should this work, despite its many imperfections, lead other investigators, Indian and non-Indian, further to explore the—as yet—largely-unworked gold-mine of the Marāṭhā Poet-Saints, I shall feel amply compensated.

BYCULLA, BOMBAY
December, 1921

J. F. EDWARDS.

CONTENTS

B

ILLUSTRATIONS

FOREWORD

Saint Tukārām has so deeply entered the soul of the people of Mahārāshtra that the attempt made by Mr. Edwards and the late Mr. Fraser in this book on the life, teachings and influence of this saint deserves to be cordially welcomed by those who work for India's good and greatness. In these days when more than ever before it has become necessary for the East and the West to grasp each other's hands in the spirit of brotherhood and promote the world's peace, we can only serve that end by finding the throbbings of that spirit in each country's poets and saints that have been. Of no country is that true more than of India; and of the poets who were also saints and who have more than anyone else striven to give her, and through her to the world, the best of thoughts and life, the poet-saints of Mahārāshtra appeal to us peculiarly by their directness and sturdiness of teaching and life. Dnyāneshwar, Nāmdev, Eknāth and last but not least of all, Tukārām, the subject of the following pages—to name but a few and those few who are familiar as household words in Mahārāshtra—are the glory of the Marāthā race; and of these Tukārām is the most popular.

Nearly sixty years ago the late Sir Alexander Grant,[1] then Principal of Elphinstone College, Bombay, read a paper on Tukārām as a poet of Mahārāshtra at a meeting of the Bombay Branch of the Royal Asiatic Society with a view to acquaint Europeans with the character of the saint's teachings. A few years later the late Rev. Dr. Murray Mitchell,[2] of the Free Church of Scotland, published a pamphlet, giving his (Dr. Mitchell's) view, from the Christian standpoint, of the religious principles taught by Tukārām and the influence his teachings had on his people. Both these attempts to interest Europeans and Americans in the saint's worth and work were but of a fragmentary character. Rev. Dr. Macnicol of Poona,[3] who has made it for years his life's mission to live and move among the people of the Mahārāshtra country and whose genuine sympathies for those people have endeared him to a large number of them, has brought more close to the European mind the beauty of Tukārām's saintliness by a sweet rendering into English verse of some of the hymns of the saint. These, read by the light of the Wilson Philological Lectures of the late Mr. W. B. Patwardhan, Principal, Fergusson College, Poona, delivered at the University of Bombay a few years ago, ought to go a great way

1 *See* pp. 165, 185, 190 of the present work.

2 *See* 'Authors' Index' for references in this book, especially Appendix III.

3 For references in this work *see* 'Authors' Index',

to instruct and interest Europeans and Americans in the character of the vast influence which Tukārām has exercized for nearly four hundred years over the masses of people in the Marāṭhā country. The present book by Mr. Edwards and Mr. Fraser is even a more valuable addition to the English literature on Tukārām, inasmuch as it goes more exhaustively into life and teachings of the saint, and analyses with care the different stages of Tukārām's religious faith and the spell he has held over the mind and heart of Mahārāshtra.

The Growth of the Soul of India

To understand Tukārām aright it is necessary, I venture to think, to trace the origin of the Devotional School of religion in India to which he belonged. That School was but a natural and necessary stage in the growth of the Soul of India, and its influence cannot be discerned in its true perspective unless we examine the conditions which gave it birth and led to its rise. Broadly viewed from the historic point the religious and social life of India, so far as its lines can be traced with distinctness, divides itself into four successive stages, viz., (1) the Age of the Vedas, (2) the Age of the Upanishads, (3) the Age of Buddha and Buddhism, and (4) the Age of the *bhakti* or Devotional School of which Tukārām stands as one of the most prominent members. But for the *Vedas* there would be no Upanishads; but for the Upanishads there would be no Buddha. These four stages are interdependent. Each led to the next and all the first three culminated in the *bhakti* or Devotional School.

The Vedic Ideal

The Vedic ideal of life, as we gather from the Vedas, so-called, and in particular the *Ṛig Veda*, may be said to have consisted, generally speaking, in the joyousness of life. The world to the Vedic age with all its mysteries and miseries was made for man to acquire wealth, enjoy life and make the best of this world's goods. Their prayer was, in the words of a Vedic hymn, 'Give me health, wealth, children and cattle.' To the question, who is the righteous man? the Vedas answered: 'He who is active, acquires wealth and then offers libations and performs sacrifices.' This view of life arose from what our Vedic ancestors in the infancy of their life saw of external Nature. Witnessing its operations they held that the universe was made by one Primordial Spirit whom they called Brahma the Creator, and who having created the universe made over its government to various gods, as his agents. Of Brahma, this primordial Spirit, they thought and said nothing beyond this, that he was the Creator, the Eternal, the truth, the only truth and reality that always exists. Man's direct concern—so they reasoned—is with the gods to whom Brahma has delegated the government of the world. In the operations of external Nature they witnessed regularity and fixed order of ceaseless activity. 'Why do not waters, seeking after truth, ever repose? Why does not the wind rest?' asks a hymn in the Vedas. So questioning they concluded that this ceaseless activity of the gods reigning in external Nature produced food and other means of life, happiness and enjoyment in this world for men. This moral law of order and activity the Vedas called *Rita*, the equivalent of which in English is 'the law of right', the principle of righteousness. The author of that law, according to the Vedas, is the god dwelling in and governing from the sky, 'the head' or brain of the primordial spirit Brahma. This Varuna, who laid down the law of *Rita* or right, is described in the Vedas as 'the righteous lord, who wields the supreme sceptre of universal sway. Both men and gods obey his law and the haughtiest yield to his decree'. Him therefore they regarded as the king of all kings among the gods whose ordinances are fixed and steadfast and who having laid down the law of *Rita*, has taken a vow, from which he has pledged himself never to depart but to abide by it unflinchingly. On that account and in that belief they called him *Dridha-Vrita*, 'firm vowed'. Further, the Vedas reasoned that Varuna's law being the law of *right*, and as it serves to give men food and other means of a life of happiness and enjoyment, men are bound to obey that law by following the example of external Nature as their teacher and like it leading a life of work and activity on the one hand and on the other acquiring as its result wealth which is the god Varuna's boon to all who observe his law of *Rita* or right with blind and unquestioning obedience. As we do not know more of this Varuna than that his law of *Rita* is a law of orderliness, prescribing work activity and enjoyment of the good things of this world, resulting from them, that is the only portion of *Truth* given for man to know and follow. *Satya* or truth, which is Brahma, is the root; *Rita*, right or righteousness, is its fruit. Of the root what can we know—it is behind the gods and therefore beyond our ken except that it bids us obey the law of *Rita*, or moral order governing the universe? Ours is merely to praise truth, and live in obedience to that law and work, enjoy and earn paradise after death by a life of cheer and work in this world. This law of *Rita*, which the Vedas discern in external Nature, calling man to a life of work, wealth, and enjoyment, is described in a hymn of the *Rig Veda*. Of that hymn and its discovery of the law of moral order in the universe operating as the law of righteousness the late Prof. Max Muller in his *Studies in Sanskrit Literature* has said that there is nothing like it in either Greek or Roman literature. Imperfectly conceived though it was by the Vedas, this law of *Rita* or moral order became for subsequent ages in India the starting point for the further quest of truth.

The Age of the Upanishads

The second stage of the Indian evolution of truth was the age of the Upanishads. If the Vedas defined Truth as Brahma the Creator, the only reality because the only imperishable life, that was, is, and shall be, incomprehensible to men, behind the law of *Rita* or righteousness reigning as moral order in the universe, the Upanishads turned from Nature outwards to the mind of man inwards. Adopting from the Vedas their doctrine that the law of *Rita* was the fruit, and Brahma, i.e., Truth, its root, they maintained that man was able to see that law in external Nature just and only because the Truth lay in his own soul dwelling in the secret cavity of his heart, and discernible there by his mind, as the eye of that soul. Therefore, while by no means contemning the gospel of an active life of work, wealth and enjoyment taught by the Vedas in obedience to the law of *Rita* as a portion of Truth, but on the other hand accepting that gospel as laying down a necessary law for man's life in this world, the Upanishads maintained that not Nature external but the soul of man is the Truth. To it, they declared, he must retire by contemplation to realize it in actual life. It is by meditation upon this indwelling soul, (said they) and not by mere works or acquisition of wealth or sacrifice of animals to gods, that man can know and do the the Truth. To the theory of the Vedas that behind the god Varuna, who laid down the law of *Rita* or moral order, there was one primordial spirit, the Creator of the whole Universe whom they called Brahma the Truth, but who they declared was beyond the comprehension of man, the Upanishads said that that primordial spirit was comprehensible, if not fully, at least sufficiently for life's purpose, by steady contemplation, because He dwells in every human heart as man's Soul. This teaching of the Upanishads that Truth means the Soul is best comprehended, if, from amidst all that they have said in a variety of ways on the subject, we turn to the homely conversation between the Indian sage Yajnyavalkya and his wife Maitreyi recorded in one of those ancient scriptures of India. Yajnyavalkya figures there as a householder, who, while leading a family life, served his country as its spiritual guide and also philosopher. Having grown old in that service and having felt that the evening of life was closing on him, he one day called his wife Maitreyi to his side and opened to her the cherished wish of his heart to give up home and country and society, now that he had done all he could to serve them, and to retire into the forests to lead there alone and by himself a life devoted to the contemplation of God until death parted him from this mortal existence. Yajnyavalkya, who had (so we gather from this story) trained his wife in the philosophy of the Soul as Truth, used that philosophy to win her consent to his wish. His reply to his wife contains the faith of the Upanishads: 'Know the Soul alone. Leave off all other talk.'

And he expanded that idea in his own words which may be paraphrased as follows: 'Maitreyi, my dearest, you are right when you tell me that we have loved each other as husband and wife. But have you thought over this question? What is that love, whence is it, and for what is it? When the husband loves the wife and the wife the husband, do you mean to say that the husband *qua* husband loves the wife *qua* wife and *vice versa*? If that were so, it could be no love at all. The relation of wife and husband is the relation of the Soul of the one to that of the other. So is it with all other human relations. They are schools for training us in Soul-Love and thereby going to the Soul of all Souls, viz. God. The Soul of each human being mixes with the Souls of others and forms the tie of those human relations which we call home, society, country, etc., because it is the bond which unites us all, makes us members of one another, and leads us by its passage of human love to Love Divine, which is God, the Over-Soul. It is our duty therefore, to win that Over-Soul by contemplation in solitude. And therefore, having trained my Soul by its human relations of home, etc., I have now arrived at a period of life when I should seek repose by lonely contemplation of the Soul of all Souls.' This soul-doctrine of the Upanishads, which they express through Yajnyavalkya, is the same that we find over and over again expounded by the poet Browning, and nowhere more lucidly expressed than in his *Cristina*:

> Ages past the soul existed,
> Here an age 'tis resting merely,
> And hence fleets again for ages,
> While the true end, sole and single,
> It stops here for is, this love-way,
> With some other soul to mingle.

The reader will detect in this doctrine of the Soul as Truth and comprehensible by contemplation and realizable by the human relations of husband and wife, parents and children, citizen and state, country and patriot, the humanistic motive, a tone of pragmatism, leading to the inference, that, in spite of the fact that the Upanishads emphasize in so many words that Truth is absolute because the Soul is absolute as being the same with Brahma, the Creator, the Over-Soul, the Upanishads deal with Truth as if it is not absolute, because there are passages in them to indicate that it is as relative as it is instrumental, as human as it is useful. That is the inference which the late Mr. Josiah Royce, the American philosopher of the Absolute, has drawn in writing about the enquiry of the Upanishads into the problem of Truth. The explanation of that seeming contradiction is that the authors of the Upanishads as successors of the age of the Vedas did not wish to break away from the past to which they had succeeded but, like all wise sages and reformers of their country, aimed at building upon that past and thereby improving it. The theory of Truth in the Vedas was humanistic and pragmatic, inasmuch as that was Truth for them which proved useful in human life as preserving that life and rendering it stable by winning success, as the world ordinarily understands it. The Upanishads did not oppose that theory; they proclaimed that the humanistic and pragmatic motive of Truth gave only a partial view of it, and that, if man would but turn to his Soul within by contemplation, he should find that Truth transcended the limits imposed by that motive and had its birth and source in the Absolute, of which the Soul was the best expression. Therefore, they laid stress on contemplation as the highest means of realizing by degrees Truth as Soul Force and and defined Truth as the Soul. They taught that to know the Soul as Truth by meditation is not only a form of worship but it is real worship.

Buddha's Gospel of Nirvana

But, notwithstanding the teaching of the Upanishads, the people of India continued, generally speaking, to be dominated by the humanistic motive of Truth. The acquisition of riches and material comforts, the pursuit of life for enjoyment, the killing of animals as sacrifices to the gods for the purpose of winning their favour and securing health, wealth, and happiness in this world and the next, went on as during the Vedic age. That rush for life figured side by side with suffering and misery. This led Buddha to preach his gospel of *Nirvāṇa* or renunciation. He did not condemn either the Vedas or the Upanishads for their respective interpretations of Truth. But he denounced the killing of animals for sacrifices as sinful. Hence his doctrine of *Ahimsā* (abstention from injury) to all creatures as the highest religion. He did not differ from the Upanishads as to the great value of *contemplation*. Rather, he accepted it and emphasized its necessity, but he discerned that the contemplation doctrine of the Upanishads, which taught men to realize Truth by meditation of the Soul, because the Soul was Truth, only led to the creation of an intellectual aristocracy in India, divorcing it in point of fellow-feeling from the masses, and did not serve to lift from off their lives the oppressive burden of misery and sin which lay heavily on them and made this world a scene of woe. Of what use is it to ask people to realize Truth in the Soul by contemplation so long as the passions and appetites of the body make a brute of him, lead him to the infliction of suffering on himself and others and to sacrifice animals to gratify his tastes and pacify the gods in the name of religion? So reasoning, Buddha put his greatest emphasis on the body of man as man's enemy. He preached: 'Overcome the body; extinguish its burning lusts that consume man.' And both by precept and his own example he proclaimed his gospel of *Nirvāṇa*, basing it upon his view of the world that 'all is void'. By *Nirvāṇa*, literally meaning extinction of self, he understood as explained by Buddhistic scholars, not the extinction of the Soul but the expulsion of the craving of carnal appetites and of the three passions of lust, hatred, and delusion. And how according to Buddha is the self to be so extinguished? His answer was by contemplation leading to kind deeds and compassion for all creatures in all the details of practical life. That he called *Ahimsā*, which, meaning literally abstention from injury, he explained as cultivation of 'good-will to all beings without measure, unhindered love and friendliness towards the whole world, above, below, around' (Rhys David's Lectures on *The Origin and Growth of Religion*, p. 111). All this, he maintained, must be attained by the extinction of the carnal appetites. That is *Nirvāṇa*. That, then, was Truth for Buddha—there is no other truth that man can know and realize.

India's Devotional School

This definition of Truth as *Nirvāṇa* or extinction of the self was bound to fail to make Buddhism the people's cult in India. If the Upanishad conception of Truth as the Soul, realizable by contemplation was too intellectual for the masses, Buddha's conception of it was too rigid, ascetic, and cold for them. Buddhism after having for some hundreds of years prevailed mainly because of its democratic character—its sympathy for all and its protest against caste—was driven out by Śrī Śankarācārya, the greatest apostle of Hinduism known to India. It had done its best work; it had brought the killing of animals as sacrifice and for food into disrepute; it had made people love peace and hate war; it had popularized the principles of meekness and charity. But the masses felt that Buddhism was a negative creed—it taught extinction of the self without putting in man anything positive instead. Śrī Śankarācārya professed himself a follower of the devotional school of religion which had begun to rise in India before his birth. The country had produced saints previously who had appealed to the masses more feelingly than other schools because they taught the doctrine of God as Truth, and Truth as Love for all without distinction of caste for creed. These saints came after Śankarā from all castes and creeds, even from the lowest castes, which to this day are despised by the higher castes as untouchable and unapproachable and subjected to utter social degradation. These saints took up the problem of Truth where Buddha had left it and improved upon it and also the Vedic and Upanishad conception of it. They accepted the view of the four Vedas that life should be one of activity and enjoyment but they counselled moderation of enjoyment. They praised family life and looked askance at asceticism which abandoned the world. They differed from the Vedas which said that God is as incomprehensible as Truth. Agreeing with the Upanishads they held that truth was in man's Soul; but that mere contemplation was not enough to realize that truth for man, God being Love and that Love shining in the Soul it should lead to deeds of peace, forgiveness, and mercy; Where these are, there only is God the Truth.' That sums up their creed in essence. Then as to Buddha, the saints accepted his gospel of *Ahimsā* (abstention from injury); also his condemnation of caste; but they ruled out his theory of the body as the enemy of man as impracticable for the very purpose of the human-hearted and universal love and good-will to all without measure, which he had preached and practised.

Their teachings on this head may be put in some such language as this; 'You, Buddha, start by holding the body as man's enemy because of its passions and you ask man to extinguish them first by contemplation and then by good deeds of love to all without measure. But how can man contemplate and do deeds of love, mercy and good-will without his body? Those who seek to find salvation by merely burning their passions in the fire of contemplation are like a man who walks on the shelterless, slippery and sundered edge of a mountain precipice. Those who again seek to burn them in that fire by contemplation of something vague and indefinable such as your *Nirvāna* are like an unmarried woman, seeking salvation by doing *Satī*, i.e., burning herself in the pyre of an imaginary husband to find salvation. You say the body is man's enemy because of its passions and that therefore the passions must be expelled. That you call *Nirvāna*. But if the passions are our enemies, are they not also our friends? Is it not because of our passions turned to good thoughts and thereby to good deeds that we are able to do what you, Buddha, enjoin, viz., a life of benevolence and love to all? The germ of these thoughts and deeds which is in man's self—whence is it? It must be from some higher self. Look at the river. It comes from the springs in mountains formed by the rain water from the sea, flows outside, fertilizes fields and serves men, and at last joins the great Ocean from whence it had taken its birth in the springs. Similar is the case of man's Self called the Soul encased in his body. Turn that Soul to its source—have God as Truth as your goal—run your life's course with that goal always in view and that is real *Nirvāṇa*. That alone is Peace. What is peace but doing good to all, even those that have done evil to you? But such peace can become accessible to all, high or low, only if they yoke the Soul to the Over-Soul by love to Him and through Him to all His creatures.'

Reasoning in this manner and borrowing the best and discarding the rest from the Vedas, the Upanishads, and Buddha, the saints of India, gave her and the world the following definition of Truth: 'Truth is *sama darshana*', i.e., 'Truth is loving others as thy own self.' Because *Rita*, the law of righteousness discovered by the Vedas first, flowed from Brahma as Truth, the Saints identified *Rita* with Truth and called falsehood *Anrita*, that which is not *Rita*. Because the Upanishads defined Truth as the Soul, residing in man's heart, they held that it is the Soul which binds us all through the Over-Soul, God, and therefore is the seat of Love. Hence Truth is Love.

Saints and Scriptures of Maharashtra

This definition of Truth as *Love of others as thy own self* is given in the *Bhāgavat Purāṇa* which is universally regarded as the standard authority of the devotional school second only to the *Bhagavadgītā* or the Celestial Song, worshipped as India's New Testament. In fact the former is in substance a rendition of the latter. The *Bhagavadgītā* nowhere defines it. But in so many words *truth* as the *Bhāgavat Purāṇa* defines it. But in several places it expressedly declares that he is the highest *Yogi* (man of contemplation and action) who looks upon and treats others as his own self. Taking up that teaching, Dnyāneshwar, the premier saint of Mahārāshtra, to whom all succeeding saints thereof, including Tukārām, owed a good deal of their religion, and who is regarded as the progenitor of Marāthā nationality, which culminated in the great Śivājī's Marātha Empire, declared that there is no acquisition equal to that of *Samya*, i.e., the power of regarding others and treating them as your own self. If we interpret that by the light of the texts in the Upanishads and the books of our Saints, which say that there is nothing higher than or even equal to Truth, we come to the same idea of Truth as that defined in the *Bhāgavat Purāṇa*. That is made clear beyond doubt by *Śivājī*'s spiritual adviser, Saint Rāmdās, who defined Truth in the Marāthī language of Western India as *Ananyapaṇā*, i.e., 'the condition of loving others as thy own self'. These Saints reverenced the Vedas and the Upanishads but they declared that those scriptures were *partial* to the three twice-born castes and neglected women and the lowest fourth caste called *Śudra* or servile, consisting of persons whose lot it was to serve the former, remain in ignorance, and live a life of servility. The Marāṭhā Saint, Dnyāneshwar, himself a Brāhman, who lived in the thirteenth century after Christ, says in his poetic gloss on the *Bhagavadgītā* which preaches the doctrine of devotion to God as the highest and the easiest way to salvation because it is open to all, not merely to the twice-born but to women and *Śudras* as well: 'The *Bhagavadgītā* is but the Vedas transformed into liberality. Therefore, it is superior to the Vedas. True, the Veda is wealthy; but there is no miser like him and that because he whispered his doctrines into the ears of the three twice-born castes only. And then he sat quiet, pretending he had no time to communicate his secret to people, like women and *Śudras*, who are distressed by the pain and the miseries of this life and its cares. But, methinks, that, as time wore on, the Veda's conscience pricked him and exposed to him his own littleness. Therefore, feeling that he should cast it off and acquire true glory, he proclaimed himself to all classes and castes even to women and *Śudras* without distinction. So he, the Veda, took the form of the *Bhagavadgītā* and brought salvation to all.' These Saints further taught that the golden age for India is not in the past but in the present and the future. The *Bhāgavat Purāna* distinctly praises the present and future as superior to the past, because of the doctrine of equality of all castes and of women and men, held up as their hope by the gospel of truth defined as love of others as one's own self. For instance the Marātha Saint Tukārām sang in that strain and proclaimed: 'The fulness of salvation has come for all. Its market is free. Come one, come all, partake of it with rejoicing. Here there is no distinction of caste, high or low, man or woman, Brāhman or *Śudra*.' What does it mean but that the age of Truth was not that of the Vedas, or of the Upanishads, or of Buddha, but that of the Saints who held that Truth means not mere truth-telling but the practical regulation of life by deeds of love to all as one's own self turned to God as Truth and therefore Love. These Saints who so defined Truth were not dreaming optimists. Their teachings abound with counsel that in this world we should enjoy life by work, rest and sobriety of enjoyment and attain to Truth by stages of steady, persevering, continuous practice in the art of contemplation and deeds of love. Man, they said, cannot like a bird fly up and at once pluck a fruit hanging on a branch of a tree. He must climb up to the fruit by steady steps. By such practice (they said) man can conquer Nature—he can cross mountains, navigate rivers, bridge distances of space and time and even learn to fly in the air. Here in this declaration the Saints anticipated and by necessary implication paid a tribute of respect to and admiration for man's discoveries, such as the telegraph, the aeroplane and all those arts of life of modern civilization which some condemn as materialistic. They took 'the forward view of life' (to use an expression which Meredith has made familiar to us); to them 'the golden age' is not the Past but the Future. Far from sharing the popular belief which has prevailed for centuries in India that the present Age is the Age of *Kali*, of decay and degeneration, they hold that this is the best Age, because it has made God accessible to all and opened the gate of life to even the most degraded and sinful. This optimistic faith finds its most terse expression in Tukārām; and—to use the words of one of his most inspiring hymns: 'Who dare disregard the devotee of God who holds by that faith unflinchingly?'

N. G. CHANDAVARKAR.

ABBREVIATIONS USED

B. G. *Bombay Gazetteer*, Bombay, 1885.

E. R. E. *Encyclopaedia of Religion and Ethics*, vols. i–xii, Edinburgh, edited by Dr. Hastings, 1908–21.

F. and M. Fraser and Marāṭhe's *Poems of Tukārām*, 3 vols. Madras, 1909–15.

F. C. M. *Fergusson College Magazine*, Poona, 1910–21.

H. M. P. *History of the Marāthā People*, vol. i, by Kincaid and Parasnis, Bombay, 1918.

I. I. *Indian Interpreter*, a Quarterly Magazine, Madras, 1906–21. C. L. S.

I. P. *Indu Prakāsh* edition of Tukārām's Poems in Marāṭhi, Bombay, 1869.

I. R. M. *International Review of Missions*, a Monthly Magazine, London, 1911–21.

J. R. A. S. Bo. *Journal of the Royal Asiatic Society, Bombay Branch*.

M. Mahīpati, Tukārām's Biographer. *See* pp. 69 ff.

M. Sar. *Mahārāshtra Sāraswat* (History of Marāthī Literature, From its beginnings to 1818), a Marāthi work by V. L. Bhāve, Poona, 1919,

M. W. Marāṭhī Writings and Lectures of Dr. Sir R. G. Bhandārkar, a Marāṭhi work edited by D. G. Vaidya, with Life of Dr. Bhandārkar by Sir. N. G. Chandāvarkar, Bombay, 1919.

O. R. L. I. *Outline of the Religious Literature of India* Dr. J. N. Farquhar, London, 1919.

P. M. S. *Psalms of Marāṭhā Saints*, Dr. N. Macnicol, Calcutta, 1919.

S. T. C. *Śrī Tukārāmāce Caritra* (Life of Tukārām in Marāthī), Mr. L. R. Pāngārkar, Poona, 1920.

V. S. M. R. S. *Vaishnavism, Śaivism and Minor Religious Systems*, Dr. Sir R. G. Bhandārkar, vol. iii, part 6 in the *Grundriss, or Encyclopedia of Indo-Aryan Research*, Strassburg, 1913.

CORRIGENDA

Page 6 line 3 *for* eldest *read* youngest and posthumous
„ 6 „ 43 *for* 1650 *read* 1650 (but see p. 77)
„ 9 „ 33 *for* Apte in *read* Āpte and Mr. V. W. Bhide in
„ 18 „ 13 (and 31) *for* 1650 *read* 1650 (but see p. 77)
„ 20 „ 36 *for* Mahīpatī *read* Mahīpati
„ 21 „ 4 (and 10) *for* Mahīpatī *read* Mahīpati
„ 21 „ 12 *for* Nabaji *read* Nābhājī
„ 27 „ 9 *for* *Bhagavadgītā* *read* Mahābhārata
„ 29 „ 10 *for* September, 1919 *read* Feb. 1, 1920
„ „ „ 18 *for* *Purāna* read *Purṇa* (full)
„ „ „ 18 *for* *Āmcā* read *Amsha* (partial)
„ 30 „ 30 *for* Veda *read* Vedas
„ 40 „ 44 *for* Vithobā, *read* Viṭhobā.'[2]
„ 40 footnote 1 *for* [1] G.R. Navalkar, etc. *read* [1] *Rise of th Marāthā Power*, pp. 9–11.
[2] G R. Navalkar, etc.
„ 42 line 31 *for Mhanoni read Mhaṇoni*
„ 49 footnote 4 *for* para. 1 *read* para. 2
„ 50 footnote 1 *for* Chap. 8 *read* Chap. 5.
„ „ „ 1 *for* under 2 *read* under 4
„ 51 line 35 *for* para. 11 *read* para. 10
„ 55 „ 27 *for* section 6 *read* section 7
„ „ „ 28 *for* 7 *read* 8,
„ 76 „ 35 *for* *māntra* read *mantra*
„ 87 „ 32 *for* beads *read* garland
„ 98 „ 44 *for* chapter 6, section 9, *read* chap. x, p. 265
„ 99 „ 29 *for* him. *read* him'.[5]
„ 99 footnote 6 *for* part II, sect. 3 *read* pp. 123–5.
„ 105 line 33 *for* Kelūskar *read* Kelūskar
„ 137 „ 11 *for* brings *read* brings'
„ 143 „ 21 *for* viii. 3 *read* viii. 2
„ 150 footnote 4 *for* 152–3 *read* 155–6
„ 159 line 42 *for* 1227 *read* 1727
„ 174 „ 11 *for* Part II *read* pp. 188–9
„ 177 headline *for* II *read* VII
„ 188 line 37 *for* 218–9 *read* 216–7
„ 194 „ 16 *for* 225–7 *read* 223–5
„ 195 „ 20 *for* 218–9 *read* 216–7
„ 216 „ 35 *for* 227, 230 *read* 225, 228
„ 244 „ 8 *for* Prabhākarrao ; *read* Prabhākarrao's
„ 278 „ 10 *for* place *read* places
„ 282 „ 32 *for* resemblances *read* resemblance
„ 296 „ 8 *for* letters *read* titles
298 „ 25 *for* 75 *read* 76

System of Transliteration

अ a, आ ā, इ i, ई ī, उ u, ऊ ū, ऋ ṛ, ए e, ऐ ai, ओ o, औ au, क k, ख kh, ग g, घ gh, ङ ṅ; च c, छ ch, ज j, झ jh, ञ ñ; ट ṭ, ठ ṭh, ड ḍ, ढ ḍh, ण ṇ; त t, थ th, द d, ध dh, न n; प p, फ ph, ब b, भ bh, म m; य y, र r, ल l, व v, श ś, ष ṣ, स s, ह h, ळ ḷ.

'Abhang': Definition and method of quotation.

Abhaṅg is the Marāṭhī word for hymn or lyrical poem. *Abhaṅgs* have peculiar metres of their own, and rhyme and divide their verses irregularly, the last couplet opening usually with the author's name, e.g., 'Tukā says.' *Abhaṅgs* may be limited to two or four lines, or they may have as many as thirty, and even more.

Whenever, in this book, *abhaṅgs* are quoted with merely a number following in brackets, e.g., on p. 135 where half a dozen are thus referred to, the reference is always to Fraser and Marāṭhe's English translations, *The Poems of Tukārām*, 3 vols.

THE GREAT HEARTED

Who day and night are from all passion free—
Within their holy hearts I love to be,
Dwelling in sanctity

They bathe in Wisdom, then their hunger stay
With Perfectness, lo, all in green array,
The leaves of Peace are they.

With pearls of Peace their limbs they beautify;
Within their minds as in a scabbard I,
The All-Indweller, lie

Therefore their love waxes unceasingly—
These greatsouled ones; not the least rift can be
Between their hearts and me

Translated from Dnyāneshwar (13th Century)
P M. S. p. 35

'O HASTE AND COME'

Dost thou behold me perishing?
O haste and come, my God and king.

I die unless thou succour bring
O haste and come, my God and king.

To help me is a trifling thing,
Yet thou must haste, my God and king.

O come (how Nāma's clamours ring)
O haste and come, my God and king

Translated from Nāmdev (14th Century)
P M. S. p. 43.

RELIGIOUS UNREALITY

Ah, he speaks the words of heaven
With a heart to murder given—
Loudly praise to God he sings,
But his soul to lucre clings—
Tukā says—A wretch so base—
Smite him, slap him on the face!

Translated from Tukārām (1608-49) by Dr. J. Murray Mitchell,
The Indian Antiquary, March, 1882, p. 61.

Chapter I

The Land and People of Tukaram

1. Maharashtra

THE land of Tukārām is that region of Western India which bears the ancient name of Mahārāshtra. By old tradition it comprises the Western Deccan, from Nāśik and Poona to Satāra and Kolhapur. 'In shape a triangle, its base is the sea from Daman to Karwar, the perpendicular side a line running from Daman beyond Nagpur, the hypotenuse an irregular line from beyond Nagpur to Karwar. The area of this tract is over 100,000 square miles and its population exceeds thirty millions.'[1] Speaking quite strictly, it does not include the country below the Ghāts, the Konkaṇ. The people of the latter speak the language of Mahārāshtra and its history has at times been closely connected with that of the table-land above the Ghāts, but it probably witnessed no part of Tukārām's life and we need give little thought to it here. It is a country of flat rice-fields with groves of trees here and there and straggling villages beneath their shade. The whole year is hot and moist and for several months everything is drenched in rain. Above the Ghāṭs we are in a different world. The sea disappears from our thoughts; all round us on every hand stretches the Deccan plain. Sometimes it is perfectly flat and treeless, but more often it rises and falls in gentle undulations and it is seldom that hills or mountains are not seen rising in the distance. Tukārām's home was not very far from the edge of the table-land and the Ghāts themselves. A few miles from Dehū, his birthplace, the cultivated fields run up to the mountains and quite close to the village there are solitary hills. Trees are not wanting, the thorny *bābhal* on the waste land and mangoes near the village being cultivated for their shade and their much-appreciated fruit. When the fields are green with crops the whole scene is pleasant to a visitor's eye, and the contrast of mountain and plain is stimulating. The air too is fresh and pure and the visitor for a moment may easily dream that he has lighted on one of the happiest retreats on earth.

The dream, however, would be dispelled by reflection. The Deccan soil for the most part is poor, the rain is uncertain, and scarcity of food has always been a recurring incident in men's lives. The extreme heat and the extreme cold are both trying, and the plagues of tropical life, fever, guinea-worm and so forth, molest the people of Mahārāshtra as much as others.

[1] *H.M.P.*, p. 1

The people inhabiting Mahārāshtra had no early history of importance. On the sea-coast arose prosperous ports, like Kalyān, but inland there was no seat of empire till the bounds of Mahārāshtra were passed. We must think of the early Marāṭhās as a village people leading hard industrious lives and waiting for a later hour to summon them to take part in history.

2. The Maharashtriyans or Marathas

Who were the Marāthās? In Asoka's inscriptions the people of the Western Deccan are called Rāthikās (Sanskrit *Rāshtrika*). Soon after his time they passed under the Āndhras, a 'Dravidian' people of Southern India who ruled the peninsula from sea to sea till the third century after Christ. These were followed in time by various 'Rajput' kings, of whose origin we know nothing. One of their dynasties, the Rāshtrakūtas, ruled at Nāśik, and lasted till the Muhammadan invasions. It is tempting, of course, to connect this name with that of Mahārāshtra, but all that is certain about the latter is that it came into general use after the invasions; how much older it was we do not know.

Kincaid and Parasnis, in their *History of the Marāthā People*, have shown that far back in the early history of Western India, Mahārāshtra bore the name of Dandakāranya or the Daṇḍaka Forest. Indeed, even still, whenever Marāthī-speaking Brāhmans in their religious sacrifices refer to the country, they do not call it Mahārāshtra but Dandakāranya. How then did Dandakāranya come to be called Mahārāshtra? Its inhabitants maintain that Mahārāshtra means the great country, while Mr. Molesworth, the well-known Marāthī scholar, hints that the name may mean the country of the Mahārs, but there are sufficient grounds for rejecting this view. The Mahārs are not a people but are merely a debased section, and their name is a corruption of the word *Mrityuhar* or 'remover of the dead'. Surely from so abject a community no country would take its name. Moreover, the words *Mrityuhar Rāshtra* could not, according to the ordinary laws of linguistic corruption, become the name Mahārāshtra. Instead of armies, Asoka sent forth in every direction ministers of religion to teach the principles of Buddha. These missions are recorded in inscriptions carved on rocks all over Northern India, and on no less than four of those still surviving Asoka states 'that he had sent missionaries to the Rāstikas. These Rāstikas or Rāshtrikas were the dwellers in the Dandaka Forest. Proud of their independence, or for some kindred reason, they came in later years to call themselves Mahārāshtrikas, and so the country which they occupied came to be known as Mahārāshtra and its people as Marāṭhās'.[1] In Mr. Rajwade's

[1] *H. M. P.*, pp. 4-7

Mahārāshtrāchā Vasāhat Kāl (the colonization of Mahārāshtra) the position is laid down that Mahārāshtra comes from Rāshtrikas, *i e.*, the leading men of the Rāshtra, or country, and that the word Mahārāshtrikas refers to chiefs among the leading men.

3. The Shaka Era of A. D. 78

Following on the Buddhist Empire which terminated in 185 B C. after the death of Asoka, 'the Āndhra kings' who were formerly vassals of the Buddhist Emperors overran the whole of Mahārāshtra and remained in power for about three centuries, their dominance receiving a check at the hands of a tribe named the Shakas, or Scythians, who gave their name to the Shaka era by which legal and religious documents of Hindus in N. and S. India are dated. The Shaka era began seventy-eight years later than the Christian, and Kincaid and Parasnis point out, relying on the 'surmises' of Dr. R.G. Bhandarkar in his *Ancient History of the Deccan*, that 'the resemblance between the word Shaka and the Shaka era . . . could hardly be fortuitous. Now if the Shaka era was founded by the Shakas, they did it in all probability to celebrate some great achievement. Thus the Shakas probably conquered the Deccan when the Shaka era began, that is to say in A.D. 78. . . . These foreign kings did not long vex Mahārāshtra . . . Before A.D. 150 Shaka rule in Mahārāshtra had vanished. . . . In A.D. 78 the Shaka chief forced his way either through the Vindhyas or along the Konkaṇ sea-board. For some fifty years he and his descendants occupied Mahārāshtra'.[1] It seems unlikely that an era of '*foreign* kings' should have been used for religious purposes in so ancient a religion as the Hinduism of Mahārāshtra especially when that 'foreign' rule was only fifty years in duration. This same view, however, is held by Sir J. F. Fleet who pronounces as 'fiction' the popular belief that the Shaka era was founded by a King Shālivāhan who reigned A. D. 78 at Pratishthāna the modern Paithan on the Godāveri.[2]

4. The Marathi Language

The language of the Marāthās has been classified by science as 'Aryan'. But no one has really enquired how much it has in common with the tongue of the Rig Veda, and the view may be hazarded that its non-Aryan elements are large and significant. Mr. V. L. Bhawe believes it to be extremely probable that there must have been a kind of mutual influence and admixture of the language of the highly intellectual Aryans and of the language

[1] *H. M. P.*, p. 10

[2] *E. R E*, Vol. xi. p. 96, also *Encyclopædia Britannica* (11th edition), Vol. xiii. pp. 497–8.

spoken by the aboriginal dwellers in Mahārāshtra, that the language thus formed was called 'Mahārāshtrī' and that from this has arisen the language known to-day as 'Mahārāshtrī' or 'Marāthī' or 'Deshī'.[1]

On this subject Professor Patwardhan observes in his *Wilson Philological Lectures:* 'There is hardly anything of a reliable character established beyond the possibility of question or controversy as regards the time and date of the makers of Marāthī and Marāṭhī Literature. . . . Nothing is definitely known, it must be admitted at the outset, as regards the origin of the Marāthās and Marāthī. Mahārāshtra and Mahārāshtrī are very old words indeed. . . . Mahārāshtrī was a current language in the days of Vararuchī . . . . Vararuchī wrote . . . . about 380 years before Christ. In that case . . . . the word Mahārāshtrī is as old as 388 B.C. if not older still . . . . From the third century B.C. to the tenth century A.D. the literary history of Mahārāshtra is yet to be written. With the exception of few literary remains we have practically no material to hand to bridge the gulf. And yet it appears, on the face of it, improbable that there was no literature. For the literature of a people rises or falls according as the people themselves rise or fall. . . . That Marāṭhī in its Marāṭhī form has come from Mahārāshtrī, is only a developed form of Mahārāshtrī, is generally admitted, and may be clear to any one who compares the vocabulary of Marāṭhī with that of Mahārāshtrī and especially certain pronominal forms, indeclinables, verbal roots, in the two. But when exactly the Marāṭhī forms, Marāthī idiom, and Marāthī words sprang into being from the original Mahārāshtrī it is difficult to say. There are, I understand, only four or five inscriptions wherein Marāṭhī forms of words and Marāthī structure of sentences can be identified. But nothing of a literary character that belongs to the period before the tenth century after Christ has so far been discovered.'[2]

Closely connected with this question of philology, and illustrating the early beginnings of the Marāṭhī language, is a legend given by Kincaid and Parasnis which shows the Āndhra period to have been one not only of military and mercantile, but also of literary, activity. A certain ghost named Kānābhūti brought to one Gunādhya, a minister of King Shālivāhan, seven volumes of stories all written in blood. Gunāḍhya accepted these and offered them as a gift to his royal master. Disgusted with the strange language and the stranger script, King Shālivāhan returned the books to his minister who, furious at the failure of his present, burnt six of the seven volumes. The remaining volume fell into the hands of Gunādhya's pupils or clerks who being acquainted with the ghost language pronounced the book charming. When

[1] See V. L. Bhawe, *M. Sār*, p. 8

[2] W. B. Patwardhan, *F. C. M.*, Vol viii, No. 3, Dec. 1917, pp. 104-110

THE VIEW FROM DEHŪ, TUKĀRĀM'S BIRTHPLACE

their verdict came to Shālivāhan's ear he made a further effort to read Kāṇābhūti's stories, and once he had mastered the difficulties of Kāṇābhūti's literary medium he was as charmed with the tales as Guṇāḍhya's pupils. It seems probable that the ghost language of Kāṇābhūti was the Mahārāshtrī dialect, born of the efforts of the Rāshtrikas to speak Sanskrit, and that the reign of Shālivāhan, that is, the period when the Āndhra kings held sway, first saw the use for literary purposes of that 'vigorous, supple, graceful and copious tongue' which we call Marāthī.

5. Dehu, Tukaram's Village: Past and Present

The village life of the Deccan has changed in some details during British rule but the present is still so much like the past that thoughtful observers can easily recall the latter as it was in Tukārām's day. To do something of the kind let us go to Dehū, the poet's birthplace on the right and south bank of the Indrāyaṇī, a large stream flowing into the Bhīma. In the rains this stream is broad and rapid; in the dry weather it is little more than a chain of pools with a rill of turbid water sometimes connecting them, sometimes vanishing in its pebbly bed. Round the village are still visible fragments of the old wall, emerging from thickets of prickly pear. Within it the houses, of bricks or mud, stand thickly crowded together. There is only one passage that can be called a street. Here are a few shops that deal in grain or cloth but they are not the only centres of trade in the village, for on market days a bāzār is opened under the peepal tree and various products are exchanged. One of the changes since Tukārām's day is probably the greater importance of the shopkeeper and the diminished importance of the bāzār. The ruinous, uncared-for appearance of the village probably recalls his own time. Nothing in India is ever repaired; and the houses in an Indian village, like the trees in the jungle, run their natural course from youth to age and death without interference from man. If this fills the village with eyesores nobody much minds them, any more than people mind the boulders in the unpaved, unlevelled pathways or the smells of an age preceding sanitation.

Accessible to the modern sightseer, Tukārām's birthplace is situated three miles from the Bombay-Poona trunk road at the very end of a country lane branching off from the former near the 98th milestone from Bombay and the 15th from Poona, less than ten minutes' walk from Shelarvādi railway station. When we visited the village on October 25, 1920 the motor-car took us right up to the walls of Vithobā's temple overlooking the Indrāyanī. An expert on anthropological research in Hinduism has laid down the following golden rules on visiting Hindu temples: 'You must have a pair of holeless stockings, some knowledge of the vernacular and charming manners; armed with these, you can enter anywhere. . . . Even if it is not absolutely necessary, take your shoes off; that is an outward and visible sign which any Indian can read that you are visiting the temple in a spirit of sympathy. Explain to the priest exactly what you want to see, and if you are writing a book, tell him so.'[1] By a stroke of good fortune the first priest we met was the leading *Gosāvī*[2] among Tukārām's direct descendants who number some 250 out of Dehū's present population of 1722. The great pride with which everything relating to the 17th century poet-saint is preserved and explained was at once manifest. In at least three directions, indeed, this natural pride goes to an extreme against which we have little doubt Tukārām would have made his remonstrance, *viz.*, worship of himself, polytheism, and caste-prejudice, though we shall see later how often our *bhakti* poet 'limped between two opinions'. To-day, despite his vehement protests in some of his poems against certain forms of idolatry, Tukārām is not only made an object of worship himself, in Dehū, but within the same sacred enclosure there is a veritable pantheon dedicated to Rāma, Māruti, Ganpati, Garud, etc. in addition to the poet's own Vithobā, from whose threshold people accounted of low-caste origin are kept away, *darshan* in such cases having to be taken at a distance. The inconsistency of this last with Tukārām's own somewhat democratic inclinations we ventured to point out to our *Gosāvī* guide who took our gentle expostulation good-naturedly. A short distance from Vithobā's shrine we came to the inevitable temple with its inevitable worship of Tukārām, on the spot where four centuries ago stood the poet's humble hut, and a few paces away was the small cottage dedicated to the worship of Jijabāī his longsuffering wife. We then saw the tomb of Tukārām's eldest son, Narāyanrao, who like Dnyāneshwar before him took *sthala-samādhī* (getting oneself buried alive). Immediately behind this rest the ashes of several famous *Gosāvīs* in Tukārām's line. Lastly, less than half a mile away we came upon the shrine visited yearly on certain days in Phālgun, the twelfth Hindu month[3], by a festival crowd that numbers anything from twenty to forty thousand people; the reason for their coming being given in a Marāthi inscription which translated reads. 'From this place Tukārām took the form of Brahma and ascended to Vaikuṇṭha (Paradise)'. We noted however that opposite this spot deemed most holy by millions of intelligent Hindus, is the deepest part of the Indrāyaṇī—a part which *always* has deep water, said our guide, and we wondered therefore whether a more natural explanation for the 'ascension' of 1650 might not fit the facts.[4]

[1] Mrs. Sinclair Stevenson, *I R M.* October, 1920.

[2] A *Gosāvī* is 'a Śūdra (and sometimes a Brāhman) who has renounced worldly business, pleasures and affections', J. T Molesworth, *Marāthi and English Dictionary*, p 249, col. 1

[3] This year (1920) these days came on March 6–8

[4] See the end of Section ii, Chapter iv

6. Deccan Villages—Then and Now

As for life's experiences in the Deccan, past and present are much the same. The same crops are planted and by the same methods; the thoughts of men are centred on weather and prices. The present differs from the past in its greater security. When the rain fails in any district life is not immediately threatened. Local war is no more a feature of the times. The outlook of men has also broadened. The cheap post, newspaper and day-school have made themselves felt in the village: there is some knowledge of the world. The isolation of the people has been disturbed. The public services in police, education and other matters, bring it into touch with other villages and remind it that there is a central power directing things for a common good. In Tukārām's day certainly such a central power existed, that of the Mogul Emperors directed from Ahmednagar, but its proceedings were far less methodical than those of modern government and if it sometimes interfered in small affairs which to-day would be left alone, in many directions where the official hand is now felt daily the village went its way without interference.

It seems idle to ask the question whether people were happier in those days than in our own, and we may leave the comparison to those bold enough to make it. No doubt local interests were stronger in the days of primitive isolation, and local gossip was more absorbing. This means also that local feuds were more bitter, and these feuds have always been the curse of Indian village life. We may suppose, if we like, that simple piety was commoner; but dark superstitions were common too, the dread of evil spirits more burdensome, dark and cruel rites more prevalent. Of all this, as we shall see, Tukārām's poems furnish their own evidence.

What is true of India as a whole is true of that part of India called the Deccan: if you would influence the people of India you must get to know something of the 750,000 villages in which nine-tenths of India's mighty population live. This was well put in a paper on *Spiritual Forces in India* by Dr. Macnicol in the *Contemporary Review*[1] some years ago. 'Every one who would touch the heart and mould the life of India must go down among the silent masses of the people. They must turn their backs upon the cities and the life of the cities. It is a commonplace of commonplaces in regard to India to say that it is a land of villages. It is this fact, no less than the tenacity of their minds and the elusiveness of their thoughts, that has made it appear so often as if messages conveyed to the people of this land were writ on water. For the most part it is probable that they never reached their ears. If anyone would know what India will be, if he would guess what forces are still dormant in her and of what she dreams, and especially if he desires to move and mould her future, he must sit with

[1] September 1900, pp. 284–294.

the villager at his hut-door, buy with him and sell at his weekly market, and journey with him when he takes his pilgrim's staff and sets forth to some distant shrine. If he is a foreigner it is difficult indeed for him to come close enough to those simple children of the earth to form any true conception of the dim thoughts and impulses that move them. The nearest he can come to them, perhaps, is when he pitches his tent close by their village and gathers them around him to speak with them of whatever troubles them, and, by what means he may, to win their hearts. It is no easy thing to do in India'.

7. Maratha Religious Life

It will be best therefore at this point to give some proportionate account of the religious life and organization of a Marāṭhā village. That life is best viewed in its general aspect as a life of domestic religious rites. Every respectable Hindu family has in its house a small shrine for domestic worship, where the head of the family every day performs the ceremonies needed for its wellbeing. There will be found the images of the chief gods, and especially of any god to whom by tradition the worship of that family is offered. Over these images scented oil is poured, then they are bathed in a saucer kept close by for sacred purposes, dried, replaced, besmeared with a sandal-wood preparation, after which flowers are offered them, lights are waved round them, a small bell is rung and food is presented to them before the family sit down to their own meal. During this *puja* (worship) prayers are uttered; the whole ceremony, which must be performed either by the male head of the household or by the family priest, occupying about half an hour before the morning meal, the chief meal of the day. These sacred images, however, do not take their places or receive these observances till they are duly consecrated by the Brāhmans. So here the services of the priest are needed, as they are needed at every special ceremony in the life of a Hindu (on which see Mrs. Sinclair Stevenson's *Rites Of The Twice-Born*). They are not needed, on the other hand, when he visits a shrine where some image of a god stands in public waiting for its worshippers. As in his own house, he approaches it directly, salutes it and departs. Almost all images, however, have their Brāhman attendants and no pious worshipper will neglect these, if they are present. Small popular shrines where no attendant waits, the red-coloured images of Māruti or Hanumān who watches over all Deccan villages, are visited by their votaries who paint them and place garlands on them when they feel disposed. The little temple of Śiva, found in every Deccan village, is visited morning and evening by all whose inclinations lead them there.

These ceremonies and visits to temples make up the round of ordinary worship. Once a year there is a special occasion of quite another kind, the *shrāddh*, or offering to the spirits of departed ancestors. This arises partly from the view that departed souls require nourishment and partly from the belief that they must expiate in hell the offences of their last incarnation till, the penalty having been duly paid, they depart to enjoy the reward of their merits for a period in heaven. The faith of their descendants manifested in the *shrāddh* accelerates their liberation, and the rite is esteemed by all Hindus as one of the most serious duties of religion. In addition, the daily round of temple visits is often supplemented by pilgrimages to famous shrines.

Correcting a misconception by no means rare in the West, Dr. Macnicol, whose authority in this matter will at once be recognised by Western readers, remarks: 'No greater mistake could be made than to suppose that there is no strength of purpose or resolution in the people of India. How else have those hill-sides been furrowed so deep by the feet of pilgrims that have come and gone throughout a thousand years? What strength of soul was theirs who, in the still more distant past, carved deep out of the solid rock cells for themselves and great cathedrals for their gods . . . . Wherever one goes, the prints of pilgrims' feet are "numberless and holy all about him". No doubt much of the reality and power that lay in former days behind those facts has passed away from them to-day . . . . Nor can one wonder, with the constant pressure of poverty upon them, that in the case of the great majority of all classes their worship, in the expressive language of a proverb, is given first to "Poṭobā, and only then to Vithobā," and perhaps there is more excuse for such worship in India than in most other lands'.[1] These worshippers of 'Potobā', so accurately described in the Pauline phrase 'whose god is their belly,' may serve as a reminder to foreigners—both missionaries and officials—that a useful point of contact with the people is provided by the study of Marāṭhī proverbs, on which Mr. Manwaring in English and Mr. Apte in Marāṭhī have written excellent books.

8. Deccan Temples

It is difficult to obtain any correct idea either of the number of Hindu temples in those early times or of the proportion of temples given up to the various Hindu deities. In an examination of 'the Selections from the *Peshwā's Diaries*' by Justice Ranade, we read the following: 'The last portion of the Selections gives a list of some 250 temples, which were of sufficient importance to receive State-help in 1810–11. The relative popularity of the several deities will appear from the analysis which shows that there were fifty-two temples of Māruti, the attendant of Rāma, while Rāma himself had eighteen places of worship. The temples

[1] *The Contemporary Review*, Sept. 1900, pp. 284–91.

dedicated to Vishṇū were nine, to Vithobā thirty-four, to Krishna as Balajī twelve. Rāma and Krishna incarnations had thus seventy-three places of worship. The most popular gods with the Brāhmans were Mahādeo who had forty temples, and Ganpati who had thirty-six temples. Judged by the number of temples, the worshippers of Siva and Vishṇū were thus nearly equal. The old aboriginal gods had in all thirty-two places of worship; the Devī had ten, Dattātreya had only one temple for his worship, and there were eight places of Muhammadan Dargas held in veneration'.[1]

9. Bhajans and Kirtans

The formalism of Hindu ritual, now as in Tukārām's day, is counterbalanced by meetings for common worship in which no priest takes any leading part or is necessarily present at all. Such meetings need not even be held in a temple. It is solely a matter of convenience where they are held and often the courtyard of some large house is the scene of a *bhajan*, *kathā* or *kīrtan*. *Bhajan* is the name of a choral service in which all present take an equal part: a *kīrtan* is a service in which one leader expounds the theme and invites the company to join him in song: a *kathā* seeks to inspire patriotic and religious fervour by narrating the exploits of gods and heroes. The leader on all such occasions may be a Brāhman but this is by no means necessary, perhaps not even usual. A *kīrtankār* is simply a man of respectable station who has felt drawn to the religious life, possesses the gift of exposition, and, what in India is closely allied to it, the gift of song. He is as it were a Moody and a Sankey in one. He may or may not make religious teaching the sole business of his life, but no doubt the most successful among the *kīrtankārs* occupy themselves with nothing else. There is nothing in the way of a school or centre for training but to some extent they learn from each other. Among them are men of great reputation, who attract very large gatherings and undoubtedly exercise a real influence for good. And it appears that they very seldom make any charge for their services or accept anything more from their friends than subsistence.

Services of this kind may be connected with the worship of any god but in practice they are chiefly held to magnify Rāma, Kṛishṇa and Vishṇū. They have been developed by the followers of the *Bhakti-Marga*, the path of loving devotion. To a Protestant eye they are the most edifying of Hindu religious observances. They combine something of the oratorio with something of the service of song, and no one whose inclinations lead him in these directions will fail to enjoy or even to take some involuntary part if he is present in a *kīrtan*. (See the section on this subject in chapter 7)

[1] Justice M. G Ranade, *Miscellaneous Writings*, 1915, pp 375–6.

10. Religious Superstition

On the other hand it is not to be forgotten that religious sentiment led and leads many of these same villagers in very different directions. It leads them for instance to propitiate evil spirits. There is much less of this practice in Mahārāshtra than in many parts of India; it exists, however, and outside the town or village often stands the shrine of Vetāḷ, the prince of these demons[1]. To this repair those who believe themselves in trouble from his myrmidons, and by the offering of a cocoanut (representing perhaps the human head of a remote antiquity) seek to purchase life. A foreigner of course can offer no opinion how often this happens, but probably it does not as often happen in Mahārāshtra as elsewhere. In times of special trouble, such as cholera or plague, an image of the cholera or plague spirit may be set up outside the village and honoured there in the hope that it may not come inside, and there are some quaint ways of inducing it to turn its attentions to other villages.

As for witches and wizards and dealers in spells and curses, potions and incantations, they are not unknown in the Deccan but probably much less is heard of them than in Southern India. Such persons are seldom found to reside in one place like the village witch of old England who has scarcely any counterpart in old India. The sorcerers of the country belong to the vast order of wandering ascetics, for ever coming and going, frightening women very much and occasionally doing great harm. But the Deccan on the whole is much more free from these troublers of men's spiritual peace than other parts of India

In a deeply interesting section entitled 'Superstitions' relating to the Marāthā Government of the Peshwās, Justice Ranade supplies the following facts: 'Belief in omens and prognostics was common to all classes. It is recorded that a student cut off his tongue and another Gujarāthī devotee cut off his head by way of offering it to the deity he worshipped, and in both cases, the events were reported to the Government by the local officials, and large sums were spent to purify the temples and ward off the dangers threatened by these unholy sacrifices. People were filled with alarm, when it was reported that an earthquake had disturbed the Kalyān Tālukā. A fortress on the Ghāts was believed to have suffered injury from the influence of evil sight, and another fortress a few years later was rendered unfit for occupation by the prevalence of an unaccountable disease. In all these three cases, steps were taken to pacify the elements by general purification. The donee of a Jahāgir village prayed to Government to resume the grant and exchange it for some other, as the gift became undesirable on account of the prevalence of evil spirits. Partial and

[1] 'Rings of white stones representing Vetāl, the ghost-king, and his troopers are often to be seen outside Deccan villages' (*H. M. P.*, p. 11). Inside these rings village athletes both wrestle and worship.

local famines gave frequent trouble in those days, and large sums were spent in employing Brāhmins to drown the gods, or pour water over them for days and weeks together. Sacrifice of buffaloes to a goddess at Trimbak, which had been stopped for some years, was resumed by the order of the Government at the instance of Brāhmin devotees. When a man-eating tiger appeared on the Saptashringī Hill in the Nāśik District, the Kamāvīsdār was ordered to consult the pleasure of the goddess, and if she consented, to employ men to shoot it. A lizard having fallen on the body of the idol at Paṇḍharpūr, a great penance was ordered in which Brāhmins took part. The sale of cows to butchers was strictly prohibited throughout the country. Some Muhammadans, who were guilty of breaking the law, were severely punished, and a Brāhmin, who cut off the tail of a cow, was sent to prison.'[1]

11. Social Life and General Culture

Mahārāshtra is, probably, on the whole, the most orderly corner of Hindu society. The village system is more clearly defined than it is elsewhere, the status and mutual services of the castes are placed on a clearer footing, there are fewer of the miserable hangers-on, the forlorn classes, than there are in the Hinduism of other parts. And the dress of Mahārāshtra is the most practical and for women the most becoming dress worn by the peasantry of India. On the other hand it is the least courtly part of the country, perhaps the least artistic. The Marāṭhās during all their history built nothing whatever, and art does not seem to owe anything to their patronage. They have one hero and one heroic period but in the leading position which they then assumed they did little of lasting value for India as a whole. Beginning with plundering the Moguls they freed the country, it is true, from Muhammadan rule, but created no system worthy of their vigour or of their shrewdness of character. When, through their own ceaseless quarrels, the sceptre departed from them, the mass of the people retained nothing inspiring from two centuries of martial authority.

On the other hand, recent investigation shows that in every stage of society, high and low, poets were highly honoured and received the popular homage. (See section 20 of this chapter on the 'Democratizing Influence of Marāṭhā Poets.') Moreover, the Peshwās all encouraged learning and education. Mr. V. L. Bhawe points out that in the case of every Marāṭhā author of importance either he or his descendants received a gift from the Peshwās to encourage him in his literary work.[2] Mr. K. V. Subramanya Aiyar, the author of *Historical Sketches of Ancient Deccan*, has pointed

[1] Justice M. G. Ranade, *Miscellaneous Writings*, pp. 374–5.
[2] See Mr. V. L. Bhawe, *M. Sār.*, e.g. p. 379, Mahipatī's case; p. 316, Niranjan's case.

out the interesting fact that in the ancient Deccan 'the poet was better favoured than even the king's nearest relations and there was nothing to compare with his status, honour and esteem.'[1] This fact helps us to understand Tukārām's popularity both in his own day and now.

As for the tastes of the Marāthā people of the present day, 'I may be forgiven if I pause to combat the disastrous idea', says Mr. Sedgwick, one of the all too few Englishmen who know the richness of Marāthī literature, 'that Marathī poetry is neither read by Marāthī speaking gentlemen, nor worth reading. Literature for its own sake is perhaps not so much followed in the East as in the West. But such students of literature as there are in the Deccan read the Marāthī poets. *Abhangs* and *pothīs* are sung or read at every festival. Children in the smallest as well as the largest schools are taught the poetical language as soon as they can read and write reasonably correctly. A not inconsiderable amount of research work and literary criticism is being done in Marāṭhī through the medium of periodicals. . . Last but not least we have at the present moment in Poona a group of Indian scholars calling themselves the *Tukārām-maṇḍalī*, which is preparing a critical edition of the works of Tukārām with an exhaustive and scholarly commentary. All this is indicative of the fact that Marāṭhī poetry is read and studied more than ever before'.[2]

Even the rank and file have their literary interests of a kind. It has been truly said that 'in every town and village in the Deccan and Konkan, especially during the rains, the pious Marāṭhā will be found listening with his family and friends to a recitation of the *Pothī* of Shrīdhar (1678–1728), and enjoying it indeed. Except an occasional gentle laugh, or a sigh, or a tear, not a sound disturbs the rapt silence of the audience, unless when one of those passages of supreme pathos is reached, which affects the whole of the listeners simultaneously with an outburst of emotion which drowns the voice of the reader'.[3]

12. The Power of the Brahmans

The Brāhmans undoubtedly retain the tradition that they are the class entitled to control and direct affairs. In this part of India they have assumed a position quite unique, furnishing the priests, politicians and, formerly, the warriors of the country. Their position as priests may be parallelled elsewhere, but nowhere have they monopolized all administrative power as they have done here. Even in the Marāṭhā army many of the officers were Brāhmans, and they filled almost all posts in the civil service. It is difficult to account for this, and difficult to say how exactly it

[1] *Indian Social Reformer*, August 4, 1919, p. 614.
[2] Mr. L. J. Sedgwick, I. C. S., *J. R. A. S. Bo.*, 1910, Vol. 23, No. 65, p. 110
[3] Acworth's *Ballads*, xxvii.

affected the country or the Brāhmans themselves. On the whole there was probably not much friction between them and the other classes; their predominance was accepted both in secular and spiritual affairs. Though exclusive they were not offensively arrogant or at least were not felt to be such by the non-Brāhman classes who felt the Brāhman influence to be humanizing after the harsh cruelties of Muhammadan rule. Non-Brāhmans became content to leave politics alone and when the Government of Bombay, regarding the Peshwā as incorrigible, annexed his territories the peasantry did not feel that any rights of theirs were being taken away. In religious matters, as we have seen, the common people had always a large sphere of their own and one in which they found a leading interest of their lives. Doubtless the view they took of Brāhmans at that time approximated to the view taken of them by low-caste people to-day, as expressed in the saying: 'Brāhmans are like palm-trees, very high, but giving little shade to us poor people'.

Careful observers have pointed out that Marāthā Brāhmans are among 'the most capable Hindus in the Empire'.[1] This, moreover, is the view they take of their own position 'Marāthā Brāhmans . . . regard themselves as the élite of mankind, not only because they are Brāhmans, but also because they believe themselves superior to all other Brāhmans in India. To them Gujrāth Brāhmans (the Brāhmans of Gujarāt) are only a caste of water-carriers, and Telang Brāhmans (Tilanga or Carnatic Brāhmans) are a caste of cooks. They look upon Sārasvat Brāhmans and the Brāhmans of Northern India as degenerate because the latter are "fish-eaters". They again believe that all other Brāhmans, like those of Northern India, are unable to pronounce Sanskrit speech correctly. On account of their pretensions to political and scholarly wisdom the Marāthā Brāhmans are far from popular . . . They have a power of conferring Vedic and Purāṇic sacraments, as they are the priests of the nation, but the possibilities of this power, and the good uses to which this power can be applied, are not yet fully realized by them . . . The Peshwās are gone, and so is the power of the Shāstrīs and Pundits in Poona. They still like to play their excommunication formalities. They often excommunicate persons, either those who have returned from England, or married a widow, or drank tea with Englishmen.'[2] Those acquainted with recent Indian history will recall the instance of the late Mr. Bāl Gangādhar Ṭilak who only a few weeks before his death on August 1, 1920 underwent the ceremony of *prāyaśchit* (purification) in consequence of visiting England. On Western India Brāhmans Mr. R. E. Enthoven's *Tribes and Castes of Bombay*, Vol. 1, pp. 213–54 should be carefully studied.

[1] *E. R. E.* article *Bombay*, Vol. 2, p. 788 (a)
[2] *E. R. E.* article *Hinduism*, Vol. 6, pp. 692–3

13. The Maratha Character

Marāthās should be thought of chiefly as a hard-working, home-keeping, religious people. This judgement departs widely from that usual in our histories. Tennyson has fixed for us the Marāthā character in one of his trenchant phrases, 'the wild Marāthā battle', and the name of Assaye (however little the common man knows about it) stands for a day-long struggle against a host of indomitable swordsmen. Now the Marāthās undoubtedly did a good deal of fighting. But in the last days of their exploits, when we examine the roll of their troops, it is astonishing how many of them were Arab mercenaries or predatory scoundrels from all parts of India. And without doubting that the famous cavalry always included the more adventurous of the young Marāṭhās it is very uncertain how long after Shivājī's time the Marāṭhā army continued to be a really national force. Perhaps it is enough to say here that in this as in all reflections on character, whether national or individual, we soon light on those contradictions which further knowledge seems only to emphasize. A certain shrewd and pushing worldliness being quite characteristic of the country, especially among those Brāhmans who have taken to worldly life, a roving, sword-clashing sort of Marāṭhā there must once have been, but the conception with which this paragraph started comes ultimately as near the central type as any other. Of course we constantly fail to allow for varieties of type within a people, but Tukārām's pages in themselves are sufficient proof that very different characters might have been found within the walls of any village in his day.

How the Marāthā army came to be so largely mercenary Justice Ranade has shown in his exhaustive examination of the *Peshwā's Diaries*. 'The army', says he, 'in fact represented the Marāṭhā nation more faithfully than any other single section of the population. Shivājī commenced his work of conquest of the forts round about Poona and in the Konkaṇ with the help of the Māvaḷes and the Hetkarīs. The army then consisted only of the Hasham Infantry, who were armed generally with swords and matchlocks. When, later on, he descended into the plains, the cavalry became the chief agency of offensive warfare in the hands of the Marāthās. The old Māvales and Hetkarīs were retained, but chiefly in command of the hill-forts. The cavalry, thus brought into existence, fought with the Moguls under Aurangzīb, and spread the terror of the Marāthā name throughout India. They were not mercenaries in the usual sense of the word. They enlisted in the army either singly, or with their horses and men, for the fair season of the year, and when the rains approached, they returned to their homes, and cultivated their ancestral lands . . . The strength of the Marāthā cavalry continued to be the most distinguishing feature till about the year 1750, when contact with the French and British armies . . . induced the Marāthā leaders to have recourse to this new agency, . . . the Gārdīs or the trained battalions. The weakness of this new addition to the military force consisted in the fact that unlike the Māvales or the Shilledārs, who each owned his plot of land and served the State, not as mercenaries, but as militia, the Gārdīs were mercenaries, pure and simple, made up of foreign recruits of different nationalities, who had to be paid fixed salaries all the year round, and only owed loyalty to the commanders who paid them their wages. There was no national element in this new force . . . The army, instead of being national, became mercenary in the worst sense of the word. Attached to the regular armies, there was a licensed host of free-booters, called Pendhārīs who . . . made a living by pillage of the enemy, and ultimately of their own people . . . The old infantry and cavalry had lost their stamina, and the new mercenaries, without leaders and without any knowledge of military science except the drill, were as ineffective as the Pendhārīs who accompanied them. It was this change which paralyzed the nation'.[1]

Later history has shown what wonderful fighters modern Marāṭhās are and the world itself has resounded with the deeds of Marāthā gallantry on many fields of action. Speaking in the Viceroy's Council shortly before the conclusion of the world-war in 1918, the Hon. Mr. C. A. Kincaid observed : 'Resourcefulness, courage, fertility of invention, endurance, all these qualities have been abundantly shown by Marāthā regiments at the front . . . I felt a glow of pride and pleasure when I learnt of the gallant deeds of the Marāthā regiments who sailed . . . to Irak, who occupied Basra, who took Kurna and won at Śaiba . . . They fought in a way which would have roused the envy of the veterans of the Bhosles and the comrades of Chimṇājī Āppā'.[2]

14. Maratha Family Life and its Women

The Marāṭhā bond is in all cases a strong one. In the case of the Brāhmans it brings together various families under one roof in a common life to which Western institutions have no parallel. The imagination of a Western critic cannot in the least conceive in detail the positions and sentiments to which this gives rise; they belong to a world into which he has no means of entering. The only thing that need be said about it is one which is obvious, that it fetters the movements of its members, especially in youth, to a degree unknown among ourselves. That the movements of a Hindū are closely prescribed for him is indeed a matter of general knowledge but perhaps this knowledge usually takes account only

[1] Justice M. G. Ranade, *Miscellaneous Writings*, pp. 352—55
[2] *Dnyānodaya*, 'Marāṭhā Gallantry', November 28, 1918.

of the incidence of rules regarding food and so forth. To this we have to add such things as the influence of a horoscope and above all the social pressure of the joint-family system, which even in practical affairs never leaves a boy a moment's freedom from the hour of his birth. It seems a marvel how any one born in this system can retain any sort of enterprise or self-determination, but we have always to remember that human nature reasserts itself in the most unexpected ways. As to what has actually happened in the Hindū families we are much in the dark. No people have ever been so little given to self-revelation.

Marāthā women are of course not personally known to the foreigner. The women of the upper classes stay within their houses as much as possible; the peasant women may be seen at work everywhere and if you can speak their language are not always averse to a brief chat with you. Their language is racy and unrestrained and fully imbued with that humour which—though some people may not think so—is engrained in most Hindūs. It would appear that they have, if not votes, yet substantial rights secured by custom, and are well able if these are invaded to defend themselves. Whatever tyranny is suffered by the child-wife or child-widow, it is at least inflicted chiefly by their own sex.

15. Heroic Age of the Marathas

We stated above that the Marāthā people had one hero, Shivājī, and one heroic age which was approaching when Tukārām was born in 1608. According to the commonly accepted date Shivājī was born in 1627, though as Jadunāth Sarkār says: 'The *Zedhe Chronology*, which gives original and surprisingly correct dates about later events in Shivājī's life-story, places his birth in February 1630'.[1] Investigation has established Shivājī's character both as a man and a ruler. By one of those revolutions which the spirit of history loves he appears on the scene a few years after the great Akbār, from whom India seems about to receive an impulse towards unity, political and religious, that will mould all her future history. The hope thus held forth is at once by destiny dispelled. With Akbār the Mogul system culminates and with him it disappears. His principles and visions vanish. His narrow-minded successor sweeps all away, and creating nothing to replace what he destroys, leaves chaos behind him after two generations of power. The reconstructing force comes from a quarter where no one looks for it—the Deccan, regarded by Aurangzīb as 'infidels' land'.

16. Shivaji, Tukaram and Ramdas

Mahārāshtra cannot have seemed a region specially fitted to produce a revived and energetic Hinduism. But it was there that

[1] *Shivājī and His Times* published by M. C. Sarkar & Sons, Calcutta.

the hour found the man. Among the few good families of the country was that of a small *jagīrdār* near Poona in which Shivājī was born. He was from his earliest years a strict and earnest Hindū and among the sentiments of his early manhood was a keen resentment against the slights and injuries which his faith suffered from the Government of Aurangzīb (1658–1707). He knew the natural sources of military strength in the Deccan, and what is even more important there breathed through his actions a rude democratic spirit which woke his countrymen into vigorous life and made them devoted and fearless soldiers. It would be outside the scope of these pages to follow his career. We need at present only notice that Tukārām lived in the darkness preceding this dawn. He died in 1650 when Shivājī was dreaming dreams of a perilous future. There is nothing in Tukārām's poems to show that he gave much thought to the Mahommedans or considered that what the times needed was a political revolution. His brief connection with Shivājī will be discussed elsewhere.

Born in the same year as Tukārām, the poet Rāmdās (1608–1681) outlived him by more than thirty years. Just as Shivājī's connexion with Tukārām is surrounded with a measure of uncertainty, so also experts have differed as to the extent of the relation between Shivājī and Rāmdās. Some have held that Rāmdās was the 'guide and inspirer' of Shivājī's whole policy through the critical years which led up to Shivājī's kingship, thus wielding potent influence in the building up of the Marāṭhā kingdom. Others hold it to be 'proved conclusively that Rāmdās had nothing to do with the great work of winning independence from the Mahommedan which Shivājī had undertaken and brought to a successful issue even before they met in 1672'. If this latter conclusion be accepted then the reference to Rāmdās in the letter to Shivājī from Tukārām—who died in 1650—must be regarded as an interpolation. The whole subject, however, is still under discussion.[1]

17. The Greeting of Hindus

Though it probably takes us beyond Tukārām's day there is one story told of Shivājī and Rāmdās which is worth repeating since it refers to the supposed origin of those well-known words *Rām Rām* by which Marāthās in Western India greet one another. It is said that Shivājī begged Rāmdās to live with him and let him serve

[1] See Prof. Bhate's Marāthī book, *Sajjangad and Samarth Rāmdās*, I. I. Jan 1919, vol xiii, pp. 157–68 where the authorities on both sides are given; Jan. 1916 vol. ix, pp 197–8, Mr. G. K Chandorkar in *Kesari*, June 26, 1906, Mr. K. A. Keluskar's *Life of Shivājī* in Marāthi, pp 507–14, 551–62 where other conclusive evidence is adduced, Kincaid and Parasnis, in *H. M. P.* pp. 191–2, and Mr. V. L Bhawe in *M. Sā.*, (pp 219, 415), with the Marāthī daily *Lōk Sangraha* for April 25, 1920 giving a lecture by Mr. D. Potdar.

him as he had done for a single day at Jaranda. Rāmdās requested in return that, instead of serving him, Shivājī would grant him three boons. Shivājī said that he would do so gladly. The third one was that Shivājī should honour the hero god Rāmchandra by ordering his subjects when they met to say to each other by way of greeting, *Rām Rām*. Shivājī granted these boons and *Rām Rām* are still the words of greeting used by Marāthās when they meet, Mahārs, Chāmbhārs and other depressed castes using the word *Johār*,[1] the ancient form of salutation, just as Brāhmans use *Namaskār*.[2] The above legend may have to be rejected as unhistorical, seeing that Tukārām himself has an *abhang* with the words of this same greeting, though of course the *abhang* itself may be an interpolation.

18. The Maratha National Movement

It only remains to note the fact, all-important for gaining any true conception of the heroic age of the Marāthās, that in the days of Tukārām, Shivājī and Rāmdās there was a linking together of the forces of the Marāthā nation, both material and moral, which contributed to a movement of enduring significance in Indian history. This has been very happily expressed by Prof. Limaye: 'We are inclined to hold that there were two factors in the national movement of Mahārāshtra. That representing material power was contributed by the Marāthā nobles who opposed Shivājī in the first instance. The moral force of the movement was derived from the preaching of the great saints, while Shivājī stands for the synthesis of the two. Himself the son of a great Marāṭhā nobleman and as such possessed of power and influence, he was thoroughly imbued with the spirit of the teaching of the saints. Inspired by their high ideals, he strove to realize them in his life, and, in doing so, was prepared to risk both his power and position. That is the significance of Shivājī's life-work, and it is this which entitles him to rank by the side of the greatest of the world's heroes'.[3] Hence it can be said with truth that 'the Marāthās are a nation, and from the Brāhman to the ryot they glory in the fact.'[4]

If, then, Shivājī's glory consists in the fact that he welded the scattered Marāṭhās into a kingdom, why was this kingdom so short-lived, suffering disruption less than nine years after Shivājī's death? Dr. Rabindranath Tagore thus explains: 'Shivājī aimed at preserving the rents and holes in our body social; he wished to save from the Mogul attack a Hindū society of which ceremonial distinctions and isolation of castes are the very breath of life. He wanted to make this heterogeneous society triumphant over all India! He wove ropes of sand; he attempted the impossible. It is

1 Originally a war-cry of the Rajputs.
2 *H. M. P.*, pp. 91–2.
3 Professor H G. Limaye, M.A., *F. C. M.*, February 1919, p. 167.
4 Acworth's *Powadas*, or Marāthī Ballads, celebrating the exploits of Marāṭhā heroes, iii.

beyond the power of any man, it is opposed to the divine law of the universe, to establish the *swarāj* of such a caste-ridden, isolated, internally-torn sect over a vast continent like India.'[1]

With this diagnosis agrees that of the Marāṭhā historian, Justice Ranade, who has shown that while the kingdom of the Peshwās anticipated some of the modern Marāṭhā movements for social reform, it contained within itself the seeds of its own decay. The later decline must not, however, be allowed to obscure the view first advocated by the late Hon. Mr. Justice Telang in his *Gleanings from the Bakhars* that the Marāṭhā rulers showed 'greater moral courage and liberality of sentiment' than people have been disposed to give them credit for.[2] Nevertheless, 'it is a matter of history that the Marāṭhā Confederacy or Empire—the most considerable Hindū national achievement in historic times—broke on the rock of caste', the effect of this being felt 'even to-day in the embittered feelings between the Brāhmins and the Marāṭhās round about Poona'.[3]

19. The Literature of the Maratha Bhaktas (Saints)

If we are to understand the true origin and force of the Marāṭhā movement and its significance for the India of to-day we must add to the 'two factors' of Prof. Limaye a third force which was at work—that of literature and specially the literature of the *Bhakti* movement in Mahārāshtra. There can be no question that this literature has been greatly underrated by Western scholars, but of late years it has been coming to its own. Prof. Patwardhan in his *Wilson Philological Lectures* has shown that 'Marāṭhī literature, even before it came into contact with the literature of the West, had reached a state of development and growth both quantitatively and qualitatively that the people of Mahārāshtra may well be proud of,'[4] and much the same has been said by Mr. L. J. Sedgwick, I.C.S.:[5] 'Western scholars may hardly be aware that there exists in Marāṭhī a *bhakti* literature, which in age, in volume, and in quality can equal, if not surpass, the Hindi. Indeed I would go further, and say that viewed from any standpoint of criticism the *ovi* poems of Mahīpatī, and the *abhangs* of Nāmdev, Eknāth, Tukārām and Rāmdās must be placed among the finest of the poetic productions of the world .... We are in the presence of a strange world of saints and poets, ... a religion which had dominated the thoughts of the lower and middle classes in the Deccan. *Bhakti* in this part of India centres entirely round this

[1] Quoted by Jadunāth Sarkār in *Shivājī and His Times*, pp. 483–4
[2] Justice M. G. Ranade, *Miscellaneous Writings*, pp. 372–80.
[3] *The Indian Social Reformer*, October 17, 1920.
[4] *F.C.M.*, July 1912, pp. 31–2.
[5] *J.R.A.S. Bo.*, Vol. 23, No. 65, pp. 109–10.

one god—the god Vithobā . . . . Upon the worship of this deity there has been built up in Marāthī a literature of great extent and beauty. It covers a period from about A.D. 1290, to the present day, but the best period ends with the death of Mahīpatī in 1791 A.D. It may be divided into two main portions: hymns, mostly in the metrical form known as *abhangs* but also partly in other forms, and especially narrative-lives of the saints in the metre known as the *ovi*. Of the former the four great exponents are Nāmdev, Eknāth, Tukārām and Rāmdās (the last-named being a Rāma worshipper), while the latter is represented mainly by Mahīpatī, whose *Bhaktivijāya*, *Bhaktilīlāmrita*, etc. were suggested by the *Bhaktamāla* of Nabaji, the Hindū poet. . . . Of the three *Vitthala-bhakta abhang* writers Tukārām is by the far the most popular.'

20. Democratizing Influence of the Maratha Poets

The unique service rendered by the saints and prophets of Mahārāshtra was long ago pointed out by the late Justice M. G. Ranade who showed that as a result of their work 'there came into existence the beginnings of a national feeling' which represented nothing less than 'spiritual emancipation of the national mind'. This has been dealt with more recently by Prof. Patwardhan who states: 'For five successive centuries Mahārāshtra was the abode of that noblest and truest of all democracies, the democracy of the *Bhakti* school. The whole of the Marāthī Literature of those centuries is a literature of Spiritual Democracy—it breathes the breath of equality, of fraternity and of spiritual liberty. . . . The *Bhakti* school democratized literature, so that all those that would, could and did bear their share in the building up of the grand edifice. There were Brāhmans, Śūdras, Shimpīs or tailors, Kumbhārs or potters, Nhāvīs or barbers, even Mahārs or low castes, that felt the call of the Divine Muse, and contributed their own little streamlet to the general flood . . . The democratization of Literature had one inevitable result. It was to nationalize it. . . . The literature was no longer of the Brāhmans or Śūdras or Mahārs. It was Marāthī Literature and every one, whatever his caste or creed, trade or profession, learned to love it and labour for it. . . . The *Bhakti* school poets thus not only made the literature but also made the people a nation They nationalized the literature'.[1] How far these facts bear on the modern history of India has been shown by Jadunāth Sarkār: 'The Marāthās have a historic advantage of unique importance in the India of to-day. Their near ancestors had faced death on a hundred battlefields, had led armies and debated in the chamber of diplomacy, had managed the finances of kingdoms and grappled with the problems of empire; they had helped to make Indian history.'[2]

[1] *F. C. M* July 1919, pp. 34–5.
[2] *Shivāji and His Times*, pp. 20–21.

Sir C. Sankaran Nair has similarly explained the uniqueness of Marāṭhā influence in the making of India. In a remarkable address at Leeds University, September 7, 1920, after speaking of the 'great national revival in the Marāṭhā country', he quoted with approval the following opinion of Major Evans Bell: 'The last chapters of self-development and self-independence in India belong to the Western region. The Marāṭhā Confederation emancipated the Hindus and . . . set up religious and social tolerance. . . . The Hindū revival of the seventeenth and eighteenth centuries which paved the way for British intervention, was a movement of social and political progress, in which the Marāṭhās took the lead, it may be said, unconsciously, instinctively, without premeditation or prevision.'[1]

If the political 'courage' of the city of Bombay is evidenced by its 'anxiety to enfranchise five million (Indian) women at the same time as five million men' as was affirmed by Sir J. D. Rees,[2] a courage, he added, which is in deep contrast with 'the conservatism of rural India'; and if Lord Sinha, first Indian Governor, could say that 'it was to the political leaders of Bombay that he always looked for instruction and guidance';[3] then such high political distinction is to be traced back to the nationalizing and democratizing influence of the Marāṭhā poet-saints. The greatest of these nationalizing and democratizing forces in the life of Western India—Tukārām—we are to study in this book.

[1] *The Indian Social Reformer*, Nov. 14, 1920.
[2] *Fortnightly Review*, 1920.
[3] A speech in Bombay, Dec. 5, 1920.

Vaishnavism is admittedly what is called the *Bhakti* or Devotional worship which is inconsistent with the spirit of caste.

Sir C. Sankaran Nair at Leeds University, September 7, 1920

THE BESETTING GOD

Of God my meat and drink I make,
  God is the bed on which I lie
God is whate'er I give or take,
  God's constant fellowship have I
For God is here and God is there—
  No place that empty is of him.
Yea, lady Vithā, I declare,
  I fill the world up to the brim.

Translated from Janābāī, Nāmdev's domestic servant (14th century), by Dr. Macnicol, *Psalms of Marāthā Saints*, p 50.

THE SCORNER

Who praises and who scorns me too,
Both are my mother. Ay, I view
My scorners as my mother true.

For such are kind to me. They say
Hard words that wash my soil away,
As does a mother's bathing They

Are friends indeed and strength supply
To me. Were I to blame them, why,
The guilty one would then be I.

O sweet is scorning, setting free
From bondage of duality.
A gracious benefactor he.

Before the scorner bow we low.
Blest be his mother, for I know
Who suffer scorn to Freedom go.

Translated from *Bhāvārtha Rāmāyana* (chap 1) of Ekanāth (1548–99) by Dr. Macnicol, *Psalms of Marāthā Saints*, p. 53.

Chapter 2

The Vaishnava Hinduism of Tukaram's Day

Before introducing Tukārām it is necessary to say something about the religious system with which he was connected.

1. Characteristics of Hinduism in General

It was not until the Mohammedan invasions that the name 'Hindū' passed into use for the people of India. Occasionally lawgivers have found themselves compelled to try to define a Hindū. The attempt has always failed, since, in practice, those Indians are Hindūs who are neither Mohammedans nor Jews nor Parsis nor Christians nor members of any other Indian community that can be defined or disposed of. Nevertheless, something may be done to understand a word so often used, if we are careful not to beg any questions. If we use the word of the prevalent type of life and belief which the Mohammedans found in India we may describe Hindūs as marked by the following characteristics. Their social system is based on caste and they recognize the spiritual ascendancy of the Brāhmans. They venerate the Vedas and the cow. They worship and believe in one or more of the usual Hindū gods, in Vishṇu or his *avatāras*, in Śiva or in others. They believe in the cycle of rebirth. They use images in religious worship. To these characteristics others might be added, frequently but not invariably associated with them.[1]

Research is made difficult by the great paucity of Indian historical works. 'Hindūs wrote no formal history at any period; for the early centuries there are no archæological remains that throw any light on the course of events; nor is any definite information provided by nations outside India'.[2] Nor is research made any easier by the pantheistic bent of the Indian mind. It might be said with truth that the popular mind is always careless of distinctions, but this indifference is more prevalent in India than in any other country. In points of daily routine vital to the caste system the sense of distinction is acute and active but in other matters it hardly exists. Sir R. G. Bhandarkar has more than once pointed out this weakness of Indian research. In his *Vaishṇavism* he writes: 'Unfortunately the historical spirit has

1 See Dr. Farquhar's concise *Primer of Hinduism*, especially chapters xii and xiv on 'What it is to be a Hindu to-day' and 'The religion of the lower classes'.

2 J. N. Farquhar, *O.R.L.I.*, p. 3.

by no means been the distinguishing feature of the intellectual life of us Indians, and we often confuse different persons together and attribute to one what belongs to another'.[1] In a remarkable paper prepared for the Oriental Conference held in Poona, November, 1919, he diagnosed this weakness as follows: 'A young man, the editor of a good many Sanskrit works, asks me with a derisive smile what the necessity was of naming a MS., of showing the country it came from and the age in which it was written. He did not know that when a judge noted down the age of a witness appearing before him, the name of the caste, or the community, or country to which he belonged, he got information from him which had a value in the estimate of the evidence. Similarly another young man, not fully acquainted with the critical method, said that Nāmdev and Dnyāndev were contemporaries, but that difference between their languages was due to the mistakes of successive scribes. Marāthī literature which has come down to us is full of such strange theories. It is a very disagreeable matter to dwell at this length on the faults of our Indian scholars, but it is an allegiance which I owe to truth.'

This spirit in religious enquiries means that you soon reach the point where you are told that one god is the same as another, or that God is the same as the world—Pantheism, which is not so much a system as a bent of mind.

One more characteristic mark of a Hindū worth noting here, and one which illuminates one aspect of the enduring religiousness of India, is his willingness to believe that every man should follow the dictates, and observe the practices, of that religion in which he was born. This helps to explain on the one hand his tolerance of the Christian religion and on the other hand his slowness to accept any form of faith other than that handed down from his forefathers.

2. Vishnu's Place in the Hindu System

Among the puzzling problems of the Hindū religion one of the most puzzling and interesting is the question who Vishṇu is and what part he has played in the Hindū system. The question is all the more important because the type of Hinduism prevalent in Tukārām's land, and the popular literature of Tukārām's people, both belonged largely to the Vaishṇava school.[2] It is a question taking us to the very heart of the religion of Tukārām, for the name Viṭhobā itself, the name of the god so closely identified with Kriṣṇa and so dear to Tukārām, is viewed by the best authorities as a corruption of the name Vishṇu.

Vishṇu is a Vedic god, being regarded as one of the upper gods in the Vedas. He is by no means supreme even in the two great

[1] *V S M R.S., etc.*, p. 92.
[2] Vaishnava is the adjective from Vishnu.

epics of India, the *Mahābhārata* and the *Rāmāyana*, though both books were written with a view to exalting his position. 'He is the centre of the first real sect, the Vaishṇavas, who derive their name from him, and who gave forth a book which has come to be regarded as India's most sacred book—the *Bhagavadgīta*. By means of this book the followers of Vishṇu created the first Hindū theism, their method being to unite Vishṇu on the one hand with Brahman and on the other with Kriṣṇa. The chapter in the *Bhagavadgītā* containing the thousand names of Vishṇu is one of the greatest treasures of devout Vaishṇavas.[1]

Since 'the Vaishṇavas of the Marāṭhā country are Bhāgavatas'[2] it is well to note specially the place occupied by Vishṇu in the religion of the Bhāgavatas. 'The word Bhāgavata has two meanings in modern Hinduism. It is first an epithet used of Vaishṇavas generally, as those who use the Bhāgavat-śāstra, or body of works which revere Vishṇu as Bhagavān. It is used, in the second place, of a special community of Vaishnavas . . . who really adore Vishṇu, but recognise the equality of the two gods', Vishṇu and Śiva, and retain Vedic rites.[3] When we realise that it was probably between A. D. 200 and A. D. 550 that the worship of Vishṇu and Śiva as equal, or as one, was instituted, we might agree to the theory that 'the worship of Śiva and Vishṇu as one was a compromise meant to reconcile warring sectaries'. Investigators, however, suggest another explanation, viz., that 'the metaphysical equality of Vishṇu and Śiva' had its origin in the Bhāgavata community referred to above. How very closely connected all this is with the subject of this book is shown by another excerpt. 'The Bhāgavatas of the Marāṭhā country to-day form a popular *bhakti* movement. . . . The god is Viṭṭhal or Viṭhobā; both these names are local variations of Vishṇu. The chief centres are Paṇḍharpūr, Ālandī and Dehū, but there are numerous shrines throughout the country. In the chief temple of Paṇḍharpūr, Viṭṭhal wears a curious sort of crown which the priests say is Śiva's *linga*; so that the image, standing for both gods, is truly Bhāgavata'.[4] (See a paragraph on Śiva in chap. 6).

How Viṭhobā of Pandharpūr, so dear to Tukārām, comes to have any connection with Vishṇu will become clearer in light of later paragraphs.

3. The Vaishnava Idea of *Avatāra*

One of the most interesting features of Vishṇu is his recurring *avatāras*. The conception will bear more enquiry than it has received, for 'we do not know how the Vaishṇavas were led to

1 See J. N. Farquhar, *O.R.L.I.*, Index under the word 'Vishṇu', p. 449.
2 *Ibid.*, p. 234.
3 *Ibid.*, p. 142
4 *Ibid.*, p. 301.

develop the doctrine. The idea appears suddenly.'[1] We have here three aspects calling for elucidation, viz., the exact meaning of the word *avatāra*—one of the most important words in Vaishṇavite Hinduism; the important place occupied in the Vaishnavite religion of Tukārām by the idea of *avatāra*; the fundamental difference between this idea and the Christian doctrine of incarnation. The first two we deal with now, the last in a brief appendix (see *Appendix* I).

i. The word *avatāra* means by derivation a descent or appearance on a scene. It has been used and might still be used of the appearance of mortal men; e.g., Tukārām is commonly regarded as an *avatāra* of his predecessor Nāmdev.

ii. It is specifically used of the sudden appearance of a *deva* (god). The *devas* (gods) in general were conceived as possessing the power of rendering themselves visible or invisible at will, and of transporting themselves at will to any part of the world. We read of various deities doing this, even minor deities.

iii. In the case of Vishṇu we have the added idea that his manifestations were always for the purpose of helping men (or animals like the elephant Gajendra) in distress.

iv. The word *avatāra* thus became specially connected with Vishnu It is now seldom used in connection with any other deity.

v. The English term 'incarnation' is a dangerous equivalent for it: the questions which this word suggests never presented themselves to the Hindū mind. An *avatāra* is a very simple expedient.

vi. As to the origin of the conception it is not necessary to trouble ourselves much. It is not Vedic. It is, however, very natural and one rather wonders that more is not heard of *avatāras* among other races. The Greeks, for instance, found it easy to believe that the gods appeared on the battle-field to help men: Hercules in the story appears to the distressed carter. These are *avatāras*, but such occurrences play no great part in Greek legend as a whole. We may say perhaps that the work performed by the Hindū *avatāras* is performed for the Greeks by heroes—the slaying of demons and so forth. The Greeks were a self-reliant race.

vii. It may be asked if the *deva* (god) is related to the body which he assumes in the same way as the human spirit is related to its bodily tenement. Probably, however, the question has not struck Hindū theologians.

4. Elasticity of the Vaishnava Term *Avatāra*

In modern times the chief *avatāras* of Vishnu have been listed and fixed at ten: fish, tortoise, boar, the man-lion, the dwarf, Parashurām, Rāma, Krisṇa, Buddha, Kalkī. This, however,

[1] See J. N. Farquhar, *O.R.L.I.*, pp. 84–5.

is quite a modern idea. In older writers the number varies a good deal. It is a curious fact that Buddha has somehow found a place in the list. Who would suppose that Buddha was the formidable enemy of Vishnu and indeed of all gods? Now, however, that all danger from Buddha has passed away, due respect is paid to his eminence by transforming him into a god himself! A positivist might sigh for the accommodating disposition of the popular mind which solves a cardinal problem with such ease. How the number ten actually obtained currency does not seem to be known.

In *The Indian Social Reformer* of September 1919, Mr. Manilal Parekh, in a letter which the editor published under the heading 'The Hindū Appreciation of Christ,' observed: 'The word *avatāra* is very loosely used by the majority of Hindūs. Most people entirely overlook the serious differences that have been made between one *avatāra* and another by such Theistic schools of thought as the Vaishṇava. Most of these schools, which alone can consistently use that term, look upon only Kṛiṣṇa as the *Purāna Avatāra*, and others as *Āmcā avatāra*. This practically means that Kriṣṇa is the *avatāra* for them in the same sense in which Christ is the *avatāra* for the Christians.' The same journal,[1] as an illustration of what 'represents the attitude of India to Christ', stated: 'One of the most powerful Hindū religious reformers of recent years was the late Swāmi Vivekānanda. He had a profound reverence for Christ, and so had his Master, Rāmkrishna Paramahamsa. Pandit Sivanāth Śāstry in his book *Men I Have Seen* relates that a Christian preacher who was the Pandit's friend once accompanied him on a visit to Rāmkrishna. When he introduced his friend to the Paramahamsa, Rāmkrishna bowed his head to the ground and said, "I bow again and again at the feet of Jesus." The Christian gentlemen asked: "How is it, Sir, that you bow at the feet of Christ? What do you think of Him?" "Why, I look upon him as an incarnation of God—an incarnation like our Rāma or Kriṣṇa. Don't you know there is a passage in the *Bhāgwat* where it is said that the incarnations of Vishṇu or the Supreme Being are innumerable?"'

How fundamental to Vaishnava Hinduism is the theory of repeated *avatāras* and how great a part it has played in India's religious history Dr. Soderblom shows:[2] 'The conception of the solitary incarnation of deity is peculiar to Christianity. In India the development of the idea resulted in an exactly opposite view, . . . constant increase in the number of embodiments—we find successively the figure ten, twelve, twenty-two, twenty-four, twenty-eight—until at length they are spoken of as innumerable so that the great teachers of any religion whatever . . . could be numbered among the *avatāras*.' Prof. Jacobi remarks,[3] that 'when a local

[1] *The Indian Social Reformer*, September 14, 1919
[2] *E. R. E.* Vol. vii, p. 184.
[3] *E. R. E.* Vol. vii, p. 197.

saint has a proper shrine where he is worshipped, and his fame continues to increase, a legend is sure to be fabricated which declares him an *avatāra* of some god or *rishi*.' Every part of India can provide its own illustrations of the above.

5. Vishnu's Most Popular *Avatāra*

We may next consider what is commonly stated to be the most popular *avatāra* of Vishṇu. Vāsudeva appears as a common name of Vishṇu and as an epithet of Kṛiṣṇa. There is scanty but genuine evidence of a worship of Vāsudeva which Sir R. G. Bhandarkar is inclined to date very early and to rate very highly as an impulse towards monotheism, which played an important part in later Hinduism. In the Veda Kṛiṣṇa is only the name of a *ṛishi* or sage and it is uncertain whether at the later stage Vāsudeva is to be considered as personally identified with the *rishi* Kṛiṣṇa. If Kriṣṇa the warrior prince whom we meet in the *Bhagavadgītā* was a historic personage, then he has been transformed into a religious teacher and an *avatāra* of the supreme spirit Vishṇu. Sir R. G. Bhandarkar surmises that there may have been a historic Kṛiṣṇa born among the pastoral tribe called the Āhirs, and his fame may have led to his identification with Kṛiṣṇa, the warrior prince, who was already identified with the much older Vishṇu and Vāsudeva.[1] Kriṣṇa and Vāsudeva on this theory are distinct, the latter teaching his people monotheism as early as the sixth century B.C. Some scholars hold this view to be unhistorical on the ground that 'there is certainly no clear evidence of the existence of a monotheistic faith during those early centuries'.[2]

6. The 'Historicity' of Krishna

The whole question of Kriṣṇa and his 'historicity' has in recent years been engaging the attention of Indian scholars. In the month of July, 1920 Pandit Sitanāth Tattvabhushan contributed to *The Indian Messenger*, the organ of the Sādhāran Brāhmo Samāj, a series of articles on 'The Bhāgavat Dharma', described as 'a grand and far-reaching movement' which 'has affected all Indian forms of religion'. The purpose of the articles was stated thus: 'Vāsudeva was originally only a particular conception of God and not a historical person and Kṛiṣṇa's historicity as a religious teacher is more than doubtful.' After speaking of the 'fictitious nature of the *Mahābhārata* story, specially of its central figure, Kṛiṣṇa,' the Pandit went on to say: 'As to Kṛiṣna, his relation with the main story of the *Mahābhārata* is slight, and in the original narration of the war he may have been quite absent. Even when introduced into the poem, he was

[1] *V.S.M R.S.*, p. 37
[2] J. N. Farquhar, *O.R.L.I.*, p. 50.

perhaps only a hero and politician, and not God incarnate. The *Bhagavadgītā* and the other *Gītās* and religious dissertations in the *Mahābhārata* in which Krṣṇa appears prominently as a religious teacher and God incarnate, are evidently very late additions to the original epic. This is clear from the abrupt way in which some of them, specially the *Bhagavadgītā*, are introduced into the body of the poem, like patches of new cloth sewn with an old piece, and from the knowledge of later times, manners and religious doctrines which they betray. But there are indications, however slight, to show that the worship of Kṛṣna as a hero or demi-god existed in the country as early as 300 B.C. . . . The temptation to invent a god or to develop and popularize a god already receiving worship from some people, was very great. The secret of the spread of Buddhism must soon have been found out by the Brāhmans. It was the position of Buddha as the central figure in his religion. The śāstras appeal only to the learned few; a person—one realizing to some extent at least the popular ideals of excellence—appeals to all. Before the rise or popularization of Krișna-worship the rapid progress of Buddhism must have deeply alarmed the leaders of Vedic society and set them thinking of the best way to stem the tide. Besides the other methods adopted, of which we need not speak, the setting up of a rival to Buddha must have commended itself as the most important . . . And as Buddha was by birth a Kshatriya and by character a religious teacher, so was his rival, Krṣṇa, conceived to be, though perhaps the warlike predilections of the epic poets made him more of a warrior than became his mission as a religious teacher. This seems to us to be the origin of the so-called Bhāgavat Dharma, which was indebted not only for many of its teachings, but also for the conception of its central figure, to Buddhism. Kṛișna Vāsudeva was not its author, but its product . . . How then was Vedic theism to be conserved? On what line should it develop? How were the broken forces of Brāhmanism to be rallied? The Bhāgavat Dharma, or, to call it by its more correct name, Vaishnavism, was an answer to these questions . . . It was given mostly in the name of one fancied teacher, that of Krișna Vāsudeva. The earlier Vaishṇavas knew he was not historical.' We have seen no answer to this statement.

7. Modern Indian Views of the Krishna Legend

If the Vaishnavite or devotee of *bhakti* has not been burdened with relics of nature-worship which cling to some forms of Hinduism, he has had his own burden in the legends connected with Krṣṇa as the 'cowherd'.[1] Perhaps indeed we ought not to call

[1] For an English translation of Tukārām's poems on this unsavoury topic see *F.* and *M.*, Vol. ii, pp 1-29.

them a burden, for they have been immensely popular, but the more elevated spirits in Hinduism have wondered what to make of them Of course they have tried allegory, that easy refuge of the interpreter, but they have probably wished the problem did not lie before them. Perhaps, indeed, the most interesting difference that has arisen between the various Vaishnava schools has been the problem as to what attitude they should adopt towards these legends depicting Krişna as taking supreme pleasure in sexual intercourse and enjoying it on a vast scale, especially with a favourite mistress named Rādhā. It is possible to allegorize all this, and to say that ultimately nothing is meant except that to the pure all things are pure. In practice, however, the prominence given by some Vaishnavas to this aspect of Krişṇa's activities has had most unpleasant results and the nobler spirits in Hinduism have turned their thoughts to other aspects of his story. Some suppose these legends are *deliberate* allegory. Now allegory has certainly played a part in the expository methods of Hinduism as of some other faiths, but as to how large that part was or how far it may have determined the developments of Hinduism there is room for vast difference of opinion. We will only say that the critic who tries to explain things allegorically is a lost man. It is so easy, so tempting a procedure that he soon sets no limits to its use: he considers it a way out of every difficulty. Certainly if the Krişṇa legends were allegories, those who devised them conferred a great disadvantage on their system.

Sir R. G. Bhandarkar has described the 'frolic' legends as 'an after-growth' in the remarkable sentence: 'The dalliance of Krişṇa with cowherdesses, which introduced an element inconsistent with the advance of morality into the Vāsudeva religion, was also "an after-growth."'[1] Mr. M. K. Gandhi has applied the allegorizing method to the *Gītā* so far as to say that 'the *Gītā* is an allegory in favour of the doctrine of non-resistance.' On this *The Indian Social Reformer* for August 24, 1919 made the pertinent comment: 'This is sheer casuistry.' Concerning the moral difficulty surrounding Krişṇa's name the *Reformer* remarked: 'If people would use their common sense—even apart from all question of charity—it must be obvious that the "eroticism" of Krişṇa's youth is merely the exuberance of the poetic chroniclers.' But even the most bountiful supply, whether of 'common sense' or of 'charity', will not solve what is one of the most baffling problems connected with the historical developments of India's chief religion and to fall back upon 'the obvious' is to give up the case in sheer despair. This book is not the place for entering at length on 'such questions as whether there was such a person as Krişṇa, whether the Krişṇa of the *Gītā* was the Krişṇa of the *Purāṇa*, whether the *Gītā* was composed by Krişṇa at all, whether Krişṇa is a Hinduised edition of Christ.'[2] Still further is it from the purpose of

[1] *V.S.M.R.S.*, p. 38.
[2] *Indian Social Reformer*, September 7, 1919.

this book to go about 'trying to discredit names and ideas held in deep veneration by the people'.[1] When, however, we are told positively that 'Krişna was the great leader and teacher who at a time of dire peril and confusion gave India the watchword which has preserved her to this day', something is stated as a historic fact which by such a first-rate authority as Sir R. G. Bhandarkar is only hazarded as a possibility and even then only by virtue of 'the Hindū habit of thought of identifying one god with another by regarding the latter either as forms or incarnations of the former and thus evolving monotheism out of polytheism.'[2]

8. The Text-Book of Vaishnavite Bhakti

The teachings by which the figure of Vishņu-Krişņa has kept its place in India are found in their authoritative form in the *Bhagavadgītā*. Though not very short, this is condensed and intricate and presupposes ages of philosophic discussion. Some have held it to be at the bottom a compromise between different views, but see below for other possibilities. Its method has been compared with that of the Anglican Prayer-book, in the form for the rite of the Eucharist, where the consecrated bread is handed to the worshipper with a formula which places side by side two opposite views of its nature. The result has been—whether intentionally or not—that just as members of the Church have been divided as to which view the Church holds, so Hindūs are divided as to whether the *Gītā* takes the *dvaita* or the *advaita* (pantheistic) view of the divine nature.

Without pretending to expound the *Gītā* or to sum up its views we may safely call it the text-book of *bhakti*, a word which means loving devotion, the *bhakti* school being those who hold that man's salvation (however this may be defined) is accomplished by loving devotion to God as personal. Whether the author of the *Gītā* was trying to reconcile the various schools of thought in his day, or whether his is the fountain from which those schools subsequently flowed, the ideas of the book, once launched into the Hindū world, have had a long history and a powerful influence over men.

Dr. Farquhar considers the enquiry concerning 'the far-famed *Bhagavadgītā*' has advanced a distinct stage. He states that 'most modern scholars recognize that, in its present form, it can scarcely be earlier than the first or second century A.D.,' whereas the late Justice Telang and Sir R. G. Bhandarkar have held it belonged to the fourth century B.C. The Vaishnavas or worshippers of Vishņu, at first only a heterodox sect, were finally established as a real force in Hinduism under the powerful influence of the two great reformation movements represented by

[1] *Indian Social Reformer*, September 7th, 1919.
[2] *V. S. M. R. S.*, p. 19.

Buddhism and Jainism, and the *Gītā* is their product. If it is 'the expression of the earliest attempt made in India to rise to a theistic faith and theology,' then the earliest Indian Theism is much later than has been hitherto supposed. The poem seeks to give all Vaishnavas a truly spiritual religion by bringing 'release' within reach of all men and women of the four chief castes, in itself a religious revolution, the *Gītā* thus becoming 'the layman's Upanishad'. This it does by instituting a new method in Hinduism, the *bhakti-marga* or path of loving devotion. Viewed at first as a heterodox book, since it sprang from 'the young Vaishnava sect' itself then viewed as heterodox, the *Gītā* is now read by half the population of India as 'the very cream of orthodoxy', and it is 'probable that the poem is purely of Indian origin' without any Christian influence.[1]

9. Vaishnava and Orthodox Hinduism

It is worth noting the relation of this influential Vaishnava sect in Hinduism to those viewing themselves as orthodox. The Vaishnava devotees have sometimes been described as revolting from orthodox Hinduism in some such way as Protestant reformers from the Church of Rome. This view of them is, however, only partly correct and is mostly misleading. Side by side with Vaishṇava Hinduism ran another line, the line of Śaivite worship holding the *advaita* creed (pantheism) in its extreme form. Naturally the Vaishnava system with the *dvaita* (duality) creed that accompanies it has occasionally looked like a reformation or a reaction against the other, but there does not seem to have been any acute conflict between the two.

We may admit an occasional clash. The Vaishṇava system tends to reject caste and of course the Brāhman ascendancy. But it never carries the tendency far. A foreign observer is astonished that it does not follow out its apparent principles, but though it stumbles across the objection to caste it does not act on it. There were revolts against caste in the history of Hinduism but the remarkable thing is they have seldom proceeded from the Vaishṇavites.

Vaishnava saints have written more in the vernacular than the *advaita* philosophers and this reminds the European of the Protestant movement. There is some real resemblance, yet it may easily be exaggerated and it should be observed that the Vaishnava writers did not pretend to publish the truth of the Vedas in the vernacular so much as attempt to provide the unlearned man with a simple devotional literature. So far the Brāhmans had no objection to their programme and we must not think of the Brāhmans fighting the *bhakti-marga* or the Vaishṇava saint with the

[1] See *O. R. L. I.*, pp. 86–92

feelings of a Roman towards a Protestant There was plenty of wrangling between the *dvaita* and *advaita* schools of philosophy but each school had its Brāhman champions. And the Brāhmans always took possession of the Vaishṇava shrines and administered them; an amicable arrangement was observed, 'either by the appointment of real Vaishnavas as ministrants, or by the recognition of the actual incumbents as Vaishnavas.'[1]

This leads to the question as to how the Brāhman priests acquired their great ascendancy even in the reformed type of Hinduism which Vaishṇavism presents to our view. Probably the simplest and truest explanation of this priestly ascendancy in Vaishnava Hinduism is the fact that adaptation to the changing circumstances has ever been the law of the Brāhmans.[2]

Whatever the status of priests in Aryan or pre-Aryan days the priest of later Hinduism was the recognised head of all the castes, and one much wonders how he got and kept the place. Even so, the Brāhman position has not been equally strong in all parts of India. In Bengal, for instance, the Brāhmans appear to be almost a depressed class compared with what they have been in the Deccan. Some dissenting bodies of Hinduism, the Lingāyats, for instance, have their priests, but they keep them in their place. The Parsīs have priests but do not yield them any ascendancy, and it appears to be perhaps an accident of destiny that so high a rank has been conceded to the Brāhman.[3]

10. Differing Elements in Vaishnavite Bhakti

It will already have become clear that the influence of Vaishnava *bhakti* has neither been simple nor has it given rise to a united school of believers. The erotic manifestations of *bhakti* in some parts have presented a *bhakti* of an essentially different type from that in Mahārāshtra, where its literature has exercised an influence of a democratizing national value. Side by side with these types other developments have arisen sometimes resembling the Vaishṇavite system, but certainly often differing from it, and *bhakti* belief and practice have often absorbed alien elements. This is so in the religion of every country, for men are not and cannot be wholly consistent in their religious and moral systems, but in India the capacity for inconsistency is greater than elsewhere.

Dr. Farquhar has shown that for nearly five hundred years (A. D. 900 to 1350) the development of Hinduism was largely influenced by the various sects that arose and that these sects were themselves greatly influenced by 'wandering singers' and their

[1] *O. R. L. I.*, p. 51

[2] On the 'unfailing adaptability' of the Brāhman see Sir Valentine Chirol in *Indian Unrest*, p. 31 and Sir Alfred Lyall, p. xii in the same book.

[3] See also section 12, chap. 1

'enthusiastic *bhakti*'. This development went on until the middle of the sixteenth century by which time these religious sects were very considerable in both numbers and influence. From 1700 this important factor of the religious sects became a diminishing quantity. 'Multitudes have drifted back to undifferenced polytheism, carrying with them the merest shreds of the old thought. Uneducated *pūjārīs* (temple-ministrants) with their numerous images and mongrel ritual strengthen the reactionary movement. The mass of Śūdras belonged to no sect but worshipped now one god, now another.'[1] In these long centuries the important *Bhāgavat* religion, with its *bhakti* and its equalizing of Vishnu and Śiva, was laying hold of the country, and since Marāthā saints were Bhāgavatas it behoves us to understand what the nature of this religion was. Of its chief scripture, the *Bhāgavata Purāna*, Dr. Farquhar says. 'What distinguishes it from all earlier literature is its new theory of *bhakti*; and therein lies its true greatness. Some of its utterances on this subject are worthy of a place in the best literature of mysticism and devotion. A careful study of those passages will convince the student that they are expressions of a living religious experience. . . . In this rich religious element lies the chief source of the power of the *Bhāgavata*. Hence the hold it has had on some of the best Vaishṇava communities and on many of the noble minds of India.'[2]

Such facts as the foregoing will help us to understand something of the religious condition of India, as we watch the rising influence of the various *bhakti* sects in South, North and Western India.

II. Early Bhakti of South India Vaishnavism

While the earliest references to the worship of Vāsudeva appear to belong geographically to North-West India, to Rājputāna and to the Marāthā country, the Vaishṇavite *bhakti* system seems to have reached its vigour earlier in the South than elsewhere. This was due to the influence exerted by a set of Vaishṇava poet-musicians named the Ālvārs whose religion was one of passionate emotion and who wandered from shrine to shrine in the Tamil country, composing hymns and singing them in ecstasy. Though they were the leaders and teachers of the Śrī-Vaishṇava sect, a sect very strict in all caste matters, they yet taught Śūdras and out-castes as well as caste people. Not only are their hymns collected and arranged to-day, but their images are even worshipped in the temples. The teaching of the Ālvārs culminated in Rāmānuja, whose birth is fixed in A. D. 1016 and his death in 1137 at 120 years of age. He was a Brāhman of Conjeeveram, and is

[1] *O. R. L. I.*, pp 292, 220, 82.
[2] *Ibid*, pp. 229-230.

regarded as 'the philosophical theologian of the *bhakti* school' supporting the Vaishnava worship with an interpretation of the ancient writings which preserves the personality of God as an ultimate truth. This leaves the devotee free to believe that *bhakti* or personal adoration is actually offered to the Supreme and human worship can go no further. Rāmānuja was followed by Madhva who established much the same conclusion by different trains of reasoning. These two are the two great theologians of the Vaishṇava school, though they are not, as an example of life, so cherished as are other less learned saints, and having written in Sanskrit they are not understood of the people. [1]

12. The Bhakti of North India Vaishnavism

Of the sect of Rāmānuja, and some three and a half centuries later, was Rāmānanda (circ. 1400–1470) a famous ascetic of Benares whose name is still surrounded with obscurity.[2] He taught that all God's servants are brothers, that faith in God, and neither caste nor position, is the thing that matters. 'Let no one ask a man's caste or with whom he eats. If a man shows love to God he is God's own'. Of his twelve apostles two were women, Padmāvati and Surasuri.

In Northern India the Vaishnava creed received a great impulse towards the end of the sixteenth century, its chief exponent being Tulsī Dās (1532–1623), who devoted himself to Rāma, an *avatāra* of Vishnu, and identified the cult with a spirited and noble morality. If Krisna is the most popular Hindū hero, 'Rāma is, perhaps, the most venerated', as embodying the highest Hindū ideals. 'The pole-stars of his life are devotion to duty and self-sacrifice. He gives up a kingdom to maintain his father's word. He gives up a peerless wife to please his people.' But he embodies the Hindū social polity also in 'some of its weaknesses such as the surrender of judgement to popular clamour and the unquestioned acceptance of the current system as divinely ordained.'[3]

Vallabha and Chaitanya worshipped Krisna, the latter (1486–1534) spreading the Krisna cult through Bengal, where the bloody sacrifices to Kālī and the dark superstitions of the tantra worship struck him with horror. He must be reckoned a reformer, but his presentation of the Vaishnava system is in many ways unedifying. On the one hand he spins endless subtleties about the different kinds of love enjoyed by Krisna and Rādhā, thus reproducing the very atmosphere of dialectic which the *bhakti* school wishes to leave behind. On the other hand, his corrective seems to have been an

1 On Rāmānuja and Madhva see Dr. Macnicol's *Indian Theism*, chaps. vii and viii.

2 Farquhar, *O.R.L.I.*, p. 323.

3 *Indian Social Reformer*, August 24, 1919.

endless round of dancing and swooning before the god. Chaitanya's emotion leads to something like hysteria, while sensuality results from that of the Vallabhas. The unbridled emotionalism of the latter sect was exposed in the Bombay Courts in 1863, as it had long before been expressed by Mīrā Bāī, queen of Udaipur in the fifteenth century 'There is but one male in existence, namely my beloved Kanai Lāl (Krişna), and all besides are females.'[1]

Chaitanya seems to have been related to the shrine at Jagannāth much as Tukārām was to Pandharpūr. This famous shrine is better known to Europeans than Paṇdharpūr, probably because it is nearer to a city like Calcutta, and because somebody at some time or other invented the fantastic myth about Jagannāth's car. The poems about Jagannāth at Puri are all cries for mercy, resembling those of Tukārām, when in that frame of mind. They are, however wanting in the moral sturdiness of Tukārām.

13. Maratha Bhaktas and Their Bhakti

It is into a very different atmosphere we pass when we begin to study the *bhakti* school of Mahārāshtra, where the chief names are Dnyāneshwar of the thirteenth century, Nāmdev of the fourteenth, Eknāth of the sixteenth and Tukārām of the first half of the seventeenth.

The first of these, *Dnyāneshwar*, commonly referred to as 'the father of Marathi poetry', is famous as the author of the Marāthī poetical commentary on the *Bhagavadgītā* called the *Dnyāneshwarī* and as the one whose name is to-day coupled with that of Tukārām by pilgrims on their way to Pandharpūr as they march on chanting the names of their two greatest teachers: Dnyānobā, Tukobā; Dnyānobā, Tukobā[2] The lofty spirit of Dnyāneshwar's teaching may be inferred from his prayer at the close of the *Dnyāneshwarī*, a portion of which runs as follows:[3] 'May God the Universal Soul be well-pleased with the offering of my words, and being pleased, may He grant me this favour—that sin may depart from the wicked; that in them the love of good works may increase, and that mutual friendship may grow in the whole of the race. May the darkness of sin disappear, may the Universe behold the sun of righteousness, and may the longings of mankind attain satisfaction. May all three worlds be perfected in joy and for ever worship the Supreme Being'.

Nāmdev, who was famous among his own people as the *kutumb-kavi* because every member of his family, even the maid-servant, could compose poetry, is the first Marathā poet to denounce idolatry with real force. With him it was always plain

[1] *E R E.* Vol. 9 p 116 b.

[2] Sometimes varied as Dnyāndev, Tukārām, or, Gyāndev, Tukārām

[3] Questions of text arise in some of the following phrases, the translation of which would need to be modified accordingly.

speech: 'They are fools lost to anything good who worship gods of stone: those who say and those who believe that a god made of stone speaks to his devotee are both stupid'. *But* Nāmdev continued the use of idols! The legend is told of Nāmdev that, being a robber, he was driven to 'make a friend of repentance' by the sorrows of a lonely widow whose husband had been killed by Nāmdev's band. Finding 'no mercy in a Śaivite temple, he plunged a knife into his own head as he stood before Śiva, the blood spurting forth and defiling the god. Cast out in anger by the people, he heard in his bitterness a voice bidding him go to Paṇdharpūr: 'Its patron god, Viṭṭhal, will purge thee of thy sins, and thou shalt not only obtain salvation, but renown as one of God's saints'.

Eknāth had his poems publicly thrown into the Godāvari river because he practised the principle laid down in the *Bhāgavadgītā* that 'a man of knowledge looks with the same eye upon a Brāhman well-versed in learning, upon a cow, or an elephant or a dog or an out-caste'. So completely was this principle observed by Eknāth the Vedantist, the Brāhman, the idolater, that on one occasion he lifted on to his own shoulder an out-caste Mahār boy whose feet were burning on the hot sand; on another occasion he took and befriended a Mahār thief after the latter's release from punishment in the stocks; on a third occasion some poor Mahārs having expressed a longing for a feast similar to one Eknāth had prepared for a company of Brāhmans, they were invited to join in and at his wife's suggestion the whole of the Māhār community were later fed in Eknāth's compound; while on a fourth occasion Eknāth went so far as to accept an invitation to dine at the house of a Mahār, though in the account of this last incident his biographer makes out that Eknāth's god took Eknāth's form. The following story is also told of him. Returning from his morning bath in the holy Godāvari, a Mohammedan spat on him. Without a word he went back and bathed again. Once more the man met him and repeated the insult. As Eknāth calmly turned round and walked back towards the river a bystander asked him why did he not curse the wretch. 'Why should I curse my benefactor?' was the reply; 'but for him I should have bathed only once in the sacred stream. Now I have bathed twice, and I must needs go again.'

Though all these Deccan *bhaktas* have something of true nobility, none has the deep personal interest of Tukārām. He must have known their writings well and no doubt owes to them many of his phrases. It is curious, however, that he does not often directly mention this debt: it was perhaps sufficiently known to his audience. Tukārām describes himself as initiated into the Vaishnava order by a wandering devotee whose name was Bābājī: this man in turn gave the names of his own teachers as Rāghava-Chāitanya and Keshava-Chaitanya, but there is nothing to show who these men were.

14. Vaishnavite Revival in Vithoba's Land

How great and far-reaching was the influence exerted by these *bhaktas* of the Deccan has been set forth by the late Justice M. G. Ranade who shows that the political revolution which stirred Mahārāshtra towards the close of the sixteenth century was preceded and in fact to some extent caused, by a religious and social upheaval which moved the entire population. As in Europe in the sixteenth century, so the contemporary Reformation in the Deccan was religious, social and literary, not Brahmanical in its orthodoxy, but ethical and heterodox in the spirit of protest against all distinctions based on birth, a reformation which was the work of the people, of the masses not of the classes. The movement was led by saints and prophets, poets and philosophers, who sprang chiefly from the lower orders of society—tailors, carpenters, potters, gardeners, shop-keepers, barbers and even Mahārs. 'What Protestantism did for Western Europe in the matter of civil liberty was accomplished on a smaller scale in Western India. The impulse was felt in art, in religion, in the growth of the vernacular literature, in communal freedom of life, in increase of self-reliance and toleration.'[1] From the twelfth to the seventeenth centuries there are no less than fifty names of popular leaders in this great movement.

For the explanation of this reviving, purifying and democratizing of the Hinduism of the Deccan we have to go to Paṇḍharpūr and there learn what little the muse of history will reveal concerning that god who was enshrined in the thought and affection of the poet-saint of Dehū. If we could forget Tukārām's veneration for the image of Vithobā we could hail him as a fellow-Protestant, but that would be to forget half of Tukārām's spiritual life, wrapped up as it is so closely with the condescending love which he supposed God to have shown in accepting the incarnation at Paṇḍharī. We cannot afford to forget that if he were alive to-day Tukārām might show himself disagreeably obstinate about the historic authentic character of Vithobā's *avatāra*, for he regarded Paṇḍharpūr as a holy place because it was at Pandharpūr that Vishṇu seemed to stand incarnate and visible, Tukārām in some way identifying that incarnation with the figure on the brick, exactly how, he does not say. He 'wanted some material effigies on which he could set his eyes and which he could clasp with his hands; and he found that satisfaction in the stone god Vithobā. He daily visited him; he decked him with flowers, offered incense to him, and pressed him tenderly to his bosom, addressing him in language of fond affection. Hence the mad devotion of Tukārām for Viṭhobā.'

[1] G R. Navalkar, *Tukārām, The Mahārāshtrian Poet and Saint*, pp. 29, 30, 32 and 33.

15. The Name Vithoba—Its Origin and Significance

Efforts have been made by scholars to elucidate the problem of the origin of the god Viṭhobā and the etymology of the name.

(1) Sir R. G. Bhandarkar believes 'the full name of the god is Viṭṭhal' and that the corruption of the Sanskrit name Vishṇu in the Kanarese language is probably Viṭṭhu, the terminations *kā* and *lā* being appended to the name Vishṇu or Vitthu to indicate the sense of tenderness or reverence.[1]

(2) This is supported by Pandit Bhagwānlāl Indrajī[2] who holds the name Viṭhobā to be a short form of Viṭhalbāva, that is, Father or Dear Viṭṭhal, the Yādav inscriptions making it probable that the oldest of these names is Vitthal and probably Kanarese.

(3) Similar to this is the conclusion reached by Dr. William Crooke[3] who suggests the name may be 'a corruption of Vishṇu-pati, lord Vishṇu', through a local form Bistu or Biṭṭu, the name Pāṇḍurang, usually understood to mean 'white coloured', being probably a Sanskritized form of Paṇḍaraga, 'belonging to Paṇḍarge', the old name of the place. According to this view Viṭhobā would appear to be a local deity admitted into Hinduism as a form of Vishṇu. The term Viṭhobā thus being traced back to Viṭṭhal, what of the latter?

(4) Mr. L. J. Sedgwick sets forth three possible etymologies for the word Viṭṭhal, one being that it stands for *Ishti-sthal*, *ishti* being used for a brick and also a special form of sacrifice; another being that it comes from the Marāthī words *viṭ*=*loathing*, and *ṭālṇe*=*to avoid*; a third being that it is connected simply with the Marāthī word *iṭ*=a brick (often pronounced *viṭ*), and meaning 'the Vishṇu of the brick'. On the story of Pundalīka, whose filial devotion Kṛiṣṇa is said to have so appreciated as to consent to become incarnate in an image which should always 'stand on a brick' (=Viṭhobā),[4] Mr. Sedgwick theorizes that about the middle of the 12th century Pundalīka brought to Panḍharpūr a statue found in some other part of India and under the name of Viṭṭhala set it up in a disused temple of Mahādev. If it be asked why did Pundalīka call the statue Viṭṭhala, Mr. Sedgwick concludes this may have been the name of Pundalīka's father and that 'the statue was intended by him to be merely a commemoration of his deceased parent' whom he worshipped to the end of his life.[5]

(5) Rao Sahib P. B. Joshi hints that the name Viṭṭhala may come from *Vishtrashravas*, 'the far-renowned', this being a rare classical epithet of Vishṇu and Kṛiṣṇa, Vistara and Viṭṭhala being philological parallels. But it is not proved either that the

1 *V.S.M.R.S.*, p. 87.
2 *B.G.* Vol. xx, p. 423.
3 Art. *Panḍhārpur* in *E.R.E.*, Vol. ix, pp. 601-2.
4 See *F.* and *M. Poems of Tukārām*, Vol 2, p. 452.
5 *J.R.A.S. Bo.*, Vol. 23, No. 65, pp. 123-5.

Paṇḍharpūr statue was ever called *Vishtrashravas*, or that the first half of the word, which is meaningless, usurped the place of the whole.[1]

(6) Most picturesque of all is the derivation given by Molesworth in his monumental *Marāṭhī and English Dictionary*[2] and accepted by the Rev. Ganpatrao R. Navalkar[3] who points out that to Brāhmans 'the initial letter *Vi* of the name Viṭṭhala indicates knowledge or understanding, it being a form of the Sanskrit root *vid*, to know or understand ; *tha* means a cypher, i.e., privation, destitution ; and *la* stands for *lāte*, he takes'. In this way *Viṭ*, *ṭha*, *la* form Viṭṭhala and the word may be interpreted to mean : 'Receiver of the ignorant and those destitute of understanding', or in Scriptural terminology, 'the Friend of publicans and sinners', as it has been rendered in poetry :

Sinners are we—I and you ;
Viṭhobā alone is true,
He receives the fallen too.

(7) In support of the second etymology under para (4) above it may be pointed out that Pundalīka is said to have been reclaimed from an irreligious life by the earnest piety of a Chāmbhār or cobbler and this heterogeneous character of Viṭhobā's worshippers is witnessed on festive occasions in the fusion of all castes. With the Brāhmans politically dominant in the country they must have felt a deep resentment against the god whose worship caused such pollution, a *viṭāḷ* on so great a scale. What wonder they called this god *Viṭāḷ* (pollution), the impersonation of defilement and abomination ! So runs the popular argument.

(8) It is worthy of note that some authorities attach the highest importance to Tukārām's own couplet on Vithobā's name,

Vicā kelā ṭhobā
Mhanoni nāva to Vithobā

numbered 4118 in the *Indu Prakāsh* edition and translated by Fraser and Marāthe (2828, vol. iii) : 'a pillar of wisdom he made himself, hence his name is Viṭhobā.' Translating the Marāṭhī note by Mr. V. N. Joga, the late Brāhman leader of the *Wārkarīs*, in his valuable commentary on Tukārām's *abhangs* (vol. 2, p. 314) we get the following English rendering of Tukārām's lines : *Vi* has become *thobā* and thus His (God's) name is Vithobā. Of the two important Marāṭhī words in the first line, *vi* stands for *vid*, knowledge, as in para (6) on this page, while *ṭhobā* (a meaningless term whose nearest Marāthī word is *ṭhombā*, a shapeless block of wood) takes the sense of *ākār*, shape or form. Tukārām's couplet would thus appear to mean that the Formless (Brahma) has assumed a form, that Divine Knowledge (*vid*) has taken concrete visible shape,

[1] *J.R.A.S. Bo.*, Vol 23, No. 65, p. 234.
[2] See under the word *Viṭṭhal*, p 757, col. 2.
[3] *Tukārām, Mahārāshṭrian Poet and Saint*, pp. 5-6.

that the Impersonal has become Personal, that God Impersonal and Unseen has become Personal and Manifest. This interesting interpretation, if it can be sustained, is in complete harmony with the conception of the Divine Being and its manifestation held by the Vaishnava *bhakti* school dealt with in this chapter. Some students of Tukārām, however, taking *ṭhobā* in Tukārām's couplet to refer to *thombā* in the other sense of the latter word which makes it refer to 'an ignorant fellow', hold that Tukārām makes the name Viṭhobā signify that *Vi*, Knowledge or the All-Knowing, has condescended to manifest or incarnate Itself in what to outward seeming is an ignorant and unthinking material object. See further on *Tukārām's Idolatry*, chapter 6, section 1.

We are bound to conclude, however that the difficult problem of the origin of the god Vithobā and the etymology of the name must be regarded as yet unsolved.

Our study thus far has brought us to Pandharpūr, the home of Vithobā and the pilgrim city of Tukārām. In our next chapter we shall with him 'go to Paṇḍharpūr' and in imagination 'be a pilgrim there'.

A REMONSTRANCE[1]

Graciously thy heart incline :—
Open to me, brother mine !

He's a saint who knoweth how
To the world's abuse to bow.

. . . .

Surely he whose soul is great
Is to all compassionate.

Thou pervading Brahman art
How should anger fill thy heart ?

Such a poiséd soul be thine.
Open to me, brother mine !

Muktābāī (13th century) *P. M. S.*, p. 41.

A BITTER CRY

When will the end of these things be ?
Ah, tell me, Lord of Paṇḍharī.
When wilt thou save unhappy me ?

O tell me, tell me true, for I
Cry to thee with a bitter cry.

Why speakest thou not ? Ah, Viṭṭhal, why
Thus silent ? Whither shall I fly ?

Who else will bear my sore distress ?
Smite me not in my helplessness.

As to the child is wholly sweet
His mother,—so to me thy feet.

. . . . .

Nāmdev (14th century) *P. M S.*, p. 44.

GOD WHO IS OUR HOME

To the child how dull the Fair
If his mother be not there !

So my heart apart from thee,
O thou Lord of Pandharī !

. . .

As the stream to fishes thou,
As is to the calf the cow.

To a faithful wife how dear
Tidings of her Lord to hear !

How a miser's heart is set
On the wealth he hopes to get !

Such, says Tukā, such am I !
But for thee, I'd surely die.

Tukārām 1608-50 *P. M. S.*, p. 57.

[1] This *Abhang* is said to have been addressed by Muktābāī to her brother Dynānesvar on an occasion when the door of his hut was closed against her and she supposed him to be angry.

Chapter III

The Pilgrimage To Pandharpur
A Study in India's Religious Aspiration

1. Tukaram and the Pilgrim City

Paṇḍharpūr having exercised a unique influence both on Tukārām's personal experiences and on his writings, it is important to consider what is known of this great pilgrim centre. How Tukārām viewed the pilgrims with whom he must so often have journeyed is shown in Fraser and Marāthe's translation of the following *abhangs*: 1499, 1500, 1512–14, 1523, 1530–9 in vol. II. On Paṇḍharpūr as a pilgrim centre, whole sections are taken up with it, e.g., section xv. in vol. III beginning with the words, 'Go, go to Paṇḍharpūr; be, be a pilgrim there!' Before, however, we consider the subject of pilgrimage in Tukārām's day and in the city so dear to him it may be well, by way of preface, to consider the subject of Indian Pilgrimage in general and note how passionate is that religious aspiration to which it is an index.

2. Moksha and Self-Torture

For three thousand tragic years *Moksha* has been the religious quest of India. This supreme aspiration after union with God, which is rightly considered 'the pith and kernel of the religious faiths of India', runs through the *Bhagavadgītā*, that sacred book held dear by no less than one hundred and fifty millions of India's people. This great desire—often despite unworthy accompaniments—is the inspiring motive of India's astonishing asceticism, with its five and a half million mendicants, *Sādhus* and ascetics, whose self-mortification goes to extremes which are disastrous both socially and religiously. These austerities are practised both by Śaivite and Vaishṇava Hindūs but mostly by the former. What soul can remain unmoved as it contemplates the indescribable self-torture inflicted to win emancipation? As part of their *tapascharyā* or austerities some lower grades of *sādhus*, and occasionally *sādhvīs* (female ascetics) too, practise self-mortifications repellent and disgusting in the extreme, though with a motive investing them with noble pathos Such are the *Panchatapas* or *Panchadhūni* whose penance consists in enduring the heat of five fires around them, the fifth sometimes being that of the sun with its fierce heat pouring down on their unclothed bodies; the *Ūrdhvabāhu* who extend one or both arms over their head until rigid and atrophied; the *Ūrdhvamukhin* or *Bhūmimukhin* who for half an hour or more hang downwards from the bough of a tree, head nearly touching the ground; the *Akāśmukhin* who keep the neck bent back as they gaze on a sky of brass; the *Nakhin* who let finger-nails grow to inordinate lengths; the *Jalaśāyī* who spend the whole night immersed in water; the *Phalāhāri* who subsist on fruits; and the *Dudhāhāri* who live solely on milk. Other forms of self-torture consist in sitting or sleeping on a couch studded with nails or on a bed of spikes (a Brāhman ascetic at Benāres lay naked thus for thirty-five years); while others observe a vow of silence for years, or chew live coals, or thrust knives or skewers into their flesh, or tread on glowing ashes, or allow themselves to be buried alive. Some of the higher grades of *Sannyāsīs*, especially the *Daṇḍī Sannyāsīs*—so named from the wand (*daṇd*) which they carry—have to undergo a probation of twelve years which is spent in wandering about in all weathers; some of them go naked, others refuse food unless supplied by the hands of a virgin. There are others who practise *ashṭadandvata*, measuring the ground by prostrations of the eight parts of the body—forehead, breast, hands, knees and insteps, in this way taking long pilgrimages to sacred places by slow marches which necessitate hundreds of thousands of painful prostrations. In such cases the pilgrims' hands are sometimes covered with padded wooden clogs, the soles being studded with hob-nails, some devotees in the performance of vows crawling the last stage on their sides or on their ankles, completing the journey by standing on their heads before the idol.[1]

An impressive example in the Marāṭhi country, illustrating the deep pathos of India's religious quest, is supplied by the case of Joga Paramānand, a poet and *bhakta* of Vithobā, long before Tukārām's day. One day, when measuring his body from his house in Barsi to the temple of Bhagwān in the town, at each prostration repeating a *sloka* from the *Bhagavadgītā*, as was his daily custom, a rich merchant vowed he would give him a costly silk garment if he got a son. On the arrival of a son the vow was fulfilled and Joga had to wear the costly covering in place of his rags. Prostrating himself as usual, but more carefully, lest the garment be spoiled, the saint reached the temple a few moments after morning *pūjā* (worship) was over. Whereupon he bitterly blamed the newly acquired garment, tore it to pieces, and ever after wore his rags.[2]

[1] *E.R.E*, Vol 2, pp 87–96, Art. *Asceticism (Hindu)*, A. S. Geden; Vol. 6, p. 701 b, Art. *Hinduism*, W. Crooke, Vol 10, p. 26a, Art. *Pilgrimage (Indian)*. W. Crooke; Vol 11, p. 330a, Art *Sects (Hindu)*, W. Crooke; and J. C. Oman, *Cults, Customs, and Superstitions of India*, p. 9.

[2] V. L. Bhave, *M. Sar.*, p. 70.

3. Pilgrim Centres in Western India

A brief consideration of what goes on in at least two other pilgrim centres in Tukārām's India—Mahārāshtra—will enable us better to appreciate Paṇḍharpūr.[1]

Nāśik is an object of pilgrimage because situated on one of India's sacred rivers, the Godāverī. According to one estimate no less than thirty million pilgrims are expected to visit Nāśik during the *Sinhasth*, a festival which occurs every twelve years when Jupiter is in the constellation of Leo, a season considered by Hindū authorities a favourable period for the washing away of sins. In the present year (1920), this 'duodecennial' festival which usually lasts eighteen months and which started on July 14 was practically over before Christmas, that is in less than five months. The disappointed *Pujārīs* (ministrants) gave two reasons for the failure, viz., famine conditions and the spread of education, some *Sādhus* bemoaning the fact that many of their clients who used to come from a distance by train and motor-car had not appeared this year.

Jejurī, on the Southern Māhratta Railway thirty-two miles south-east of Poona, is sacred to Khaṇḍobā, a god worshipped by the middle and low castes of Mahārāshtra and the cause of much obscenity. Khaṇḍobā is of the family of Śiva who represents all that is most repulsive in India's worship, who attracted to himself much of the sordid worship of the aborigines of the land, and who about the 12th century appears to have instigated a terrible persecution of Vaishṇavas, Buddhists and Jains. The 'dogs of Khandobā', as his devotees are called, are slaves of passion; boys born after a vow to Khaṇḍobā merely adding to the number of India's 'holy beggars', while girls are doomed to lifelong degradation.[2] See also chapter 5, II, 10 on 'doubtful religious characters'.

If Khaṇḍobā, the Śaivite god of Jejurī, shows Hinduism on its darker side, the Vaishṇava idol Vithobā represents Hinduism almost at its best. Far and away the most sacred city of Mahārāshtra is *Paṇḍharpūr* in the Sholapūr District of the Marāthā country, on which we are to concentrate our attention in order to learn with what passionate purpose Hindūs in Western India seek after *moksha*. 'You can buy liberation there for nothing' is the verdict of Tukārām, the most famous of the singers of Paṇḍharpūr. The chief sacred days are those in Āshādh (June or July) and Kārtik (October or November) when most of the visitors come from the Deccan, and with railway facilities the number is very large. At the

[1] This is not a section on 'sacred places', otherwise we should have to deal with many places, e. g., *Wāī*, on the Kṛṣṇa river, with a large Brāhman population, many temples and bathing *ghāts*, and notable in Śivājī's wanderings, one incident in Golewādī village near by illustrating the purity of his personal character. See *H M. P.*, p 153

[2] On Jejurī see *B G*, Vol xviii, part iii, pp 132–9, and part i, pp. 476–7 also *Contemporary Review*, September 1909, pp. 289–90.

Āshāḍhī Fair of 1919 no less than 140,000 pilgrims[1] entered the town, nearly 12,000 taking *darshan* daily, many of these taking the recognised pilgrim route which includes Dehū, Tukārām's birthplace[2] and Ālandī, the *samādhi* of Dnyāneśwar, and thence to Paṇḍharpūr. The god Vithobā, whose *darshan* so many eager souls aspire after, and said to be standing on the brick thrown to Kṛṣṇa by Pundalīka when the former told the latter to worship him as Viṭhobā (in other words as 'him who stood upon the brick'), has for its companion in the innermost shrine the image of Rukhminī, Kṛṣṇa's consort, since her flight and subsequent discovery were the cause of Kṛṣṇa's visit to Paṇḍharpūr. It is from this event that the town dates its importance in the history of Vaishṇava religion.[3]

4. On the Way to Pandharpur

How do Vithobā's 140,000 pilgrims reach Pandharpūr? The answer to this question not only vindicates the claim that Vaishnavism is the most genuine religion in Hinduism, but shows how closely linked with song is India's spiritual development. A section in our last chapter gave the names of the chief poets enshrined in the heart of the Marāṭhā nation. The depth of the people's devotion to their poet-saints is seen in the part the songs of these saints play in the annual pilgrimages. Pilgrims reach Paṇḍharpūr from all quarters and each company carries its own *pālkhī* (palanquin) containing the *pādukā* (or footprints) and as is believed the spirit of their bygone saint, whose praise they sing in his own or some other poet's verse, the leading refrain of these pilgrim songs being *Dnyānobā, Tukobā*. A prominent member of the Bombay Prarthanā Samāj, in an article describing his visit to the Āshāḍhī festival on June 26, 1920, writes: 'For the last three or four centuries, it has become customary to send on this *Ekādashī* day Pālkhīs or Palanquins from several places in Mahārāshtra and Berar connected with saints like Tukārām, Dnyāndev, Muktābāī and others. Stone images or *pādukās* of these saints are carried in these pālkhīs and a large number of pilgrims numbering from 100 to 2,000 accompany them. They come from long distances of fifty to a hundred miles travelling at the rate of eight to ten miles daily. They all come to a place five miles from Paṇḍharpūr on the morning of the *Ekādashī* day. In the evening these pālkhīs

[1] The 1920 Āshādhī Fair was attended by 124,775 pilgrims, the decline being attributed to the 'Sinhasth' Fair (Government of Bombay, General Department, Order No. 941, January 26, 1921).

[2] See section 5, Chap. 1

[3] See *H.M.P* Chap. xi, 'The Paṇḍharpūr Movement, A. D. 1271 to 1640', where the information given needs supplementing by study of the Marāṭhī sources.

start in a procession under police supervision so as to reach Paṇḍharpūr by 8 p.m. It is a really inspiring sight to see this procession. It lasts for nearly four hours. In front of each Pālkhī there are trumpets playing and wind-pipes blowing followed by *kīrtan*-parties enthusiastically singing and dancing, clapping their hands.'[1]

Official figures show that out of Vithobā's 140,000 worshippers attending the Āshāḍhī Fair, 55,923 travelled there by train. Pilgrimage by railway train is one example of changing India. This means that over 84,000 came by road and what pilgrimage to Paṇḍharpūr meant for some of them is indicated by the *Bombay Gazetteer* in its seventy pages on Paṇḍharpūr. Its section on *Pilgrims* contains the following: 'As soon as the pinnacle of Vithobā's temple comes in sight, the pilgrim stops and throws himself on the ground in honour of the god. Some pilgrims, who have taken a vow to that effect, continue to prostrate till they reach the town, or throw themselves at full length on the ground making a mark ahead as far as their hands can reach, then rise, walk up to the mark again, prostrate themselves, and so in this way reach the holy city. Some pilgrims roll on the ground all the way from Barsi Road (31 miles) or Jeūr (45 miles). Cases are said to have occurred of pilgrims rolling from Benāres, Nāgpūr, and Haidarabād in fulfilment of vows'.[2] Dr. J. Murray Mitchell gives a similar account of what he saw in 1881, telling of one man who 'had come, rolling like a log at the rate of two miles a day, from the neighbourhood of Nāgpūr, occupying about two years in the achievement.'[3] As recently as 1919 a Mamlatdar in government service, a devoted Vaishnava of B.A. attainments, distressed by his brother's mysterious disappearance, vowed he would go to Pandharpur by the method of *dandavat* (personal prostrations) if only his missing brother were found. To his astonishment he discovered the latter that very day, so bracing himself up for the hardship and possible ridicule, after a few days' practice of *dandavat* he obtained leave and made prostrations all the way from Hubli to Paṇḍharpūr, the journey taking several weeks.

These tragic methods of religious quest adopted in Hinduism against which the Ārya and Prārthanā Samājes utter so honourable a protest must have been well-known to our *bhakti* saint and poet Tukārām who if he ever practised them, which is more than doubtful, did so only to reject them, for he knew that by none of these things could his accusing conscience find rest.[4]

5. The Self-Accusations of Deccan Pilgrims

How stinging these accusations, despite Tukārām's personal popularity, his *abhaṅg* numbered 1334 in the *Induprakāsh*

[1] *Subodh Patrikā*, July 18, 1920.
[2] *B. G.* Vol. xx, p 470.
[3] *The Indian Antiquary*, Vol. xi, 1882, p. 155.
[4] See chap. 6, sect. 2, chap 8, sect. IV, para. 1, also chap. 9, sects. 8 and 11.

edition and 126 in Fraser and Marāthe shows: 'Oh sages, hear this what I say; I am a great fallen sinner, Why do ye love me with such tenderness? My heart is witness to me that I am not redeemed?' Or take his *abhang* numbered 476 in the above edition and translated by Fraser and Marāthe (number 343) in words which, though expressive, cannot convey the pathos and plaintiveness of the original Marāṭhī: 'Fallen of fallen, thrice fallen am I; but do Thou raise me by Thy power. I have neither purity of heart, nor a faith firmly set at Thy feet: I am created out of sin. How often shall I repeat it? says Tukā.' And listen yet again to the piercing cry: 'How can I be saved? Tell me O ye saints, and pacify my mind. How shall the sum of my past perish? I know not the secret, and hence I despair. How can I make myself pure? I weigh this thought continually day and night; I am disquieted. Tukā says, I have no strength of my own, to bring me to this final repose.'[1]

Nor was Tukārām alone, among Hindū pilgrims, in the possession of a sense of sin. 'Not to lay too much stress on a mere matter of words, the whole Karmic philosophy of Hinduism, the pilgrimages to rivers and shrines, the conception of heavens and hills, the innumerable *prāyaschittams* that abound in the moral code, all these testify to the presence of a sense of moral unworthiness.'[2] The Nāśik festival of the *Sinhasth* referred to above affords incidental proof that the sense of sin is by no means absent from the consciousness of the earnest Hindū pilgrim. This same festival affords also interesting evidence as to what the Hindū pilgrim feels he must do for the washing away of his sins. During this favourable period, says Sir Ramkrishna Gopal Bhandarkar, 'Hindūs go to holy places, such as Nāśik, shave their heads and moustaches and bathe in the river.'[3] How clearly Tukārām saw the futility of such methods and how fearlessly he criticized them is shown by his striking *abhang* numbered 2,869 in the *Indu-Prakāsh* edition and translated by Sir R. G. Bhandarkar as follows: 'When the auspicious juncture of Sinhasth comes, it brings fortune only to barbers and priests. There are crores of sins in the heart, but externally a man shaves the hair on the head and the beard. What has been shaved off, has disappeared. Tell me what else has changed. The vicious habits are not changed, which might be regarded as a mark of the destruction of sins; says Tukā, without devotion and faith everything else is useless trouble.'[4]

[1] *F. and M.* 363; *Induprakāsh* 619. See further Chap. 8 section iii, paras under 2 on Tukārām's Sense of Sin.

[2] *Christian Patriot*, Madras, June 19, 1920.

[3] *V. S. M. R. S.*, p. 94.

[4] For other renderings of this see *P. M. S.*, No. ciii, p. 88, and *F. and M.*, No. 2599, Vol. ii. p. 415.

6. Pandharpur and its Temples

The town of Paṇḍharpūr stands on the West bank of the Bhīma in the hollow of a great bend of the river. The bank itself is high and steep and below it there is a vast expanse of sand and gravel. On this are several temples in the usual Deccan style approached from the town by flights of steps or ghāts. From the opposite bank the little town half-buried in trees presents a picturesque sight with spires of temples emerging from among the tree-tops. The pilgrim coming from distant villages by road crosses the river by a ford, unless the water is too high, in which case there are large barges with curious equine figure-heads painted a bright red waiting to transport him.

The town itself wears a thriving appearance. Some small manufactures are carried on, a kind of decorated cloth being one of them. A mixture of resin is squeezed on to the cloth through a stencil and mica is dusted over the resin. The result is a bright glittering pattern. Pandharpūr's resident population in the census of March 18, 1921 was about 25,530.

Paṇḍharpūr, however, from the religious point of view is not a town but a holy place where many temples have been built, and we must begin our serious acquaintance with it by visiting these temples. They are numerous. Every god of importance has his place or places of worship. The following is a conspectus of the chief among them, there being many others not mentioned here.[1]

Shiva : There are many temples, large and small, insignificant and famous, of Śiva. Perhaps his most popular manifestation is simply the *liṅga* set up by Pundalīka, known as Pundalīka's temple. These are gracious manifestations, but there is also the temple of *Kāla-bhairāva*, with an image in black stone where the menacing aspect is displayed. His consort has shrines under the names of *Shākambarī*, *Ambābāī* and *Mahiṣāsura-mardinī*. These two latter represent her as a friend of man, the destroyer of the buffalo demon.

Khandoba : There is also a temple of the warrior god of the Deccan, about which no more need be said than appears in section 3 above, and in para 11, section II of chapter 5.

Ramchandra's Temple : This temple contains the images of Ganpati, Rāma, Lakshman, and Sīta. There is also a portrait image of Ahalyābāī, the builder. Such images are very rare in connection with Hinduism.

Ganpati's Temple : The original temple of Ganpati was destroyed by the Mahommedans, the present one being built in the reign of the last Peshwā. A stone marks the grave of Cokhāmeḷā, a Mahār devotee of Viṭhobā.

The Chophala Temple : This contains the *Panchāyatan*, or five images of Viṣnu, Amba, Ganpati, Mahādev and Surya.

[1] Full details are to be found in *B.G.*, Vol. xx. in its fine section on Pandharpūr to which we are indebted for much in this chapter

This is a popular combination bringing together the gods whose temples are usually separated.

Vyasa: The author of the *Mahābhārata* is honoured with a temple to himself.

Chandrabhaga: The spirit of the river is represented by a black stone image of a woman. On the top of the porch is (among other figures) a representation of the four-headed Bramha, who never has a temple to himself, though he is quite familiar as a figure on other gods' temples. Chandrabhāga is the name given to the river Bhīma in and around Pandharpūr because the bend of the river at this point assumes the form of the crescent moon (*chandra*). This and other details concerning Paṇdharpūr are given by Mahipatī in his book *Pāṇdurang Mahātmya* written in 1766.[1]

Maruti: This popular guardian of Deccan towns and villages, the famous monkey god, has two shrines or rather images, one black and one red. The red one owes its colour to the red paint lavished upon it and it is a conspicuous sight under a peepal tree in the town of Pandharpūr.

Vishnu: Besides the temple of Viṭhobā there are various other shrines of Viṣṇu. A little to the south of the town in the bend of the river there is a holy spot known as Vishṇupada. Here on the rocks there are a few rough cup-shaped indentations, which are said to be the foot-prints left by Kriṣṇa's cows when he brought them here on his wanderings in search of Rukminī. It was here he found her and here a feast was held to celebrate their reconciliation. Accordingly a temple has been built here and here *shrāddh* ceremonies are performed. Not far from this spot is the village of Gopālpūr, where there is another temple of Kriṣṇa, a fairly large structure in a courtyard enclosed by cloisters. Here we are shown a big jar where Yashodā used to make butter and the place is connected with Kṛiṣṇa's name by various tales. In Paṇdharpūr itself there is a temple of Kṛiṣṇa represented as Murlidhar, the flute-player: there is also one of the Dattātreya incarnation of Viṣṇu.

All the temples mentioned above are places of note: smaller temples and shrines abound. In some cases their origin is known, in others it is not, in no case does it appear to be of any interest or connected with any legend except that of the Tākpiṭhyā Viṭhobā. This is the name of a small image erected by a Brāhman widow who was crowded out of the temple and sat disappointed and fasting for fifteen days after which she fell asleep and on waking found this image miraculously presented to her by the god.

7. The Temple of Vithoba

We may now proceed to visit the sacred temple of Vithobā itself. It stands in the very centre of *Paṇḍhrī-kshetra*, the holy city of Paṇdharī. Round it is a courtyard, measuring 350

[1] See V. L Bhave, *M. Sar.*, pp. 382–3.

VIṬHOBĀ OF PAṆḌHARPŪR

feet by 170. The chief entrance to this is by the East gate called the Nāmdev gate. As the floor of the courtyard is above the level of the surrounding ground the gate is reached by twelve steps. On the lowest of these steps is placed a brass bust of Nāmdev who with his family took *samādhi* there, the step being plated with brass on which are stamped the figures of Nāmdev holding a *Kīrtan* and of the women of his family clapping their hands in accompaniment to his music. Inside the courtyard are many little shrines, to Ganpati, Māruti and Rāma and even Śiva and Bhairāva, and there are small living rooms, storehouses and other chambers for purposes connected with the temple. The central shrine has been constructed at various times. Its core appears to have been in the Hemadpanti style of the twelfth century, a style which though simple is one of the truly artistic styles of Hindū architecture. The shrine itself is approached by a long vestibule, with a flat roof and Westerners are allowed access to this roof from which part of the courtyard can be seen. It is all that they see of the interior, which is rigidly closed to all but Hindūs. This is in contrast with our experience at Dehū where on October 25, 1920, we were allowed to stand on the temple threshold examining by the aid of a hand-mirror the faces of Viṭhobā and Rukminī; at Pandharpur, however, access to the central shrine can only be gained by crossing the above-mentioned courtyard where un-Hindū feet never tread.

8. The god Vithoba

Western eyes, accordingly, do not gaze on the sacred image of Viṭhobā at Paṇḍharpūr and his shrine is small and dark, little being distinguished except by lamplight. Copies of the image are made and sold, one of which may be examined in the picture opposite. It is probably not unlike the original. This is three feet nine inches high, cut, probably, out of black trap rock. The upper part of the body is usually nude; round the waist is a waist-cloth; on his neck the god wears a collar with a jewel set in it; in his ears are the fish ear-rings. The image stands with arms akimbo and hands on hips, one hand carrying a conch-shell, the other a discus, Viṣṇu's emblems. On his forehead is the sextarial mark of Viṣṇu. His feet are evenly set on the square brick so often mentioned in the poems. Perhaps the most remarkable fact of all, and one we learned from a *Pujārī* (ministrant) on the spot during our visit on October 27, 1920, is the fact that Vithobā wears a curious tope-like crown, which the priests say is Śiva's *linga*; as is affirmed also in an *abhang* of Nivṛittināth, the older brother of Dnyāneśwar, and in a well-known line of Rāmdās's *Manobodh*.[1]

The copy of the image here presented is probably if anything superior to the original as a work of art and Western critics might conclude that whatever impression Vithobā has produced

[1] See chap. 6, sect. 4 on Śiva

upon mankind is not due to any aid from plastic art. With reference to the same picture in Dr. Macnicol's *Psalms of Marāthā Saints*, Miss Evelyn Underhill writes as follows: 'To the Western mind it seems almost incredible that the image of Vithobā, which forms the frontispiece of this volume, could arouse ardent feeling of any kind save that of repulsion; but we must remember that an ancient Greek would probably have found a Byzantine crucifix equally grotesque, and been wholly unable to understand the emotional glamour with which devotion has surrounded it.'[1] It may be that Hindūs are desirous of emphasizing their theory that their idols or sculptures are *swayambhū*, self-formed or self-created. This was what Dr. J. Murray Mitchell was told about Viṭhobā on his visit to Pandharpūr in December 1881: 'We were told it had not been fashioned by human hands but was *swayambhū* i.e., self-produced.[2] We were further informed that in the morning it looked like a child, at noon like a full-grown man, in the evening like an old man.'[3] On some occasions during the pressure of *Ashādh* and *Kārtik* observances the god 'is popularly represented as being tired out and his bed-chamber is closed.'[4]

9. Vithoba and Caste-Distinction

On the question of the equal privileges of all castes at Paṇḍharpūr there may easily be confusion. While it is quite correct to say that history shows 'Vitthala is quite free to all castes' and that 'in the 13th to 16th centuries distinction of caste was not observed in and about the temple precincts at Paṇḍharpūr,'[5] it is yet true that the Mahār poet and saint Cokhāmelā who is said to have died in 1338 (traditional date) was forbidden to enter Vithobā's temple? The only reason assigned is that he was an 'untouchable', a Mahār 'out-caste', and that 'out-castes' as such have never been allowed within the sacred precincts. This agrees with what Dr. J. Murray Mitchell saw on the spot: 'It is often asserted that caste is disregarded at Paṇḍharpūr; but we found that Mahārs were not allowed to approach beyond a certain point. This led us to ask for an explanation: and we quoted one of Tukārām's most remarkable *abhangs*, beginning

'Twixt the low and lofty, God no difference knoweth,
Still to faith He sheweth
All his glory,

[1] *Westminster Gazette*, Feb. 14, 1920. The review from which the above is taken is not signed with Miss Underhill's name but 'E U' is sufficient indication of the writer.

[2] The present writer was told the same in October, 1920

[3] *The Indian Antiquary*, Vol xi., 1882, p 151.

[4] L. J Sedgwick, I C S., *J. R. A. S. Bo*, Vol. 23, No 65, p. 126.

[5] *Ibid*, p 134.

in which the poet declares that the god Vithobā assisted the Mahār devotee Cokhāmeḷā even to bear off dead cattle—which is one of the most humiliating of employments. "Why then," we asked, "exclude Mahār worshippers now?" "That was all very well for the god," was the reply; "he may do as he pleases; but men must obey the rules of caste."[1]

The principle applied always at Paṇḍharpūr, the understanding of which will prevent any possible confusion as to the practice obtaining there, is that *low* castes are admitted to Vithobā's shrine, while *out*-castes or 'untouchables' are excluded, and always have been. Nevertheless, all that was said at the close of chapter I on 'the democratizing influence' of the Marāṭhā *bhaktas* holds true, with the result that in Vithobā's presence there is a cosmopolitanism found very rarely in Indian temples. This fact doubtless largely explains Vithobā's popularity with the masses of the people. Even those *Wārkarīs*[2] who are of low-caste origin, as well as other low-caste devotees of Vithobā, are allowed to embrace him in his innermost shrine, just like those of higher birth. It seems all the more unfortunate therefore that *out*-castes are not allowed at all within the precincts of Vithobā's temple, but must worship at the image of the Mahār saint Cokhāmeḷā on the other side of the street opposite Nāmdev's staircase.

It must be regarded as one of the many irreconcilable inconsistencies of Hinduism that in spite of *bhakti's* 'democratizing influence 'no out-caste is admitted to Bhāgavata temples in Mahārāshtra'.[3] And Vithoba's temple is a Bhāgavata temple.[4] On this subject see also section 6, 'Tukārām as Reformer,' and section 7, Tukārām and Caste,' in chapter 6.

10. Vithoba's Temple-service

It will be of interest to note what are the services performed in Vithobā's temple and who perform them. It would appear that no other Vaishṇava temple in India possesses a similar image, served as it is by a colony of *Deśastha* Brāhmans, including priests (*badvās*), ministrants, choristers, bath-men, singers, barbers, mace-bearers, and lamp lighters. Five times every twenty-four hours the round of service is performed. About three a.m. a priest begs the god to wake. The door being opened, food placed in the bed-chamber the previous day is removed, butter and sugar-candy are laid before the god, and a torch made of muslin soaked in butter is waved before him from head to foot. Many votaries come to behold Vithobā at this time, after which he is again fed, butter and sugar being placed in his mouth. Lights perfumed with camphor are waved, faded garlands are removed, the feet of the image are

[1] *The Indian Antiquary*, Vol. xi., 1882, pp. 151-2.
[2] See section on these in Chapter 7.
[3] *O.R.L.I*, p. 301. [4] See para 2, chapter 2, p. 27.

washed first in milk and then in water, and the service proper (*pūjā*) then begins. The image is unrobed and bathed, a sheet being held before the door while he is naked. Before the 1873 attack on Vithobā by the Śaivite enthusiast (see section 14 below) the god was washed in warm water, but since the left leg had to be cemented it is said that cold water mixed with saffron has been used. After his bath he is dried and dressed in new robes, his face being wiped and rubbed with scented oil until it shines. A turban is bound round his head and garlands of flowers are hung on his neck, while the barber holds a mirror before him. His feet are washed and rubbed with sandal, and sandal paste is applied to his brow. About three in the afternoon the god is again dressed, the ministrant bathing and adorning him. Wednesday and Saturday are days specially sacred to the god unless these fall at the conjunction of sun and moon or at ominous conjunctions of planets, and as with all Vaishnavas, the eleventh day in each fortnight of the lunar month (*ekādashī*) is a fast day.[1]

11. The Pilgrim's Priest and Ceremonies

Having learned what there is to see with the bodily eye at Paṇḍharpūr we may now follow the pilgrims on their arrival there and observe what use they make of their time. Each pilgrim on arrival is bound by custom to enroll himself as the client of some priest. Strictly speaking, indeed, he should engage three priests, a *Badvā* to conduct him to Vithobā, an *Utpat* to conduct him to Rukminī, and an ordinary local Brāhman to perform the river-side ceremonies. To mix with the crowd and salute the god in passing requires no priestly help, but most pilgrims come desirous to accomplish something more. They have no difficulty in finding priests, for records are kept of all visitors and the priest who has once served a family has a right, and his family inherit a right, to serve its descendants. Every pilgrim is met on his arrival and handed over to his proper priest, who generally makes all necessary arrangements for his stay.

Early on the morning after his arrival the pilgrim goes down to the river to perform the *Gangā-bheṭ*, the ceremony of meeting the Ganges, as the Bhīmā is called for the time being. He places on the ground a cocoanut, some sandal paste, tulsi leaves and a few grains of rice. He addresses the river thus: 'I offer a cocoanut, sandal paste, tulsi leaves and rice,' and at the same time he places these articles on the sand before him. The priest then says: 'I bow, Gangā, to thy lotus feet: I bow to thee, Chandrabhāga'. The ritual which follows is a little more complicated if the pilgrim is a Brāhman than if he belongs to the lower castes. In the former case he enters the water till his head is submerged, faces the East, sips water thrice from the palm of his hand and

[1] See *B. G.*, Vol. xx, pp. 415 ff; *E.R.E.*, Vol. ix, p. 602 a,

repeats the twenty-four names of Viṣṇu which he invokes in his daily devotions. He then sprinkles water on the river and prays in Sanskrit. 'Come, Sun, with thy thousand rays, thou mass of glory, and ruler of the world, accept this my worship and this offering of water: I bow to thee.' He takes a little earth from the bed of the river and rubs it on his chest, saying in Sanskrit; 'Earth! free me from my sins and misdeeds, that my sins being destroyed by thee I may win heaven.' He makes another dip in the water and turning to the West takes a little cow-dung from the priest and rubs it on his body saying in Sanskrit: 'Cow-dung, that belongest to the wives of bulls who roam from wood to wood eating herbs, thou that dost cleanse the body, remove for ever all my ailments and sorrows.' He dips again in the water, rubs ashes on his chest, and recites a Vedic hymn. Then still standing in the water he takes water in both hands and pours it out as an offering to the river, saying: 'In this South-flowing Bhīmā on the West bank, in the holy Lohadand, in the holy town of Paṇdhrī, near Pundalīk, near the holy *pipal* Narāyan, and near the cow and the Brāhman, O Bhīmā! by thy favour guard me, who am the image of sin, a sinner above other sinners, whose soul is a sinner and born in sin.[1] To put away the miseries and sins whose source is the body, the speech, the mind, the touch of others or the neglecting to touch others, eating or refusing to eat, drinking or refusing to drink, and all small and secondary sins, to put away these I bathe in the Chandrabhāga on this auspicious day.' After this ceremonial bathing, if he wishes, he may proceed to personal ablutions.

If a Brāhman pilgrim has his wife with him the ends of their clothes are tied in a knot before they enter the river. The wife does not rub her body with earth, cowdung or ashes, nor does she repeat her husband's prayers: she merely follows her husband's actions in dipping in the water.

In the case of a non-Brāhman pilgrim these ceremonies are much abridged, the rubbings being omitted. The pilgrim salutes the river in the first words we have given and then enters the water while the priest says: 'In this holy place on this holy day I shall bathe in the Chandrabhāga to remove all sins of body and mind due to touch or caused by speech.'

12. The Pilgrim's Gifts

The pilgrim then, if a well-to-do man, proceeds to make certain offerings to the river: sandal-paste, rice, flowers, sugar and fruit. Offerings are also made to the priest: (i) Possibly the clothes in which the pilgrim bathed are presented to him. (ii) Some money: it is a rule that whatever else is given to a Brāhman some money must accompany it. (iii) If the pilgrim is a married man his wife

[1] *B. G.* (xx., p. 475) here inserts: 'Śiva! destroy my sins'.

may make a present to the priest's wife. This takes the form of a winnowing fan, in which are laid various articles partly symbolic, such as rice and plantains, partly valuable such as ornaments or dress. (iv) A cow may be given to the Brāhman. The pilgrim seldom is rich enough to make this present, but a pretence of making it is gone through. The priest brings forward a cow which he keeps for the purpose, the pilgrim lays a little money beside her, worships her and walks round her, while the priest says: 'All the sins and misdeeds of this and other births are destroyed at every step of the round.' Then the pilgrim grasps the cow's tail and places it in the priest's hand and the priest says on his behalf. 'The cow in whom live fourteen worlds and who therefore is able to do good in this world and the next, this cow whose god is Rudra, who has golden horns, silver hoofs, a copper back, with a milking pot and a bell round her neck, this cow I give to thee who art learned in the Vedas, who hast committed them to memory, who hast a wife, (this do) that Viṣṇu may be pleased and I may be saved from hell.' After this comes the gift of a shāligrām stone made with similar ceremonies. This gift, it appears, is more usual from pilgrims from the Southern Deccan or Telugū country.

Then comes the ceremony called *shrāddh* or funeral rite, in memory of the pilgrim's ancestors. As the Bhīmā flows into the Kriṣna and not into the sea, these 'mind-rites' at Pandharpūr are less availing than at Gāya or Nāśik. Brāhmans therefore seldom perform them at Paṇḍharpūr 'and when they do the moustache is not shaved,'[1] an additional reason being that the worshipper is viewed as still having a father and mother in the god Vithobā and the goddess Rakhumāī. The *shrāddh* ceremony should properly be performed on the banks of a river flowing into the sea, the Bhīmā being the only river allowed as an exception to this rule.

The *Bombay Gazetteer* adds that some Madras pilgrims treat Paṇḍharpūr as they treat Benāres or Gāya. 'The women, though their husbands are alive, make the hair offering or *veṇīdān* (*veṇī*, braid; *dān*, gift), that is, they have their heads shaved as Brāhman women's heads are shaved at Gāya. The ceremonies may either be spread over three days or crowded into one, according to the time and money the pilgrim means to spend'.[2]

13. Darshan (vision of the god)

After these duties are accomplished the pilgrim proceeds to the worship of the god. In its simplest form this is nothing more than a *darshan* or a setting of one's eyes upon him. But the usual method of *darshan* in Vithobā's temple in Paṇḍharpūr is marked by a feature said to be found nowhere else in the whole of India. No pilgrim to Vithobā at Pandharpūr considers the

[1] *B. G.* Vol. xx, p. 478.
[2] Ibid, p. 481.

darshan ceremony complete unless he touches the feet of Viṭhobā with his head. In order to ensure decorous performance of this ceremony, bars are placed beyond which only one worshipper can go at a time. *Darshan* at Pandharpūr thus includes embracing the image, laying one's head on its feet, waving money, laying money before it, placing round its neck a flower garland and *tulsī* leaves, and offering a cocoanut or sugar and incense. Till this is done the pilgrim has no rest, for to most pilgrims the sight of Vithobā is their dearest hope on earth. They beam with joy as they leave his presence, their longing to throw their arms round his knees at last realized.[1]

It often happens that a pilgrim reaching Paṇḍharpūr late in the evening goes straight to the temple and accomplishes a *dhūl-darshan* or visit for this purpose with the dust (*dhūl*) of his journey still on his feet. There is nothing formal about such a visit. But more ceremonious visits may be paid. Two of these have been recognized, the *mahāpūjā* and the *pādyapūjā*. In the former the pilgrim pours over the image the five nectars and usually presents offerings of considerable value, such as jewels. Owing to some dissensions between the priests official permission for this *mahāpūjā* has now to be obtained. The *pādyapūjā* is more common. In the course of this the pilgrim washes the feet of the image, sprinkles them with sandal-paste and rice, throws a garland of flowers round its neck, waves lighted sticks of camphor incense round it, and finally lays a cash present[2] before it. The image is then decked in its ornaments, and sweetmeats are offered to it. This being accomplished the pilgrim proceeds to worship Rukminī. Here he still has choice of forms of ceremonial corresponding to the two recognized in the case of Viṭhobā. The details are in each case much the same. It is to be noted that in 1873 various innovations were introduced into Vithobā's worship owing to the injuries inflicted on him (on which see following page).

The visit to the chief gods being finished the pilgrim makes a circuit of the holy district[3] and salutes the deities at their temples. There are two recognized routes, one longer[4] than the other.[5] Once in his life every devout worshipper makes the longer circuit, over seven miles. When he stays a day or two in Paṇḍharpūr he makes it a point to see the daily ministrations offered to the image as often as possible. Nor does he neglect to feed a company of Brāhmans, large or small according to his means, especially if his visit has been a ceremonious one. If his visit falls during the sacred seasons its closing scene will be enacted at the Gopālpūr temple, where the pilgrims partake of a mixture of dried curds together in memory of the joint-meal by Kriṣna and the cowherds.

[1] *B. G.* xx., p. 473.
[2] *Dakshinā.*
[3] *Pradakshinā.*
[4] *Nagarpradakshiṇā*, town circuit.
[5] *Devpradakshiṇā*, god-circuit.

14. Vithoba's Calamity in 1873

On Sunday, July 20, 1873, while four or five *Gosāvī*[1] mendicants were embracing the idol Viṭhobā, one of them pushed it over and as it fell it broke its legs between knees and ankles. The priests refused to divulge exactly what happened, the local belief being that the mendicant threw a stone at the idol because it did not eat fruit which he had offered. 'But this is less likely', says the *Bombay Gazetteer*, 'than the story that the image was thrown over by a shove either wilful or accidental. To avoid inquiry and noise the *Badvās* silently drove out the mendicants and kept the temple closed for two or three days. According to one story during those days a new image was installed, but examination shows that the present image is the old image patched at the break, it is said, by iron or copper rods from within. Besides being mended the image has also been strengthened by a support from behind up to the knee.'[2]

Newspapers of the time enable us to supplement the above record in various details. The *Arunodaya* published at Thana affirmed positively that a stone *was* thrown, while a Bombay correspondent after careful investigation wrote to the *Indu-Prakāsh* that the stone thrown was the size of a cocoanut, adding that a new idol of Vithobā was erected as nearly like the old one as could be made, but dissimilar in important respects which he mentions.

How terrible the presence of a broken idol at Paṇḍharpūr must have seemed will appear from a few sentences by Mrs. Sinclair Stevenson: 'If in the process of time the ear or nose of an idol, or any of its limbs, gets broken or crumbles away, the belief is that the spirit of the god escapes through the opening thus made. . . . One of the most illuminating ways to study idolatry sympathetically and scientifically is to watch what is done with a broken idol'.[3] In Vithobā's case, it was no mere 'crumbling away' but a violent attack upon him resulting in grave injury.

A sure index to the gravity of the affair is supplied by a secret meeting of the temple priests and the resolution they passed of which the following is a rough translation: 'This affair must not reach the outside world, for we have already many foes and this is a most critical occasion. Therefore without complete unanimity we cannot possibly preserve secrecy. Remembering then our ancient ancestors, let us make no more ado but all pull together and reseat Viṭhobā on his throne. Putting aside our differences regarding temple-rights let us labour with one accord, for we are all dependent solely on him. All wrangling at the time of worship should cease forthwith and we should all toil with one end in view. When people come to offer sacrifice we should ask of them gifts

[1] See second footnote, p. 6.
[2] *B.G.* Vol. xx, p. 423.
[3] *The Rites of the Twice-Born*, pp. 415–6.

only in accordance with established rules, gladly accepting what is gladly given. Whenever Vithobā is worshipped arrayed in his ornaments, all must be present, each doing service strictly according to his hereditary right. This resolution is passed unanimously and our earnest request to all *Wārkarīs* and their followers is that they read and carefully ponder over it, and that without fail they impart wisdom to the common people by pointing out the advantages of coming to Pandharpūr.' The crisis thus led to self-reformation by the priests and a consolidation of their ranks.

Needless to say, confusion reigned supreme not only in Paṇḍharpūr but throughout Mahārāshtra, for it was found impossible to conceal the fact that so grave a disaster had happened in the holy city. The iconoclast himself spread the knowledge, for he went about bragging of his deed until the angry citizens, two days later at 7–30 in the evening, set on him so furiously with cudgels that he fell senseless and the police had to remove him to hospital. Others were arrested on suspicion but released on a security the next day owing to lack of evidence. How deeply Mahārāshtra was moved is clear from the newspapers of the time—*Indu-Prakāsh*, *Arunodaya*, *Berār Samāchār*, and the *Dnyānodaya*. One Hindū gentleman writing to the proprietor of the first-mentioned paper gave expression to what must have been a widespread doubt: 'With broken leg how could Vithobā any longer be viewed as "self-existent" as indicated in the favourite term applied to him, *swayambhū*'? And among the *Warkaris*, the innermost sect of Vithobā's devotees, there was a wailing as if a member in each family lay dead.[1]

15. Pilgrims, Missionaries and Indian Reformers

Writing in *The Indian Antiquary* for June 1882 (pp. 149–156) the Rev. Dr J. Murray Mitchell gives an interesting account of a visit to Pandharpūr in which he reports that in conversing with the people and in preaching he met no bitter opposition, many expressing a desire to hear him again. The mental state of the pilgrims is illustrated by the following typical conversation. 'You good friends are very much in earnest. Some of you have come 600 miles to this festival. The expense, the labour, is very great; the risk to life not small; for you all know how frequently cholera breaks out at these gatherings. You expect much from this pilgrimage. How sad if you do not get what you want; but what *do* you want?' 'We bathe in the Bhīmā, and gaze on the god; and so all sin is removed, and much righteousness acquired', was the usual answer. 'Are you sure that bathing in the Bhīmā washes away sin?' 'Why, who doubts it? have not I come hundreds of miles to be purified so?' Dr. Mitchell reports perpetual confusion

[1] *Dnyānodaya*, Vol. 32, July 31, 1873, pp. 245–7, 251–2; August 7, 1873, pp. 237–9; Vol. 71, August 1, 1912, pp. 243–4.

between the material image and an unseen Vithobā. 'Viṭhobā', said one of the hearers, 'is almighty and omnipresent.' 'Is he in your own village?' 'To be sure.' 'Then why travel hundreds of miles to see him here?' 'Ah! but this is a special Viṭhobā; this is a *swayambhū* image.' 'Well; but is it the image, or the deity, you trust in?' 'The deity.' The doctor made efforts to discover what precise meaning was affixed to the phrase heard continually, that the waters of the Bhīmā 'washed away sin.' The pilgrims believing that the guilt of sin was removed, to discover whether they held that their *hearts* were purified questions were put. 'Unless our hearts are purified,' said one man, 'there is little good in our coming here'. But did experience show that they were purified? On one or two maintaining this, they were easily silenced by proverbs current all over India about those who go on pilgrimage generally coming back worse than before. 'Visit Benāres thrice', runs one Marāthī proverb, 'and you become a thorough scoundrel.' So the doctor asked: 'When a pilgrim visits Pandharpūr, does he not usually carry home a load of pride and self-conceit?' 'Too often,' was the reply. 'Has he then got any good by bathing in the Chandrabhāga?' 'Very little.' 'Has he not got harm?' 'Perhaps.'

A similar impression was left on the mind of an Indian Reformer belonging to the Bombay Prārthanā Samāj whose visit to Paṇḍharpūr on June 26, 1920 we have already referred to. He writes as follows: 'One cannot avoid thinking when he sees this vast humanity on *Āshādhi* Day in Pandharpur. . . . that people do not get true spiritual benefit. After all it is a religious feast which affects only the outside. The hearts of the devotees are not touched and their life is not renovated. The pilgrim does not leave the place morally or spiritually transformed He thinks his sins are washed away, but he has no determination not to err again. How to preserve this valuable asset of *bhakti* and make it spiritual is the problem to which the thoughts of a Brāhmo naturally turn when he sees this religious feast.'[1]

16. Government and Pilgrim Festivals

In the essay on Pandharpūr referred to above, Dr. Murray Mitchell writing in 1882 showed the grave need of public control in connection with the two great annual festivals. The crowding of the worshippers into Viṭhobā's small apartment often resulted in women being injured in the crush, sometimes they were subjected to indignities, sometimes had their ornaments torn off. A thoughtful English magistrate had ruled, a few years before, that as far as possible, men and women should be kept separate on the great day of any feast. Even so, the scene was one of terrible confusion, the unutterably filthy condition of the town making one of the doctor's party seriously ill. On another occasion cholera broke out, and they

[1] *Subodh Patrikā*, July 18, 1920.

had to minister to the bodies as well as the souls of the pilgrims. Happily, however, 'Pandharpūr has developed into a decent-looking, clean town, with a plentiful water-supply.'[1]

How this improved condition of affairs in this great pilgrim centre has been brought about and how it is still maintained appears from the annual Government reports on the *Āshāḍhi* Festival. In the report from the Collector of Sholapur to the Commissioner, C. D., dated the 11th November 1919, we are told supervision was exercised as usual by the Collector, the District Deputy Collector, the District Superintendent of Police, and the Deputy Sanitary Commissioner, the Sanitary Commissioner also encamping at Pandharpūr during the Fair. In addition to the ordinary police stationed at Paṇḍharpūr, a force consisting of one Inspector, eight Sub-Inspectors, six jamadārs, twenty-three Head Constables and one hundred and thirty-five constables from other parts of the District were drafted into Pandharpūr. From other districts also detectives were called in to watch their own local bad characters. Sanitary arrangements were completed in good time before the Fair in a way reported to be 'very creditable to the Municipality.' One hundred and thirty-eight extra *bhangīs* and one Sanitary Inspector were employed by the Municipality, who had arranged to stock sufficient quantities of disinfectants freely used during the Fair. Water-supply was adequate. Ten men were appointed to prevent waste, and only on one day was want of water felt in places of high levels. The usual precautions of closing step-wells, and of treating all wells on the *pālkhī* routes with permanganate of potash, were adopted. 'The pilgrims as usual took river-water in spite of advice from the police.' The medical arrangements showed twenty-eight Sub-Assistant Surgeons employed on special duty. There was no indigenous cholera at Pandharpūr, but it broke out with the Ālandī *pālkhī* and thus infection was brought to Pandharpūr, a few cases from Nāsik, Jalgaon and Umraoti also being imported. After the big day the cholera cases were almost confined to the followers of the Ālandī *pālkhī*, and three Sub-Assistant Surgeons were sent with the *pālkhīs* of Dnyānobā, Nivrittināth and Tukārām for two marches of their return journey. The Hindū division of St. John's Ambulance Brigade attended the Fair as usual and rendered great assistance.

17. The Disastrous Pilgrimage of the Last Peshwa

It would have been strange if so famous a religious centre as Pandharpūr was for probably a thousand years[2] had not figured in

[1] *The Indian Antiquary*, Vol. xi, 1882, pp. 153–6.

[2] 'In the thirteenth century Vithal was already a god of long standing. . . The general workmanship of the image is earlier than the mediaeval Rajput style of the Anhilvad Chaulukyas (943–1240), . . . or the Ājmer Chohāns (685—1193). The dress and ornament of the image belong to . . . probably not later than the 5th or 6th century after Christ.' This image of Vithobā resembles sculptures 'of the 4th century'. *B.G.*, Vol. xx, pp. 420, 424, 430.

the historical vicissitudes of the country. Within the walls of Paṇḍharpūr, a stone's throw from Vithobā's temple, Vithobā's devotees who were for the time being residing in the sacred enclosure, in 1815 committed a foul murder. This murder of Gangādhar Shāstrī, the Gaikwār's agent at the Poona court, effected with the complicity of Trimbakjī Denglia, the favourite of Bājirao the last Peshwā (1796–1817), was one of the chief causes of the downfall of Marāṭhā rule. The official chronicle runs: 'Gangādhar Shāstrī had gone to Poona under British guarantee to settle some money disputes between the Gaikwār and the Peshwā, but finding his efforts fruitless he had determined to return to Baroda and leave the settlement to British arbitration. This disconcerted Bājirao's plans, whose real object was to arrange a union with the Gaikwār against the English, and he and Trimbakjī after much persuasion induced Gangādhar to stay. In July (1815) Bājirao went to Paṇḍharpūr on a pilgrimage and took with him Trimbakjī and Gangādhar Shāstrī. On the 14th of July the Shāstrī dined with the Peshwā, and in the evening Trimbakjī asked him to Vithobā's temple where the Peshwā was. Gangādhar who was unwell excused himself, but was pressed by Trimbakjī and went to the temple with a few unarmed attendants. After a prayer to Vithobā he talked with Trimbakjī and then went to pay his respects to the Peshwā who was seated in the upper verandah of the temple and treated him with marked attention. When the visit was over, Gangādhar started for his lodging in high spirits. He had scarcely gone 300 yards when he was attacked in the street by assassins hired by Trimbakjī and was almost cut to pieces'[1]. The treacherous murder of a Brāhman in the holy city, the proved guilt of the Peshwā's representative, the intrigue and duplicity of the Peshwā himself, the assassination of one for whose security the British had pledged themselves, these things led on to war and the issue was only determined by the complete defeat of the Peshwā's army on the battlefield of Kirkee, November 5, 1817.

Having thus acquainted ourselves, in our introductory chapters, with Tukārām's land and people, with the religion of his day, and with the city he has made famous in his verse, let us now enter upon our study of the *bhakti* poet himself as far as the biographical material at our disposal will permit.

[1] *B.G.*, Vol. xx, pp. 484–5.

THE PRIDE OF KNOWLEDGE [1]

Though I'm a man of lowly birth
The saints have magnified my worth.

And so within my heart to hide
Has come the great destroyer, pride.

In my fond heart the fancy dwells
That I am wise and no one else.

O, save me, save me, Tukā prays;
Spent like the wind are all my days

WITHIN MY HEART

I know no way by which
My faith thy feet can reach
    Nor e'er depart.
How, how can I attain
That thou, O Lord, shalt reign
    Within my heart?

Lord, I beseech thee, hear
And grant to faith sincere,
    My heart within,
Thy gracious face to see,
Driving afar from me
    Deceit and sin

O come, I, Tukā, pray,
And ever with me stay,
    Mine, mine to be.
Thy mighty hand outstretch
And save a fallen wretch,
    Yea, even me.

GOD IS OURS [1]

God is ours, yea, ours is he,
Soul of all the souls that be.

God is nigh without a doubt,
Nigh to all, within, without.

God is gracious, gracious still;
Every longing he'll fulfil

God protects, protects his own.
Strife and death he casteth down.

Kind is God, ah, kind indeed;
Tukā he will guard and lead.

[1] Translated from Tukārām, *P.M.S.*, pp. 77, 62, 73.

Chapter IV

The Biography of Tukaram

Preliminary Considerations

With regard to the date of Tukārām's birth there is a difference of opinion, some Marāṭhī authorities holding it to have taken place in 1598, others in 1588, while other schools hold to 1577 or 1568. We however may adopt the traditional date of 1608 based on Mahīpati's record, until better available evidence points to the contrary.[1] This means that Tukārām Bolhobā Āmbile [2] was born the same year as John Milton. If Milton's mission was to herald the golden age both of English Protestantism and English literature, that of Milton's contemporary, Tukārām, was to give expression to the protest of India's *heart* against the Hindū scheme of things which had reduced religion to a philosophy and to express that protest in verse that was to become dear to Indian prince and peasant alike. Tukārām's value, therefore, in the words of Prof. W. B. Patwardhan of Poona, is that of 'a poet-saint who lived and moved just when Mahārāshtra was in labour over the birth of a new spirit. A new life was stirring the hearts and a new warmth was felt in the blood that surged in the veins of Marāthās of the time and it may be that non-Indian students of Marāthā history will discover material here to estimate the under-current of thought and feeling of the Mahārāshtra of the sixteenth and the seventeenth century'.[3] In the happy simile of Dr. Mackichan, Tukārām is 'the Robert Burns of India'.[4]

In writing any biographical account of Tukārām we are confronted with two serious problems. The first one arises from the fact that the existing Marāṭhī 'Lives' of Tukārām are indebted to one authority. Up to the present hour indeed (1921) almost all the available information concerning Tukārām's life comes to us from

1 See the Marāthī discussions in L. R. Pāngarkar's *S.T.C.*, (1920) pp. 7–46; in the *Vividh Dnyān Vistāra*, September 1920, pp. 105–114, and January 1921, pp. 25–36, and in *Nawa Yuga*, March 1921, pp. 137–9, summarized p. 76 below.

2 'Morē' is the family surname given by some authorities including Sir R. G. Bhandarkar (*V.S.M.R S.*, p. 92). This is traceable to the *bakhar* of Rāmdās whose authority in a matter of this kind cannot be regarded as equal to that of the official records of a Nāsik priest who used to serve Tukārām and his descendants on their visits there and whose records give the signature of Tukārām's son Nārāyan with 'Āmbile' as the family surname, 'Morē' being given as that of the family lineage (*M Sār.*, p. 172, footnote 2).

3 *I. I.*, October, 1910, p. 114.

4 *I I.*, January, 1913, p. 173.

that same source, Mahīpati, the famous biographer of the Marāthā 'saints' who wrote a century and a quarter after Tukārām's death. It is true that some of these details are confirmed by other sources, but in the main we are depended on this one authority. The other difficulty referred to concerns the fact, admitted by Hindū biographers and commentators (see below), that Mahīpati, on whom we are so dependent, has interwoven with his story much that is obviously miraculous and legendary. In view of these facts it seems best to divide this 'biographical' chapter regarding the poet and saint who marks 'the era of the efflorescence of Mahārāshtra's people'[1] into three distinct parts: I. The Value of our Sources; II. the Probable Biographical Facts; III. The Legendary Additions.

I. The Biographical Sources

1. Fact and Tradition in 'Lives' of Tukaram

Prefixed to the standard Marāṭhī edition of Tukārām's poems published by the *Indu-Prakāsh* Press, is a biographical essay by Janārdan Sakharām Gadgil where it is stated: 'The biographer's task, in writing a faithful life of any of the guiding spirits who in their time influenced the Hindū nation, is extremely difficult. The idea of recording events faithfully for the information of after-ages never existed in the nation. Whenever the influence on the succeeding generations of any of the important personages has been great enough to induce somebody to write his biography, the tendency towards deification has been so great, that the little of real events that has descended by tradition has been mixed up with fable to such a degree as almost to defy all attempts at separation . . . . . What has been aimed at, therefore, in this notice, is to bring together the several passages in the following collection bearing on the poet's life, linking them together by the light furnished by the mythological account of Mahīpati.'[2]

In the above observations there are three phrases used—'the tendency towards deification,' 'tradition mixed up with fable,' 'the mythological account of Mahīpati'—which, when joined by a fourth at the conclusion of the same essay, 'the legends of Mahīpati' (*Ibid.* p. 32), give abundant reason for caution in reading the Marāṭhī 'Lives' of Tukārām who is '*par excellence* the poet of Mahārāshtra.'[3] Should the verdict in the *Indu-Prakāsh* edition of 1869 be challenged as out of date, a similar verdict by Prof. Patwardhan in April 1912, may be more readily accepted. He says: 'We have, in the first place, no authentic and properly sifted

1 Dr. Mackichan, *I. I.*, January 1913, p 165.
2 *Poems of Tukārām*, *I.P* edition, Vol. I., p. 2.
3 *Dr. Mackichan*, *I.I*, January 1913, p. 173

account of his life. There is a mass of legends and traditions that have gathered round Tukārām. These are implicitly believed in by those who are avowedly Tukobā's followers, and equally by those who, though not followers of Tukobā's school, are innocent admirers of everything connected with the saint of Mahārāshtra.'[1] Again he says: 'As in the case of Tukārām, so in that of Nāmdev, I have to sound a note of complaint at the outset. There is hardly any authentic information available as regards his life and work. Most of the accounts that have come down to us are vitiated by adventitious matter mixed up with and added to the little that is genuine history. It is everywhere the same old story; miracle and wonder-working have obscured the field. Take any of the saint-poets of Mahārāshtra from Dnyāneshwar . . . . , his life-story is shrouded with mystery—hidden behind a dense overgrowth of superstitious tradition and fantastic invention. In the case of Tukārām we had at least some facts of historical accuracy to start with.'[2] On the other hand, 'it is a great relief,' says Dr. P. R. Bhandarkar, 'to find Tukārām working no miracles. Tradition has credited him with having performed many, but he personally does not lay claim to any.'[3]

2. Tukaram's Biographer: Mahipati

Who was this Mahīpati, concerning whose poetical accounts of the Marāthā saints the late Marāthā Christian poet Narāyan Wāman Tilak once said that they 'remind one of Foxe's *Book of Martyrs*'? And what led Mahīpati to write the 'lives' of his country's saints? Born in 1715, from his earliest days Mahīpati gave proof of a religious temperament. At five years old he joined a company of pilgrims to Paṇḍharpūr, and from that time made an annual pilgrimage to the great shrine. On his father's death he succeeded him as *kulkarnī* of Tābarābād but soon resigned Government service because the Mussulman *jāghīrdār* who was his superior forced him to work when he (Mahīpati) desired to pray. Leaving his *pūjā* and carrying out the order, he told the *jāghīrdār* when he had completed the task, 'I have obeyed your command, but no more of this'. He had learned that he could not serve two masters, the State and his god, so he laid his pen at Vithobā's feet, devoted himself to Vithobā's service for ever, and vowed that neither he nor any descendant should ever again serve the State, a vow which was kept for generations. One night Tukārām appeared to Mahīpati in a dream and bade him write the lives of Marāṭhā *bhaktas*. He began the *Bhakta Vijāya*, his

1 *I.I.*, April 1912, p. 19
2 *I.I.*, April 1913, p. 11.
3 *Two Masters, Jesus and Tukārām*, p. 28.

chief work, finishing it in A. D. 1762 or 1763. Its completion was anticipated by his *Santa Līlāmṛita* in 1757. *Kathā Sārāmṛita* was finished in 1765 and *Bhakta Līlāmṛita* in 1774. His *Santa Vijaya* was incomplete when he died in A. D. 1790.[1] His life of Tukārām occupies twenty-one chapters in all, five in the *Bhakta Vijaya* (48–52) and sixteen in *Bhakta Līlāmṛita* (25-40).

We have already quoted one English critic's estimate of Mahīpati's literary merit (see pp. 20–1). Another, Mr. C. A. Kincaid, affirms: 'Had Mahīpati used a linguistic medium more widely known than Marāthī, he would have ranked high among the world's poets. Even a foreigner can appreciate the easy flow of his stanzas, his musical rhymes and above all his unrivalled imagery.'[2] One of the greatest needs in Marāṭhī literature to-day is a critical investigation of what have been called Mahīpati's 'legends of mediaeval *bhaktas*.'[3]

3. Mahipati an Honest Author

America joins in this chorus of praise from foreign critics concerning the author of the *Acta Sanctorum* of the Marāṭhās. We are indebted to Dr. Justin E. Abbott of New Jersey, United States, and formerly of Bombay, for the following critical notes. They reached us on different dates and we give them as we received them, (*a*) and (*b*) respectively, to which we add a paragraph (*c*).

(*a*) 'Mahīpati's account of Tukārām is almost the sole source from which the different Marāṭhī "lives of Tukārām" draw. The question then is: Is Mahīpati's account true to facts? Tukārām died in 1649 (traditional date)[4] and Mahīpati wrote his account in 1774, or 125 years after Tukārām's death. Not very long, but long enough for legends to grow. I regard Mahīpati as an honest writer, that he used honestly the material at his disposal. He was not a "higher critic", but used as truth whatever came to him in the form of MSS or oral tradition. I think I can produce convincing evidence of this honesty. He had evidently a good library of manuscripts. I have the names of some he possessed, or was more or less familiar with. I find this list in his own writings. But as poet he avows the principle of expanding the facts at his disposal "as a seed expands into a tree." This is indeed a habit of Indian poets.

[1] See *M. Sār.*, pp. 378-388 for biographical details.
[2] *Tales of the Saints of Pandharpur*, pp. 3–4.
[3] L. J. Sedgwick, *J.R.A.S. Bo.*, Vol 23, No. 65, pp 127–8.
[4] The brackets are our own, as various dates are held by scholars—164 1649, 1650 and 1652 · see our note at the end of the list of dates, Part II. p. 77.

MAHĪPATI, THE BIOGRAPHER OF TUKĀRĀM

'What MSS or what oral tradition did Mahīpati use? This is as yet an unsolved problem, with this exception, that a few sources are known. Among the MSS he uses are the *Abhangs* by Tukārām's brother Kānhobā (see *Bhakta Līlāmṛita*, ch. 40. 198 and following) and *abhangs* of Rāmeshwar (*Bhakta Līlāmrita*, ch. 40. 209). There is also now published Nilobā's *Gāthā*. Nilobā was a disciple of Tukārām's.[1] He gives some account of Tukārām, and Mahīpati knew of Niḷoba, so probably knew of his *abhangs* (*Bhakta Līlāmṛita*, ch. 40. 238.) The last part of Mahīpati's chapter 40, which describes Tukārām's "ascension," mentions many individuals who must have passed on to the next generation their knowledge of Tukārām.

'It still remains true that all modern accounts of Tukārām's life are to be traced to Mahīpati as the practically sole source of information. Perhaps some time Mahīpati's sources will be better known.

'This being so we cannot now know what are facts and what are fiction in Mahīpati's account. It will not do merely to deduct the manifestly legendary, and call the balance facts, as seems to be the general practice. The only honest way for any modern writer, is to give Mahīpati credit for the account the writer gives, and give it as Mahīpati gives it, legend and all, leaving it to the future, for possible discoveries, to settle what are the real facts of Tukārām's life. Much of Mahīpati's account may be facts, but I think events in Tukārām's life should not be recorded *as facts* until they can be substantiated from other and earlier sources.'

(*b*) 'As I have before remarked I regard Mahīpati as an honest historian. He wrote from books before him, and from oral tradition. He anticipated the charge that he drew from his own imagination and says in *Santa Līlāmṛita* (1. 67–69): "You will raise this doubt in your mind and say: You have drawn on your own imagination. This is not so. Listen. Great poet-saints have written books in many languages. It is on their authority that I write this *Santa Līlāmṛita*. If I wrote on my own authority my statements would not be respected. The Husband of Rukminī is witness to this, who knows all hearts."

'In *Bhakta Vijāya* (1.37) he says: "You will say I have compiled this book on my own authority. This indeed is not so. Hold no doubts in your minds." He then quotes Nābhājī and Udhavchidghan as authorities: "Joining these two together, *Bhakta Vijāya* was begun" (1. 39). For a list of saints with whose names and books Mahīpati was familiar see *Bhakta Vijāya* (1. 19), *Bhakta Vijāya* (57. 169–201) and *Bhakta Līlāmṛita*, chap. 51, where there are 127 saints mentioned by name.

'His story of Dnyāneshwar in *Bhakta Vijāya* (chap. 8) he took from *Dyāndevāchī Ādi* (Dnyāndev's Origin) by Nāmdev. His

[1] A posthumous disciple: see sect. 4 (6), p. 73 below.

story of Mirābāī in *Bhakta Vijāya* (chap. 38) he took from *Mirābāīche Charitra* (Life of Mirābāī) by Nāmdev. His story of Gora Kumbhār in *Bhakta Vijāya* (chap. 17) he took from *Goraba Kumbhārāche Charitra* (Life of Gorobā Kumbhār) by Nāmdev.'

'So far as evidence goes he conscientiously used his sources, as an honest recorder of what he believed to be true. If he expanded meagre statements into fuller detail it was not to add facts but to give a fuller understanding of them To use his own words he "expanded facts just as a tree is the expansion of a seed." By this I understand that he embellished but did not add imaginary accounts, that what he wrote he felt he had good authority for.

'The faithfulness of Mahīpati in recording the traditions received by him, either through books or oral sources, does not ensure the truth of those traditions, which must be established on other grounds, but it is satisfaction that one can depend with good assurance on his honesty as a writer, and that he did not draw on his imagination more than he felt necessary for poetic reasons.'

(c) In addition to the above from Dr. Abbott on the honesty and trustworthiness of our chief authority, Mahīpati, we shall do well to note a striking illustration of Mahīpati's candour as provided by his faithful account of the attitude adopted towards caste by one of his Brāhman 'saints'. Dr. Sir R. G. Bhandarkar has pointed out that Mahīpati makes 'one of his Brāhman saints declare that there is no caste among devotees of God and represents him to have drunk the holy water given to him by a *chāmbhār* or leather-worker'.[1] That Mahīpati, a 'Rigvedī Vāsiśtha Gotrī Deśasth Brāhman,'[2] should have faithfully recorded that another Brāhman winked at caste in relation to religious matters and should have portrayed him as receiving water at the hands of one of the lowest of India's out-castes is a remarkable illustration of Mahīpati's honesty as an author. He sometimes even revises an earlier account of his own (see footnote 2 on sect. 15, Part II).

4. Sources Earlier than Mahipati

What are the possibilities of substantiating or correcting Mahīpati's account 'from other and earlier sources'?

(1) First and most important of all we must never forget the rich mine of information in Tukārām's own autobiographical poems, the investigation concerning which we leave until the chapter on Tukārām's Autobiography (see chap. 5, Part I).

(2) Next in real value come the *abhangs* of Rāmeshwar Bhatt, a leading disciple of Tukārām's referred to in the notes from Dr. Abbott on the previous page as one of Mahīpati's own sources.

[1] *I. I.*, April 1914, p. 26. [2] *M. Sār.*, p. 378.

The importance of Rāmeshwar Bhatt in this connexion is threefold: (*a*) as having been used by Mahīpati we are able to test the accuracy of the latter, (*b*) as being one of Tukārām's own circle we have invaluable contemporary *data*, and (*c*) as formerly keenly hostile to Tukārām, and then his follower, he is in himself an abiding testimony to the influence of Tukārām's character and work in the poet-saint's own lifetime (see sections 29–30, Part II of this chapter).

(3) A third source is provided in a short life of Tukārām by his grandson (son of Tukārām's own son) named Gopāl Boā.[1]

(4) Another of Tukārām's immediate disciples, a woman named Bahinābāī (1628–1700), whose Marāthī shows her to have had some literary ability, dictated her autobiography to her son.[2] Among other things she confirms the incident concerning Mumbājī (see sect. 31, Part II, present chap.) whose house she occupied but from which she says she was expelled because she attended Tukārām's *kīrtans*. Not only does she confirm the account of Mumbājī's hostility to Tukārām but she gives the names of some of the leading personalities in Tukārām's circle, including that of the *Pāṭīl* (chief village officer) and others.[3]

(5) In 1674, only a little more than twenty years after Tukārām's death, there was written a book on Keshav Chaitanya Sampradāya by one named Krishnajī Bairāgya. This authority is quoted by name and his facts are given in detail by one Niranjan who supplies from this source priceless information from which we come to know the succession of gurus—Keshav, Rāghav and Bābājī—leading up to the 'call' of Tukārām. It was from the last of these that Tukārām says he obtained in a dream his *guru-mantra*[4] which not only initiated him finally into Hinduism, investing him with complete authority, but was felt by him to be a divine afflatus marking out his future career. The fundamentally important dates of this crucial spiritual experience and of Tukārām's birth itself are regarded as being settled by this ancient authority, which takes us back to a source nearly a century earlier than Mahīpati.[5]

(6) Almost equally ancient is Niḷobā of Pimpalner, one of the most famous of *Warkarī* leaders, the priest (*joshī*) and revenue officer (*kuḷkarnī*) of his ancestral Sirur in the Poona district, who has left *abhangs* descriptive of Tukārām dated no later than thirty years after Tukārām's death. From his 'Life' which Mr. Pāngārkar has borrowed from descendants and examined, it appears Niḷoba was born after Tukārām died, that he saw Tukārām in a

[1] *M. Sār.*, p. 186 footnote.

[2] See 'The Autobiography of Bahinābāī' in Marāthī published by Mr. D. V. Umarkhāne (Chitra Shāḷā Press, Poona) and an English Note on this in the *Dynānodaya*, March 10, 1921.

[3] *M. Sār.*, pp. 242–5. 193, and L. R Pangarkar, *S.T.C.*, pp. 468–74.

[4] See sect. 22, Part II of this chapter, and Muzumdar's view given there.

[5] *M. Sār.*, p. 190, note 1.

dream about 1675–80, healed the *Pāṭīl* (chief village officer) of Pimpalner, on going to live there received the honours of a *sādhu*, gave up secular service because it interfered with his devotions,[1] and wrote a *Gāthā* of which 1551 *abhangs* are published, many of them, especially Nos. 869–890, being written in praise of Tukārām and his *kīrtans*, thus confirming Mahīpati's narrative of nearly a century later in this important matter.[2]

Some authorities would add a seventh source other than Mahīpati—Narahari Mālu, author of *Bhakti Kathāmṛita*, who wrote fifty years later. He must, however, be pronounced an utterly untrustworthy guide though he has unfortunately been followed by various Marāṭhā writers.[3]

5. The Biography on the whole Trustworthy

How far then may the existing biography of Tukārām be regarded as reliable? In view of Tukārām's picture of himself in his own moving poems, the contemporary evidence of his own disciples, the record of a by no means distant relative, and the important testimony surrounding his *guru-mantra*, we are justified in believing that while there is much unsifted tradition, 'miracle and wonder-working,' Mahīpati's interesting account has a solid substratum of historical accuracy. As far as we can test his sources he gives us a large body of fact on which we can safely rely. We are confirmed in reaching such a conclusion when we learn that Mahīpati went, for example, to Tukārām's own descendants and obtained from them what evidence he could,[4] in one case information concerning the facts of Tukārām's youth and early manhood between the ages of 13 and 21, at which age and during a severe famine Tukārām's father died. Of these and other facts we have independent confirmatory evidence. Our confidence in Mahīpati is strengthened when we further discover that in writing his 'lives of the saints' he used the works of earlier authorities with such discrimination that when he found any of them not as informing or as useful as he had expected he laid them aside, e.g., Nābhājī, the Nāgar Brāhman of the late 17th century whose *Bhakta Mālā* was of service when Mahīpati 'began' his *Bhakta Vijaya*, but whom he set aside later because of his preference in favour of better authorities.[5]

1 See the parallel of Mahīpati in sect. 2 above.

2 See *Bhakta Vijaya*, chap 56, 147–187, L. R. Pāngārkar, *S.T.C.*, pp. 474–80 and *The Gāthā of Nilobā's Abhangs*, by Trimbak Hari Awte, esp. pp. 195–200.

3 *M. Sār.*, p 391.

4 *M. Sār.*, p. 381.

5 See *M. Sār.*, pp 372–4; on the whole question of Mahīpati's sources, *M. Sār.*, pp 378–88 are worthy of careful study.

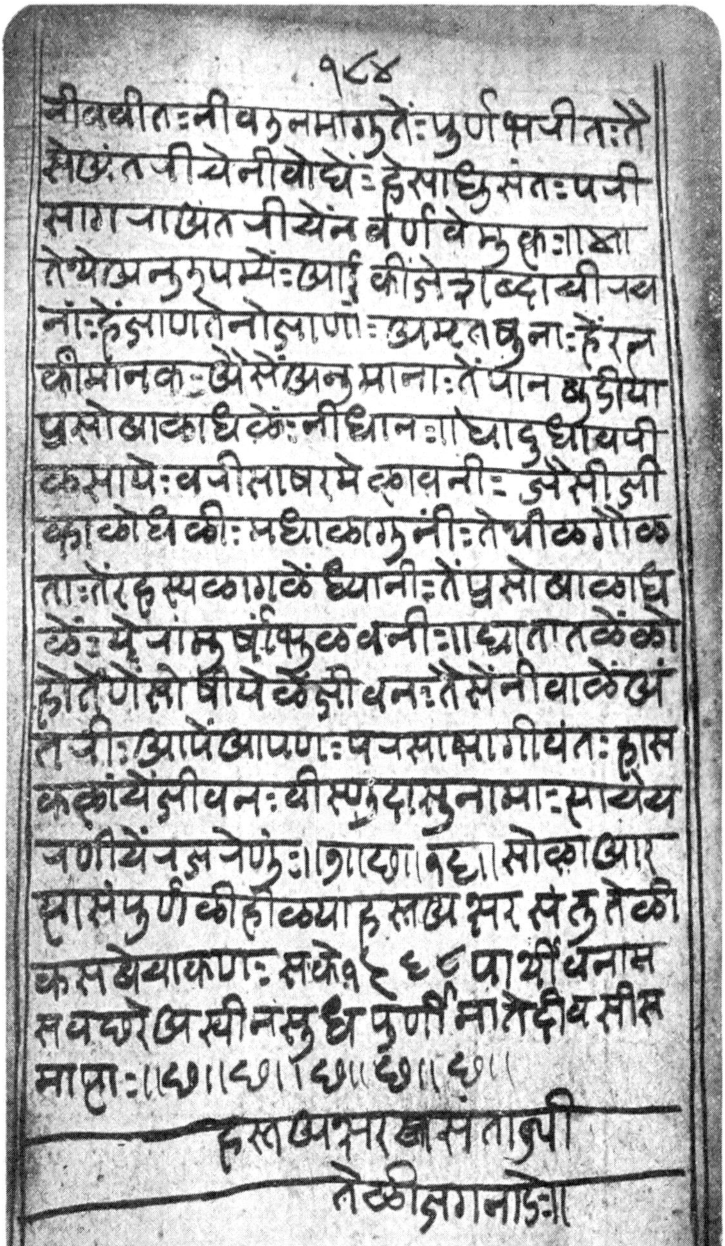

A PAGE OF SANTĀJĪ TEḶĪ JAGANĀḌE'S MS OF TUKĀRĀM'S *abhangs*

With such a conclusion before us we are surely justified in separating the probable historical element in the material that has come down to us from what appears to be legendary, as we do in the two remaining parts (II and III) of this chapter, always remembering, as the reader must, the possibility of error in the results presented. This course we follow, though Dr. Abbott would himself prefer to have the account 'as Mahīpati gave it, legend and all', leaving the future to settle what are the true facts of Tukārām's life. We have however, adopted a compromise—see Part II, the italic type at the close of section 1. The Western reader needs the additional reminder that even the probable biographical facts, in part II, are of necessity presented in that Hindū dress with which Tukārām's Hindū biographer has clothed them, Parts II and III being in the form of translated excerpts from Mahīpati's 'biographical' record in *Bhakta Līlāmrita* (chaps. 25-40) and *Bhakta Vijaya* (chaps. 48-52).

II. The Probable Biographical Facts in the Life of Tukaram

1. Chief Events with Approximate Dates[1]

A. D.

1608. Tukārām's Birth (see sect. 3 below).

This is the traditional date, being the one adopted by Mahīpati in *Bhakta Līlāmrita* (ch. 28. 132–8); the late Janārdan Rāmchandra held to 1588; the genealogical records at Dehū and Paṇḍharpūr give 1598; other authorities affirm 1577; while Prof. Rājwāḍe, on the basis of an ancient genealogy found with a *Wārkarī* near Wāī, maintains 1568. At present certainty is impossible. See Bhawe, *M. Sār.*, p. 194, note; Pāngārkar, *S.T.C.*, pp. 20–32; Gadre in *Vividh Dnyān Vistāra*, September 1920, pp. 105–114, and Bhide in January 1921, pp. 25–36; also P. R. Bhandarkar, *Nawa Yuga*, March 1921, pp. 137–9.

1621. Tukārām's father turns over to him the burden of the business (see sect. 5).

1621–3 (*circ.*) Tukārām is married to Rakhmābāī and then to Āvalībāī, otherwise called Jijābāī (see sect. 8).

1625. Death of Tukārām's parents and of his eldest brother's wife (see sect. 10).

1626. His eldest brother Sāvajī becomes a sanyāsī (see sect. 10).

1628. Tukārām resolves to put aside his indifference to worldly affairs and to give himself to the management of his business in company with his two wives and his eldest son (see sects. 5, 7–8).

1629. Business failure and bankruptcy. Beginning of a famine (see sects. 10–11).

1630. Famine at its worst, during which Rakhmābāī dies of hunger; death of eldest son, after which, in utter indifference to worldly things, he retires to Bhāmbanāth Hill and receives a 'revelation' (see sects. 10–11).

1631. Rebuilding of the temple in Dehū; continuous attendance at *Kīrtans* (sect. 13).

1632–5. Tukārām's call to become a poet (sect. 19); he receives the *guru-māntra*[2] (sect. 22). See however footnote, sect. 30, for Dr. P. R. Bhandarkar's view.

[1] These dates are taken from the Marāthī 'Life' by Mr. L. R. Pāngārkar (1920), pp. 45–6, embodying the results of a careful discussion of Tukārām chronology. We have added in brackets after each event a reference to our own sections in the following Part II and a note where we differ.

[2] We have here taken a slightly different order from Pāngārkar in accordance with what we believe to be Mahīpati's order.

1638 (*circ.*) Tukārām persecuted by Rāmeshwar Bhaṭṭ and sustained by a special 'revelation' (sects. 29–30).

1649 Tukārām's end.

This is the date given by Tukārām's grandson Gopāl Boā and Mahīpati in his *Bhakta Līlāmṛita* (chap. 40, 183); Mr. Pāngārkar adopts March 9, 1650; Prof. Rājwāde holds to 1648; while Mr. Bhawe prefers 1652. On this difficult question, which with present available material, is probably insoluble, see Bhawe, *M. Sār*, pp. 189, 186n, *Assal Gāthā*, p. 13; Pāngārkar, *S.T.C.*, pp. 14–20; Gadre in *Vividh Dnyān Vistāra*, September 1920, pp. 105–114, and Bhide in January 1921, p. 27; also P. R. Bhandarkar in *Nawa Yuga*, March 1921, pp. 138–9.

In the following narrative, footnotes are given to indicate where lines or paragraphs have been deleted, as belonging to what the best authorities would probably agree are 'legendary additions'. These lines and paragraphs omitted from Part II are inserted in Part III ('Legendary Additions') of this Chapter and anyone desirous of reading Mahīpati's story consecutively may do so by following the guidance of the footnotes. Occasionally this 'legendary' dress will be found clinging even to the narrative in Part II. In most such cases we have either introduced Mahīpati's name or the device of quotation marks or that of a special footnote. In the last-mentioned the letter 'M' refers to Mahīpati, and it is to be carefully distinguished from 'F and M' which refers to Fraser and Marāṭhe's Translation of Tukārām's 'Poems,' 3 vols, and from 'M. Sār.' which refers to V. L. Bhawe's 'Mahārāshtra Sāraswat'.

2. Tukaram's Ancestry

Our knowledge of Tukārām begins with a forefather named Viśvambhara who was a tradesman at Dehū and at the same time a devout worshipper of Viṭhobā. He was a truthful and fair-dealing man; his business throve, so he spent his profits entertaining holy men and Brāhmans who were bound on pilgrimage. By night he would assemble his neighbours and sing the lives of Rām and Kṛiṣṇa till all worldly impulses died away in him.

At length he was advised by his mother to follow an old custom of his family and make the pilgrimage to Paṇḍharpūr. He listened to her advice, visited Paṇḍharī, subdued his mind to a frame of repentance, bathed in the Chandrabhāga, gazed on the god and returned home filled with joy. After his return he had no peace for thinking of Paṇḍharī. His eyes were for ever full of tears, sobs choked his throat; he was like a miser brooding on his gold or a cow on her calf. So he returned to Paṇḍharī and there told his distress. 'Know you not that there is no place void of me even for a moment?' was the voice he seemed to hear. 'Wherever you call upon my name, there assuredly I am present.'

Then Viśvambhara went home, but every fortnight he made a pilgrimage to Paṇḍharī, and after nine months, one night in a dream he saw Hari[1] who said: 'Viśvambhara, my friend, you have made me your debtor, and I have come here to stay with you.' So saying, he vanished, and[2] Viśvambhara took and set up an image near the river Indrāyaṇī; then calling in Brāhmans skilled in vedic lore they performed the installation ceremony,[3] poured over the image the *panchāmrita*[4] and arranged it in silk, with a crown and earrings, offered it food and sang a song of praise.

Viśvambhara then begged of Vithobā that his family might always serve him; and some time later he passed away leaving behind him a wife Amabāī and two sons, Hari and Mukunda. His wife was a devout woman, who asked heaven for no worldly blessings, and though she showed no interest or special skill in business, everything for a time went smoothly in her house. Amabāī's two sons were worldly men; they persuaded her to leave Dehū, and soon after they perished in war. She too lost everything and one of her daughters-in-law burned herself with her husband's (Mukunda's) corpse Her other daughter-in-law (wife of Hari) had meanwhile given birth to a son, Vithobā, by whom the family was continued.

3. Birth and Naming

The 'family tree' gives us the names Vithobā, Padājī, Śankar, Kānhaya and Bolhobā sometimes called Bolhājī, this last, whose wife was named Kanakāī, becoming the father of Tukārām. Bolhobā spent twenty years in pilgrimages and other religious acts, at the end of which period he had three sons.[5]

For the birth of her second child, Tukārām, Kanakāī went to a lonely temple, and when she looked on his face an incredible lustre dazzled her eyes, and she read in his countenance a rapture of devotion and peace.

Twelve days later she took the child to the temple, laid it at the feet of Pānḍuraṅg and asked that he might be named. Receiving the assurance that every blessing should attend him, she laid him in a cradle and this cradle song was sung for him:—

'Where the Eternal, the Undeveloped, the Void of name and form rejoices, sleep there, O child of mine! Where 'I am I' and

[1] One of Krisna's names popularly understood to mean 'sin-remover'.

[2] When Viśvambhara awoke, M. says, he called together all the worshippers of Vishṇu, and paying no heed to scoffers and scorners, went with them in procession, singing Hari's praises, to a mango-grove near Dehū. They found it pervaded by a wondrous fragrance coming from an image of Pāṇḍuraṅg with Rukminī beside him.

[3] See Chapter 6, sect 1 on Tukārām's 'Idolatry' for the significance of this ceremony which is called *prān pratisthā*.

[4] The *Panchāmrita* is an anointing by curd, milk, honey, ghee and sugar being poured over all images, both in temples and in Brāhman houses.

[5] See sect. '1. Tukārām's Birth' in Part III of this chapter.

'I am he' are heard no more, where monism and dualism are each half true, sleep there, O child of mine! Where Knower, Knowledge and Known cease to exist, sleep there, O child of mine! On the place where the saints declare knowledge to be perfect knowledge, the place where desire is not, in the home where delight is the soul's own delight, setting *there* your heart, sleep there, O child of mine! On the feet of Pāndurang, where the Undeveloped, the Unknowable, through his worshippers' love has assumed a form, setting there your affection, sleep there, O child of mine!'

Then she called the child Tukārām.

4. Home Influences

Her husband never failed to worship the Lord of Pandharī, and God gave wealth and children, 'the fruit of ancient merit.' Three sons were born to them—Sāvajī, Tukārām and Kānhobā. Their natures were like others but they were destined to lead mankind to devotion and repose. Friends increased around them, the Brāhmans wedded them with lavish outlay, and their mother rejoiced. A son, a son's wife, possessions, and a living husband, these are what Hindū women delight in and she had them all. The Merciful One suffered nothing to go amiss with them. While attending duly to their affairs they forgot not the highest purpose of life; he truly is severed from the world who never says to himself, 'It is I who do this.' The saints, like other men, carry on business but their feelings towards it are different. The ignorant imagine that their own efforts bear fruit and that their own skill saves them from confusion. They are imprisoned in their self-conceit; but the wise are they who know that God[1] alone acts. Such a one was Bolhobā. As the lotus grows in the pool, yet no water clings to it; as the sun is reflected in the water-vessel, yet it is not wetted; so the servants of God[2] live under the illusion of the world and traffic therein, yet they forget not Him.

On Dehū, the scene of Tukārām's early home-life, see pages 5 and 6.

5. Tukaram enters Business

When Bolhobā grew old, he called his eldest son and bade him take charge of the business. But Sāvajī, when he heard his father's words, and looked at the stock and ledger, fell at his father's feet, and declared that he abhorred the world and its ways.

The father then turned to Tukārām, who accepted the task, and won praise from everybody by his management of the business.

[1] M's word is Hari, a name of Vishṇu (see footnote 1 on previous page).
[2] M's word is Vishṇu.

His father's mind was at peace and for a few years Tukārām appears to have prospered. But grief follows joy—this is a truth immemorial; darkness follows day; scarcity follows a good harvest; sickness good health; and so it was with Tukārām. His father and mother passed away. Sāvajī's wife died and Sāvajī became a religious mendicant: he subdued the flesh and attained to happiness and peace. Tukārām found himself losing money in the business, his capital disappearing like clouds in summer. But he felt his duty as head of the family and he made every effort to succeed. He toiled day and night, loading the bullocks with his own hands, enduring heat and cold and loss of sleep. He raised fresh capital and started new transactions; but he made no profit.[1] All the time, however, he dealt with his customers honestly; he never gave anyone short measure; he never uttered a falsehood; Hari's name was ever on his lips; and his actions towards all creatures were compassionate.

At last all his own means were exhausted. His friends met and set him up once more with a little money. They also offered him their advice: 'Day and night you are crying on Hari's name, this is what has ruined you. A devotee of Vishṇu cannot thrive in the world. Our fathers always said so and now you know it is true; you have brought yourself to beggary.' His wife added her complaints. Still Tukārām called on Hari's name and still misfortune followed him. Mahīpati adds: 'Hári was trying to see if Tukārām would give him up.'

6. The Fallen Sack and the Sympathetic Stranger

One night as he was travelling in the way of business, his companions having gone on ahead, a dreadful storm fell upon him, a storm of wind and rain and lightning, and he saw beasts of prey around. Then his sorrows broke forth and he cried: 'The filthy world! I have embraced it! Hence my troubles! My father is dead; my brother has abandoned everything; I am bankrupt; hence my shame. Here I am; my companions have left me; no one will lend me a hand with this sack! O Hari, god of gods, I have no friend but thee! Run to help me!' As he spoke he saw a wayfaring man beside him—'it was Hari who had come to help him,' says Mahīpati. 'Who are you?' asked the stranger, 'blocking up the road in this way?' 'I am a dealer in grain,' said Tukārām; 'Here's a sack fallen and I have no one to help me with it; and my companions are gone ahead.' Then, according to our authority, the sympathetic stranger put forth his hand and in a moment laid the sack on the ox. After that he stepped forward and showed Tukārām the way, till they came to the Indrāyaṇī river

[1] M. gives as the reason. 'Hari never helped him.'

which was high in flood, but the stranger led the way and they crossed safely. Tukārām stood amazed and 'suddenly', says Mahīpati triumphantly, 'a flash of lightning showed Tukārām that his companion wore the *pitāmber* (the usual yellow silk robe of Vishṇu), that at his throat a *kaustubh* jewel sparkled, and a rosary of Tuḷsī beads hung round his neck.' Nothing was said, however, and they went on to Dehū together, where Tukārām's companion left him.

7. In the Chilly Trade

There is always enmity between the world and spiritual aspiration, and Tukārām continued solitary among his fellow-villagers. They went on scoffing at him. Then the rains failed and a sore drought prevailed. In the hope therefore of making a little money Tukārām set out with bags of chillies [1] for the Konkan and as he went along, the name of Vitthal [2] was ever on his lips. When he reached the sea he unloaded his oxen beneath a peepal tree, near the temple of Śiva, and spread his wares on the ground. Then he sat down beside them, forgetting all about himself and thinking on nothing but the form of Pāṇḍuraṅg. The villagers came and asked his prices. He answered: 'You know the usual price, don't you? Take what you want,' and he let them fill the measure themselves. At first they feared he would check them, but his thoughts were far away, and he never interfered with them. The news spread through the village, and people came tumbling over each other. 'We will pay you later on,' said they. 'Very good,' said Tukārām. Some took handfuls, others maunds, according to their strength, and at last one rascal made the remark: 'I have plenty of money at home, I want a sack of chillies.' 'I will trust you,' said Tukārām. Even so pious men understand God's purposes, but not the hard hearts of the wicked.

Now Tukārām felt pleased to think he had finished his business, so he set a little rice cooking and sat watching it with a thankful heart. Meanwhile [3] the kindly stranger who on the stormy night some time before had helped him now entered the village, represented himself as belonging to Tukārām and said politely to the people: 'It is time we were going, please let us have our money.' 'What money?' said they; 'he never measured anything out to us, we don't know what we owe him.' Then he told each one exactly what he had taken and they were

[1] Dr. Murray Mitchell's translation of Mahīpati's *Bhakta Līlāmṛita* in *J.R.A.S. Bo.*, January 1849, pp. 15–29, at this point says: 'Tukārām filled three sacks with *pepper* and proceeded to the Konkan'. There are two mistakes here, one a confusing of the word *mirchī* (chillies) with *mirī* (pepper), the other that Tukārām would not take pepper to the Konkan where pepper was grown and sold. this would be like 'taking coals to Newcastle'

[2] Another name for Viṭhobā, see sect. 15, chap. 2, pp. 41–3.

[3] Hari took the form of a man, says M.

stupified; they paid up at once. So he went through all the village and collected all Tukārām's debts.[1] There remained only the rascal who carried off the whole sack. 'He is the worst of the lot' said Tukārām's representative, 'what am I to do with him?' So he took a rope and tied it round his neck and cried, 'Pay me or I will hang myself and ruin your whole village!' Then the villagers all cried, 'Shame on the rogue,' and they fell on the rascal with kicks and fisticuffs till he paid up in full. So off went the stranger to Tukārām, and gave him the price of his chillies. Tukārām mistook him for the village watchman, and begged him to go and buy him a little ghee. He brought so much that Tukārām was astonished and he said, 'Ghee is very cheap here! Stay and share my meal.' 'Very good,' said he, and with them also sat down an unbidden guest.[2] Tukārām bade him welcome, and when the meal was finished both[3] departed and were seen no more. But when the villagers came to see Tukārām and learned that he sent no one to collect his debts, there was great astonishment and Tukārām could say nothing but 'Unfathomable are the ways of Hari.'

8. The Rogue with Gilded Bracelets

So Tukārām went off singing Hari's name and on his way he met a rogue who had some gilded bracelets,[4] and these he offered him for sale. Tukārām protested he was too poor to buy them, but the rogue offered to take part payment in cash and trust him for the rest. Tukārām accordingly bought them; he went home and tied up his oxen, and went to pay off his debt to money-lenders. But when they tried his bracelets on the touchstone there was a loud laugh, and scorn was poured on Tukārām and Viṭhobā and he must needs go woefully home.

Now Tukārām had two wives. The elder one named Rakhmābāī had become 'constitutionally asthmatic'[5] and so he had married another, the daughter of Āppājī Gulve, a well-to-do shopkeeper of Poona.[6] The younger wife Āvalī, who was also called Jijābāī, lamented loudly the misfortune of the brass bracelets. Bringing forth her own jewels she pledged them and raised two hundred pieces of silver. With these she bade Tukārām go forth and trade, and he purchased a commodity of salt and took it to Baleghāṭ. Much she admonished him as he went, to take care of his money and not lavish it on beggars. And Tukārām reached Baleghāt and sold his salt, and bought sugar and sold it again for cash.

1 Hari never thinks of his own dignity, he forgets everything but his worshipper's love, says M.

2 Who according to M. was 'Śiva.'

3 M. means Hari and Śiva.

4 M says these bracelets were of brass gilded over.

5 W. B. Patwardhan, *F.C.M.*, vol. 1, No. 3, p. 1, Bhawe, *M. Sār*. p. 172.

6 In accordance with Hindū practice, these marriages would be arranged by Tukārām's father, Tukārām being 13 or 14. See *S.T.C.*, p. 77 where Pāngārkar's figures do not harmonise with those on his p. 46.

9. Helping a Brahman Debtor

In one city which he entered he met a Brāhman with a long untrimmed beard, a wooden plough strung round his neck,[1] and who cried to everyone, 'Help! Help!' The avaricious people of the town gave him a few coppers, but Tukārām asked the reason of his plight. Whereupon the Brāhman answered: 'My kinsmen have wrested my inheritance from me; they bribed the court and threw me into prison. The rājā was a man of no judgement and I was fined three hundred rupees. Fifty I have paid, and the rest I am begging; there is a constable in charge of me and he gives me no rest.' Tukārām was moved with compassion and he gave two hundred and fifty rupees to the Brāhman who sent the constable with it to the court. Then Tukārām had the Brāhman shaved and fed his family and ten other Brāhmans[2] and they all gave him their blessing. 'The villagers of Dehū were now satisfied that Tukārām was a lunatic When he returned home, they put a necklace of onions round his neck, mounted him on a donkey and paraded him through the streets to be mocked at by the crowd.'[3]

10. Adversity and Self-Dedication

After this a sore famine broke out, the great famine of Tukārām's life-time being in 1629, and it is to this that Tukārām[4] probably refers in *abhang* No. 113 of Fraser and Marāṭhe's translation. The rains failed utterly and the cattle died of hunger. Tukārām's family began to starve and in vain he entreated neighbours to help him. One day he sold his last possessions, a few old sacks and a pack-saddle, and purchasing a little grain he made some thin porridge for his family. When that was finished the neighbours asked scornfully what Vitthal was doing for him? He felt as a man feels when an ulcer is opened up with a lancet, but he answered them quietly. The husbandman's toil is long and weary but he rejoices when the harvest ripens; 'even so the spiritual struggle is long drawn out but it ends in the joy of experience. This is what Tukārām found.' At 13 he entered business; when 17 his parents died and soon afterwards occurred the death of his sister-in-law, Sāvajī's wife. When Tukārām was 18 this elder brother Sāvajī became a sanyāsī and said good-bye to Dehū

[1] This is in accordance with an ancient custom still prevalent in some parts of India, debtors being compelled to wear a small hand-size plough around the neck as the sign to all they meet or from whom they beg that they are in debt. Such a debtor is usually pursued by some representative of his creditor with whom he must share all his takings, whether food or money.

[2] Highly meritorious acts.

[3] *H. M. P.* p. 181.

[4] See V. L. Bhave's *M. Sār.* p. 192.

and his family. Now at 21 Tukārām had become 'bankrupt'[1] and —'sorrow's crown of sorrow' in India—he had to face famine, bankruptcy and bereavements. He lost his eldest son; his favourite wife Rakhmābāī died crying for bread; and he began to reflect on the world[2]: 'How many years I have wasted! The time that is left let me give to Hari.' Reflecting thus, he closed his eyes and cried: 'Hari, O Lord, can I behold thee? How can I bring thee before my eyes? How shall I deal with the world?' So crying, he called to memory the image of Pāṇḍuraṅg, and for seven days he sat with his eyelids closed. The silence was at length broken, says Mahīpati, by a divine voice. How the bankrupt and grief-stricken merchant of Dehū came to view all this painful discipline, and how sorrow and self-dedication became strangely mingled, we shall see in our next chapter.

II. Tukaram withdraws from Business

Tukārām then went to a waste place and his younger brother Kānhobā went to look for him, night and day searching among the hills. At last he came to Bhāmbanāth and there he saw an amazing sight: Tukārām was rapt in worship.[3] In the words of Dr. P. R. Bhandarkar: 'It was on the hill named Bhāmbanāth, Tukārām tells us, that he had the revelation in which "formless Viṭhobā appeared unto him".'[4]

The two brothers went back to Dehū together. As soon as they got home Tukārām threw into the river the papers which showed that people owed his father money. 'It is idle to read books,' said he, 'unless we learn by experience to appreciate them. I am resolved myself to be a beggar; as for the business, *you* must carry it on.' And Kānhobā did so, while Tukārām withdrew from the world. Very little food he ate, so that his limbs wasted away. He allowed himself neither sleep nor rest and poured himself out in repentance. In the morning he would bathe and visit Pāṇḍuraṅg's temple, then he would go to the forest. West of Dehū is Bhaṇḍārā Hill where he would sit alone rapt in contemplation. 'Since God has visited you,' men would say, 'why need you subdue your senses?' 'When the sun rises,' replied Tukārām, 'every eye beholds him, but no one can keep him from his course a moment. God indeed has visited me once, but I mean to keep Him with me always. The Ganges flows into the sea not once but continually, so must God's worshippers part from Him only to meet Him again.' In short, he gave up the world entirely, and worshipped

1 'I became bankrupt and was crushed by the famine' are his words in *abhaṅg* 113 (F and M).

2 See sect. '2. Adversity and Self-Dedication' in Part III of this Chapter.

3 For the detail by M. see sect. 3 in Part III of this Chapter.

4 *Two Masters; Jesus and Tukārām*, p. 12.

God day and night. 'I trust in Thy name alone: it is to me family and wealth, and the merit of fierce austerities; its glory is known to all the saints.' Each evening Tukārām would return to Dehū. Many voices spoke, some approving and some disapproving, but none of them troubled his mind. He was like an elephant walking on a royal road, with dogs barking at his heels.

12. How he watched the Cornfield

Near the place of his meditations a peasant had a crop of corn and one day he made Tukārām a proposal. 'Sit and watch my field,' said he, 'I will give you half a maund of grain. You can go on worshipping Hari.' 'Very good,' said Tukārām, for he was always ready to help any one. So the peasant led him off and gave him a sling, and he promised to stay till the crop ripened.

There was a watchman's scaffold in the field and Tukārām sat himself down on it. Soon came the birds and settled for a meal, and Tukārām said to himself: 'These too are God's creatures and all of them hungry; last year there was famine, this year God has sent us a crop; I call myself a worshipper of Vishṇu; I must not chase these away or I shall be guilty of wrongdoing.' When two watches of the day had passed, the birds began to sing sweetly; they had filled their stomachs and they flew away to drink. Meanwhile Tukārām's wife wondered where he was, and she sent her daughter to look for him. Kaśī ran and found him, but Tukārām refused to go home, so Āvaḷī sent him some food to the field. And there he stayed day and night, save for his morning visit to the temple. Every evening he said to the birds, 'Be off! Be off! It will be dark soon and you will not be able to see your way! Come back to-morrow morning.' And he looked on them with admiration and said, 'They eat only a few grains here and take nothing home with them. When, O God, wilt Thou let me live like them? Away with the illusions that bind me; let me trample on names and forms, let me see my own self in every one and forget my body. As dead leaves are whirled about by the wind, such be my comings and goings; let me look on gold and pebbles as the same; keep evil hopes far from me; let me listen neither to praise nor censure; let me see the Life of the World in all living things.'

While he was thus meditating all the birds in the village flocked to the field. Tukārām rejoiced to see them feed, as a generous man rejoices to feed rows of Brāhmans, but later on came the peasant and he found every ear in his field empty! He visited every corner of it, and everywhere birds flew away, like Brāhmans at the approach of an out-caste. 'You have ruined me!' he cried to Tukārām, and he dragged him off to the *panchāyat* (village jury). Tukārām told his story very simply and everyone burst into laughter. 'How much have you lost?' said the jury to the peasant. 'Two *khaṅdīs*[1]', he replied. Then the jury agreed that Tukārām must make it good, or the Government official would be displeased, since he was insisting on payment of the taxes due from the grain. So the jury went off to estimate the damage, but—so runs the story of Mahīpati—when they reached the field, lo! every ear was full of grain, not a trace of damage could be seen! And when the field was reaped, seventeen *khaṅḍīs* of grain were recovered from it; such a harvest had never been seen before. There were many opinions what should be done with it, but finally it was agreed by the jury that Vithobā had sent it for Tukārām and that two *khandīs* should be given the peasant, the rest to Tukārām. He however refused to take it, 'for to expect no fruit of our actions is the chief sign that a man is a true devotee and that his spirit is at peace.' Many are ready to serve such a man—and such a man was Tukārām. The balance of fifteen *khaṅḍīs* of grain were left in custody of Mahādājīpant Deshpānde, the revenue official already referred to.

13. Tukaram and the Temple Repairs

Tukārām's wife was very bitter over his refusal to accept the grain, but Tukārām heeded her not. He turned his thoughts to the old temple of Pāṇḍurang in the village which was falling down through age. He took a pickaxe in his hand and also set to work mixing clay and water Mahādājīpant at this time had a dream in which he seemed to hear Hari bidding him help Tukārām. He obeyed the call and sent workmen to repair the temple, paying their wages out of the balance of grain left in his hands. Tukārām reflected sadly that he ought now to feed Brāhmans, and he had no means of doing so. Once more Mahādājīpant remembered[2] that Tukārām had never been paid his half maund for watching the field. The village jury was again summoned and they called on the peasant to pay up his debt. Many of them added something themselves, and Tukārām finished his labours on the temple by feasting the Brāhmans, while a consecration ceremony[3] was performed for the image.

Tukārām then formed the idea of conducting *Kīrtans*, and he began by committing to memory the lines of old saints like Nāmdev and Kabīr, Dnyāneshwar and Eknāth. He sat on Bhanḍārā Hill and learned them. He read the *Bhagvadgītā* and searched out its meaning, his wife bringing him food daily. To be sure, she was a shrew, but she respected her husband and laid all the blame for his foolishness on Viṭṭhal.

[1] A *khaṅdī* is 20 Bombay maunds by measure, roughly lbs. 1600 or over cwts 14.

[2] M says: 'Hari reminded Mahādājīpant'.

[3] The *Prāṇ Pratiṣṭha* ceremony, on which see chapter 6, sect. 1 on 'Tukārām's Idolatry'.

IMAGE OF JIJĀBĀĪ (OR ĀVAḶĪBĀĪ) TUKĀRĀM'S WIFE, NOW WORSHIPPED AT DEHŪ

14. The Troubles of His Wife

Well, one day Āvalī was carrying him bread and a gourd full of water. The sun was very hot, the path very rough and thorny, and she was almost fainting with fatigue. She spilt the water and her bitterness broke forth in loud complaints. A thorn got into her foot and she could walk no further, when suddenly it was as if there stood by her side one glittering in silk and jewels. 'The wretch!' said Āvaḷī, 'what does he want? He has driven my husband mad, and he has come to laugh at my troubles.' So she turned away, but, whichever way she looked, it seemed as though Hari was reflected in a house full of mirrors. She closed her eyes, but a voice seemed to say, 'My daughter, why do you take me for an enemy? You say I have turned your husband against the world; not so, it is only that the plant has borne its own fruit, and the wind has blown it from the tree. How am I to blame in this?' And with this Āvalī felt the thorn had left her foot. Then she stood and cried: 'I am losing time; that lunatic is sitting there on the hill,' and off she started, finding some fresh water and supplying her husband's needs."[1]

15. Avali Loses Her Robe

One day she was bathing and had hung on a wall her one and only robe, while her husband despite their deep poverty was sitting near singing of Hari. Just then there came past a poor old Brāhman woman[2] who begged Tukārām for a dress. His heart was filled with pity and he signed to her to take the robe; she did so and gave him her blessing and departed. Then Tukārām went off to the Indrāyaṇī, leaving Āvaḷī much perplexed by the loss of her robe.[3] At length the children told her what had happened and her lamentations were loud and long. 'Curse the old woman,' she said, 'he's given her my clothes and gone off to the forest without a word to me! My husband indeed! I never ate the food he earned. He tied the beads[4] on me and made himself my master; he never did anything for me. One wife of his died in the famine; she was very lucky to go before me.' Just at that moment relatives called inviting her to a wedding ceremony and this added fuel to the fire of her wrath. Just as she was all aflame with passion, says Mahīpati, she had a vision of Hari standing offering her a silk robe—and the vision acted like rain on the fire! She put on the dress and went abroad,

[1] For M's embellishments see sect. 4 in Part III of this chapter.

[2] So says M. in *Bhakta Vijāya*, but in his later *Bhakta Līlāmrita* he says Rakhumāī came in the guise of a Mahārāṇī.

[3] *S.T.C.* has a chapter (14) on 'Tukohā and Jijābāī' (Āvaḷī) which raised in the press a fruitless discussion on 'Who was to blame?'

[4] A necklace of flowers, like the ring in the European ritual, is the symbol of marriage among Hindūs.

her friends astonished to see her splendour. One said: 'She must always have kept it hidden!' And another: 'Tukārām pretends to be an ascetic, but look what he's given his wife!'

16. Tukaram as a Vaishnava Saint

Gradually Tukārām became known as a Vaishṇava and even Brāhmans began to honour him, but his humility did not forsake him. When other Vaishṇavas gathered to dance and sing he would sweep away the pebbles from the ground with his own hands and stand behind them and take up the refrain. All his actions were those of a true saint. 'What is a true saint?' asks Mahīpati. 'One who grieves equally whether his own child or another man's cries, who is not vexed when a thief carries off his goods, who feels equally honoured when a king gives him a jewel and a peasant a few vegetables. Such was Tukārām.' He would sit by the river humbling himself before God and when night came on he would return to the temple. Sometimes he would determine to keep awake all night in meditation, but he would find himself growing sleepy. 'For though a man may have left the world, yet some weaknesses of the flesh will cling to him, as a fragrance lingers where camphor has been burnt, or as the potter's wheel goes on whirling when he has withdrawn the stick, or as leaves tremble when the storm is over, or twilight lingers when the sun has set.' What did 'the prince of Vaishṇavas' do? In order to ensure constancy of devotion he tied his *shendī*—the sacred lock of long hair worn by a Hindū—to a nail above him, and thus for four days he abstained from sleep, and for four days he banished all thoughts of ease. 'Probably Mahīpati has based his statement on tradition; but if it be his own invention, he must evidently have made a close study of Tukārām's works, a fact which is borne out by other evidence also. For Tukārām feelingly refers again and again to his own laziness and the loss of time in sleep, so that nobody need wonder if he actually tried the arrangement which some over-zealous students sometimes resort to even in these days.'[1]

In every possible way Tukārām served other men. He assisted pilgrims. When he found in the jungle old cattle turned loose to shift for themselves, he brought them grass and water and fondled them. In hot weather he provided water for wayfarers and when he found any sick he brought them into the temple and gave them medicine. In short, he performed any service required of him and he never failed in his word.

17. His Commission in Oil

Once when he was sitting on the bank of the Indrāyaṇī, people going to market bade him come with them. 'Very good,' said

[1] Dr. P. R. Bhandarkar, *Two Masters: Jesus and Tukārām*, p. 19.

Tukārām, and he joined them, but so as not to be idle a moment, he sang as he walked. Now there was an old Brāhman woman in the company, very feeble on her legs, and Tukārām felt so sorry for her that he offered to carry her on his back. 'Better if you went to the bāzār for me, and brought me my oil!' 'Véry good,' said Tukārām, and next day he brought her oil. And some days later she was telling everyone that the oil never ended! And some people said: 'He ought to be ashamed of himself! His own children haven't enough to eat.' But others sought to turn the occasion to their own advantage, and they sent Tukārām to buy oil for *them*, loading him up with many vessels and bottles. He accepted the commission, and went to the bāzār, where he helped visitors to stall and feed their horses, then going to the temple to worship. Afterwards he took the vessels to the dealer in oil and handed him his money, but he had no idea how much oil ought to go in each vessel.

Tukārām's wife was very bitter when she saw him working for others and others taking advantage of him. But her friends said: 'Every man suffers for his qualities; the parrot wouldn't be imprisoned if he couldn't talk; if a cow has a white tail we cut it off.' And so Āvalī was silenced, but she was very discontented.

18. The Holy Day of His Forefathers

Āvalī addressed him one day and said: 'To-day is the holy day of your forefathers and we have nothing to offer them.' 'I will go to the forest,' said Tukārām, 'and bring some herbs for an offering. You may eat them and feast our forefathers.' So off he went, singing loudly the name of Hari: 'My burden is all on thy head; do with me as thou wilt.' As he passed by a spot where some reapers were at work, they shouted to him to come and help them. They were labourers who were working half-heartedly but Tukārām helped them with all his might. He forgot all about the herb he wanted.[1]

After some hours Tukārām came home from his labours, with a bundle of wheat the reapers had given him. And as he passed along he disturbed a bees' nest, and the bees swarmed out and settled on him. But Tukārām would not drive them off. 'This body of mine,' said he, 'is doomed to perish; let it spend itself in the service of other creatures. To-day is the holy day of my forefathers; peradventure they have come to visit me in the form of these bees.' Then the bees left off troubling him and he reached home without more annoyance.[2] Bidding his wife cook the corn and make a feast for their forefathers, he prayed: 'O merciful Mother

[1] For another aspect of this episode see sect. 5 in part III of this chapter.
[2] M. says 'Hari drove the bees away.'

Viṭhobā, unless thou dine with me I will not dine!' 'Then,' says Mahīpati, 'Hari heard his words and appeared, and he and his Lord sat down together. This was the work and effect of faith. God ate with him and vanished from his sight.'[1]

19. His Call to Become a Poet

The breathing into Tukārām of the spirit of poetry took place in a dream in which Nāmdev in the company of Hari appeared to Tukārām.[2] 'Rise up, Tukā,' said a voice to him, 'and listen to me. Behold Nāma, my worshipper, who vowed he would write me a hundred crores of *abhaṅgs*. Before he finished his task he passed away. Now you finish it for him.' When Tukārām awoke he felt mightily rejoiced, and set to work at once, making himself books of rough paper and learning the *Bālbhodh* letters.[3] Nine hundred[4] verses he wrote and they were heard with delight by Hari's worshippers. Then he began to compose *abhaṅgs* and fast they flowed from him: 'As when the rain pours down, unnumbered shoots of grass spring up, even so verses poured forth' from Tukārām.[5]

20. His Daily Offering

Tukārām used to give milk daily to Viṭhobā, pouring it over his image. Āvaḷī greatly disapproved of this. She said: 'He gives that black fellow a pot of milk daily; why ever does he do it? We have a troop of children at home; and not enough milk left to make a little curd for them.' Now her little daughter Bhāgīrathi always went with Tukārām to the temple, so Āvaḷī said to her: 'The milk your father takes to the temple, does that black fellow really drink it?' 'Indeed he does,' said the little girl, 'and if there is any left he gives me some and drinks the rest himself.' Āvaḷī was

[1] The last few lines offer a striking Hindū parallel to the Christian's 'grace before meat' and to Brother Lawrence's *Practice of the Presence of God.*

[2] This story is recorded in Tukārām's own *Gāthā*, *abhaṅgs* 1320–1321, *Indu Prakāsh* edition and 103–4 F. and M., but Dr. P. R. Bhandarkar rejects them and this story also on the ground that in *abhaṅg* 1333 in which Tukārām gives a summary of his life, 'this dream is not referred to while the other one (see section 22 below) in which his *guru* appeared is mentioned.' This seems to us inconclusive, for Tukārām was not bound to give every detail of his life in this one *abhaṅg*; moreover the incident of the *guru-mantra* referred to by him was by far the more important of the two. See *Two Masters: Jesus and Tukaram*, p. 9.

[3] In which Sanskrit is usually written.

[4] Only 102 of these have been published. They are given in the *I. P.* edition, Vol. 2, pp. 655–717.

[5] On the subject of this sect. and sect. 22 below, see L. R. Pāngārkar. *S.T.C.*, chap. 7, and P. R. Bhandarkar's later view in footnote, sect. 30 below.

astonished, and one day she said to Tukārām, 'I am going to give him some milk myself.' 'Very good,' replied Tukārām. Mahīpati adds: 'The Lord of Pandharī was perplexed. He knew Āvalī had no faith in him and if he did show any sign or wonder, she would only torment her poor husband.' Now when Āvaḷī brought the milk it was too hot, but she had no gentle feelings towards the god, and she never thought of cooling it. So when she put the vessel next to his lips 'and burned them', she was greatly astonished, and said: 'This black fellow looks like a stone, but there seems to be life in him for all that.' Then Tukārām was sorely distressed and went off to the temple, where tears streamed from his eyes. 'Even as he wept, however, the blister went down,' adds the devoted biographer of the Marāthā saints.

21. The Healing of His Sick Boy

Tukārām had now two sons, Mahādev and Viṭhobā and one time Mahādev fell very ill. Āvalī tried many remedies, whatever were proposed to her, and she sent for adepts who were masters of evil spirits. She tied threads and charms on the boy and waved holy lights round him. All was idle, however; the boy wasted away, though drugs were poured down his throat. The neighbours told her that it was Hari that had sent the misfortune, and her feelings were roused to the uttermost. She took her dying son and went off to the temple to beat Pāṇḍuraṅg. Having reached the temple Āvaḷī listened in amazement to the prayers and looking upon her son she saw that he was healed. So she took him home and fed him and his sickness returned no more. But when Tukārām heard of this he exclaimed: 'Alas! you have laid a burden on the Lord of Paṇḍharī.'

22. Tukaram's Dream and the Mantra

A small band of followers now began to write down his poems, which task was entrusted to Santājī Jaganāḍe the oilman.[1] There was also a Brāhman member of the band named Gangājī Mavāḷa; day and night they went to the temple to sing and to worship Hari. At that time Tukārām dreamed that he met a saint while going to bathe. Laying his hand on Tukārām's head the saint imparted to him the *mantra*: 'Rām-Kṛiṣṇa-Hari,' adding that his own name was Bābājī and his predecessors Rāghav Chaitanya and Keshav Chaitanya. Tukārām then begged that he would go home with

1 Some of these poems are now published from Santājī's manuscripts by Mr. V. L. Bhawe in his *Tukārāmāce Assal* (original) *Gāthā*, 1920–1, see our chap. 5, I, sect. 1.

him and sanctify his house; he would give him food and he should cook it himself, 'Give me, then,' said the saint in the dream, 'a quarter-seer of ghee and I will come with you.' This far went Tukārām's dream and he awoke.[1] 'Mahīpati suggests that Tukārām did not like to resort to a *guru*, because according to the usual custom the latter would have put forth for the acceptance of his disciple the doctrine of *advaitism* or pantheism, for which he had a great repugnance. The difficulty was solved when Tukārām had a dream, in which appeared a person who declared his name to be Bābājī Chaitanya of the line of Rāghava Chaitanya and Keshav Chaitanya and who gave him the sacred formula, not 'tattwamasi',[2] but "Rām, Kṛṣṇa, Hari". "The Prince of Teachers," says Tukārām, told me the simple sacred formula of my liking that will not lead to any entanglement anywhere"'[3]

In a paper before the *Bhārata Itihāsa Sanshodhaka Maṇḍaḷa*, Poona, May 29, 1921, Mr. A. Muzumdar said four newly-discovered *sanads* showed Keshav and Bābājī as one and not two individuals, that Bābājī died *shake* 1493, Tukārām receiving the *gurumantra* in *shake* 1523. This view runs counter both to the traditional date of Tukārām's birth and to the definite statement of Bahinābāī—see I, 4 (4) above—that Rāghav, Keshav, Bābājī were three distinct persons.

23. Avali and Her Moods

His wife's conduct much chagrined him, and much he remonstrated with her. 'Pāṇḍuraṅg,' said he, 'is our father; he will not suffer us to want anything If you will listen to me, we shall gain a glorious name in this world. Cast aside worldly hopes; forget that you have any children: go to the saints for protection, and call on the name of Vīthobā.' Eleven *abhangs* in this strain he addressed to her.[4] For a time she was moved by his own spirit of devotion, and one day, early in the morning, she called in a party of Brāhmans, and bade them carry off all their household goods; she even gave the ashes on the fireplace to a sanyāsi, to smear his body withal. After this she went to the temple and there came up an old Mahār woman, a beggar, and asked for a cast-off dress, whereupon Tukārām gave her one of Āvaḷī's that was hanging on the wall. The children of the village told this to Āvaḷī, and she was bitterly incensed; she took a stone and went to the temple to break the image. There Āvaḷi poured out her wrongs against Rukhminī.[5] (See footnote 3. Sect. 15).

[1] See footnotes at the end of sect. 19 above, and on sect. 30 below.
[2] The Sanskrit for 'Thou art that'
[3] Dr. P. R. Bhandarkar, *Two Masters: Jesus and Tukaram*, p. 9.
[4] *Abhangs* numbered 1573a to 1573k in volume 2 of F. and M.
[5] M. says Rukminī gave her a handful of gold pieces and a dress, but when Tukārām saw her returning he said, 'Greedy creature!' took the gold pieces and gave them away to Brāhmans.

24. Dining with the Chinchwad Brahman

At Chinchwad lived a Brāhman named Chiṇtāmaṇi Dev, who, hearing of Tukārām's fame, sent him an invitation to dine with him. Tukārām reached the house just as Chintāmani Dev was at his morning devotions. He approached unperceived and heard Chintāmani in the midst of recitations giving orders to the gardener and scolding him for neglecting the plants. When Chintāmani came forth, Tukārām laid himself in the dust before him; but Chintāmani scorned to make any reverence to a Śūdra. 'I am glad to see you,' said he, 'when did you come?' 'I came,' said Tukārām, 'when you were seated at your morning devotions and just as you (mentally) went into the garden.' Chintāmaṇi's conscience smote him. 'Truly,' remarked he, 'you are well said to be a searcher of hearts. But tell me! They say Vishnu eats in your company! Is it so? Will you show me this marvel?' So saying he offered Tukārām a seat and a plate, for even a beggar has a right to such if he comes at the moment when the fire oblation is offered. Howbeit, Tukārām's plate was set four cubits' distance from the Brāhman's. Then Tukārām set out two other plates and Chintāmani asked him for whom they were. 'One,' said Tukārām, 'is for my god Hari, the other for your god Gaṇpati. Now you call on Ganpati to join us.' And Chintāmaṇi did so, but in vain, whereupon Tukārām said: 'Know that, while you were calling, a devotee of Gaṇpati was drowning; he remembered Ganpati, who ran forthwith to save him. If you doubt this, wait a while and see.' And according to the picturesque narrative of Mahīpati, 'an hour afterward Gaṇpati came to join them, his silken robes dripping with salt water,' and Tukārām bade Chintāmaṇi invite him to dinner. 'How can he dine with us?' said Chintāmaṇi, 'when we offer him sacred food, he accepts but the odour.' 'I shall not be comforted,' said Tukārām, 'unless he dines with us.' And he 'turned to Ganpati' and saluted him: 'Glory to thee! Giver of all accomplishment, saviour of thy worshippers in all extremities, dispeller of the ensnaring world?' Then, so runs the Hindū story, did Gaṇpati, 'a visible presence, sit down before them; and Tukārām closing his eyes called on Pāṇḍuraṅg, and he came in all his glory and joined them. And they ate and were satisfied and departed.' Then Chintāmani laid himself in the dust before Tukārām but Tukārām raised him up and said. 'My lord, it is more fitting that I should reverence your feet.'

This remarkable event can best be understood by reading carefully Tukārām's own *abhangs* 1573 L to 1573 P in the second volume of the Poems,[1] especially 1573 O, where Tukārām says: 'It is Nārāyan who eats the food. At every mouthful let us utter the name of Govinda, it is enough that the worshippers eat—God eats

[1] F. and M.

through them.' Or as Dr. P. R. Bhandarkar translates this important *abhang*.[1] 'If at every mouthful a man has faith then God dines in his person. Keep hold of the essential thing which is to remember God, then the distance between is not great. If you enjoy a meal in faith, God sits down to dine with you.' The Hindū story thus supplies an interesting parallel to the sacramental significance given by Quakers to every meal.

25. Tukaram's Six Children

Now Tukārām had the following children: three daughters—Kāśībāī, Bhāgīrathī, and Gangābāī, and three sons—Mahādev, Vithobā, and Narāyan.[2] His daughters had come to be of marriageable age, and Āvalī pressed their marriage upon him. So one day Tukārām went into the road and there saw three boys of his own caste playing together; he called them to the house, sent for a Brāhman and forthwith he got them married to his daughters. Friends met and a marriage feast was duly held, Tukārām's fellow-devotees making contributions towards the expenses of the four days' wedding festivities. 'Truly God protects those who make friends of Him; and the world shows itself merciful to them,' is the comment of Tukārām's biographer.

26. The Haughty Brahman Deshpande

A Brāhman named Deshpānde there was who sat and fasted and practised austerities, in the hope that he might comprehend the Purānas. Ten days he sat fasting, till in a dream he heard Hari bid him go and worship at Ālandī. To Ālandī therefore he went and twelve days he fasted before Dnyāneshwar's tomb, till he was bidden rise and visit Tukārām. Then Deshpānde awoke and the counsel displeased him, for Tukārām was a Śudra. Nevertheless he went to Dehū and told his tale to Tukārām, who said in dismay: 'O Hari! all that I utter is but the words thou dost whisper in my ear. What can I do to instruct this man?' And he composed for him eleven *abhangs* under the title 'The Best Knowledge', and with these gave him a cocoanut; but the Brāhman was wroth and said: 'It is the old Purānas I desire to comprehend, not this *Prākṛit*[3] of yours.' And he refused Tukārām's offering of fruit and away he went back to Ālandī and complained to Dnyāneshwar. But again he heard the same voice as before, this time saying: 'Your base suspicions are the fruit of your own past. You sat

[1] *Two Masters: Jesus and Tukārām*, p. 31.
[2] Narāyan was born four months after Tukārām's death (see Part III, sect. 18).
[3] The common dialect of the people as contrasted with the sacred Sanskrit.

under the tree of wishes and tied up your wallet and disdained to put therein what it gave you. In Tukārām's *abhangs* is the very essence of the holy scriptures, but you despised them because they were written in *Prākrit*.'

27. The Pearls in the Cocoanut

Thus it was in Deshpānde's case. But there was another Brāhman named Kondobā, a stout jolly fellow, unlettered and void of self-conceit, who did reverence to Tukārām and accepted from him the cocoanut which Deshpānde had refused. *He* found inside it a number of costly pearls valued at a lakh of rupees! For a banker of Ahmedabād had offered these pearls to Dnyāneshwar at Ālandī and he had been told at Dnyāneshwar's tomb to give them to Tukārām. In sending them to Tukārām the banker put them inside a cocoanut, knowing as he did that Tukārām *must* accept a cocoanut in accordance with the courtesies of the country, whereas he would be sure to refuse pearls. This cocoanut Tukārām then gave to the Brāhman, and as the story goes, along with these precious pearls inside the cocoanut Kondobā received the knowledge of Sanskrit.

28. Tukaram's Kirtans at Lohogaon

Tukārām's fame continued to spread and one day the people of Lohogaon begged him to pay them a visit and sanctify their village. He consented and went and held a *kīrtan* there. One month he stayed with them, and at last a Brāhman widow begged him to perform a *kīrtan* in her house. When he saw her devotion he consented, but before the day came there was a storm of rain and the wall of her neighbour's house threatened to fall in. She went to Tukāram in great distress, but he assured her the wall should not fall until the service was finished So four days passed safely, the service was completed, the feast was held, the house was emptied and then the wall fell. Tukārām bade the people build her a new house, and he held a service there too.

29. Rameshwar Bhatt

Some men, however, cannot bear the sight of goodness, just as the fevered stomach rejects milk; such an one was the Brāhman Rāmeshwar Bhaṭṭ. A learned student of the scriptures, he lived at Wāgholi, and Tukārām's fame moved him to anger. Resolving to drive him from the countryside, he sent a complaint to the Court, [1]

[1] A Mahommedan Court, the country at that time being subject to Aurangzīb. The Court might presumably take cognisance of any actions that disturbed existing customs and so threatened the public peace,

that Tukārām, a Śudra, was studying the scriptures and holding *kīrtans* and that even Brāhmans were saluting him. The simple people were deluded when they heard this complaint, even the District Officer being incensed, so he ordered the *Pātīl* of Dehū to drive forth the offending poet-saint. On this being made known, Tukārām went to see Rāmeshwar Bhatt and deprecated his wrath. But Rāmeshwar told him unauthorized preachers such as he would go to hell and he enjoined silence upon him. 'You Brāhmans,' said Tukārām, 'are visible images of the Lord; I will obey your command; I will speak no more. But what of those poems of mine that are written down?' 'Throw them into the river,' said Rāmeshwar. 'Very good,' said Tukārām.

So back went he to Dehū, and entering the temple, there cried: 'O thou that doest all deeds, at thy behest I have uttered these irregular words; now I must throw them in the river.' Then with his own hands he committed every sheet to the water, tying them in a cloth and sinking them with a stone, calling on the name of God[1] as he did so. And the malicious said: 'Ha! the butterfly has lost his colours! Rāmeshwar is a wise man; like a second sun he has chased away the darkness of falsehood' Tukārām was at first quite cheerful, and for five days he continued praising God as before; at last, however, he began to feel men's derision. 'You threw away the deeds of your property; now you've thrown away your poems. Aren't you ashamed to look us in the face?' When he heard these biting words, his heart failed him, and he sat down on a stone outside the temple, feeling ashamed before the world. 'Speak a word, O Vitthal,' he cried, 'ere yet I destroy myself; if I do not reach thee I must perish.' And he closed his eyes, firmly fixed his thoughts on God[2], ate not nor drank nor gave any sign of life. In his silence he composed a number of moving *abhangs* about the sad event.[3]

Though Rāmeshwar was a learned Brāhman, yet, in the words of our narrator, 'his enmity towards Vishṇu's worshipper destroyed the merit he had won'.[4] One day he came to Poona to salute Śiva—let us see what happened to him. At Poona there lived a great *fakīr*, Anagādashāh by name; Rāmeshwar Bhatt unwittingly entered his garden and seeing before him a pool of clear water began to bathe. The *fakīr* heard him at his devotions and he was mightily incensed. 'You have polluted my sanctified water,' said he, 'your body shall be burned without fire.' And as the story goes, Rāmeshwar Bhatt soon felt himself aflame; sleeping, rising or walking, an inward fire consumed him; he knew not what to do.[5] Thoughtful people said, however, 'This is the wrath of

1 'Vitthala,' says M.
2 'Hari's feet,' says M.
3 These *abhangs* are 1519–73 in F. and M., with commento, p. 439, vol. II.
4 As a Westerner would say 'He was ruined by his jealousy.'
5 I. e., his conscience became a hell of torment.

God; Anagādashāh is His instrument.' And at last he went to Ālandī and sat in mute entreaty before the image of Dnyāndev.

30. Recovery of Tukaram's Poems from the River

Meanwhile God[1] laid His comforting hand on Tukārām, saying: 'I am thy protection. Many saints have I protected'. And He settled 'like a bee in the lotus of the poet's heart', and Tukārām felt glad once more. That night He showed himself in a dream to many of the village and said to them: 'I have kept dry all Tukārām's papers; they are even now coming to the surface of the river. Make haste and take them out'. So in the morning they hurried to the river, and, behold! the papers were floating like gourds on the water. Great was the joy among the poet's friends as some of them swam out and brought the papers to shore. And Tukārām opened his eyes and sang a hymn of praise: 'One fault I acknowledge,' said he, 'that I have troubled Him who wears the woodland wreath. I have no right to lay my burden upon Him.'[2]

The *Indu Prakāsh* edition[3] presents the above remarkable story as follows, adding[4] that the difficulty arising 'can easily be explained on rational grounds': 'Tukārām threw the books into the river Indrāyanī with his own hand, taking care, says Mahīpati, to cover them on either side with thin slates of stone and wrapping them up in a cloth. . . With his poems all drowned in the river, and he forbidden to compose any new ones, he seemed destined to live a life of nonentity, . . . leaving the world to his persecutors, who evidently thought they had gained everything they wanted. But no; by that inherent force of truth to triumph and to outlive, and by that unforeseen and unexpected succour which the truly faithful and sincere receive from quarters unknown, call it miracle or anything else, Tukārām and his poems outlived his persecutors and inculcated in the Marāthā nation the great doctrine of Salvation by Faith. On the 13th day according to Mahīpati's account of the event, the drowned books began to float on the surface of the water and were taken out by the people.' Such considerations will weigh differently with different minds. Some might be disposed to consider favourably the possibility that after several days in the river the cloth

[1] Hari, says M.

[2] Dr. P. R. Bhandārkar would here insert the narrative of Tukārām's call to become a poet already given in sect. 19 above, urging as he does that the 'call' came after the recovery of Tukārām's poems from the river, and that for the occasion Vishnu came to the poet under the guise of a child. But it is clear that Tukārām was already famous as a poet *before* the poems were consigned to the river, as sect. 29 above shows, and to put his call to be a poet *after* the recovery of poems which had made him famous seems an unjustifiable reversing of Mahīpati's order of narrative (*Nawayuga*, March 1921, pp. 145–9).

[3] *I. P.*, Vol. I., p. 11–12.

[4] *Ibid* p. 20.

wrapping may have been washed away, followed shortly after by the 'thin slates of stone;' the bundle of papers then increasing in bulk, as suggested by Mr. V. L. Bhawe's word [1] *phugīn*=swollen, they would naturally rise to the surface. A modern parallel was the recovery from the sea of MSS belonging to the late Archdeacon Dennis of the Niger Mission, who, returning to England in August 1917 on the S. S. *Karina* was sunk by a German submarine. His sunken MSS—linguistic notes and the bulky typescript of his English-Ibo dictionary— were sometime after washed up on the coast of Wales and are now at Salisbury Square, London.

The story spread abroad like the fragrance of a bed of flowers, while all the time Rāmeshwar Bhatt was sitting at Ālandī. At last in the temple of Dnyāneshwar he received this message: 'If you assail the servants of Hari no sacred waters will wash your guilt away; you must go and implore Tukārām for help and your misery will end'. Then Rāmeshwar repented and wrote a letter, sending it Tukārām by the hand of one of his disciples saying: 'I write to you in fear and trembling for I have greatly wronged you.' Tukārām was moved by compassion, and he sent him an *abhang*: 'If your mind is pure, your enemies will be your friends, tigers and serpents will approach you but they will not devour you. If men revile you, you will think they are speaking gently to you; flames of fire will feel cool to you.[2]

When Rāmeshwar read this, he rose and went to visit Tukārām and praised his greatness and goodness. But Tukārām said: 'I am a man of low degree; I beg you will show me your kindness and favour'. And the other answered. 'I shall go home no more but shall make my home for ever at your feet'. And so he did.[3]

Shortly afterwards the *fakīr* heard the story, and he set out to visit Tukārām. When he arrived at Tukārām's house, Āvalī received him with a curse, but little Gangā, Tukārām's daughter, dropped a little flower into his bowl. The child's mother, Āvalī, thereupon grasped Gangā's hand, seizing some of the flour left there, but Gangā managed to throw a little more, filling the *fakīr's* vessel. 'What! and are you Tukārām?' he asked in astonishment. 'Are you a fool?' replied Gangā, 'Tukārām is in the temple'. Hearing this he went to the temple and paid Tukārām a visit, laying himself in the dust before him. Two days he stayed listening to Tukārām's *kīrtans* and then he went back home.

Among those who came to the Dehū temple was a young woman, a stranger, and very beautiful, who one day when she found Tukārām alone besought him to sin. Whereupon he trembled with horror, spoke to her two *abhangs*—121 and 122 on which see chapter 6, section 9—and rebuked her.

1 *M. Sār.*, p. 178
2 See *Abhang* 1466, Fraser and Marāthe
3 M. here gives 'The Coppersmith and His Wife' in sect. 6, part iii

31. Mumbaji the Jealous Brahman[1]

There was living at Chinchwad a Brāhman named Mumbājī who became an ascetic and changed his place of abode to Dehū. As Tukārām's fame increased Mumbājī despised him as being a Śudra by caste and a grocer by vocation. Now it happened that Āvalī's father had given her a buffalo, and one day this creature went into Mumbājī's garden and ate some of the plants there. Mumbājī cursed the buffalo and closed the path to his garden with thorns. In so doing, however, he also closed the way round the temple, and next *Ekādashī*[2] when the pilgrims came, Tukārām opened it. Mumbājī burst into furious wrath, seized Tukārām and severely beat him. Tukārām offered no resistance and no word of remonstrance, merely calling devotedly on the name of Hari. But Mumbājī went on beating him as a thresher beats ears of corn?

When all was over Tukārām went into the temple.[3] It was soon time to begin the service, but Tukārām insisted they should wait for Mumbājī. When they sent to remind him, however, he sent word that he could not come. His body was aching all over! On hearing this, Tukārām went himself to the house of Mumbājī, gently rubbed the aching body of the man who a short time before had been thrashing him, and then brought Mumbājī to the temple service. Thus was Mumbājī put to shame by Tukārām's meekness and spirit of forgiveness. Dr. P. R. Bhandarkar well says that it was 'a realization of the precept of Jesus "that ye resist not evil" in Matthew v. 39–40.'[4] Mahīpati rightly adds: 'Towards friend and foe alike Tukārām showed the same kindly disposition. Free from ill-feeling or resentment of any kind he won the love of all around him'.[5]

32. Shivaji and Tukaram[6]

Tukārām's fame now came to the ears of the future Marāṭhā King Śivājī, who said: 'I will call Tukārām here and listen to his *kīrtan* myself.' So he sent a horse with a torch and umbrella and

[1] This story of Mumbājī, in all the Marāṭhī 'lives' of Tukārām, is placed very much earlier, before the incident of Rāmeshwar Bhaṭṭ and the loss and recovery of Tukārām's poems. On the evidence of Bahīnābāī—recently brought to light (see page 73 above and *M. Sār*, p. 193)—who distinctly states that previous to the Mumbājī incident Rāmeshwar Bhaṭṭ was a disciple of Tukārām, we have placed this story after that of Rāmeshwar Bhaṭṭ.

[2] For definition see p. 56.

[3] On a glance from Hari all his wounds were healed, adds M.

[4] *Two Masters Jesus and Tukārām*, p. 10.

[5] M here relates 'Vithobā and the Thieves', sect. 7, part iii

[6] On the historicity of this event see Chapter V, part II, sect. 3.

a clerk in charge of them. The clerk found Tukārām at Lohogaon and delivered him the Rājā's message. He was much distressed when he heard it, and wrote four *abhangs* excusing himself, which he gave the clerk to take. 'Sit on the horse', said he, 'you will soon get back.' 'I dare not sit on him', replied the clerk, 'he is too fiery in his temper.' Then Tukārām patting the horse, his temper was subdued, and the clerk took the following message:

'Torches, umbrellas, and horses, these are not among things good for me. Why, O Lord of Pandharī, dost thou entangle me amongst such? O God, says Tukārām, run to set me free from this. . . . I feel that I should avoid society. . . . It is my pressing request that you will not even talk of seeing me. The rock is an excellent bed to sleep on and I have the sky above me for a cloak. If I saw fine apparel and men wearing jewels, it would at once be the death of me. Let me tell you this surprising news, there is no happiness like the beggar's. . . . There is one thing that brings a blessing, and its purport is this, learn to see one spirit in all created things.'[1]

Śivājī was amazed when he read the message and he resolved to visit Tukārām himself. He set out in full state, with all his ministers in attendance and went to Lohogaon. He made his way at once to Tukārām and laid himself in the dust before him. Then with his own hands he put a garland of *tulsī* on his neck, and laid a plate of gold coins before him. With a struggle Tukārām spoke and said: 'What need have I of gold? Vitthal is enough for me. Thy fame, my lord, I know well; to-day I know thy generosity. Yet a man needs no lamp when he has the sun to give him light; the Himālaya needs no fan to keep him cool; the wealth you have brought me is as cow's flesh to my senses. Now let me give you this counsel, to ensure you peace; let your only ornament be the *tulsī* garland, your only observance the *ekādashī*,[2] and call yourself the servant of Vithobā.' At this the Rājā was well-pleased, and the money he had brought he gave to Brāhmans. That night he spent listening to Tukārām's *kīrtan*. 'The world is perishable', so he sang; 'it will perish; it will pass away; worship God[3], and you will save yourself and your fathers'. As the Rājā listened, the message sank into his mind and he said to himself: 'I will renounce my kingdom and sit in the forest praising God[4]', and he took off his headdress[5] and laid it on the ground. Next morning he sent away his ministers and gave himself up to the bliss of devotion.

[1] We have given Tukārām's message to Śivājī in summary only, the message being given fully in vol. 2 of F. and M., *abhangs* 1468–1474.

[2] For definition see p. 56.

[3] 'Vithobā', says M.

[4] 'Hari', says M.

[5] Dr. J. Murray Mitchell (*J.R.A.S. Bo.*, Jany. 1849, p. 23) wrongly translates 'crown', the Marathī word meaning simply a head-covering.

33. Message to Shivaji

Then they wrote and told Śivājī's mother what had happened, and Jijabāī exclaimed, 'This is bad news;- Tukārām has ruined the kingdom?' Nor was it long before she reached Lohogaon and flung herself on the ground before the poet. 'My son,' she said, 'has given up the world; he has no child, and who will guide the kingdom?' So Tukārām bade her take comfort. That evening after the *kīrtan* he thus addressed the Rājā: 'To cross the sea of the world there is but one rule; observe the duties of your own station. Should fish leave the water for the air, or birds the air for the water? Should an Arab horse be set to draw a plough, or a soldier to ride a bullock? Has not God set the sea round the earth to contain it? He has appointed to the Brāhman in his student days to learn the scriptures, as a householder to perform the six rites[1], and as a recluse to overcome his passions; now listen while I tell you the duties of a *kshattriya*. He must conquer his enemies and protect his own faith; reverence the Brāhmans; see the Supreme in all creatures; oppress none; delight in worship; speak no falsehood; feed the hungry; and remember God[2] continually. Such an one may live without misgiving in the world—why should he go to the jungle? God visits him in his own house'.

When the Rājā heard these words tears came into his eyes, and he took up his clothes from the ground. His mother fell at Tukārām's feet, exclaiming, 'How can I ever repay you?' Four days later Śivājī departed, but, ere he went, he begged a boon of the poet, that he would give him as a present a piece of bread if the kingdom was to be delivered, and a piece of cocoanut if he was to have a son. Howbeit Tukārām gave him both.[3]

34. Tukaram's Disciples; Way with Pilgrims

By this time Tukārām had a circle of disciples, several of whom had been his bitterest enemies, the principal ones being Rāmeshwar Bhatt whose change of attitude is related in sections 29–30 above; Kānhobā the poet's own younger brother who relieved him of all business cares as stated in section 11; Gangārām Mavāḷa Kaḍūskar the Brāhman, and Santājī Telī Jaganāde who were his two chief assistant *kīrtankārs* and writers, Santājī's MS. having recently been published;[4] Konḍoba, Brāhmān reader of *Purāṇas* who took Tukārām's messages to distant holy places—see section 17 in part III; Nāvajī the flower-seller; Śivabā Kāsār the coppersmith of whom the story is told in section 6, part III; Māḷajī Gāḍe,

[1] The six rites are study, teaching, sacrificing, causing sacrifices to be made, bestowing gifts, receiving gifts.

[2] 'Hari', says M.

[3] M. here gives 'The Kunbī's Cucumber' in sect. 8, part III.

[4] See sect. 1, part I, chap 5.

husband of Bhāgīrathī, Tukārām's daughter; Malhārpant, one of his cymbal players; Mahādājīpant the *kulkārnī* of Dehū referred to in section 12 above; Ambājīpant the *kulkarnī* and fortune-teller of Lohogaon; Kaceswar, a Brāhman versed in Vedic lore; Bahinābāī—see paragraph (4), section 4, part I, and Gavarśet the Lingāyat grocer referred to in section 19 of part III.[1]

Four months later there passed Tukārām's house a company of pilgrims bound for Bhīmāśankar and when he saw them he laid himself in the dust before them. He found among them Chintāmani Dev and they were glad to meet each other again. Chintāmani asked him for a mark of his favour, whereupon Tukārām brought forth flour and herbs. Enough for one only he brought forth, but every pilgrim begged for a portion. Then the saint was perplexed, and he prayed that his little store might be enough for all, whereupon, so runs the story, when Tukārām's flour was divided each had a full share. Then the pilgrims embraced him lovingly, prepared a meal, sat down and made Tukārām join them.[2]

Again he succoured another company of pilgrims which had to pass through a wild country where there was a fierce overgrown dog that no one could master. Tukārām went along the path and the dog flew at him, but the saint was undismayed. 'I do not growl at you,' said he, 'why do you growl at me?' As he spoke the dog was pacified and lay down like a tame cat. So the pilgrims passed on, and when Tukārām returned, the dog followed him and ever afterwards attended his *kīrtans*.[3]

35. Protest Against Pantheism

Once it chanced that a certain Brāhman had copied Mukund Rāja's Hindū book *Vivek Sindhū*[1] expounding the Vedānta, and he visited Tukārām and sought permission to read this book to him. Now Tukārām would not dishonour the Brāhman, so he granted him permission and sat down before him, but he kept his head shrouded in a blanket, for, said he, the sight of the world disturbed his attention. For an hour the Brāhman read, and Tukārām stirred not nor spoke, till at length the Brāhman lifted the blanket, and behold! Tukārām sat with his fingers in his ears! 'What is this', said the Brahman, 'why are you wasting my time?' 'I cannot listen', said Tukārām, 'to the doctrine that God and His worshipper are one.[5] If everything is a form of Bramha, then why this howl

[1] On these disciples see L. R. Pāngārkar, *S.T.C.*, chap 13.

[2] Here M has sect. '9, How Tukarām Helped the Needy', Part III,

[3] Here come the stories 10–14 in Part III entitled 'A Brahman Boy Healed', 'A Scribe's Unauthorized Alteration', 'A Miraculous Visit From Śiva', 'Tukārām's Letter of Apology to Vithobā', 'Supplying Oil and Alms.'

[1] Dated A D 1188 see *M. Sār*, p 26.

[5] The *advaita* or *pantheistic* doctrine.

about gain or loss? Between Himself and His worshippers God has drawn a line; that line we must recognize. A man may have perfect insight into God's nature, but he does not acquire God's power to create, preserve and destroy; these attributes belong to God alone. So long as God in His three forms exercises these powers Himself let us mortals be humble and claim no identity with Him.'

There lived at Lohogaon a certain Vaishnava who was devoted to Tukārām and thereby offended his wife She resolved to test the saint, and one day when her husband was away she cooked some bitter gourds and invited Tukārām to her house to eat them. But Tukārām had fully conquered his senses; he knew nothing of what happened to his body; and he ate the bitter gourds with pleasure and even asked for more.[1]

36. External Methods Unavailing for Salvation

Once upon a time, according to a story that runs everywhere in Mahārāshtra, several of Tukārām's devotees were to visit the seven holy places of India and Tukārām gave them a bitter gourd, bidding them bathe it in every sacred river they visited. On their return a feast was held in celebration of the event and Tukārām bade them divide the gourd among the assembled guests at the feast. Each guest exclaimed that it was just as bitter as before and asked in surprise why bathing it in holy rivers had not taken away its bitterness. Whereupon Tukārām pointed the moral that all external means, including sacred rivers, would thus fail miserably in effecting their salvation.

37. Shivaji's Escape from Tukaram's Kirtan

It happened once that Śivājī came to Poona to visit Tukārām. Śivājī fell at his feet, and the *kīrtan* began, nothing wanting to complete the general delight. But it chanced that the Mahommedan official at Chākan heard of Śivājī's visit and he sent a troop of soldiers to seize him. News was brought to Śivājī and he rose to leave the *kīrtan*. Then Tukārām prayed aloud for help: 'I fear not death myself, but I cannot bear to see all round me troubled.' And a message[2] came and comforted him; 'Be at ease; go on with the service; I, the Life of the World, will protect Śivājī'. According to Mahīpati, Hari 'took on himself the form of Śivājī, and so multiplied himself that when the Pathāns entered, whichever

1 M. here has sects. 15-16 'The Fortune-Teller's Son Raised' and 'Tukārām and the Sanyāsīs' in Part III.

2 Hari, says M.

way they looked, they saw Śivājī[1]. And as they pursued he led them on, till within an hour they were miles away in the forest.' Meanwhile Tukārām full joyously was singing the praise of God in a stream of names which he poured forth, while his throat was choked with sobs, and tears streamed from his eyes.[2]

Śivājī was amazed at his escape, and he set off himself for Singhad. But first he asked Tukārām for a mark of his favour, and the saint gave him a handful of horse-dung. This Śivājī accepted with humble thankfulness and Tukārām returned to Lohogaon.[3]

38. Other-Worldliness

Tukārām was now victor over all enemies of the flesh. All earthly riches he rejected; but little he ate and at every mouthful he called on the name of God.[4] Sometimes he would visit another village, but if anyone asked him where he was going he would ever answer: 'To the City of Vaikuntha.'[5] He never spoke save in *abhaṅg* verse, and was received by all as a true saint. Often he would go and humble his soul in the temple, confessing his sins and rebuking himself. One day some birds flew away from him and he became so distressed at their being afraid of him that he said: 'I look on all the world as myself, and yet the birds fly away from me! Truly all I have done is wasted. I have renounced name and family, I have offered my body to Him to Whom it belongs. Yet all is wasted; the birds fly away from me! There must be some duplicity in me'. So he became very down-hearted, and again rousing himself and giving himself up to religious contemplation he cried; 'O Merciful Lord! As a blind man leans on his guide, so do I lean on thee, I follow thee to salvation; yet I have stumbled into a devious path, save me! O save me!' So saying he stood still without breath or motion, till the birds settled on him without fear, and though he moved they were no more startled than they are startled by a moving bough.[6]

1 The story of 'angels at Mons' is an interesting parallel to this story, whether or no we believe either story.

2 In view of the 'legendary' atmosphere of Mahīpati's story as given above it is worthy of note that the modern historian confirms it. 'One of the most picturesque stories of his career', says Professor H. G. Rawlinson in his book *Śivājī The Marātha* (p. 31), 'relates how, at the risk of his life, he once stole through the Mussulman lines, into the heart of his enemy's camp at Poona, to listen to a *kathā*'. And again 'The story is well known, how, when Shayista Khan held Poona, Śivājī stole down through the enemy's lines to attend a festival at which Tukārām's hymns were chanted' (p. 86)

3 Here comes M's story in section 17, part III on 'The Coin and Letters to Holy Places'.

4 'Hari' says M

5 The nearest Hindū parallel to the Jewish Paradise.

6 This story is rejected by Rev Nehemiah Goreh (*Tenets of Tukārām*, p. 72) on what appear inadequate grounds.

THE RIVER INDRĀYAṆĪ WHERE TUKĀRĀM THREW HIS POEMS AND WHERE HE 'DISAPPEARED'

39. Tukaram's End

Mahīpati has expended all his powers in describing the end of Tukārām and the account will be found in its proper place at the conclusion of Part III.[1] The only safe verdict, however, is that of the *Indu Prakāsh* edition: 'Very great obscurity prevails as to the end of Tukārām's earthly existence. The popular Hindū belief is that he ascended alive to Heaven in the Car of Vishṇu . . . A consistent meaning might be made out of the *abhangs*[2] and they would seem to point out, that Tukārām . . . thought that his worldly duty was over, wished to be rid of that visible existence which. . . separates man from the everlating, . . . and therefore went on pilgrimage with the intention of never returning to Dehū, and probably of putting an end to his existence.'[3] With this agrees Dr. P. R. Bhandarkar's suggestion 'that he ended his life by means of *jalasamādhi*, drowning himself in the neighbouring river. Some of Tukārām's own *abhangs* show that he was aware of his approaching separation from the people and was constantly expecting God to come and take him away; and other evidence makes it probable that he met his death by drowning. But whether the drowning was a pre-arranged affair, that is to say a *jalasamādhi*, or whether the constant expectation of God's coming to fetch him away produced an illusion, and in obeying a fancied call from the opposite bank he ran into the river and was drowned, it is very difficult to say. But taking into consideration all facts, I am inclined to take the latter view, that is to say, if we are to believe that Tukārām met his death by drowning."[4] 'It is believed', says the Rev. Ganpatrao R. Navalkar, 'that he drowned himself in the holy river of his native village, as is the custom of the Indian *sādhus*.'[5] Parallel instances of Indian saints who have ended their lives by *jalasamādhi* will occur to students of Marāṭhā history, e.g., Eknāth in 1599, Nijānand the *guru* and father of Ranganāth in 1642, Brahmānand in 1775 and in recent years a Mr. and Mrs. Keḷūskar who both took *jalasamādhi* simultaneously. An equally striking instance is that of Dnyāneshwar, the father of Marāthī poetry, who took *sthalasamādhi* (getting oneself buried alive) in 1296, the moving story of which event may be read in Mr. Bhāve's fascinating Marāthī work.[6] On the date of Tukārām's end see section 1, Part II (p. 77) and footnote to section 18, Part III (p. 116).

An interesting feature of Tukārām's disappearance is the discovery of his blanket and cymbals a few days later, which fact

1 See section 18, Part III, '"Ascension" of Tukārām', which should be read at this point.

2 Numbered 1444 to 1459, F. and M.

3 *Indu-Prakāsh* edition, pp. 21–23.

4 *Two Masters: Jesus and Tukārām*, p. 11.

5 *Tukārām, the Mahārāshtrian Poet and Saint*, p. 2.

6 *M. Sār.* p. 51–2.

some would adduce as evidence in favour of the theory of drowning, while the biographer of the 'Saints', whose narrative is given in section 18 of Part III, regards it as proof that 'he had been received into Vaikuntha', a phrase which the modernist Hindū might be justified in explaining as a Hindū poetic way of saying that Tukārām's 'spirit had taken its flight'.

On Tukārām's supposed 'influence after death' see section 19 in Part III of this chapter.

III. The 'Legendary' Element in Tukaram's Biography

The order and numbering of sections are explained on page 77, Part II of this chapter. Doubtless many of the 'traditions' given here have a substratum of fact, e.g., *much of section* 16 *below. They are given in the form of a fairly literal translation from Mahīpati's Marāthī narrative, without comment of our own.*

1. Tukaram's Birth [1]

After some generations it happened on one occasion when the great devotees were seated round Hari in Vaikuntha—like stars round the moon, or ascetics round Śiva, or mountains round Mount Meru—that Hari addressed them and said: 'In the family of Viśvambhara there is now a saint named Bolhobā; I am resolved to present him with a son who shall be a world-saviour and a world-teacher.' The saints acclaimed this resolution, and Hari then led aside Nāma [2] and reminded him that he had never finished the hundred crores of *abhangs* he promised to write; this then should be his opportunity to assume the flesh again and finish the task. Nāma replied that in this Kali Yuga, Kṛṣna had assumed his Buddha form and gave no answer to mankind.[3] But Kṛṣṇa answered that he would show himself to the world again if Nāma would return there. Thereupon Nāma fell at his feet, and he raised him up and embraced him. Thus Tukārām, who dwelt in God's heart, was set in Nāma's heart: whereby God filled Nāma's heart with the nectar of love, and God offered Nāma his own power of creation and destruction, and that devotion which lies beyond liberation. This peculiar treasure of His, Tukārām who was part of His innermost nature, He thus by an embrace conveyed to Nāma, and as He did so, He said: 'Help each other to know what love is.' Then said Nāma, 'Where shall I assume flesh? Tell me some holy family,' and Hari pointed out to him Viśvambhara's house

Then even as the Lord of *avatāras* descends into the ocean shells and forms pearls therein, even so the Spirit of Loving Devotion entered the womb of Kanakāī and Tukārām was conceived.

[1] To be read in connexion with sect. 3, Part II of this chapter, p. 78.

[2] 'Nāma' refers to Nāmdev, the Marāthā poet saint of the 14th century.

[3] This silence of the Buddha form of Kṛṣṇa is entirely characteristic of Buddha, one of the names of Buddha meaning, 'meditator' or, 'one who remains dumb.'

2. Adversity and Self-Dedication [1]

Then did Hari make himself like the Great Serpent of Śiva, and He encompassed Tukārām, loudly hissing with his hood uplifted, and he bade Tukārām open his eyes and look upon him. But he answered: 'If God has visited me in this Serpent form, assuredly I will not look upon Him. I am a servant of Pāṇḍuraṇg, no other will I behold.' When Hari thus learned Tukārām's innermost thoughts, he came before him in his true form, with his four arms, his conch and disc, and Tukārām opened his eyes and beheld him. 'My darling,' said he, 'I have never forgotten you.'

3. Withdrawal from Business [2]

When at last Kānhobā came to Bhāmbanātha he saw there an amazing sight—Hari glittering in his robes and jewels, with Tukārām seated on his thigh, and he heard Hari say: 'From age to age I show myself in the world: it is for my votary's sake. For Pundalika's sake [3] I stand by the Bhīmā with my hands upon my hips; for Viśvambhara's sake I stayed at Dehū? And Tukārām fell at his feet—the spot is known to this day; Kānhobā carved a pair of feet there.

4. The Troubles of His Wife [4]

Off Āvaḷī started, 'with Hari behind her,' if we are to follow Mahīpati. Tukārām, the prince of Vaiṣṇavas, when he saw them was astonished but also very pleased, and all three sat down together. Then Tukārām bade Āvaḷī offer him food, but she answered, 'I have brought only one cake, it will not be enough for two.' Āvaḷī in confusion opened the bundle, and lo! it was full of dishes, for Hari had previously eaten. 'Surely,' she said, 'my family god has come to help me.' But nevertheless she found it hard to believe in his power. So she went on serving her husband in silence, till he needed water. Now she had spilt her water on the way, and there was none on the hill. Hari suggested her going to the dell and when she went and lifted a stone, she found a spring of clear water and brought and gave it 'them' to drink.

5. The Holy Day of His Forefathers [5]

Tukārām having forgotten all about the herb he wanted, Hari took pity on him and assuming the form of Tukārām, went to his

[1] To be read with sect. 10, Part II according to footnote 2, p. 84

[2] To be read with sect. 11, Part II, see footnote 3, p. 84

[3] See pp 41-2, 48, 51 and chap 6, sect. 4.

[4] To follow on sect 14, Part II of this Chapter; see footnote 1, p. 87.

[5] To be read with sect. 18, Part II; see footnote 1, p. 89.

house with a load on his head, gave the stuff to Āvaḷī and told her to start cooking. Wheat and pulse and ghee he gave her and every sort of sugar and spice. Then he went through the village and invited everyone to the feast. He brought them to the Indrāyaṇī and showed them all due respect, set them down and pressed upon each of them the food he preferred. And they said to Āvaḷī: 'This is astonishing! Tukārām has turned his thoughts to the world again.' 'My mind misgives me,' said Āvaḷī. Then the Mahārs and the beggars came forward for a share which they obtained. At last Hari saw the dishes washed, restored his own dish to every guest and then vanished.

6. The Coppersmith and His Wife [1]

A Brāhman, having to pay a debt of ten thousand rupees, was sitting in supplication before Dnyānobā's temple. In a vision he was instructed to go to Tukārām. He did so and was again sent to a *kāsār* (coppersmith) who gave him two small copper coins in charity. Tukārām took them, and touching them with a stone turned them into gold; but as this was not sufficient, he turned his copper sacrificial vessels also into gold. The *kāsār* seeing this thought Tukārām must be possessed of the *parisa*;[2] and began to pay him court in every possible way. After a year, a wonderful event occurred. The *kāsār* had procured thirty-six bullock loads of tin from Bombay, all of which was turned into silver. On this the *kāsār* gave up the world, became Tukārām's disciple and, with his money, built a well, still called 'the *kāsār's* well.' The wife of the *kāsār* was exceedingly angry with Tukārām on account of the change that had taken place in her husband. She one day pretended to make a feast on his account, and when he went to bathe, she poured down upon him vessel after vessel of boiling water. The god however turned it into cold water. She then set food before him, with poison in it; but that too the god rendered harmless. Over the body of this woman there immediately appeared leprosy, and she was exceedingly distressed. She then obtained relief by taking (at the suggestion of Rāmeshwar Bhaṭṭ) some of the clay from the place where Tukārām had bathed, and anointing her body with it.[3]

7. Vithoba and the Thieves [4]

The buffalo given by Āvaḷī's father and which had done the damage in Mumbājī's garden was once carried off by two thieves.

1 This sect comes in sect. 30 of Part II, see footnote 3, p. 98.

2 A stone, the touch of which turns metals into gold

3 Sects. 6–11 and 14 are here given as translated by Dr. J. Murray Mitchell in *J.R.A.S.Bo.*, 1849, Vol III; pp 19–26.

4 This story comes between sects. 31 and 32 in Part II; see footnote 5, p. 99. The story of Mumbājī being placed in part II later than is usual (see footnote 1, sect. 31 in Part II) necessitates also our placing later than is usual this 'buffalo' story.

They had gone a considerable distance when Vithobā appeared in the shape of a tall black figure, with a huge cudgel over his shoulder, right in front of them. The thieves turned to one side, but so did it. Whenever they tried to turn off, the terrible *bhūt* (ghost)-looking shape posted itself in the way. The thieves became terrified, and taking back the buffalo, bound it in the place whence they had carried it off. 'Now' thought they, 'we shall get off.' But no! for there stood the ghost, as frightful as ever. So they went to Tukārām, and confessed all they had done. 'If you want the bullock, take it,' said Tukārām. 'No,' said they, 'we only want to be delivered from that frightful ghost.' On this Tukārām, by mental vision, perceived that the god was not there and he began to invoke his presence. Whereupon, in the sight of all, Viṭhobā entered the temple, with a huge cudgel over his shoulder.

8. The Kunbi's Cucumber [1]

A certain *Kuṇbī* (peasant) was a very religious man. He brought a small cucumber to Tukārām out of affection. Tukārām divided it into four parts, and had eaten three of them when his disciples said, 'Kindly give us part of the fruit.' Tukārām replied, 'This is not good to eat; but never mind; take this, and give the dumb Brāhman half.' As the Brāhman ate, his speech returned. When the other disciples began to eat the other half, they all cried: 'Oh, how bitter!' and secretly spit it out.

9. How Tukaram Helped the Needy [2]

A Brāhman who wished to pay off a debt was sitting before Dnyānobā's temple, and by him was sent to Tukārām, who again sent him to the *Kāsār* mentioned above. The *Kāsār* gave him four iron *pās* (bars), a load which the Brāhman could not carry, so that he hid three, and came with one to Dehū. Tukārām turned it into gold; whereupon the Brāhman went back, and searched for the three others, which however he could not find.

10. A Brahman Boy Healed [3]

About this time too a Brahman sent for Tukāram to his house and entreated him to help his son. He was a boy of eight years, who was dumb from his birth, and his thread ceremony could not be performed. Tukārām caused the boy to be brought to him and bade him cry 'Vitthal' and immediately the boy spoke.

1 To be read with sect. 33, Part II; see footnote 3, p. 101.
2 To be read with sect. 34, Part II; see footnote 2, p. 102.
3 Stories 10–14 follow section 34, Part II; see footnote 3, p. 102.

11. A Scribe's Unauthorized Alteration[1]

Tukārām was composing *abhaṅgs*, and in celebrating the sports of Kriśna, he said, 'His face was dirty.' Rāmeshwar Bhaṭṭ thought this would never answer, and he changed it to 'His face was pale.' Whereupon the god appeared to him in a vision and reproved him. 'Was I afraid?' said the god. 'What could make me pale? My face was dirty; in my childhood I was eating dust; Tukārām was quite right.' So Rāmeshwar corrected to what Tukārām had written.

12. A Miraculous Visit from Siva[1]

Once in the month of *Chaitra* Tukārām went on a pilgrimage to a temple of Śivā; the journey took six days and on the seventh they descried the temple. Then Tukārām faithfully greeted it with a prostration. Kothaleshwar was the name of the hill whereon it stood; at its foot there was a tank, where people bathed before visiting the temple. But ere they climbed the hill Tukārām bade them cook a meal and conceiving his purpose they cooked a meal and set out dishes for four. Then suddenly a naked form, sky-clothed, appeared before them, the very Lord of *Kailāsa*, with braided locks and ashes smeared upon him. 'Give me food,' said he, 'I am hungry.' 'Very good,' said Tukārām, and he bade his companions serve the guest first. Then did the Lord of *Kailāsa* refresh himself, and he ate all the food that Tukārām and his friends had prepared for the party, and after that he blessed them and went his way. They must needs send to the village for more victuals, but when they opened their pots (for they had tied them up to keep the flies off), behold they were full of food!

So Tukārām and his friends knew that undoubtedly it was Śiva who had visited them, and they ate themselves and climbed the hill and saluted the god. And then they returned and on their way they met a householder who was troubled by a Brāhman ghost. Now the ghost had said to him: 'Offer a solemn sacrifice, and bestow on me the merit thereof, and I will trouble thee no more.' But the householder was too poor to offer the sacrifice, and his spirit sank at the words of the ghost. Wandering from house to house, he begged men to help him, and many regions he had passed through before he reached Lohogaon. 'If any has the merit of a sacrifice, pray let him give it to me,' he cried, and there was one that heard him, a follower of Tukārām, that uttered the name of Viṭṭhal as he passed along the road, and every time he did so tied a knot in a cord. When he heard him he cut off a knot and bade

[1] See footnote on sect. 10 above.

him steep it in water and drink it. And he did so, and the instant he drank it the evil spirit departed from him and he fell down as one dead.

13. Tukaram's Letter of Apology to Vithoba [1]

Once it chanced that Tukārām fell sick and on the eleventh day he could not visit Paṇdharī. So he wrote a letter and sent it by the hand of a pilgrim. He laid before Hari all his longings and the weakness of his limbs and he cried to him for help. The pilgrim took the letter and went with his company to Paṇdharī, and there he read it before Vithobā. Then Vithobā felt his throat choke with sobs, and he said to Rukhmiṇī, 'Tukārām, my faithful servant, is ill; he cannot come to Paṇḍharī; shall I go and visit him?' And Rukhmiṇī answered, 'Nay, rather send Garuḍ and bring Tukārām here.' So Hari called for Garud, who came and did obeisance to him, and he sent him whirring away to Dehū. He found Tukārām with little life in him, but all his thoughts devotedly fixed on the Lord of Pandharī. Gently he roused him and gave him a letter from Viṭṭhal, bidding him take his seat on the sacred bird. But tears came into Tukārām's eyes. 'How can I presume to do this?' said he, 'it is your office to bear my lord; I beseech you, tell my lord how I am, and beg him to visit me.' And Garuḍ went and told Hari, and Hari came flashing through the sky in all his splendour, and he alighted and embraced Tukārām. And Tukārām slowly opened his eyes, and when he saw his lord before him he fell down and kissed his feet.

Then Hari taking Tukārām's hand went into the house with him—a broken-down hut it was, open to the wind on every side. 'I am hungry,' said the god of gods, 'give me a meal.' And Āvalī gave him a simple meal, such as the Bhīl woman once gave him and he ate till he was satisfied and then departed.

14. Supplying Oil and Alms [1]

A Brāhman made a feast for Tukārām on a Monday. At the proper time of dining, the oil was deficient, and the lamp was going out. The Brāhman was distressed, but Tukārām said, 'Look into the skin-bottle and see.' His wife went to look, and saw a large quantity of oil, and the oil lasted afterwards as long as the Brāhman and his wife lived.

There was a stone before the door of a *pātīl's* house in that village, on which Tukārām used to sit. He was sitting there one

[1] See footnote on sect. 10 above.

day when a very poor man came and asked alms. At Tukārām's command he went and begged in the village, and some pieces of iron were given him. Coming back, he said, 'I have got this iron,' and laid a piece down before Tukārām on the stone. It was immediately changed into gold. He put down another, and another which were changed in like manner. The people of the village seeing this wonder, brought pieces of iron and laid them on the stone but no change took place in these.

15. The Fortune-Teller's Son Raised

Many miracles did Tukārām perform.[2] He turned salt water sweet and filled vessels with oil for the needy and faithful. And once at Lohogaon when he was holding a *kīrtan* the *joshī's* (soothsayer's) son died, and the father said to him: 'If you are truly a servant of Vishnu, raise up my son again.' Thus the service was interrupted and the worshippers were distressed. Then Tukārām closed his eyes, and centred all his thoughts on the Lord of Panḍharī. 'From of old,' said he, 'the saints have given thee a good name, do thou establish it now in the sight of us all. If thou comest not now to our help I will not consent to live more'. Then the Lord of Pandharī came speedily, and he roused Tukārām and said: 'O crest-jewel of devotion! have you not in the worship of Hari the very water of life?' Then Tukārām rejoiced and he called on the worshippers to sing, and for an hour they glorified Hari till Tukārām's spirit dwelt no more in his body. Meanwhile the corpse was laid in the assembly and when the hour had passed it lived again, and the young man sat up and praised Hari.

16. Tukaram and the Sanyasis[3]

Two Sanyāsīs heard the recitation of Tukārām, and going to Dadu Kond Deva, a high authority in Poona, complained that Tukārām was destroying the *Karma Mārga*, and that Brāhmans were falling down at his feet. Dadu Kond Deva, on this, fined the Brāhmans of Lohogaon fifty rupees and summoned Tukārām. The Brāhmans said: 'How can we pay fifty rupees?' Then they accompanied Tukārām. At the Sangam where they rested, people came to see Tukārām in numbers like an army; and Dadu Kond Deva himself proceeded to pay reverence to him. In the first

1 This story and the next one (section 16) follow on section 35 in Part II see footnote 1, p. 103.

2 On this claim see the last sentence in first paragraph, p. 69.

3 See footnote 1 on preceding section 15.

recitation a great *avadhūta* [1] appeared, naked, with his body shining with dazzling brightness and with the ensigns of a *Gosāvī* [2]. He embraced Tukārām, and made obeisance to him. 'I longed to see you,' said the wonderful visitant, 'now I have done so.' So saying he went up into heaven. Thereupon the people said: 'Surely that was Mahādev or Dattātreya.'

Next night, in Poona during the recitation—the Sanyāsis that complained, as well as a great number of other people, being present —the Sanyāsīs were seen to rise up and prostrate before Tukārām. Dadu Kond Deva was exceedingly angry that the men who complained so bitterly of Tukārām should do this. 'But,' said they, 'he now appeared to us in the form of Narāyan (Vishṇu) four-armed and resplendant.' On this Dadu Kond Deva ordered them to have their hair shaved off in five lines, to be mounted on the back of an ass and led round the city. All was ready for this, but Tukārām interceded on their behalf and the punishment was not inflicted.[3]

17. The Coin and Letters to Holy Places [4]

There went from Lohogaon a disciple of Tukārām's named Kondobā as a pilgrim to *Kāśī* and Tukārām wrote and sent *abhangs* as letters with him. To help the pilgrim on his visits Tukārām gave him a gold coin saying, 'When you change this, always set aside one piece for next time, binding it carefully, and it will become a gold coin too.'

The first letter was to the 'Lord of Creation': 'This marvellous universe, this is thou, O Lord of Kailāsa, therefore thou art called Lord of the world. Pity then the feeble and lowly that approach thee. O Asākī with the braided locks, give me a morsel of thy favour!' And the second letter Tukārām wrote to Bhagīrathī:[5] 'O mistress of all holy waters! The very sight of thee cleanses from the greatest sins; and he attains to liberation who believes and bathes in thee. I, Tukārām, the foster child of the saints, send thee a flower of speech.' And the third letter he wrote to Vishṇupad: 'Greater art thou than Gāya! Whoso lays a ball of rice on thee, he pays off all the debt he owes his fathers.' These three letters Kondobā took to Benāres, and he first read the letter to Bhagīrathī. Then a hand rose from the water, with a

1 A term describing a roaming, naked Brāhmin or *Gosāvī* (on which term see p. 6, footnote 2) who is considered to be an *avatāra* of Śiva or Dattātreya and who recites metrical pieces from the *Bhāgavata Purāṇa*.

2 See p. 6, footnote 2

3 Translation of this sect. 16 is taken from *J.R.A.S. Bo.*, p. 26–27 by Dr. J. Murray Mitchell.

4 This story follows section 37, Part II, see footnote 3, p. 104.

5 i e, a part of the Ganges, see *F.* and *M.* 1462–3 with 'Notes', vol. 2, p. 438.

jewelled arm glittering like the sun, and Kondobā placed within the hand the letter and it closed on it and disappeared. Then Kondobā read the letter to Śiva, and the Holder of the Trident slowly moved from side to side, while a shower of bell-flowers fell from heaven. And last, at Gāya, he performed a *śrāddh*, and then came back to his own country. When Kondobā returned home Tukārām asked him for the gold coin. Kondobā falsely told him it was lost. When he went home and looked for it, the coin had really disappeared, but the knot in which he had tied it, was still there.

18. 'Ascension' of Tukaram [1]

Now if you ask, what was the divine purpose of Tukārām's incarnation, I reply: [2] What avails a mirror if there be none to observe his features in it? What avails a scented flower, if there be no nostril to smell it? God's mighty power is nothing unless there be a worshipper to recognize it; for this reason, then, God has divided Himself, that He might worship Himself. Hence did Tukārām assume his incarnation that he might show, as the *Bhāgawat* declares, that Loving Devotion is the highest worship.

And the Lord of the World, with the saints around Him, took their seats in their chariots and descending to the earth they came to Dehū, embracing Tukārām and saying to him: 'Without thee Vaikuntha is a wilderness!' And for five days they held high festival by the Iṇdrāyaṇī unseen by all save Tukārām. Nevertheless, all the village sat listening to Tukārām; and though the *Shimgā* [3] fell at that time no one joined in the *Shimgā* mirth; a spirit of peace and heavenly joy possessed them all.

Then Hari bade Tukārām accompany him, but he fell at Hari's feet and said: 'Nay, my lord, here is Paṇḍharpūr, a very Vaikuntha on earth—why need I go hence?' 'Pay me but one visit,' said Hari; 'I will show thee my glory on the sea of milk; if thou livest for ever in the world the fond desires of men will be unsatisfied.' Then Tukārām answered in four *abhangs*,[4] proclaiming his freedom from the earth and earthly passions, and the gods listened to him with joy and wonder; 'Blest, indeed,' said they, 'is our lot that hear him.'

Then said Hari, 'Let us go to Vaikuntha,' and Tukārām sent for his wife and said to her, 'Behold, I go to Vaikuntha! Come with me'. But she answered: 'I am five months gone with child— there's a buffalo at home to look after—the children, too,

[1] This section should be read before section 39, Part II on pp. 105–6.

[2] Says Mahīpati.

[3] A Hindu annual festival called 'The Holi'.

[4] See *F.* and *M.* 1389, 587, 1586—three remarkable *abhangs*, whose genuineness is doubtful, one *abhang* not being in the *I. P.* edition and therefore not translated in *F.* and *M.*

who will take care of them ?' And the saint was amazed and said, 'She is still in love with her house; the Lord of Vaikuntha calls her, but she will not go with him!' Yet it was not her own fault, for often Tukārām had said, when she asked where he was going, 'I am going to Vaikuntha'. So now once more she only thought, 'The fool is going to some village or other.'

Then Tukārām moved away, but his followers understood not that he was leaving them for ever, they supposed he was setting off on a pilgrimage. 'He is weary of us,' they said, 'so he journeys to the Himālaya Mountains.' And other *abhangs* he spoke [1] till a great marvel took place, chariots appearing in the sky, wherein were seated Nārad and Tumbāra singing, and Parvatī and the Lord of Kailāsa, and Brahma and Vishṇu and Rudra. The lustre of the sun was dimmed by their splendour and mortal men closed their eyes, as they close them when lightning flashes in the sky. Then Tukārām sat himself in a chariot, and began his journey through the sky.

When his followers opened their eyes, behold! he was with them no more.[2] Loud were the voices of lamentation; and Āvaḷī lamented with them, crying: 'He told me to come with him, but I thought he was lying. The fiery flame of his renunciation burned my own body, and, before our eyes, he has gone away; if I had known he was going I should have clung to his robe.' And she fell on the ground and swooned.

Three days and three nights Tukārām's followers sat lamenting for him when suddenly there fell from the sky his cymbals and his blanket. Then they knew he had been received into Vaikuntha, for his cymbals were sent them as a sign of farewell.

On Tukārām's End see further the last eight lines on page 126.

19. Influence after Death

Tukārām while yet on earth had promised a Lingayat *Wānī* to appear to him at his death.[3] Accordingly when the *Wānī* felt his death approaching, he sent to Dehū for Rāmeshwar, for Tukārām's

[1] Of these some are translated in *F* and *M* edition (e.g., 513) Some are in the *I. P.* Ed. (e.g. 10, 28, 8, 9, 11) but not translated by *F.* and *M.*; others are not in the *I. P.* Ed. None has any special propriety in this context.

[2] The date is given · In the year 1571 of the Śake era, the year Virodhi, on Monday the second day of the latter half of the month of Phalgūn (Feb-March) between 6 a.m. and 9 a.m This has usually been thought to indicate A.D. 1649 as the year of Tukārām's end, but L R Pāngārkar's book published in 1920 (p. 19, footnote) concludes in favour of March 9, 1650, while on the evidence of Santājī the oilman, and the Hindu almanacs (as he writes in a personal letter), V. L. Bhāve, *Tukārāmāce Assal Gāthā*, vol 2, p, 13, *M Sar*, p. 189, believes Tukārām 'left this world' when Shaka 1572 was completed, that is, in Shaka 1573 or 16th Feb. 1652. See further Sect. 1, Part II.

[3] Modern parallels to this are provided by the cases of dying saints who assure grief-stricken loved ones that in some way or other they will help them.

younger brother, and for his younger son. When they arrived, Tukārām appeared. The *Wānī* alone perceived him and made obeisance to him and put sweet-smelling powder on his forehead and garlands on his neck. The two then spoke together, and all around marvelled, for they saw nothing but the garlands of flowers, which seemed as if suspended in the air. To faithful men Tukārām still appears. Of this we have many witnesses. To Niloba *Gosāvī* of Pimpalner, to Bahinabāī, and Gangādhar he appeared in vision, and gave them instruction.[1] The last three lines may be viewed as an anticipation of modern spiritualism by the eighteenth century biographer of the Marāṭhā saints.

1 Up to this point this sect. (19) is from Dr. Mitchell's translation, *J.R.A.S. Bo.*, Vol. III, p. 29.

ME MISERABLE

Since little wit have I,
O hear my mournful cry.

Grant now, O grant to me
That I thy feet may see.

I have no steadfastness,
Nārāyan,[1] I confess.

Have mercy, Tukā prays,
On my unhappy case

BEYOND THE MOUNTAINS, GOD

Here tower the hills of passion and of lust,—
Far off the Infinite!
No path I find and all impassable
Fronts me the hostile height.

Ah, God is lost, my friend. Nārāyan[1] now
How can I e'er attain?
Thus it appears that all my life, so dear,
I've spent, alas, in vain

THOUGH HE SLAY ME

Now I submit me to thy will,
Whether thou save or whether kill;
Keep thou me near or send me hence,
Or plunge me in the war of sense,

Thee in my ignorance I sought,
Of true devotion knowing nought.
Little could I, a dullard, know,
Myself the lowest of the low

My mind I cannot steadfast hold,
My senses wander uncontrolled.
Ah, I have sought and sought for peace.
In vain, for me there's no release.

Now bring I thee a faith complete
And lay my life before thy feet.
Do thou, O God, what seemeth best;
In thee, in thee alone is rest.

In thee I trust, and, hapless weight.
Cling to thy skirts with all my might.
My strength is spent, I, Tukā say;
Now upon thee this task I lay.

[1] That is, the Supreme Being.

The poems on this page are translations from Tukārām's *Abhangs*, *P.M.S* pp. 62, 67, 69.

Chapter V

Tukaram's Autobiography

From the writings of Mahīpati we pass to the poems of Tukārām himself, so many of which are purely autobiographical. The treatment of Tukārām's autobiography as found in his *abhaṅgs* presents itself naturally under three aspects: First, the critical problem arising in connection with Tukārām's autobiographical poetry; second, the literary characteristics of the autobiography; and third, Tukārām's picture of himself.

I. The Critical Problem

1. Variant Editions of Tukaram's Poems

One of the most serious difficulties confronting the student of Tukārām arises from the existence of several different collections of his poems, each of which has a system of numbering of its own. The edition which has been widely accepted as the best, the *Indu Prakāsh* edition of 1869, subsidized by the Bombay Government at a cost, it is said, of no less than Rs. 24,000[1] has for many years been out of print. With other editions adopting different texts and numberings of the poems, these being arranged variously by different editors on their own principles, we have a perfect illustration of 'the disorganized state of the literary world of India'.[2] Truly a heavy task, and a worthy one, awaits the *Tukārām Mandaḷī* and the *Bhārata Itihās Sanshodhaka Manḍaḷa* of Poona. Until a really scientific attempt has been made to settle the true authentic text of Tukārām's *abhaṅgs* many fundamental problems affecting his biography must remain unsolved and any correct estimate of him is impossible. An interesting discussion of the question, without anything new, appeared in the *Subodh Patrikā* of Dec. 14, 1919.

The following is a list of the various editions of Tukārām's poems with their dates and other details[3] the last one in the list being added by us. By 'editions' in the whole of this discussion is meant

1 V. L. Bhāve, *Tukārāmāce Assal Gāthā*, vol. 2, p. 2
2 Preface to Vol. III, *F.* and *M.*
3 The list is taken from V. L. Bhāve's *Tukārāmāce Assal Gāthā*, Vol. 2, p. 1.

of course Marāthī editions, the only English edition being that by Fraser and Marāṭhe which contains translations of 3721 *abhangs.*

No.	Date of publication.	Place of Publication.	Name of Publishing Press.	Name of Editor.	Number of abhangs
1	1867	Bombay	*G. Krishnājī* .	G. Krishnājī ...	4500
2	1869	do	*Indu Prakāsh*...	Shankar Pāndurang ...	4621
3	1886	do	*Nirnaya Sāgar*	V. Mādgaokar	4645
4	1889	do	*Subodh Prakāsh*	Tukārām Tātya	8441
5	1901	Poona	*Indua* ...	Messrs. Jog & Gulve ...	4575
6	1903	Bombay	*Indu Prakāsh & Chandrodaya* (*Poona*)	K. Heralekar ...	4476
7	1909	Poona	*Jagaddhitechhu*	V. N. Joga ...	4149
8	1912	Bombay	*Nirnaya Sagar*	V, L. Pānsikar ...	4505
9	1913	Poona	*Aryabhushan* ...	Dravid and Āpte	4092
10	1913	Poona	*Jagaddhitechhu*	V N. Godbole ...	4499
11	1920	Thana and Poona	*Aryabhushaṇ* ..	V. L. Bhāve ...	1323 (incomplete)

Since the publication of the above list in Mr. Bhāve's book and whilst our own book is passing through the press a 12th edition has been published, in Bombay, by S. Narayan & Co., edited by R. T. Padwal, containing 9,000 *abhangs.*

Of these variant editions three call for special mention. (1) The *Indu Prakāsh* collection, referred to as No. 2 above, containing 4621 *abhangs* and—*rara avis*—has a 'critical preface'. Even in this edition, however, the problem of a critically ascertained text of Tukārām's poems, one of the most difficult and most important problems in the whole range of Marāthī literature, is dismissed in a page and a half. Moreover, the principles followed leave much to be desired. None of the MSS on which the editors base their text is described in any detail. Of these the best would appear to be the 'Dehū MS' and the 'Kadusa MS' the others being the 'Talegaon MS' and the 'Pandharpūr MS'. The two former are superior only because the Dehū MS is '*said* to have been written' by Tukārām's eldest son, Mahādev, no proof of any kind being adduced, and because the Kadusa MS is 'said to have been written' by Gangājī Mavāla—who is described as 'the person who put down in writing what Tukārām composed'. As for Mahādev, had he indeed written his father's *abhangs*, as is affirmed, surely Mahīpati would have known and mentioned the fact. As for Gangājī Mavāḷa, he cannot be allowed to occupy his position of solitary distinction as Tukārām's amanuensis, for there were at least two others who are mentioned as having done similar work—Rāmeshwar Bhatt and Santājī the Oilman,[1] and the editors do not appear to have obtained any original writing of Gangājī, while there is room for doubt whether they made the best use of what MSS they did see. Since therefore they appear to have accepted mere traditions as trustworthy evidence, our faith is somewhat shaken in the value of the critical principles adopted by them. The *Indu Prakāsh* editors are honest enough to tell us that some of the MSS on which they rely had been 'corrected', 'further corrected' and 'arranged', all of which are very damaging terms, indicating a grave diminution of value in any of the MSS so doctored. It is unsafe to conclude, therefore, that the text lying behind the *Indu Prakāsh* edition is either the best text or that it has reached us in its original form. At the same time this edition may be regarded as exceedingly well-edited, the aim of its editors being 'faithfully to reproduce' the text they considered available in 1869, and though their basal MSS should eventually have to be considered imperfect, the editors were conscientious enough 'not to leave out any word or verse even where it appeared indecent'.[2]

2. If such are the methods obtaining in the only 'critical preface' found among all the editions published up to 1920, what shall be said of those collections which conceal their methods from our view? The late Vishnuboā Joga's edition of 4149 *abhangs* (numbered 7 in the list above), with its excellent commentary, must be pronounced the best edition from the standpoint of interpretation and for that reason it is approved by the *Wārkarīs* (see chapter 7, sec. 2), though its text is probably not of the best. The edition of *Tukārām Tātya* (No. 4) is well-described by Dr. R. G. Bhandarkar[3] as 'uncritically made and oftentimes one same piece is given a second time with the opening lines omitted. Still, this. . . . contains *abhangs*. . . quite in the style of Tukārām with the usual fervent devotion and purity of thought'. For this reason the Prārthanā Samāj have taken several of their hymns from this edition. The late Hari Narayan Āpte took a leading part with Mr. Dravid in editing the collection numbered 9 in the list given above, embodying an order of the poems accepted by the *Wārkarīs* of Paṇḍharpūr but as this is based on the Paṇḍharpūr MS already referred to, and of secondary value, being characterized by the *Indu Prakāsh* editors as 'very recent', 'modernized' and 'less accurate', we may safely leave it out of our reckoning. Numbers 1 and 10 in the list are based on *Wārkarī* MSS of doubtful authority while the editions numbered 3, 5, 6 and 8 were prepared from other printed collections such as the *Indu Prakāsh*.

3. We come to the last and most recent edition in our list, the one which presents the nearest approach to critical principles,

[1] See pp. 73, 101, 111, and 122.
[2] *Indu Prakāsh*, Vol. 1, p. 2.
[3] *V. S. M. R. S.*, p. 94.

though still incomplete. It is a collection claiming to be 'Tukārām's Original Gāthā' (*Tukārāmāce Assal Gāthā*, 2 vols.), edited by Mr. V. L. Bhāve of Thana, Bombay. Two volumes only have been published, the first containing 865 *abhangs*, the second 458. In his preface to the first volume Mr. Bhāve points out that 'original' poems may be of three kinds—those written by the poet himself, those dictated by him, and those corrected by him after being written by someone else. Mr. Bhāve claims that his collection is one of poems of the second order, having been written by a disciple of Tukārām, either as Tukārām uttered them or—a modification of the same principle—as the disciple remembered them afterwards. The particular disciple in this case is one Santājī the Oilman, or, to give his name in full, Santājī Telī Jagnāḍe who along with Gangājī Mavāla and Rāmeshwar Bhaṭṭ wrote down Tukārām's verses, and one of whose MSS bears a date a few years previous to that of Tukārām's death along with what is claimed to be Santājī's signature. This MS itself has been in Mr. Bhāve's possession and photographs of the MS show up this very early date quite clearly. One is reproduced on the opposite page. Santājī's descendants affirm that he wrote four volumes of Tukārām's *abhangs* and Mr. Bhāve claims thus to have discovered an early authority consulted by no previous editor, not even the *Indu Prakāsh*. It is much too early to say whether Marāṭhā scholars will accept the authenticity and uniqueness of this MS of Santājī, and all that can be said at the present stage of investigation is that it represents a worthy attempt to solve a most baffling problem. Mr. Bhāve's 22-page critical discussion at the beginning of his second volume is, up to the time of writing (early 1921), far and away the most praiseworthy effort made at elucidating the difficult questions raised, the old spelling of Marāṭhī words also being preserved, and probably their pronunciation as in Tukārām's own day.[1]

2. Poems of Doubtful Authenticity

It appears fairly certain that of Tukārām's fourteen disciples no less than three—Rāmeshwar, Gangājī and Santājī—are known to have written down his poems as they remembered them, but how faithfully we cannot say. No doubt there were many poems which they did not preserve, many also which were preserved but did not find their way into well-known MSS, whilst other poems may have been inserted which are not authentic. Tukārām's style is easily imitated and we have seen that one collection has nearly twice as many poems as the *Indu Prakāsh* edition, many *abhangs* probably existing also which have never been printed but which pass from mouth to mouth throughout the Marāthā country.

[1] See *Dnyānodaya*, Dr. J. E. Abbott's *Notes on the Marāṭhā Saints*, No. 9, April 28, 1921.

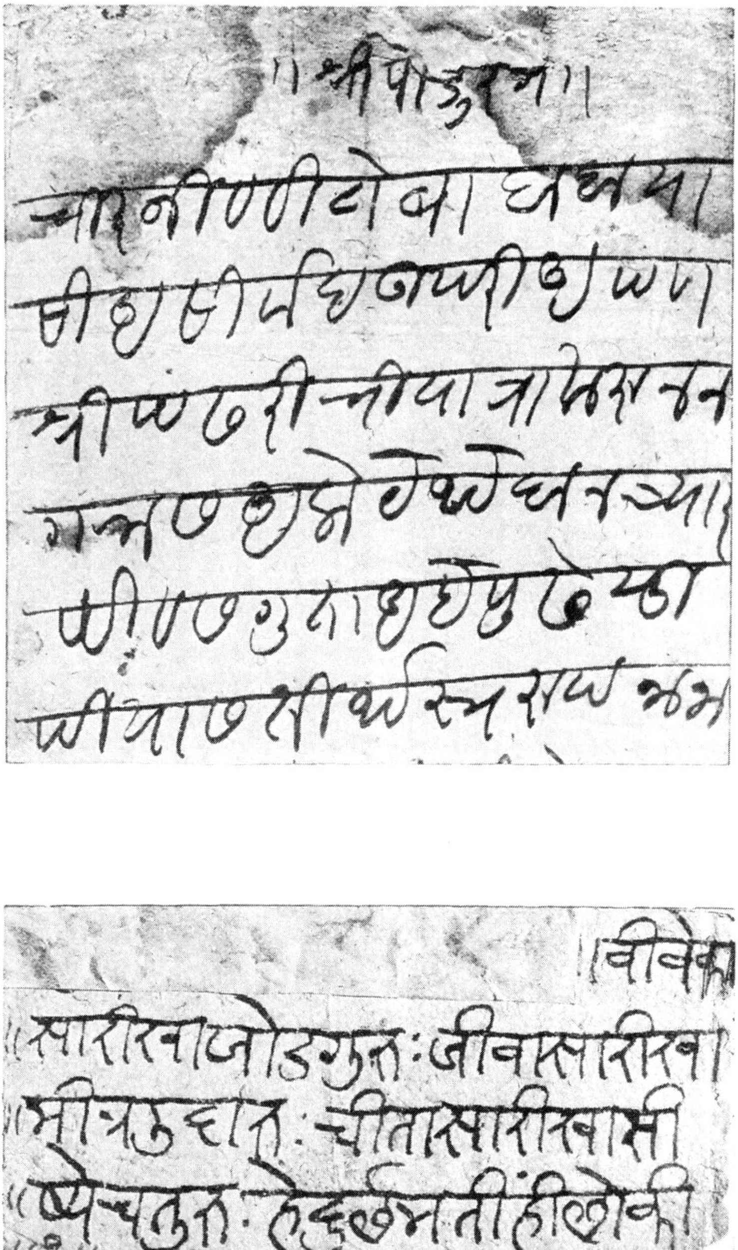

SAMPLES OF MAHĪPATI'S HANDWRITING

This state of things is annoying in two ways. First, there are many poems even in widely-accepted collections which are possibly not Tukārām's and there is no means of distinguishing them. A good judge of Marathi can sometimes form an opinion from the language, but the critic who begins in this way is soon in danger of rejecting lines because the sentiment does not seem to be Tukārām's and such a proceeding may take us any lengths.

3. Shivaji's Visit—Apocryphal or Genuine?

Put in this doubtful class sometimes are some *abhangs* whose rejection would modify seriously Tukārām's biography, those describing the visit of the rising prince and future king Śivājī (*abhangs* 1468 74 in *F.* and *M.*).[1] It is impossible in the present stage of investigation in Maratha history and literature to pronounce definitely either way. We shall therefore content ourselves with presenting the evidence as it appears to both sides in the matter, first stating the point of view of those questioning the historicity of Śivājī's visit and the authenticity of Tukarām's verses on the subject, and then giving briefly what is said in reply by those who are inclined to accept both the visit and the verses. The ground common to both sides is that Tukārām was probably born in 1608 and died sometime between 1648 and 1652, while Śivājī was born in 1627 though some think a little later (see p. 17), all these dates being subject to alteration (see pages 76 7).

Those who consider the visit and the verses apocryphal make the following points. (1) When Tukārām died Śivājī was still a young man with all his future before him. (2) In 1649 Śivājī was just beginning his operations against the Deccan hill-forts and his coronation did not take place till 1674. (3) His system of government cannot possibly have been in operation by the time when Tukaram died. (4) Had there ever been such an episode as a projected retirement of Śivaji from the world in the train of Tukārām surely he would at some time in his life have shown some interest in Paṇḍharī or Viṭhobā's shrine. But nothing of the kind is recorded. Śivaji on the contrary maintained a close connection with the family shrine of Tuljapūr and never visited Paṇḍharī. (5) Śivājī had his own *guru* in Rāmdās, a most interesting person, who forms a remarkable contrast with our poet. He was politician as well as devotee, a patriot as well as a sage, a shrewd and amusing moralist, and a more useful auxiliary to the warrior prince than Tukarām could have been. (On Rāmdās see p. 18).

Answering the above points *in seriatim*, those who are inclined to hold Śivājī requested Tukārām to go to him and that in declining to do so the poet sent the prince the verses, do so for the following reasons. (1) The first point in the above stated by a Westerner and for Western readers, sounds very plausible. When, however,

[1] See pp. 99–101 above.

it is remembered that Śivājī was very precocious as a boy, even at 8 or 9 cherishing ideas of wresting independence from the Muhammadans, that he was married at 16, had two wives before Tukārām died, and had already made a great mark in Mahārāshtra, to say that Śivājī had '*all* his future before him' is not strictly correct. (2) In reply to the second point, Śivājī had already, when Tukārām died, captured the famous Torna fort and several others, including some in Tukārām's own neighbourhood, thus extending his kingdom over the Poona district. Moreover, the *royal* title *chatrapati* is found ascribed to Śivājī as early as 1647, at least a year or two before Tukārām's death.[1] (3) The very special circumstances of the time when Śivājī and his followers were in open revolt against the Muhammadan power, rule out any dogmatic statement such as is made under (3) above. Moreover the royal title already mentioned carries with it the existence of 'ministers of state' such as Tukārām referred to in his verses. Besides which, a document dated shortly after Tukārām's death proves the full 'system of government' to have been in operation under Śivājī. (4) The 'projected retirement' referred to above was nothing but a passing mood, the result of the poet's moving *kīrtan*,[2] and there was therefore no necessity for Śivājī to visit Paṇdharpūr. But who can say for certain that he 'never' went there? This is an argument from silence, which is always perilous Śivājī's greater devotion to Tuljapūr must be accounted entirely natural because it *was* 'the family shrine'. (5) The fifth point above far outruns the evidence. Granting, however, that Śivājī had Rāmdās as his *guru* at that time—though this point is somewhat fiercely debated (see Chap. I, p. 18 of this book)—no one suggests that there was any idea of Tukārām supplanting Rāmdās as Śivājī's preceptor and guide. Indeed, assuming for the moment the authenticity of the verses, Tukārām discourages Śivājī's clinging to him and directs attention to his own *guru*: 'Fix your thoughts on the good teacher, Rāmdās: do not swerve from him.' (See *abhaṅg* 1471, *F.* and *M.*). Further, that Śivājī already had a *guru* in Rāmdās is no argument against Śivājī visiting Tukārām. Some of the greatest Hindū saints have had more than one *guru*. Indeed, Śivājī himself had accepted as *guru*, and taken a *guru-mantrā* from, a Brāhman at Mahābleshwar, the original *sanad* given by Śivājī being still in the possession of the Brāhman's descendant and now published. (6) In addition to the above are the considerations arising from the topography of the neighbourhood and Śivājī's close proximity to Tukārām at that time, the altogether unique position occupied in Marāṭhā public affairs by Śivājī's mother, Jijābāī, and the fact that she and Śivājī's preceptor Dādojī Kondadev were of such a deeply religious turn of mind. All these considerations taken together make it at least highly probable that Jijābāī and Dādojī would wish

[1] V. L. Bhāve, *M. Sāt.*, p. 186 footnote 1.
[2] See pp. 100-1.

the greatest saint of the time, and one residing so near, to give his blessing to the young prince, and it is not at all unlikely that they arranged it. (7) Śivājī's *sanad* (grant) of four villages to Tukārām's posthumous son Narāyan[1] after the poet's death must be given some significance in this connexion. (8) The preponderance of Indian opinion should be given its true value. The incident is not only recorded in Mahīpati and in MSS of Tukārām's poems considered by the *Indu Prakāsh* editors as the best, one of them being the MS 'said to be in the handwriting of the eldest son of Tukārām' and therefore probably dated before Śivājī's coronation; it is also found in those trustworthy historical authorities, the early Marāthī *bakhars* (historical memoirs). Sir R. G. Bhandarkar accepts both visit and verses (see his *Vaishnavism*, p. 94), as did also the late Christian poet Narāyan Vaman Tilak who in an unpublished essay observes: 'Śivājī had paid his homage to Tukārām and was greatly impressed by the latter's saintliness.' We may add that both visit and verses are accepted by Prof. H. G. Rawlinson in his book on *Shivājī the Marāṭhā* published in 1915 (see pp. 86, 113–4. See also L. R. Pāngārkar's Marāṭhī work, pp. 436–46) and Prof. N. S. Takākhav's English translation of Mr. K. A. Kelūskar's Marāthī *Life of Shivājī*.

On the whole we incline to think the balance of evidence is in favour of the historicity of Śivājī's request to Tukārām and subsequent visit, the authenticity of the poet's verses perhaps not being in quite so strong a position. It is due to Mr. Fraser to say that the first of the last two paragraphs—the one viewing verses and visit as apocryphal—was found among his papers just as it is given above, the latter of the two paragraphs coming entirely from the pen of his co-author.

4. No known Chronological Order

The second annoying result referred to above affects the biography in another direction, for we are unable to fix the chronological order of the autobiographical *abhangs*. This appears, indeed, well-nigh impossible in the present state of our knowledge. The effort, however, may well be made, and those making it will find that all the editions of Tukārām, without exception, have thrown to the winds all idea of any possible chronological order, and what is worse, they have modified the language by attempting to modernize it, though Mr. Bhāve's edition is an exception on this last point. This means that the task of discovering any possible chronology in Tukārām's poems is made much more difficult than it might have been. In view of these facts, therefore, we cannot say, for instance, whether Tukārām moved, as time went on,

[1] See footnote 2, p. 94.

towards or away from the *advaita* position, towards or away from idolatry. We cannot say if he found more or less peace of mind. One would like to think his devotion did not go unrewarded. But on this point as on others certainty is not possible, and indeed Tukārām's own moods and views may have gone on varying to the day of his death. In the English translation[1] the *abhangs* are presented in a sort of ideal order, the problem poems coming before the poems that find solutions, but no reader must infer that they were written in this order.

5. Genuineness of the Autobiography

Despite many unsolved problems, however, we need have no doubt that the *abhangs* describing Tukārām's feelings and habits of life are quite genuine. And they appear to be exceedingly sincere. This is not said without the full sense of the difficulty of judging the sincerity of words. The portraits which writers give of themselves are usually false, and false, one may say, in proportion to their air of candour. But Tukārām's self-revelation seems to leave no room for suspicion of pose. The things he says of his weakness and misery are not the things men say to add to their merit. What he might say to his own credit he leaves unsaid. We learn nothing for instance, from his own lines, of the unselfish kindness to his neighbours that strikes us so much in Mahīpati's biography. And the inconsistencies of view and conduct that come to light in studying them are laid before us with such simplicity that we may justifiably trust well-nigh the whole record. Unquestionably, there are incidents which never happened. We have for instance a number of *abhangs* purporting to give his last words (*abhangs* 1444–1459 F. and M) These fit in with Mahīpati's account, but cannot be received as authentic, unless the reader is ready to believe that Hari really did come whirring through the air and carried off Tukārām in a *vimān* (balloon or aeroplane). The account by Mahīpati will be found on pages 115–6 and a brief discussion on pages 105–6. We only need add here a view prevalent among Tukārām students, one helping to an intelligible understanding of the *abhangs* on the subject. It seems that when Hindū saint dies, his body is usually carried in a framework resembling a *vimān*, for burning or burial as the case may be. Tukārām's *abhangs* concerning his going to Vaikuntha ('heaven') are therefore regarded as nothing more than a symbolical forecast of his approaching death.

[1] By *F.* and *M*

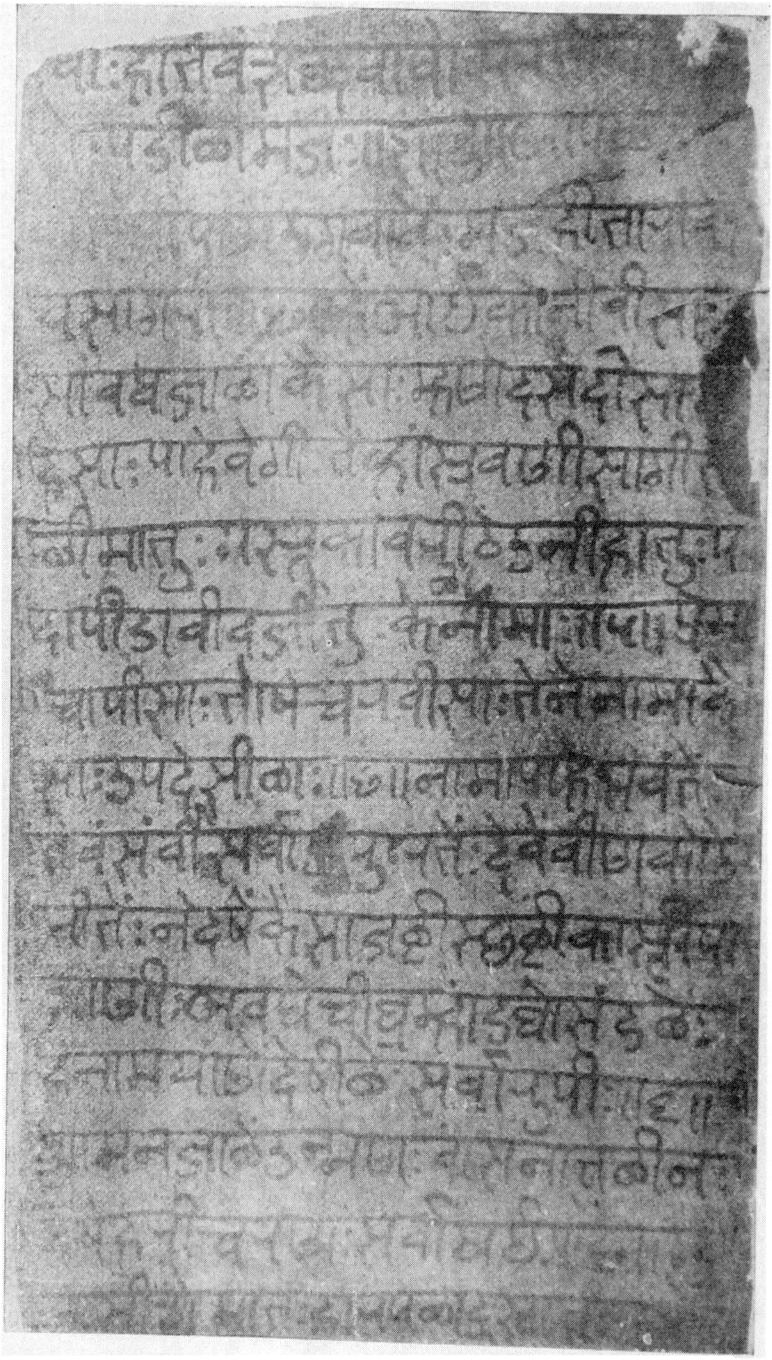

A SAMPLE OF WHAT IS CLAIMED TO BE TUKĀRĀM'S HANDWRITING

II. The Literary Characteristics of the Autobiography

1. Tukaram's Verse Extempore and Original

Tukārām's verses were probably all extempore, and there is little reason to think that he either prepared or revised them, though we have seen that a well-founded belief exists that his *abhangs* were written down by at least three disciples during his lifetime. Distinction or fame as a writer Tukārām was probably far from courting. He speaks of his own accents as stammering and childish. They are the feeble means he possesses to utter his message and make known his Master's glory. It does not occur to him that along with the message there was sent any gift of speech.

In this modest view of his literary merits the modern critic must in the main acquiesce. The *abhangs* as a whole do not rise above rustic simplicity. Many are quite prosaic. But others are fully inspired by the spirit of poetry. 'His *abhangs* are not mere paraphrases; they are original effusions, the outcome of the poet's own inward experience and of his observation of the facts of human life. They are full of shrewd and often-times humorous delineation, and they reflect unmistakably the features of the poet's character . . . They reveal a strange mixture of religious ideas, high spiritual aspirations mingled with the infatuations of idolatry, explicable partly by the underlying pantheism in all Hindū thinking and partly by the fact that Tukārām saw beyond his time and with a true spiritual instinct."[1]

2. His Debt to Predecessors

That Tukārām's poems are to be regarded as 'original effusions' does not mean that he owed no debt to the *bhakti* poets who had preceded him. On the contrary, he himself states plainly in more than one place that 'some words of the Saints he had committed to memory with reverence and with faith.'[2] On this important subject Mr. Pāngārkar has an exhaustive and informing chapter (the sixth in his book) in which he shows, on the basis of clear quotations from Tukārām's own poems and of the confirmatory testimony of Mahīpati in his *Bhakta Līlāmrita* (chapter 30) that Tukārām had given special attention to Dnyāneshwar, Nāmdev, Eknāth and Kabīr. The last-mentioned, who had preceded the poet-saint of Dehū by more than a century and a quarter, Tukārām may have come to know on his visit to Benāres referred to by him

1 Dr. Mackichan, *I. I.*, Vol. VII. No. 4, January 1913, pp. 173 and 175.
2 See *abhang* 101 in *F.* and *M.*, 1333 in *I. P.*

in his *abhaṅg* numbered 2488 in the *Indu Prakāsh* edition.[1] It is suggested that the *Bhagavadgītā* and *Bhāgavata Purāṇa*, the scriptures of the Bhāgavata Religion of Mahārāshtra (see our chapter 2, p. 27), had been the objects of Tukārām's special study[2], from which conclusion the deduction is made that Tukārām had also become sufficiently acquainted with Sanskrit to study Sanskrit works with avidity (Pāngārkar, 178, 214), some even affirming, though on what grounds is not indicated, that soon after he had renounced the world, Tukārām spent a few months at the important centre of Paiṭhan on the Godāveri river where from a devout Shastrī he learned much sacred lore.[3]

This much at least is certain, that, compared with his predecessors, Tukārām's religious ideas are both more mature and more advanced, that there is much greater variety of subject-matter, of expression and of imagery, and that Tukārām himself admits his indebtedness to those predecessors. 'Indian writers have always exhibited a marvellous power of working up into new shapes again and again the same material of metaphor and phrase',[4] and we shall see that Tukārām was no exception.

3. His Brevity, Obscurity and Metaphors

The best of Tukārām's *abhaṅgs*, from the point of view of literary merit, are those distinguished for their vigour. He is able, on occasion, to speak with good point and force. Indeed he never wastes any words, and his defect is that he sometimes falls into obscurity. To the foreigner, one may say, he is almost always obscure, the ellipses of true vernacular Marāṭhī being confounding in the extreme, but even the Indian is often perplexed by Tukārām's inconsiderate brevity. There is always a meaning inside the unpromising shell of his language, and the student (like the student of Browning) ends by admiring the form of expression. It has cost him so much labour to master that he is more inclined to love it than to pardon or to apologize for it, but perhaps he has reached a point where he may no longer speak as a literary critic. We only need add that the linguist and philologist would find a study of Tukārām's expressions repaying.

Tukārām's style is enlivened by a copious use of metaphor, most likely influenced by his close study of Dnyāneshwar and Eknāth who are masters of metaphor in Marāṭhī. The conventions of Asiatic literature do not forbid a poet enriching himself by borrowing from his predecessors, and a good metaphor once discovered becomes common property for ever. Tukārām borrows in this way quite freely, while he is also able to use his own opportunities and

1 L. R. M. Pāngārkar, *S.T.C.*, pp. 203, 95.
2 *Ibid.* pp. 161-3.
3 *Ibid.* p. 179.
4 L. J. Sedgwick, *J.R.A.S. Bo.*, Vol. 23, No. 65.

invent images for himself. The most interesting of these are the images derived from his life as a grocer, which we shall presently collect, having first brought together some examples of figures no less striking but perhaps less congenial.

4. Pictures of Life in the World

The world of sensation is a mirage; the world of desire a net; the task before us to tear up the very root of desire, so that it may never sprout again. Otherwise, desires flourish like wild creepers; it is no use hacking them down, you must dig up their roots. The victim of desire passes through one wretched life after another like the pots that ascend and descend on the Persian wheel; what he needs is to make a bonfire of the past, similar to the bonfire of the *Holī*[1]. Like a man caught in a press gang the victim of desire toils and gains nothing by his toil; like a bee with a string tied to its foot, the plaything of a child, he starts off to force himself and finds himself a prisoner. In this bondage, life slips by, and death is waiting for him like a cat waiting for a mouse. In its confusion life resembles a village fair; in its perplexity a trackless forest. Hari's name is like a moist shadow in a parched land, it is a flowing spring[2] of delight. His grace flows like the Ganges in flood, freely offered to all, like the sunlight. Life is a delirious fever; a swollen river that lies before a traveller; how can he cross it? There is a boat ready waiting for him, the boat of Hari's name; he has only to sit in it, he will be carried over the stream. This metaphor of the river is characteristically Indian, 'Perhaps the symbol that, more than any other, takes the place in Indian mysticism that is taken in the mysticism of the West by the pilgrimage of the soul is that of the crossing of the river in a boat. By the Marāṭhā saints and by Kabīr, in the meditations of Maharshi Debendranāth Tagore and in the poems of his son, this picture is again and again made use of to represent man's perilous passage to what is sometimes God's bosom and sometimes a land unknown, but what is perhaps to most, both of these at once. It is strange that to the West, death is the dark river to be crossed, but to India it is not death but life. "Your friend," says Kabīr, "stands on the other shore." Taking a wise *guru* for his ferryman, and embarking on the boat of a surrendered spirit, the traveller crosses the perilous waters safely to the place of union and of bliss.'[3]

5. The Motherhood of God

The way of God with his worshippers is like the way of a mother with her child. However ugly he may be, she loves him

[1] An annual Hindū Festival.
[2] Perhaps rather 'well'; springs are rare in India.
[3] Dr. Macnicol, *I. R. M.*, Vol. 5, No. 18, April 1916, p. 216.

none the less; she is patient with his ill humours, she interprets and fulfills his wishes and she is satisfied to be thanked in such imperfect accents as he can command. He does not understand the depth of her devotion, but he trusts her, and with this she is content. (See further chap. 6, sect. 1; and chap. 8, II, 3).

As the fruit corresponds to the seed in the field, so the fruit corresponds to the seed in spiritual things. Sow the seed of faith if you wish to gather the fruit of spiritual bliss. Listen to instruction, whoever offers it you. It is the Saints who instruct mankind by their example, as a teacher shows children how to form the letters by drawing them on a slate.

6. Similes from Animal Life and Business

Countless illustrations are drawn from animal life. The passions are like unruly cows that struggle and break into pastures and defy the herds, man's efforts being to drive them into their shed and tie them up. The snake drinks the same water as the people but his spittle turns to poison. The worldling's life is like the daily round of a blinded ox turning an oil mill. Why do ascetics pride themselves on ceremonies and needless austerities? Tukārām cries for mercy as a nestling cries with open beak for food, as a calf or a fawn in the jungle cries after its mother.

Tukārām's special property no doubt are the similes drawn from business. He often compares himself and the Saints to dealers in God's mercy; they have opened a shop where full value is given, the only coin they take is faith. There is no fear of the stock running short; it can be measured out for ever and ever and the store will never decrease. Then at other times he refers to the anxiety attending worldly business, to the perplexities of account-keeping, and to the misery of debt, and he rejoices that he has done with it all, for God manages the affairs of the godly. Also he compares himself to the measure with which corn is measured out; a thing of no value in itself, thrown aside when it is empty.

7. Tukaram's Gravity and Humour

Though usually a very grave philosopher Tukārām does occasionally smile. In this he is not unlike his countrymen. A general misconception among Europeans is that Hindūs have no sense of humour, those who have never met them supposing that they are all as sad and silent as ascetics and those who live among them being surprised that they cannot understand foreign jokes in a foreign tongue. The fact is that Hindūs are for the most part very humorous and their popular religion has a humorous vein. This is not in the least incompatible with the melancholy and pessimistic philosophy common among them. Human nature is capable of anything in the way of paradox, and the alliance of humour and melancholy is one of the most usual that it admits.

Tukārām's humour, to be sure, is seldom blithe. In a lighter moment he says: 'We beggars are lucky folk: thieves are frightened when they come near us. We have wealth and grain in every house, for we live on every one's charity.' But for the most part his humorous jests are biting sarcasms levelled, like those of Solomon, against every sort of fool. The rich man's spoiled wife (*abhaṅg* 1070), and the hen-pecked husband, are vigorously hit off here and there. The seamy side of married life seems to have caught his eye pretty often. If he laughs at it his laugh passes quickly into stern denunciation.

Allied to Tukārām's humorous vein is that in which he rallies Vithobā on his treatment of men. His favourite idea is that Vithobā is a thief, who runs away with men's property and leaves them penniless. He is a cheat, and cheats men out of their worldly goods. This is only an affectionate way of saying that Tukārām thinks they get something better instead. We notice those *abhaṅgs* here only as a point in his literary method.

8. Allegorical Value of Common Life

A curious group of poems is formed by those which make an allegorical use of images drawn from common life. Many of them are based on games. Hindū boys have many games and these must be understood in order to follow the poems, the explanations given in the notes[1] being perhaps sufficient. In general we must distinguish two kinds of games, those in which there is rivalry and those in which there is only common effort. Where there is rivalry the boys of one side are trying to catch or beat the boys of the other, probably one representative boy of the other. Such a game therefore is an image of the contest of the soul and the world. The soul is struggling to escape, the world is trying to detain it. In the poem on *Aṭyāpāṭyā*, rather unexpectedly the soul is represented by the side that guards the base (as we should say in prisoner's base), the player that struggles to get through is a passion. These images, it appears, illustrate the hard struggle that lies before the man who seeks salvation by works, good deeds or austerities or the observation of ceremonial law. Contrasted with his case is that of the devotee of Viṭṭhal who joins

[1] At the end of each volume of *F.* and *M.*

in loving union with God, just as two players do in the friendly recreation of *ṭipari*.[1]

9. Images from Low Caste People

Of the same type are poems employing images from village characters. In a Hindū village there are various low caste persons who perform services to the community, to Government, to passing strangers, and are paid by a share in the village produce. Such are the Mahārs who live on the outskirts of the village but perform services of importance, such as carrying the revenue to the treasury, a common salutation of theirs being the cry '*johār*'.[2] In *abhaṅg* 1351 the Mahār calling for the revenue typifies the world or the claim of *karma* which calls on a man for the penalty of his actions, in contrast with the devotion to Vitthal which either cuts that short or enables a man to view it with indifference. The allegory here is clear enough, but such is not always the case, indeed allegory is always a treacherous form of exposition, losing its message as soon as it comes to details.

10. Images from Doubtful Religious Characters

Tukārām employs images from religious characters, some of them religious mendicants of a sorry and disreputable kind. These have not been included in the translation by Fraser and Marāṭhe but may be mentioned here. One of the reprehensible customs of the country is that of marrying girls to a god, in which case they fall back on prostitution for a living, while at the same time they go about singing the praises of the god. We have already seen that in the Deccan the god to whom they are usually married is Khanḍobā,[3] more or less identified in popular opinion with Śiva. *Muraḷī* is the name given to these unfortunate girls, while that of the boys is *Wāghyā*, the male devotees and mendicants of Khandobā. On behalf of a woman thus devoted to this god at Jejurī, Tukārām writes a poem in which she describes her life. The language is so chosen as to suggest that instead of what she possesses or thinks she possesses she ought to turn to Viṭthal and accept the treasures which he can give. In a similar vein Tukārām writes a poem on behalf of an adulteress, making the guilty love suggest the divine love which she is neglecting. The double meaning can scarcely be rendered in English.

It is a question how far in these poems the poet is inspired by anything like the pity which a modern observer might feel for the

1 See the whole Section on Games numbered [illegible], pp. 41–50, Vol, II, *F.* and *M.* with a 'Notes', pp. 433–5.

2 See p 19.

3 See Chapter 3, page 47, also Molesworth's *Marāthi-English Dictionary*, p. xxvi, footnote.

victims of destiny. Probably this sentiment did not pass through his mind: it does not belong to his age. He would think of them as mortals besotted by the world, as a grasping tradesman or a cavilling Brāhman might be, but not specially as creatures whose case called for the philanthropist.

The interpretation of these poems is obscure, their subject unpleasant, and it is a relief to turn to others in which the fidelity of the day-labourer and of the *pāīk* (see *abhangs* 1344–54) or the joint labours of two women grinding together furnish images of sturdy piety or faithful trust. By a *pāīk* is meant an armed attendant, a peon, messenger or courtier, and around the *abhangs* on the subject (numbered 3655–3665 in Vishnuboa Joga's commentary which see) has raged a controversy in the Marāthā country as to whether Tukārām enfeebled Mahārāshtra by directing its attention exclusively to things spiritual. Those who argue that Tukārām advocated military virtues are answered by those who affirm that while the language of these *abhangs* is secular their meaning and message are distinctly spiritual.

11. Popularity of Tukaram's Style

A poet whose verse is quoted by millions of peasants as a final authority and who supplies some of India's greatest reformers with religious nourishment must be regarded as having couched his message in a popular style. And such is the case with the poet-saint of Dehū The late Christian poet, Narāyan Vāman Tilak, no mean judge either of poetic power or of popular taste, observes in an unpublished essay we have quoted elsewhere: 'That Tukārām is still the most popular Marāṭhi poet of the day even in the 20th century shows how Tukārām's literary characteristics appealed to the people of Mahārāshtra and still appeal. As Shrīdhar,[1] a poet born a generation after Tukārām's death, remarked: "I fully sympathize with the common people who do not understand the Sanskrit language; they are like thirsty persons standing by the side of a deep well without either a rope or a vessel, knowing that the well has no steps to go into it, and that their hands can never reach the surface of water in it." So Shrīdhar provided this rope and this vessel as Tukārām had done more than half a century before him. Tukārām is still unequalled among all the Marāthi poets. The flow and force of Tukārām's music is simply wonderful, his diction is easy, his illustrations are homely and exact; he had glimpses of the past, but he mainly dealt with the present and the future. He was an investigator and a painter of human nature and he did his work so well that none among the Marāthī poets merits comparison with him.'

[1] See p 1[illegible], end of Section 11, chap 1.

III. Tukaram's Picture of Himself

1. A Trustworthy Picture

From Tukārām's own poems, assisted by the pages of Mahīpati, we have no difficulty in drawing a portrait of his character which is almost as full as we could wish and as we have seen (see Part I, this Chapter), probably quite trustworthy. His own account of himself is frank and simple and clearly inspired by nothing else than a desire to be useful. There is no trace of egoism about it and no affectation of any kind. His religion was nearly his all in all. This is illustrated by what the late Narāyan Vāman Ṭilak sets forth: 'He walked with his god, talked with him, took him to task, settled quarrels with him, consulted him, shared his lot with him. None other and nothing else was so dear and so near to him as his Viṭhobā. This attitude of his mind has made his devotional flights so real that while reading his poetry one finds one's self as it were in the midst of a new life, not merely of thoughts. Excepting a few *abhangs*, all his poetry had for its theme his own experiences in his relation to the world and to his god. Thus Tukārām himself is the hero of most of his poems, and his presence goes with a reader of them, and makes them exceedingly charming. One cannot get half of Tukārām's meaning unless one has first read and studied his life thoroughly well, and unless one has learned to sympathize with him in his wisdom and folly alike.'

2. An Honest Tradesman

We notice that he did not wholly give his heart to God till he was laid prostrate by misfortune. At his father's request he took over the family business and, no doubt, had prosperity attended him he might have continued all his life a thriving and respected tradesman. An honest tradesman we need not doubt, and a devout man, but perhaps not the author of our poems. It was calamity that made him change his path in life. We may therefore contrast his experience with that of other Indian devotees who have left the world in the hour of success and glory. As for example Ramāvalabhdās, son of the Prime Minister of Devgirī (Daulatābād) and a contemporary of Tukārām, who during the plunder which followed a successful battle by chance found a copy of Eknāth's *Bhāgwat* and viewing this good fortune as a divine favour he gave himself up entirely to religious meditation.[1]

A similar example of Indian renunciation, though one connected with another of India's faiths—Jainism—and another part

[1] See V L Bhāve, *Sār*, p. 163; in the same volume see also the cases of Dāsopant, p. 117, Kesarīnāth, p. 350, and Banājī, p. 135-6, footnote.

of the country, is one many travellers have come across, viz., the Jain princes and princesses whose names are inscribed on the rock at Sravana Belgola, with a record testifying that they who took their seats upon that rock had closed their lives by starvation, because they had found that worldly pleasures were unsatisfying.

3. His Failures in Business

Of his life in the world before he retired from business Tukārām has little to say. It is summed up in *abhangs* 101–126. He does not specially complain of hard treatment from man or destiny or accuse himself of wanting the qualities needful for success. He never gives us to understand that he failed because he was too good for a wicked world. His view of the world is more detached, as he makes sufficiently plain. Human life fills him with extreme horror. 'The whole world is an eddy of misery. I cannot bear it: adamant would break beneath it: my soul is filled with trembling fear: I utterly shrink from the tale of this fetid world' (361). Many poems dwell in detail on the guilt and misery of men and there is nothing to tell us that Tukārām ever lighted on any scene with satisfaction save the assembly of Vaishnava Saints.

4. Conviction of Sin

Meditation brought a great conviction of sin. Very numerous and most earnest are the poems that speak of self-accusation. The poems on this subject number several hundreds out of the whole collection. They speak chiefly of sloth that wastes time, of desire that longs for pleasures. We need not think that Tukārām any more than John Bunyan was worse than his neighbours: he has learned to reproach himself. We cannot date these poems, and neither psychological nor chronological principles justify the supposition that they must have been written in the first days of spiritual struggle. How utterly overwhelming was Tukārām's sense of sin may be gathered from the poems. Without commenting we give a brief selection in addition to the renderings on page 50: 'O God, protect me and still my agitated soul. Cast no reproach on me; receive within thyself, says Tukā, the million offences I have committed' (347). 'Regard not my mountainous guilt' (348). 'I see that my own heart is not pure; I have fallen into the destructive power of the senses. O Hari, do thou swiftly cut off this evil that clings to me. Other evils too why need I count up? sinful illusions, evil affections. I am tortured by lust and rage; who but thou can set me free?' (353) 'Though I speak gentle words, yet lust and rage flourish within me; my spirit is not pure, as the saints describe purity' (354). 'O God,

. . . . do thou banish all in me that is deceitful and come in thy genuine nature to dwell within me. Sinful as I am, let thy power save me' (356). 'Where there is falsehood, there is a heap of sin' (364). 'O best of beings, pity my sins, past and future' (365). 'What purity have I, of descent, lineage or action, that thy secret should be revealed to me?' (372).

'I have sought thee because I was fallen' (1860). 'Why dost thou consider my faults or merits? I am altogether a heap of sins, yet am united to the Saviour of the sinful' (1870). 'We cannot see how to unwind these meshes. We are beset by the dogs of rage and lust, we are fallen into the whirlpool of temptations' (1879). 'I am vicious, guilty, how guilty, how can I tell?' (1881). 'Give me, O God, the happiness of solitude; take away all that brings ruin on my soul. I am a heap of sin, says, Tukā, O set me behind thy back' (1891). 'O ye Saints, I am a sinful man' (3009). 'Who would care to enquire into my merits? Thy name is Purifier of the Sinful. We are fast bound by greed and error. Truly I am a sinful man, but I seek shelter in thee' (3026). 'I am nothing but a heap of sins; thou art altogether the best of all beings' (3030). See also section 7 of chapter 9, also chapter 8, III.

So striking indeed is the sense of sin evinced by Tukārām that we could well imagine some of his despairing cries had been taken from the pages of the 'Penitential Psalms.' There is perhaps an even more instructive parallel in this matter of a sense of sin and unworthiness between St. Paul and Tukārām. St. Paul's description of himself as 'the least of the apostles' (1 Cor. 15 : 9), 'less than the least of all saints' (Eph. 3 : 8), and 'the chief of sinners' (1 Tim. 1: 18) finds a worthy echo in the penitential cry of Tukārām for mercy: 'I am helpless, guilty and chief among sinners' (1609); 'I am a depraved sinner, O God, and I have come to seek Thy mercy: put me not to shame. I do not know how many men thou hast saved, but this I know that I am the worst of them all . . . . I am a supplicant for Thy mercy; cleanse thou me completely from my sin, O God."[1] This sense of personal sinfulness in Tukārām is all the more impressive when we remember that there is little of this quality in the Marāthā poets before him. None of his predecessors 'was so thorough-going', says Prof. W. B. Patwardhan, 'in his rage of self-examination and self-exposition; none before him was so subtly sensible of his own defects, so keenly conscious of his evil doings and evil tendencies, of the erring habits of the mind and predilections to evil and sin. No one before him has so lively a sense of the power of passion and sensual affections, of the weakness of man when beset with temptation in the outer world and torn asunder by conflicting promptings of the flesh. His outlook upon life and the world may be right or wrong. But the intensity with which he feels the

1 Rev. G R Navalkar's translation in *Tukārām, the Mahārāshtrian Poet and Saint*, pp. 23-4.

need of divine grace and support and the anguish and agony with which he realizes the tyranny of the world on the soul of man, the imaginative vividness of his apprehension of the vanity of all pomp and splendour, of the futility of learning and logic and philosophy, the sincerity of his cry for help, and the whole heartedness of his devotion, these are points of Tukārām's life and work that cannot fail to strike any one who reads his *abhangs.*' [1]

In view of these facts we are unable to agree with Dr. Macnicol in his exquisite *Psalms of Marāthā Saints* (p. 33) where he says that in the Bible there is 'a profounder sense of human sin and the alienation that it brings than there is in Tukārām, nor can we agree to his observation that Tukārām was a stranger to the truth 'that the sacrifices of God are a broken heart'[2] (*P.M.S.* p. 33). If ever there was 'a broken heart', broken because so deeply conscious of its wrong and plague, it was the heart of Tukārām. His hundreds of *abhangs* on the subject are sufficient proof of this. We would agree that the sense of sin is not so *constant* a feature as the Christian Scriptures show, probably due to the abiding sense of the stainless purity of God in the latter, but in our view the Bible itself has no more poignant cries of shame than those which escape Tukārām's lips. For ourselves the essential difference between this Marāthā saint and the saints of the Bible lies in another direction. We would place him in the school of Romans vii. 7-24. The self-analysis there fits Tukārām's case perfectly, for he realizes most painfully his 'moral impotence'. What is missing from Tukārām is the song of *complete deliverance* in the last verse of that chapter and in chapter viii with its experience of a final moral and inward emancipation. The Christian's deep sense of sin is what the theologians call 'a saving sense' while that of Tukārām was nearly always a cry of despair: 'my heart testifies to me that I am not redeemed' (126). 'Whomever I meet on this road I enquire of him: Will God be merciful to me?' (19) That he had fleeting glimpses of something else we shall see in Section 8 below.

5. 'De Profundis': Saved by Misfortune

This conviction of personal guilt is accompanied by a dreadful sense of the inscrutable problem of the world. Some of his poems testify to an extreme depression of mind. 'False alike are laughter and tears, the false nature flees to falsehood. False is "mine", false is "thine", the false nature bears a false burden. There is falsehood in thought and falsehood in song. The false finds its way

[1] *F. C. M.* February 1919, pp. 140–1.

[2] The same idea appearing in his illuminating article on 'The Indian Poetry of Devotion' (*Hibbert Journal*, October 1917, pp. 74–88) where he says. 'the dark barrier of a sense of sin does not lower above them as it does above the saints of Israel.'

to the false. False is the life of senses and false renunciation: the ascetic is false, the world an illusion. False is Tukā, false is his faith; he speaks falsehood to the false' (2345). This is perhaps the *De Profundis* of our poet, though it possibly belongs to time when he had already begun to teach and preach. After this we can believe him when he says, 'My words are not figures of rhetoric; I beseech thee in accents of true misery' (1886).

In this harsh scene of suffering Tukārām comes before us as a common man with no claims to any kind of worldly distinction. Strenuously he repels the idea that he has any kind of unusual gift, an attitude in which he may be compared with Walt Whitman. 'I am neither learned nor skilled in debate or pure in lineage' (358). He does not even allow that by nature or early instinct (like his brother) he was drawn to the religious life. It was misfortune that saved him. 'It is well, O God, that I became bankrupt, that I was crushed by the famine; this is how I repented and turned to thee, so that the world became odious to me' (113). He began his religious life modestly, listening to the songs of the Saints and the sermons of the preacher, taking up the refrain at their meetings and finally venturing himself to preach. He spent much time outside the village in solitary meditation among the hills.

6. Sorrow and Self-Dedication

Weaving together Mahīpati's story and Tukārām's own autobiographical *abhangs* we see clearly that it was sorrow that led to his self-dedication. The death of both his parents and his brother's wife followed by that of his own wife and eldest son filled the cup of his sorrow and he decided to retire into solitude. In the words of Prof. W. B. Patwardhan: 'The vanity of human wishes and worldly pursuits came bitterly home to him and there was nothing left in the world of men which could give him peace of mind. He would seek the life that could not die, and the wealth that could not run short. He would have nothing to do with a world that had so much suffering, so much misery, so much that could not last. That which would never fade, never wither, that which cloyed not, died not, that would he seek and in that would he rest. Nothing short of the eternal and the absolutely good would satisfy him. So complete was the change of spirit that came upon him, so long and hard and potent was the conflict raging in his heart, so profound the gloom that sat brooding over his soul, that he emerged a new man, purified and chastened and illumined. Tukārām the Wānī, Tukārām the worldly, Tukārām the son, the brother, the husband, the father was no more, and there lived, moved and had his being Tukārām the spiritual seer, Tukārām the saint, Tukārām the prophet, Tukārām the moral teacher, Tukārām the servant or bondsman of Viṭhobā. . . ,

That it was the series of afflictions that befell him and the bitter experiences and the cruel reverses of fortune he was subject to that brought on the spiritual transformation is apparent from the poet's own words.'[1]

7. 'Spiritual Growth'

Tukārām's autobiography shows how steep and rugged was the ascent he climbed before he could say, 'In the Stainless One I have established my home; in the Formless One I abide' (2755); 'Tukā has his Home in the Inconceivable' (1578); 'my simple-minded faith has put an end to pilgrimage to and fro' (2773); 'rank, race, colour, creed and caste—all are gone' (2790). A worthy 'tentative' effort at delineating this long inward struggle has been made by Prof. W. B. Patwardhan in his paper on 'Tukārām's spiritual growth' which occupies nearly sixteen pages, the Marāṭhi original being given along with English translation; the following continuous extract is in his own words without indicating the explanatory context.

'For days and months and perhaps years, Tukārām appears to have been groping about for want of a sure guide. In vain did he pass from *gosāvī* to *gosāvī* with a view to secure a pilot who could steer him straight to the other and safer shore. Just then he came upon a band of Vārkaris—annual pilgrims to Paṇḍharī, contact and conversation with whom reassured him that he had hit upon the right path. "Take up the *Tāl* (a kind of musical cymbol) and the *Diṇḍī* (a stringed instrument), and dance for love of God," said they. What with the spontaneous impulses of his heart and the words of confidence from the Saints, he applied himself wholly and entirely to the pursuit of the blessing. He would sing to his god, dance to him, pray to him, and concentrate his eye upon him. With all that, he was where he had been spiritually. "I have put on this outward mask. But there has been no renunciation from within. I have no experience of awakening. My heart has not yet emerged out of the toils of the world. Devotional practices have been mechanical. They are neither spontaneous nor soul-affecting." His heart had not yet been purged of a fond attachment to the domestic and worldly life. But there were others that were deeper-seated, viz., his passions. "Sexual desire and angry passion are still alive in me. My mind has not been purified. No advance towards spiritual well-being is possible unless the heart is washed clean of all evil taint." He was an earnest seeker after God—after the Divine Presence, after Divine Love. Tukārām has now arrived at a very delicate stage. The goal is not yet in sight! The world around him, on the other hand, points the finger of scorn at him, scoffs at

[1] *F. C. M.*, Vol. I, No. 3, September 1910, pp. 2–3.

him. Friends and foes alike set him down for a madcap. Tukārām was human and like all human beings apt to lose heart and waver. His is an intensely emotional soul—timid, gentle, and yet sturdy and strong in its own sphere. What is he to do now when his doubts have grown insistent? Whom shall he consult? He will again go to his god, and ask him what he should do. "Who will put heart in me? I am neither an expert in the *Shāstras*, nor a learned man, nor again am I a member of the pure caste. I have no secure anchorage—no piece of firm ground to stand upon. Now I will take this whole-hearted resolve. I will not consult others hereafter. I will be thy subject—thy bondsman—earmarked. "That is," says Tukārām, "the firm and settled purpose of my heart." Yet the expected and long-wished-for bliss does not come. The vision makes no approach to reality. In the yearning impatience of soul he breaks into a pathetic cry: "Come O Vitthal, do come, my life bursts with imploring. Bitterly does the heart repine: it seems thou hast deliberately kept me at a distance. We are sheer orphans having no anchorage. Verily the land is come to be desolate of God." After this long trial Tukārām's long-cherished wish is realized. His spiritual craving is satisfied, and he feels within himself, with all the authority of his own experience, that eternal Love is won only by devoted patience. Now that he has discovered the way, he must show it to others. He therefore proclaims to them: "The only thing to do is to have patience. Do not give up taking food; do not retire to a wood, to solitude; only think of Narāyan in all your experiences of pain or pleasure. All other notions should be lopped off. Commit everything to the care of God and proceed—go on, neither involved in enjoyment or suffering, nor making an ado of renunciation." Here it appears to me,' says Prof. Patwardhan, 'is the process of spiritual evolution in Tukārām complete. It has been a long and laborious circle no doubt.'[1] See also chap. 10, sect. 2, where Prof. Patwardhan characterizes Tukārām's *bhakti* as 'individual' and 'one-sided'.

8. Life after Self-Dedication

Of his life after dedication we have sometimes a picture that presents him as going quietly on with his business. 'I go on with my daily business, yet I love thy feet. I keep thy form ever before my eyes, though outwardly I acknowledge the tie of the world. I govern my actions according to the occasion but with my speech I sing thy praises. Like a pressed man I walk the round of worldly duties. I am like a puppet that life sets in motion. I am resolved that my soul shall not be parted from thee' (2311). Clearly this is not a solution of the problem of life, though it shows

[1] 'Some *Abhangs* of Tukārām' F. C. M. Vol. I. No 3 September 1910, pp. 4–16

that Tukārām's thoughts were once approaching a solution, and we need not be surprised that he left the world for the life of the professed devotee. Of his sentiments then the following *abhang* speaks: 'I have grown heedless of the body; I care for one thing alone. Wealth and poverty are the same to me: I have weighed them and set them aside' (885). 'I stand outside the courtesies of life, the proceedings in which men display their pride and love of honour' (3451).

Let us note how he escaped from his slough of despond. 'I have come to know God by serving him' (566). We may take this as probably the profoundest truth that he utters, but Tukārām is perhaps too modest to repeat it often. He prefers to speak of God's generosity and condescension, of the flood of love that the worshipper feels to be poured into his soul, and of the 'ecstasy' that comes with it. To take a few sentences quite at random from one section headed 'triumphant happiness' where these are placed: 'I have found a sea of love, an inexhaustible flood, I have opened a treasure of spiritual knowledge, it diffuses the lustre of a million suns arisen in thy worshippers' souls. Unexpectedly, without an effort, I have heard the eternal secret, I have learned to know God. The very joy of peace and compassion is found in this joy that accompanies the knowledge of the being and knowing God' (573). And in this mood he speaks often as if no relapse was possible. 'I have crossed over: I have justified my confidence: I have spoken thy name: I have dismissed the world. I am tied to nothing now' (879). This mood was, however, far from abiding and would seem to have come mostly in 'gatherings of the Saints'. See chapter 9, section 12 and chapter 10, sections 6 and 8 where N. V. Tilak reminds us that such 'ecstasy' is not devotion, or salvation.

9. Changing Moods

There is an oscillation of view between a humble and a lofty view of himself. There are poems in which there is quite a note of self-esteem. 'A pebble may look beautiful till the diamond flashes forth; a lamp may look beautiful till the sun rises. Men may talk about saints till they have seen Tukā' (1422). Were these really his own words? Probably they were, but in any case they were not many. We may be sure that he speaks more in his habitual mood when he tells us how he despises himself if any feeling of self-complacency rises up in his mind. 'I have become skilful in my own conceit; I have given up faith for idle self-satisfaction' (351). And 'I dislike to hear my praises; when men extol me they weary my soul' (176). He knows his business better 'My chief duty is like a servant to forward my lord's purposes' (690).

He speaks much and no doubt with justice of his simplicity and sincerity. 'I utter fond and foolish words but they come straight from the core of my being' (3407). This remains perhaps the strongest impression that his character leaves upon us. Along with it we may place a passionate desire to save and serve mankind. There is no doubt about the horror with which he sees men 'running to hell'. He speaks of human wickedness with nothing short of horror and agony, and his language of indignant reproof is in marvellous contrast with the sweetness of persuasion with which he lays before them the bliss and rapture of the devotee's life. We may sometimes feel that he overdoes the language of mere rage and denunciation, especially when the poems of this type are collected together, but viewing the case in a just perspective we shall see that he did not rest satisfied as the censorious do with mere denunciation, but that he showed the way to something better, though sometimes in rough, and even coarse, terminology—on which coarseness see V. L. Bhāve, *M. Sār.*, p. 182.

10. Service for Others

An unselfish desire to raise the world around him is the noblest feature of Tukārām's character, and, breathing as it does from so many poems in one form or other, remains the final impression. On this question we are compelled to take a different view from that adopted by Dr. Macnicol in *Psalms of Marāṭhā Saints* (pp. 31–2) and by Dr. Farquhar in *An Outline of the Religious Literature of India* (p. 300): 'His own need and his own concerns absorb him,' says the former; 'it is his own religious life that occupies his soul,' says the latter. That Tukārām, however, had a true concern for others also is very manifest throughout the whole of Mahīpati's narrative, as will be seen from many incidents recorded in our chapter 4. There we see Tukārām spending his time helping anybody he finds in need. When we come to his autobiographical poems it is clear that for Tukārām religion does not mean a selfish concern for one's own soul or concentration on religious exercises only, for he speaks of 'wearing out his own body' by 'serving others'.[1] How emphatic a place this practical principle occupies even in his poems is shown by those classified by Fraser and Marāthe under the heading 'The Service of Others', a classification found in each of the three volumes, the following being samples from the first only. 'Whoso makes himself the friend of the oppressed, recognize him for a true saint, know that God dwells in him. He who takes the unprotected to his heart, Tukā says—how often shall I tell you?—he is the very image of the Divine?' (709). 'He who serves other creatures and shows them compassion, in him the supreme spirit dwells' (710). 'Merit

[1] *Abhang* 101, *F.* and *M.*, 1333 *I P.*

consists in service to others' (711). In 712 we have interesting examples of this practical benevolence in the lives of Kabīr, Nāmdev and Venkobā. 'Blessed in the world are the compassionate; their true home is Vaikuntha, but they have come here to serve mankind' (713). 'A benefactor knows not the difference between himself and others' (715). 'One whose mind is for ever unquiet and discontented, let me never meet such a man, he knows not the highest word of all, do good to others' (717). 'We should use our best endeavours for the afflicted' (720).

On this subject Mr. Pāngārkar has some excellent observations, particularly on pages 131–6 of his Marāthī biography of our poet-saint. He not only refers to the remarkable chapter 31 in Mahīpati's *Bhakta Līlāmṛta* which we have summarized in our own chapter 4, but he points out a striking *abhang* of Tukārām's own which Fraser and Marāthe have classified in their second volume under 'Peacefulness' and numbered 2200. In this *abhang* Tukārām propounds the problem: 'Are you in need of God?' and he supplies a twofold answer. 'The ideal method is to sing His praises with devotion, or with faith (*bhāva*)', but another method is: 'Do good to others, whether it be much or little'. (See also our Section on 'The Saints', Chapter 8, Section viii. 3, 'Their Service to Men'.

11. His Mission as a Preacher

Our last glimpse of Tukārām leaves him pictured in our memory as a preacher. In Mahīpati's pages we find him helping poor widows or working miracles, but his own portrait of himself is that of a preacher, though conscious of his unworthiness. His native equipment is small; he has little intelligence, he is wholly unlearned, he knows nothing of the Vedas. 'What knowledge have I? What authority have I?' (1134). But this question he answers—he bears a message, he is sealed with the seal of a mighty prince (70–71). He feels his language is childish and feeble, and all Tukārām can say is that God makes it sufficient to convey the message. Tukārām is but the measure that measures out the truth; 'the measure says, "I measure out all," yet its master fills it and lays it aside empty' (70). At other times, however, he seems to think his poems are powerful because they are *not* his own, because his master speaking through him inspires him with an eloquence not his own.' These are not my words, I am a hired messenger of Vithobā' (1420). He has a strong sense of the need for preaching and for good honest preachers. He denounces the professional orator who takes money for holding a *kīrtan*. Making terms and extorting money Tukārām always reprehends. The numerous poems on this topic are amusing and one gathers that religious imposters turned up in the Deccan as regularly as tramps in England or America. Like these gentlemen too they found their chief supporters among such women, as were impressed and indeed misled by their magic and false pretensions. They are often accused of over-eating—over-drinking not being a Hindū failing—and of smoking *bhāng* and of gratifying their lust with women. 'Their desires are set on shawls and pots and money' (1196). 'They shall not escape hell, says Tukā' (1195). And he adds in one place, 'If I have polluted my tongue in making these wretches ashamed of themselves, O purify me' (2028).

Inspiration is needed by the preacher. Tukārām is honest enough to admit that this rule has its exceptions: 'There are people who follow crooked paths and yet point out straight paths to others' (2398). But he does not dwell much on this paradox—indeed the subtlety of human nature is a thing that Hindū moralists hardly ever handle. He prefers to insist on the straightforward view that the teacher must be sincere. 'Matted hair and ashes are a scandal when the mind has neither patience nor forbearance' (1199). 'If God ceases to speak to a man, he too ought to be silent; Tukā says, People act very differently—when God has ceased to speak to them they go on talking *about* Him' (561). And the preacher must not spare his efforts. 'If a man stands up to preach and spares his energy who can measure his guilt?' (2525). The right conditions, however, being fulfilled, the preacher 'rescues others by the sweet perfume of his words'. But the listeners must do their part. Tukārām denounces with unsparing energy those who sleep while the speaker holds forth, those who talk and above all those who raise cavilling objections to the discourse. No doubt his patience was often tried. 'Such people sink themselves and destroy the ship of salvation.'

Our study of the biographical and autobiographical facts of Tukārām's life having brought him before us as a preacher, we are now to learn what his themes are, first by noting his attitude to contemporary Hinduism (chapter 6), second by enquiring in which directions he may be influencing men to-day (chapter 7), and third by seeking to discover what may be regarded as his religious tenets (chapter 8).

THE HYPOCRITE *

Possessed with devils they grow long their hair
No saints are they, nor trace of God they bear.
They tell of omens to a gaping crowd.
Rogues are they, Tukā says ; Govind's [1] not there

WITHOUT AND WITHIN *

Soon as the season of Sinhasth [2] comes in,
The barber and the priest—what wealth they win !
Thousands of sins may lurk within his heart,
If only he will shave his head and chin !

What is shaved off is gone, but what else, pray ?
What sign that sin is gone ? His evil way
Is still unchanged. Yea, without faith and love
All is but vanity, I, Tukā, say.

DROWNING MEN *

For men's saving I make known
These devices—this alone
My desire.

Can my heart unmovèd be
When before my eyes I see
Drowning men ?

LOVE FINDS OUT GOD *

Thy nature is beyond the grasp
Of human speech or thought
So love I've made the measure-rod,
By which I can be taught

Thus with the measure-rod of love
I mete the Infinite
In sooth, to measure him there is
None other means so fit

Not *Yoga's* power, nor sacrifice,
Nor fierce austerity,
Nor yet the strength of thought profound
Hath ever found out thee.

And so, says Tukā, graciously,
Oh Keśav,[3] take, we pray,
Love's service that with simple hearts
Before thy feet we lay

1 *Govind* = Kṛṣṇa. 2 see pp 47, 50 of this book, 3 *Keśav* = Kṛṣna.

* Translated from Tukārām, *P M S* , pp. 90, 88, 73.

Chapter VI

Tukaram's Attitude to Conventional Hinduism

This chapter is not intended to be a criticism either of Hinduism or of Tukārām but an enquiry into the relation of the latter to the former. On every side Tukārām found himself surrounded by the conventional beliefs and practices of Hinduism. The question presents itself: Which of these did he adopt or sanction? How far was he a reformer? It is a question not a little difficult to approach or solve, for inconsistencies and contradictions of thought appear on well-nigh every page. So true is this that very different schools of interpretation claim him as favouring their views. What we need to remember throughout is that he was a poet with a poet's varying moods and that he was also a Hindū, the Hindū's ability to accept positions which to others are mutually exclusive being the constant despair of the Western enquirer.

1. Tukaram's Idolatry

No better illustration can be found of the folly of trying to reduce Tukārām's attitude to one of logical consistency than his relation to the all-surrounding idolatry of his day. The lofty theistic aspirations of the small but influential community of the Prārthanā Samājists and the sordid—though sincere—idolatry of the vast multitude of Tukārām's Deccan followers to-day are both able to turn to his pages for confirmation of their respective tenets. His irreconcilable views on the subject of idolatry are accounted for by the fact that the worship of Viṭhobā, the idol at Paṇḍharpūr, with all its traditional ceremonies, Tukārām regarded as sanctioned by time and custom on the one hand and by the wish of the god on the other. At the same time he desired something very much higher than the ceremonies of the central shrine at Paṇḍharpūr, something much more inward and spiritual, but he nowhere condemns those particular ceremonies and he believes that they make some sort of impression on the divine nature.

This raises the whole question of images or idols in worship, a feature of Hinduism which has naturally struck the world but has received very little scientific attention either from the Hindū theologians or others. A few words are therefore advisable on the views and practices of Hindūs. Not long ago it was unnecessary to distinguish between the educated and uneducated in this matter, though educated men, one may suppose, cannot ever have looked on images or idols with the simple unquestioning faith of the masses.

With the Hindū masses the use of an image or idol is the natural way of approaching the divine, and for this purpose the Hindū view is that the image must be one definitely consecrated to the god and accepted by the god as a place of residence. The consecration ceremony must always be performed by a Brāhman and is called *Prānapratiṣṭhā*. This important ceremony was defined nearly a century ago by the great reformer Rām Mohun Roy in words reproduced by *The Indian Messenger*, the Sādhāran Brāhmo Samāj organ of Calcutta, which we give below. Rām Mohun Roy was refuting the position of those Hindūs who maintain that an image or idol is merely a lifeless symbol meant to remind the worshippers of the One Living God. As proof that the worshippers do not take this view the reformer stated: 'Whatever Hindū purchases an idol in the market, or constructs one with his own hands, or has one made under his superintendence, it is his invariable practice to perform certain ceremonies called *Prāṇapratiṣṭha* or the endowment of animation, by which he believes that its nature is changed from that of the mere materials of which it is formed, and that it acquires not only life but supernatural powers. Shortly afterwards, if the idol be of the masculine gender, he marries it to a feminine one with no less pomp and magnificence than he celebrates the nuptials of his own children. The mysterious process is now complete and the god and goddess are esteemed the arbiters of his destiny, and continually receive his most ardent adoration. At the same time the worshipper of the images ascribes to them at once the opposite natures of human and superhuman beings. In attention to their supposed wants as living beings, he is seen feeding them.'[1] If it be asked what is the result of such a ceremony, the Hindū reply is that a portion of the god's own nature is infused into the image. It is then possible for the worshipper to meet the god by adoring the image or idol. The god once present is always present, unless the image somehow gets polluted, in which case the god forsakes it, though it can be reconsecrated.

What is Tukārām's view? The only way to answer the question is briefly to review the facts. How utterly devoted to Kṛiṣṇa was the saint of Dehū is indicated by such *abhangs* as number 245 in Fraser and Marāthe's translation: 'Kṛiṣṇa is my mother and father, sister, brother, aunt and uncle. Kṛiṣṇa is my teacher and boat of salvation. He bears me over the river of the world. Kṛiṣṇa is my own mind, my family, and my bosom friend. Tukā says, Holy

[1] Quoted from *The Indian Messenger* in *Dnyānodaya*, April 10, 1919. On this 'life-implanting ceremony' see further Mrs. Sinclair Stevenson, *The Rites of The Twice Born*, the section entitled 'Consecration of Idols', pp. 409–15.

Kṛiṣṇa is my place of repose; I am resolved I will not be parted from him.' With questions affecting Kriṣṇa's historicity, his relation to Vishnu, etc., we have dealt on pages 29–33.[1] That Tukārām's mind dwelt sometimes on the amorous character of his god is clear from the 29 pages of *abhangs* in Fraser and Marāthe given up to this unsavoury topic, on which there is no need to add to what we have said on pages 31–33. A point of interest arising out of Tukārām's relation to Krisna is the view held by some that for a part of his life it was the idol-form of the *child* Kṛiṣṇa that he worshipped, one proof of this being the dream he had after the recovery of his poems from the river, in which dream Kṛiṣṇa appeared in the guise of a child,[2] and that there was a time when Tukārām viewed the Pandharpūr idol as being the image of Kriṣṇa's wife Rukmini, exactly at what stages of his life he held these respective views it being impossible to say, since there is little or no available historical evidence[3].

It is in the poet's relation to Viṭhobā, Krisṇa's 'incarnation' at Paṇḍharpūr, a relation alternating between rapture and despair, that his devotion to Kriṣna is chiefly manifested. For the rapture see *abhang* 136 which we quote only in part: 'Vitthal is our life, our ancestral god, treasure, family and spirit; Viṭthal is the darling of our hearts, our gracious and tender master, the embodiment of our love; our father, mother, uncle, brother, sister; apart from him we care not for our family; Tukā says, Now we have none but him'. For the despair see chap. 9, sect. 6 and chap. 10, sect. 5 To understand this relation of Tukārām to Vithobā and the development which led to Vithobā's exalted position at Paṇḍharpūr, see the various sections on Viṭhobā in chapter 2. Like most other Vaishṇavas or devotees of the *Bhāgavata* religion of Mahārāshtra, Tukārām recognized also the equality, if not the oneness, of Vishṇu and Śiva, on which see page 27 above and section 4 in this chapter on 'Śiva and Viṭhobā'.

In Tukārām's pantheon other deities were included as the objects of his praise and homage, for the *Bhāgavata* religion or Vaishṇavism of Paṇḍharpūr recognized a plurality of gods; see chapter 3, section 6. It will suffice here to refer by number only to the *abhangs* employing stories from mythology in *F. and M.* vol. 2. Those numbered 1281–94 are written in praise of Rāmā, 1295–6 in praise of Gaṇpati (or Ganesha), 1297-1300 in praise of Mārutī (or Hanumān, or Hanumant), while 1301–5 contain the amorous 'complaints' of Rādhā, Satyabhāma and Sīta. In *abhang* 1462 we learn that he offered worship some time or other to the Ganges, the Bhāgirathi there referred to as 'cleansing from sin' being a sacred tributary. Yet other deities are mentioned in 147, while in

1 See further chap 10, sect. 6, especially Pandit Tattvabhushan's view regarding Vishṇu.

2 See footnote 2, p 97.

3 Dr. P. R. Bhandarkar, *Navayuga*, March 1921, pp. 145–9, 159.

991 'the evil age' has for one of its characteristics that a man 'does not revere his village god'.

Of course it is possible, in seeking to harmonize the above facts with the lofty spiritual aspirations and monotheistic utterances of the preceding chapter (see pp. 134–144) and of our ninth chapter, to adopt the 'easy' solution offered by the Prārthanā Samājists as expressed by Dr. P. R. Bhandarkar: 'It is evident that at an early stage of his religious life Tukārām was a pure idolator and a polytheist, but it is easy to trace his progress to monotheism.'[1] It would be an inviting solution of a perplexing problem could we accept it, but formidable difficulties of chronology and the lack of a critical edition of Tukārām's writings present an insurmountable obstacle. It is doubtless allowable to use in a monotheistic sense for devotional purposes, as does the Prārthanā Samāj, *abhaṅgs* which have no specific mention of Kṛṣṇa or Viṭhobā, e. g., 'make this your gain, the contemplation of God, with a mind centred in Him' (953), though it is probable that even in such *abhaṅgs* the *bhakta's* thought was of his beloved Viṭhobā at Pandharī.

Mr. L. R. Pāngārkar categorically affirms, without any qualification, that Tukārām was an idolator outright to the very end, and he points out that in the *sanad* or government grant of property to Tukārām's son Narāyanrao at Dehū there is the definite statement that 'Tukārām the *Gosāvī*[2] used to do *pūjā* to the god with his own hand.'[3] In defending the lifelong idolatry of his hero, Mr. Pāngārkar observes that the reason idolatry is not understood by those not practising it is that its secret lies in the complete identification of the worshipper and his god. The scathing reply of the Prārthanā Samājist compares idolatry to a carriage meant for conveying the spiritually lame, the carriage to be cast aside when its invalid occupants are able to walk, otherwise they become 'confirmed invalids', who when they see anyone else moving along without any such adventitious aid infer that the carriage is hidden away in some mysterious fashion.[4] Idolatry and its evil effects have indeed no more scathing critics anywhere than the leaders of the Indian Samājes. As far as Tukārām's own attitude is concerned we are probably quite safe in concluding, despite the additional considerations given later in this section, that he was probably never quite as denunciatory of idolatry as was his predecessor Nāmdev, on whom see pp. 38–9. In the picturesque metaphor applied to him, Nāmdev burnt all his boats, (i.e., his idols), hitherto used by him in crossing life's river, while the saint of Dehū never took so daring a step.[5] Nevertheless, as we observed on page

1 *Two Masters Jesus and Tukārām*, pp 32–3, the same view appearing from the same writer in *Navayuga*, March, 1921, p. 152.
2 See p. 6, note 2, for a definition.
3 *S T. C*, pp 332–4
4 Dr. P.R Bhandarkar, *Navayuga*, March 1921, pp 152–3.
5 *Ibid*, p. 162.

39, even Nāmdev continued idolatrous practices, his denunciations notwithstanding.

Tukārām's prevailing view, therefore, as far as his poems show, is that God is really present in the image or idol and he gives reasons why he consents to this manifestation: 'He assumes name and form to protect devotion, to show how God and worship are related' (2603). Without some bodily aspect, says our poet, the moral mind cannot grasp God: 'Give something visible to pray to, let someone fulfil my helpless desires' (1153). In another place he describes himself as 'supported by the beauty of God's visible form' (2036). This is expressed in a fanciful poem where the bodily members all demand that Vithobā shall be made accessible to them: 'My mouth sings thy attributes, my ears listen; but, say the other members, such is not our case; the sight of thee alone can gratify all, whereby each shall receive his own portion' (3143). It is to comply with this longing that Vithobā takes form, but Tukārām goes on to add that Viṭhobā is not really present unless the worshipper brings faith with him: 'It was our faith that brought about your full incarnation' (288); 'the essence of the matter is faith; it is a matter of experience that stones become gods' (2605); 'men give the name "god" to a stone and faith in it can save a man' (3203); 'if a stone be placed on the highest seat it should not be treated as a common stone' (907); 'by singing his praises we have induced the formless to assume a form' (282).[1]

There are various passages showing that Tukārām was alive to the mysteries, perplexities and inconsistencies of this view and those perplexities and inconsistencies lead to moments when Tukārām's faith is so much shaken that it almost vanishes: 'we have formed a Vishnu of stone but the stone is not Vishṇu; the worship of Vishṇu is offered to Vishṇu, the stone remains in the form of a stone' (1144). Commenting on this last *abhaṅg*, the Marāthī grammarian Ganpatrao R. Navalkar, Fellow of Bombay University, observes: 'The mind is so constituted that it cannot separate in worship, the image from the object it represents, and the image itself becomes a god and receives the worship.'[2] Sir R. G. Bhandarkar, writing out of a full and sympathetic understanding of Tukārām's whole position, describes him as 'a devotee only of Vithobā of Pandharpūr and a monotheist in this sense', adding that 'though he worshipped the idol at the place, still he had always before his mind's eye the great Lord of the universe.'[3]

It is interesting to note how Tukārām recoiled from the inconsistencies we have indicated and how he retained his own hold on the Divine Personality in 'an atmosphere of idolatry'. Though God was worshipped idolatrously by all the people in Tukārām's

1 See also L. R. Pāngārkar, *S.T.C.* p. 130.
2 *Tukārām the Mahārāshtrian Poet and Saint*, p. 10.
3 *V.S.M.R.S.*, p. 95.

environment, yet the following threefold position appears from a careful survey of his poems on this subject:

(1) No special image of God is necessary: 'If you mean to worship Him then conceive Him as the Universe, it is vain to limit Him to one spot' (224); 'my spirit is at peace because I see thee in every quarry' (2588), 'wherever I look, there I see God—give me such faith as this' (3117); 'one whose god is a stone will reap fruits like his faith; preserve your faith; you will prove the sweetness of it, though hindrances arise to part you from it; God is secured by faith' (2598).

(2) The true image of God is His faithful people: 'In holy places we find water and an image of stone, but in the society of good men we have the actual presence of God' (926); 'it is the saints who are gods; images of stone are pretences' (2606); 'through love to men he dances and sings in the person of the saints' (287).

(3) Mere idolatry, accompanied by external rites without inward religion, he condemns outright: 'Why do they worship stone and brass and the eight metals? The wretches have no faith. 'Tis faith that moves us and is fitly called the means of salvation. What avails your rosary? 'Tis only pleasures of the senses you count on it. What will you do with your learned tongue? It will make you proud and conceited. What will you do with your skill in song, as long as your will is foul within you? If you serve God without faith, says Tukā, how will you become fit for Him?' (2597) 'Diversity of gods is an offspring of our own thoughts; there is no truth in it; God is one' (184); 'these gods and goddesses smeared with vermilion—who could worship such masters? . . . I have known what it is to wait on them; it is in truth a base and vile inclination; . . . only beggars call such things gods' (1169).

(4) The seemingly insoluble riddle presented by the various contradictory elements in Tukārām's belief as regards idols is perhaps brought nearest to a solution by an aspect well brought out by Prof. W. B. Patwardhan who shows that Vithobā—how, we are not told—had come to embody for Tukārām the conception of God as a Mother, which conception solved for Tukārām himself most problems about the Divine Being. 'This phase of Tukārām's faith,' says Professor Patwardhan, 'is particularly remarkable since it emphasizes the personality of God. To those who have never been idolators it is perhaps a difficult task to conceive an impersonal God in a personal aspect. But to Tukārām it was an easy thing. He had been brought up in an atmosphere of idolatry and the idol at Paṇḍharī was to him for a long time invested with a glory and splendour and grace nowhere else realized on earth, endowed with a presence and power that could be visualized only in moments of rare bliss. In course of time the ecstatic frenzy of Tukārām rose to a height wherein the idol at Paṇḍharī ceased to be an idol; the dead material image was

nowhere; and he was wrapped up in a personal presence of Viṭṭhal like that of his mother, only with a halo of glory around her. All the devotional raptures of Tukārām's poetry are due, perhaps, to this personal element in the conception of God's Motherhood."[1]

That God is our Mother is an Old Testament view (Isaiah 66: 13), just as His Fatherhood is the note of emphasis in New Testament teaching. On the Divine Motherhood it has been pointed out that 'the worship of the Mothers' has often been among the grossest forms of popular superstition. 'How far these associations mingle with Tukārām's fervent expressions of affection we cannot say, but there is little doubt that even on his lips it is an imperfectly moralised relationship.'[2] Nevertheless it is at this point that Tukārām's idea of God approximates most closely to the Christian conception; see chap. 8, II, 3.

It is impossible to leave this subject of idolatry without observing the unfortunate consequences of Tukārām's ambiguity on so vital a matter. It must be regarded as one of the saddest aspects of the popular Hinduism of Mahārāshtra, that there are millions of Marāthī-speaking Hindūs who, forgetting the lofty principles of the saint of Dehū, follow only the idolatrous part of his example, viz., his worship of the idol Viṭhobā at Paṇḍharpūr, while those who follow the nobler part of his example, viz., his earnest quest for inward purity revealed in many of his *abhaṅgs*, are probably to be counted only by thousands, possibly hundreds. It would gratify us to be shown that this diagnosis of ours is not correct and to learn that more people follow Tukārām the *bhakta* than Tukārām the idolator, but all our information points the other way.[3]

To Tukārām's ambiguity is probably due another result. During 1920 a curious development took place in the Bombay Prārthanā Samāj on the question of 'idolatrous rites', confirming one item in Dr. Farquhar's description of the Samāj[4] to the effect that there are some members who 'have banished neither idolatry nor caste from their homes'. At a meeting held in June 1920 the two following resolutions were proposed with regard to this: '(1) That at the time of becoming a member each applicant be required to declare: "I undertake to perform all domestic and other ceremonies according to theistic rites, discarding idolatry." The resolution was carried, 19 members voting for it and 12 against it. The second resolution was: (2) That the following rule be added to the rules of the Samāj: "Any member who performs a domestic or any other ceremony with idolatrous rites or worships

[1] *I. I.*, April, 1912, pp. 25–26.
[2] Macnicol, 'Indian Poetry of Devotion,' *The Hibbert Journal*, October 1917, pp. 74–88.
[3] The last twelve lines we wrote in the *Dnyānodaya* of July 1, 1920 and we have not yet (August 1921) seen them controverted.
[4] *E. R. E.*, vol. 9, Art, *Prārthanā Samāj*, p. 151–2.

any idols while performing such rites will *ipso facto* cease to be a member of the Bombay Prārthanā Samāj." The resolution was lost, only 7 members voting for it.'[1]

2. Holy Places, Holy Rivers, Holy Seasons

Another feature always conspicuous in Hinduism is the belief in pilgrimages to holy places,[2] lustrations in holy rivers and strict observance of holy seasons. The belief holds that the water of holy places can wash away sin, and it leads to vast and constant pilgrimages to such places. The sense of sin is no doubt present[3] in Hinduism, but it is mostly identified with ceremonial uncleanness, though often it has been purely moral. The whole subject raises one of the most intricate problems that the moralist can attempt. On this subject as with regard to images, Tukārām halts between two opinions. In several places he maintains the value of pilgrimages. He mentions among unacceptable people the man whose 'feet move not to holy places, and who says, Why should I spend money on them?' (1043) Several times he mentions the Ganges with respect: 'He who attributes impurity to the Ganges and to fire he is a miscreant' (1007); 'dwell alone and bathe in Ganges water, worship god and walk round the *tulśī*' (731); 'fail not to visit holy places' (722). On the other hand: 'If I go on a pilgrimage, my mind goes not with me' (615). He even condemns those who 'pride themselves on pilgrimages and austerities, they glory in a thing unreal; they are sunk in the pit of rules and prohibitions' (2531). God is present to the faithful everywhere: 'We may go to all countries: thou art ready for us' (1714) 'A man's own parents are his true *Kāśī* (Benares); he need not visit any holy place' (2230). 'Being now under the inspiration of God I need not go anywhere' (3165). 'Ill-starred is he who sets off on the path to a holy place, the very place he reaches becomes an obstacle to him' (3195). Besides his deprecation of religious austerities noticed above, we may add one interesting passage; 'Do not put an end to your own life: he knows not his own true good who throws away a treasure lodged within him' (2232).

It is fairly certain that he always observed the *ekādashī*[4] fast in spite of his objection to fixed seasons: 'He who observes not the 11th day know him for a living corpse' (1054).

Sometimes he uses language condemning unsparingly rites and practices which are merely external, proclaiming plainly their utter inability to wash away the sins of the heart, as for example in his *abhang* numbered 4733 in Tukārām Tātyā's edition

1 *Subodh Patrikā*, June 27, 1920 and *Dnyānodaya*, July 1, 1920.
2 See pp. 45–9.
3 See Chap 3 especially, pp. 49–50, also pp. 135–7, and Chap. 9, sect 7.
4 For definition see p. 56.

and translated by Sir R. G. Bhandarkar as follows: 'What hast thou done by going to a holy river? Thou hast only outwardly washed thy skin. In what way has the interior been purified? By this thou hast only added a feather to thy cap (literally, prepared a decoration for thyself). Even if the bitter *vrandāvana* fruit is coated with sugar, the settled quality of the interior (bitterness) is in no way lessened. If peace, forgiveness and sympathy do not come in, why should you take any trouble?'[1]

3. His Idea of Pandharpur and its Practices

Much that Tukārām saw at Paṇḍharpūr must have vexed his soul or at best must have seemed to him wasted devotion. The veneration of the image of the river, the red paint bestowed on the great Hanumān, all the homage to the minor deities represented on the river banks—all this lies probably outside the system which he personally regarded as fundamental. But he does not attack it, or he only does so when he sees anything definitely degrading or leading to immoral practices. His denunciations indeed are sometimes so fierce as to pass over into coarseness, on which we need add nothing to what Mr. V. L. Bhāve has said in his Marāṭhī work on the History of Marāthī Literature, page 182. Among his *abhaṅgs* are those denouncing the worship of powers that lick up bloody sacrifices or of powers that offer magical accomplishments. We have also constant denunciation of all religious impostors, among whom are the sleek rogues who cheat women, the pretenders to magical powers and the disputatious self-important pundits. These and their victims are vigorously denounced, sometimes in language of incisive sarcasm.

Paṇḍharpūr has been dealt with in an earlier chapter, but we may note here the difference between the ancient view of Paṇḍharpūr and that characteristic of Tukārām. To him the river appears nothing like as important. He seldom recommends the rite of bathing in it: 'Let your bathing be in the Chandrabhāgā' (1634) is a kind of advice very rare. He often, however, speaks of the joys of the pebbly shore, but they are the joys of the *kīrtans* held there in praise of Viṭhobā. We need not doubt that when he went to Paṇḍharī he bathed in the stream, for that would be part of the routine of the visit though in all probability he rejected the idea of the waters of the Bhīmā having any power to cleanse from sin (see pages 56-9, 61-2). But there can be few cities on earth whose praises or merit-imparting values have been more sweetly chanted than those of this city on the banks of the Bhīmā: 'Be a pilgrim and gaze on Paṇḍharī; why need you practise other means of salvation' (154); 'no guilt enters ten miles of

[1] See also the paragraph on 'Self-Accusations of Deccan Pilgrims', pp 49-50.

its circuit' (157); 'you can buy liberation[1] there for nothing, for nobody wants it' (159); 'when I see the spire of the temple, weariness, sleep and hunger will vanish' (1627); 'happy are they who dwell in Paṇḍharī; they have no pride of caste' (see pages 54–5), 'they are all emancipated souls' (2827); 'the spirit which none could control was nailed by Pundalīka to this spot' (2836).

Paṇḍharī, in his view, owes no sanctity to any such source as a triumph of the *devas* (gods) over the *asuras* (demons): it is holy as the spot where Vishnu stands 'incarnate' before his worshippers. This 'incarnation' Tukārām does not connect with the story of Rukminī's bad temper or Kriṣṇa's search for her. Such an explanation he would probably have rejected as paltry and absurd. Allegory is not in Tukārām's line nor is controversy, and these old legends he neither explains nor controverts. He has his own views and he remains content to place these before the world. To him the 'incarnation' is vouchsafed to Pundalīka in reward of his filial love, which somehow—Tukārām never says how—is identified with the figure on the brick.

4. Relation Between Shiva and Vithoba

One of the most important aspects of Vaishṇavism or the *Bhāgavata* religion in Mahārāshtra is the equality, possibly oneness, of Vishṇu and Śiva referred to on page 27 and in other places in this book, and in order to understand Tukārām's attitude on some questions, particularly his attitude towards Śiva and the Śaivites, we need briefly to dip into the far past. Inscriptions indicate that in the 12th century Paṇḍharpūr bore two names—Paundarīka Kseṭra and Pāṇḍuraṅgpūr or city of Pāṇḍuraṅg, the local name of Śiva. The most important temple on the sandy beach is that of Pundalīka (on whom and on 'the name Viṭhobā', see pages 41–3 and 48), in which temple is worshipped the Śiva-*liṅga*. How Viṭhobā or Viṭṭhal came to receive the Śaivite name of Pāṇḍuraṅg it is impossible to say, save to suggest that it possibly represents one of the many efforts of the time to unite Śiva and Vishṇu, Pundalīka being the agent in this particular effort. This is the line on which Dr. P. R. Bhandarkar attempts a solution and he suggests that as the name Viṭṭhal may be a Kanarese form of the Sanskrit Vishṇu, and as the worship of Rakhumāī (Kṛiṣṇa's wife) followed on that of Viṭṭhal, therefore the worship of Kṛiṣṇa and Rukminī must have been brought from South India where an inscription of the 10th century shows this worship to have been prevalent, confirmatory evidence being supplied by the fact that though the outward garb of Rukminī at Paṇḍharpūr is Marāṭhā in character, yet that carved on her image is undoubtedly of a South

[1] On this important word see chapter 8, part IV, section 1.

THE 'TĀKPIṬHYĀ' (IMITATION) VIṬHOBĀ AT PAṆḌHARPŪR

Indian pattern. This line of reasoning would appear to be supported by an *abhang* of Dnyāneshwar indicating that Viṭṭhal and its worship came from the Cārnatic, while another of Nivrittināth's affirms that Pundalīka 'brought Śiva with Vishṇu to Paṇḍharī',[1] a joint-worship very ancient and images of which belonging to the 8th and 9th centuries are found in various parts of India. The present image, however, is that of Vishṇu only, the severe persecution during the Mohammedan invasions, as well as other reasons, necessitating the removal of the original image which never returned.[2] A popular tale runs to the effect that the present image is the original one, stolen by some marauding king and brought back by Pundalīka at Viṭhobā's command in a dream.

These facts, taken along with others affecting the *Bhāgavata* religion of Mahārāshtra (see page 27), may help us to understand both Tukārām's recognition of Śiva and the paucity of his references to the subject: 'I love the town of Paṇḍharī, . . . the *liṅga* and Pundalīka' (2826). No need therefore, in light of the above considerations, to conclude as Fraser and Marāthe did on page 333 of vol. 3, English translations, that 'the mention of the *liṅga* is unparalleled in Tukā and suggests that this *abhaṅg* is spurious'. That it is not unparalleled, indeed, *abhang* 1579 in the *Indu Prakāsh* edition shows: 'Having worshipped the *liṅga*, Tukā stands with folded hands and makes a request to which, O Śiva! kindly pay attention: Let my mind remain always at thy feet'. And similarly, 2484 in *F. and M.*'s own translation, where in his picture of the mean man, Tukārām says 'he never dreams of worshipping the village *liṅga*'. For though the original image representing the Hari-Hara worship of Vishṇu-Śiva may not have returned, yet the *liṅga* is still present in Paṇḍharpūr, and not in Pundalīka's temple only. The tope-like crown on the head of Viṭhobā—see page 27 and the picture opposite page 53—clearly symbolizes the presence of Śiva worshipped along with the 'incarnation' of Kṛiṣṇa. That this tope-like crown is the Siva-*liṅga* is accepted as 'unquestionable'[3] by some scholars. We would humbly suggest to the latter that it is worthy of investigation whether the present one may not be the original image after all[4] and whether the mark of Śiva on Viṭhobā's head may not be what Nivṛittināth refers to in his *abhaṅg*.

It is in light of these considerations that we are to interpret Tukārām's attitude towards Śiva and the Śaivites. He often uses the common joint form of the names Hara and Hari, a feature of

1 Nivrittināth's *abhaṅg* translated reads: 'None can describe the good fortune of Pundalīka who brought Śiva along with Vishṇu to Paṇḍharī on the banks of the Bhīmā.'

2 Dr. P. R. Bhandarkar, *Navayuga*, March 1921, pp. 155-9, 168d.

3 This is Mr. L. R. Pāṅgārkar's verdict in a personal communication to us dated Feb. 1, 1921 in which, besides Nivṛittināth's *abhaṅg*, he quotes also in support a 'well-known verse' from the *Manobodh* of Rāmdās.

4 'Without prejudice' to the 'new image' theory on pp. 60 in our chap. 3.

the *Bhāgavata* religion of these parts, the former being of course a name of Mahādev or Śiva, while the latter refers to Kṛṣṇa. There are, it is true, one or two passages in Tukārām where the worship of Śiva is discountenanced, but we cannot feel sure they are genuine, for in one of the most popular of his *abhangs* Tukārām observes: 'Śiva is made of mud, but the mud itself continues to be called mud, and Śiva alone receives the worship, mind turning to mind'—see Fraser and Marāthe (1144) for another translation. In one place, indeed, Tukārām bids us 'raise no question whether Hara or Hari (i.e., Śiva and Vishnu) be different; one resides in the other as sweetness resides in sugar; . . . it is but a *vilāntī* that marks the difference' (176), the *vilāntī* being the minute Marāthī sign distinguishing between two particular vowels.

5. Shakta Worship, Sati, Brahmans

On the other hand we need not doubt that he is quite fairly represented in the attacks on *śākta* worship. This, as is well known, is a form of worship of the female energy of Śiva. Its details are repulsive, and the *śākta* meetings often appear to end in nothing but licence and gratification of any sensual passion that presents itself. Dr. Farquhar points out that the literature of the *śākta* sects shows 'some' of them have 'foul, gruesome and degrading practices.'[1] The extent of its prevalence in India is difficult to estimate, for it comes to light unexpectedly. In this matter Tukārām departs from his usual rule of not criticising his neighbours and he attacks *śākta* worship in language of the most exasperating hostility.

Passing on to the field of morals one may note with interest certain practices which Tukārām leaves quite unassailed. One is *satī*, although even as far back as the 7th century A.D. we hear a note of protest against *satī* in a well-known passage in the *Kādambarī* of Bāṇa Bhaṭṭa, a work regarded as the best extant prose in Sanskrit literature. Tukārām refers more than once to the rite as an example of fortitude. He commends the woman who walks firmly to the pyre and speaks of the holy joy which she feels in the act. But it does not occur to him that social pressure may drive women to it, that it is a form of cruelty, and that after all it is an undesirable way of testifying to faithful love. He seems to feel towards the rite just as an orthodox Hindū of those days felt, that it was a commendable piece of devotion.

There is no hostile tone in his poems towards Brāhmans. Passages even occur in which men are censured for not freely supporting them: 'We should pay reverence to sages and Brāhmans; we should not accept it ourselves' (2621). Here is his description

[1] *O. R. L. I.*, p. 167.

of a worldly man: 'To support a cow never enters into his thoughts; he never says, Let me bathe the feet of the Brāhmans' (3605). 'He who never worships holy men, visits no holy spot, he is a dowry of hell' (1066). He even goes so far as to say: 'Should a Brāhman lose all his attributes, still, says Tukā, he is supreme in the three worlds' (3352b). There are passages, however, in which Brāhmans who neglect their duties are censured. How Tukārām reverenced Brāhmans has already been made clear by several stories in his biography (see pp. 83, 93, 96-9).

We may note, also, that he has no belief in any magical or mystic power of Brāhmans. There is for instance no reference to their recognized right or privilege to consecrate an image, described earlier (p. 148) in this chapter. And in general Tukārām shows no leaning towards the occult. Of omens he says: 'All the good omens I recognise are the feet of Hari in the heart' (2254). So too of auspicious moments: 'You need not seek the proper moment for a good deed, an unsought time is the best for it' (2224); 'charms are impracticable, likewise acts and seasons prescribed' (263) He does occasionally mention mystic powers but in so slight a manner that their mention appears to be little more than a figure of speech.

6. Cows, Vedas, Puranas, Ceremonies

From several passages we see that he shared the feeling of his country about cows: 'He alone will reach the highest life, who is compassionate towards all creatures, a protector of cows, who supplies them with water when they are thirsty in the wilderness' (2313). But there appears no definite statement showing he believed that the excreta of the animal have the power to cleanse mankind from sin, a belief well-nigh universal among Hindūs.

Passages about the Vedas, like those on other subjects, fall into two divisions: 'Study the Vedas before you sing the attributes of Hari' (2620); 'Tukā looks into the arts which the Vedas teach and speaks by the favouring grace of Viṭṭhal' (527). It is uncertain if this means that Tukārām had read the Vedas or that he considered Vitthal had spared him this labour by revealing their meaning to him, but in any case it is a passage upholding their value as authorities. On the other hand Tukārām points out that the Vedas are unintelligible: 'Teachers themselves do not understand the Vedas' (265). He occasionally speaks slightingly of them and professes his own independence of this source of enlightenment: 'We waste our time over the dots and dashes of the Vedas' (1227). Finally: 'The recitation of the Vedas cannot equal this name, nor pilgrimages to *Prayāga* (Allahabad) and *Kāśi* (Benares) and all holy places' (1740); 'his name is more glorious than the Vedas' (281). Mr. L. R. Pāngārkar[1] has given references to the poems showing, first, that Tukārām felt that he had no authority himself to read the Vedas, in accordance with the view common among Hindūs that no one but Brāhmans may study the sacred books; second, that his knowledge of them he owed to reading predecessors like Dnyāneshwar; and third, that while he accepts the Vedas, the Purānas, and the words of the 'Saints' as authorities, he yet always despises those whose attitude towards these has degenerated into one of mere formalism.[2]

Here we should note that Tukārām is fully familiar with all the old *purāṇic* legends about Vishnu and Hari and accepts them all. He is fond of mentioning one after another the marvellous deeds of the 'incarnations', especially those which show the condescending kindness of God.

The general impression to which the poems lead is that we have in Tukārām a man naturally and by reflection averse to ceremonies, averse to magic and averse to everything that interposes even with the offer of aid between man and his Maker. We see him advancing with halting steps towards clear views in these matters and to watch him is an occupation of profound interest.

7. Tukaram No Reformer

Great caution is to be observed in reading him and drawing conclusions. Our uncertainty about the text prevents us from being sure on many individual points affecting his attitude to the Hinduism of his time. Since we know nothing of the chronological order of the poems we must avoid drawing conclusions as to the development of his views. It is always possible that he kept to the last some sympathy with ideas really hostile to his own and even expressed it.

We should greatly misconceive Tukārām if we thought of him as a reformer setting out to attack abuses. He is primarily a servant of Vithobā, whose object is to sing his master's praises. It is only by accident that he is led into conflict with other people's creeds or religious practices: 'You need not abandon your own order of life or the pious ways which have grown up in your own family' (1172).

Certainly there are things which he does attack. First, pretences of magical power: 'To procure intelligence of past. present or future is an achievement of worthless people' (1163). Then all *śākta* worship. Also the worship of various greedy menacing deities. Some of these gods are denounced as 'stone gods:' 'They offer vows to their stone gods' (3566). But a passage

[1] *S. T. C.*, chap. 6, pp. 148–155.
[2] See further, chap. 8, II, 4.

of this type must not be mistaken for a denunciation of idolatry. Tukārām only means that the images of these people not being consecrated by the needful faith remain but stone.

Writing of Tukārām and other Marāthā *bhaktas* the late Rev. N. V. Tilak said: 'They are considered as Hindū religious reformers by some, but in my humble opinion they were sages who had hardly any idea of reforming Hinduism on national lines, but who had lofty visions, were personally true to them, enjoyed them, tenaciously treasured them and thus became examples and *gurus* to their co-religionists. They caused a powerful religious revival among the Hindūs, and thus gave Hinduism a new impetus which preserved it from the fearful downfall which was anticipated in those days.'

Prof. Patwardhan has attempted to show that this feature, what we may call, for want of a better term, Tukārām's 'easy-going tolerance,' is characteristic both of the spirit of *bhakti* and of the Marāthā people. 'The fact is,' he says, 'that the saints of the *bhakti* school were of a pacific turn of mind and did not love controversy or contest. I may go still further and say that is the frame of mind of Mahārāshtra. The people of Mahārāshtra are imbued with the spirit of conciliation, of quiet resignation and catholic toleration. A sense of the inherent defectiveness of human reasoning, of all human systems, be they of government, of religion, of morality, or any other, is ingrained in the blood, and hence the militant dogmatism and the furious fanaticism that stir and make or mar other races or other peoples have been generally conspicuous by absence in Mahārāshtra. We Marāthās would mind our own business, and would not quarrel with our neighbour. Let him be a Parsi, a Muhammadan, a Jain, a merchant, a tailor, a government officer, a *fakīr*, a *Sādhu*, or a Sanyāsī, we would let him pursue his line unmolested as long as he does not molest us. We lack the conviction that we alone are in the right and all the rest of the world in the wrong. Consequently we are very rarely fired with the fury of the fanatic. Being the eloquent embodiment of the peace-loving spirit of Mahārāshtra, the saints of the *bhakti* school have always been eager to reconcile the conflicting systems . . . . Their principle was the principle of conciliation.'[1] And again: 'The *bhakti* school neither started as a revolt against nor aimed at the demolition of any established system. It has been the special feature of all Indian movements in the past—and especially of Marāthā movements—that they assimilated more than discarded. They disarmed opposition and contest by assimilation. It may be that India and Mahārāshtra have had to suffer in the struggle for existence and for supremacy among the nations of the world, for want of that militant spirit and self-assertive energy.'[2]

[1] *F. C. M.*, February 1919, p. 142.
[2] *Ibid*, July 1919, pp. 33–4.

8. Tukaram and Caste

We need all the illumination we can derive from Prof. Patwardhan's exposition of the Mahārāshtrian spirit of toleration in order to understand Tukārām's attitude on caste. It is a principle fundamental with Tukārām that God does not consider a man's caste, that all worshippers are equally dear to Him, and yet we find Tukārām doing practically nothing to enforce this far-reaching principle. Some of his predecessors among the *bhaktas* had uttered noble words against caste. This had been the message of Eknāth, a Deśasth Brāhman who a generation before Tukārām's day had been out-casted, his poems being thrown into the river Godāverī because he would persist in ignoring caste-distinction and in recognizing the 'luxuriant foliage of devotion to the Highest' wherever it might be found.'[1] On this matter we have some of the loftiest utterances in Tukārām's poems: 'Our Lord knows nothing of high or low birth; he stops wherever he sees devotion and faith . . . Blessed is his story' (2077)—the whole of this remarkable *abhaṅg* should be studied. Many other similarly high utterances on this subject have we from our poet-saint: 'Consider him as a Brāhman, vile though his birth may be, who utters correctly the name of Rāma Kriṣṇa' (266); 'a Vaishnava is one who loves God alone, his caste may be anything at all' (942). *Abhaṅg* 4297 in the *Indu Prakāsh* edition, too long for quotation, is specially worthy of study with its long list of 'people of the lowest castes who have been saved', including Mahars like Cokhāmelā, and 'of whom even the Purānas became the bards'.

'His name belongs to no race or creed or caste; all are free to utter it' (1744); 'Tukā has nothing to do with a man's caste; he who utters the Name is truly blest' (2395). In this group of sayings we have the plain assertion that the worship of Vithobā is open to anyone and that devotion is equally welcome to Vithobā from whatever human being it proceeds. The question then naturally arises whether Tukārām drew the practical inference that the observance of caste should be abolished. One or two *abhaṅgs* seem to show that he was moving in this direction: 'I find the whole world peopled with relatives, I see nothing to cause contamination of man by man' (832); 'is the world divided into parts to hold the various castes?' (945) 'We think not of times or seasons or of any man's caste' (2259).

We must however be cautious how we draw any extended inference from these sayings, which are few compared with the mass of the poems, and there is nothing in Tukārām's biography to suggest that he appeared as one who took any strong line against

[1] See p. 39 for Eknāth's disregard of caste in everyday life.

caste. In practice most probably he acquiesced in it, relaxing its rules only so far as to permit all worshippers of the upper castes to mix freely in the gatherings on the shore of the Bhīmā. He appears to have seen without protest the 'untouchables' excluded, as they still are, from the temple ; and probably it never entered his head that there was anything open to criticism in the ordinary treatment of the 'pariah' classes.

Sometimes the fact that Tukārām had his daughters married to men of their own caste[1] is adduced as proof that he observed caste practices. This incident, however, is probably to be viewed in the same light as the custom prevalent among people in the West according to which they generally prefer relatives to marry those of their own social rank or station. Similarly, the Prārthanā Samāj, whose aim is to abolish caste and idolatry, though but gradually as we have seen above (pp. 153–4), and one of whose chief tenets is that all men and women are children of the one Supreme God, yet marry their children within their own caste.[2]

There appears, however, no cause to doubt that Tukārām accepted caste as an institution of the Hindū world and that he looked upon it as an inevitable part of India's social organization. The only way in which it might have troubled him was that it prevented humble men from embracing Vithobā's feet and that some of his worshippers were denied the comfort and satisfaction granted to others. One feels that Tukārām was called upon to demand the right of admission to the temple for all worshippers alike. That he did not do so, and that many were denied this common right in a temple of religion, seems to be overlooked by Prof. Patwardhan when he says : 'There is no bar here in this land of *bhakti*. Here all are admitted, all have a right to enter. Love of God and service of God, hence service of man, are their birthright. Everyone, man, woman, child, rich and poor, Brāhman and non-Brāhman, is a privileged heir to this sweet legacy. It is the most romantic democracy.'[3] Romantic, true, but what of Cokhāmeḷā, cast out of the temple at Paṇḍharpūr when he had crossed its threshold moved as he claimed by a divine impulse ? We have already shown how the treatment meted out to this Mahār saint and poet bears on the question of caste prejudice : see the section entitled 'Viṭhobā and Caste Distinction', pages 54-5 in chapter 3. In addition to what is stated there, reference may be made to Mahīpati's beautiful poem on Cokhāmeḷā's persecution by the high castes after he had left his native place at Anagod near Paṇḍharpūr and, grateful for Viṭhobā's help in his Mahār duty of dragging a dead cow, had taken up his abode in the sacred city itself. Refused entrance into the central shrine

[1] See p. 94.

[2] Dr. P R Bhandarkar, *Navayuga*, March 1921, p. 152.

[3] F. C. M. vol. ix, No. iv, Feb. 1919, p. 143 ; see also our own sec: 20. Chapter 1.

by the Brāhmans, Cokhāmeḷā retorted in moving words translated by Mr. C. A. Kincaid thus:

> Base though I be, no evil have I done
> Him in whose eyes all castes and creeds are one;

and he reminded his high caste persecutors of an even deeper principle:

> But if He finds no temple in your heart,
> Close to His shrine, you yet are far apart.

Many years after Cokhāmeḷā's death, from the crashing down of an unfinished wall he was building with other Mahārs, a divine direction came to the tailor-poet Nāmdev to collect Cokhāmeḷā's bones and take them to Paṇḍharpūr where opposite Nāmdev's staircase leading up into Viṭhobā's temple, on the opposite side of the street, Cokhāmeḷā's tomb was erected. Here in Tukārām's day, as in our own, the untouchable Mahārs offered their worship to Vishṇu, worship which Viṭhobā is represented as accepting, for Tukārām clearly states: 'God does not feel ashamed to help anyone; He seeks to comfort people of all conditions'. Such cosmopolitan teaching it was that, despite the glaring contradiction of it presented by the persecution of out-castes like Cokhāmeḷā, welded the Marāṭhās into a nation as is affirmed at the close of chapter 1.[1] Hence it comes about that Tukārām can claim, in an *abhaṅg* left untranslated by Fraser and Marāṭhe: 'I have been to Benāres, Gayā and Dwārkā, but they cannot be compared with Paṇḍharī. At Paṇḍharī no one is proud and people fall at each other's feet.'[2] This last mentioned practice is still in vogue among the *Warkaris* without any distinction of caste; see page 171 below.

When, however, the fullest possible weight has been given to all the considerations in this and the preceding section, this must needs be said concerning the absence of any effective protest by Tukārām against caste, that a unique opportunity was surely missed when a man of his convictions and influence failed to demand for every worshipper the right and privilege of admission to Viṭhobā's temple, and when he failed to realize the national evil of caste as a thorough-going reformer would have done. 'In personal inward religion Tukārām was democratic enough but he was too much of the "mild Hindū" to fight the battle of religious rights and privileges'.[3] He had practically the same freedom-loving instincts as his far-off contemporary the English Milton, but training,

See *Ishtur Phakde* by C. A. Kincaid, especially chaps. V, 'An Untouchable Saint. Cokhāmelā', and VI, 'The Saints of Pandharpur: The Dawn of Marātha Power'.

2 *Abhaṅg* No 2488, *I P.* edition, 1728 in Joga, where the comment should be noted.

3 This sentence we have taken from our *art.* *Tukārām*, *E. R. E.* Vol. 12

environment, and religious system were all against him. Therefore to call Tukārām a 'revolutionist' as does M. M. Kunte[1] is to misunderstand him.

Whether, therefore, Tukārām's mild teaching against caste lapsed through lack of courage or of conviction or of inspiration, we see one consequence in the paradox with which the *bhakti* school presents us. While this movement stirred the soul of an emotional people, and while its leaders sought to abolish the priestly caste, to substitute heart-religion for ceremonial formalism, and to make the worship of God open to all irrespective of caste, the historian's verdict is that 'the movement had little real effect upon Indian life and to this day, Brāhmans who recite with admiration the verses of Tukārām hold jealously to caste-distinctions'.[2]

9. Ambiguity and Self-Contradiction

Impartial study of Tukārām's poems yields the inevitable conclusion that his spirit of compromise, ambiguity of expression, and lack of reforming zeal arise from what must be described as a lack of religious certainty, and from what Westerners cannot but regard as acquiescence in mutually exclusive principles. Both these points are characteristic not only of Tukārām but of most other Indian sages. They certainly explain much of the self-contradictoriness of Tukārām which meets us on almost every page.

In one *abhang* he will address his god in the most endearing terms, in another upbraid him with the harshest epithets imaginable; on one page he will condemn idol-worship unsparingly, on another approve it. And so we might go on compiling a list of ambiguities, many of them affecting fundamentals. We are compelled to fall back finally on Sir Alexander Grant's conclusion[3] that Tukārām 'is never really philosophical—only always moral and devout'.

Narayan Vaman Tilak, the late Christian poet, wrote eight *abhangs*[4] in which this feature of Tukārām's self-contradictoriness was well brought out. Seldom has Tukārām been extolled in warmer terms than by this Christian *bhakta* whose 'rank as a poet is very high' and who has been sometimes called the 'Rabindranāth Tagore of Western India'[5] as said Mr. N. C. Kelkar, editor of the *Kesari*. But the praise is discriminating. After pointing out that anyone who fails to recognise Tukārām as the very home of spiritual devotion is void of all sense of appreciation, he says Tukārām must be acknowledged as a king among Indian saints, but

[1] *Vicissitudes of Aryan Civilisation in India*, pp. 279, 595.
[2] *The Times of India*, Oct 8, 1919.
[3] *Fortnightly Review*, Jan. 1867.
[4] *Dnyānodaya*, May 24, 1917.
[5] *I. I.* April, 1915.

also as a seeker often given to self-contradiction. Now he views God as *mābāp* (father and mother) and lord, now as man's opponent; now God is personal, now impersonal; now He is the embodiment of sagacity, now a simpleton. The chief defect of Tukārām, says this appreciative critic, is that of moulding God according to his own changing ideas, instead of letting God mould the ideas. So at one time Tukārām appears as an idolator, while at another he is angry with the very notion. Is then Tukārām hypocritical? A thousand times no. He is merely inconsistent and self-contradictory. In one mood he says: 'Had the good God not made me a humble peasant I had been swallowed up of pride'; in another he declares that 'a Brāhman is superior in the three worlds though he fails in duty'. In his speech there is no consistency—the opinion prevailing with him to-day is just as true as will be its opposite on the morrow. Despite it all, Tukārām is true-hearted and devoted—let none doubt that. One day he may be—indeed he is—a *dvaitist*, the next day an *advaitist*, and then the third day he is found halting between the two. Nevertheless, the Christian poet solemnly declares that he will persist in regarding 'all India's saints as so many Providential boons and divinely ordained paths to God,' and to the saint of Dehū he owes a specially sacred obligation. see chapter 10, section 3.

Therefore, though Tukārām far too often speaks with two voices regarding the Hinduism of his day, he has nevertheless come to wield among his people an influence of an altogether unique kind. This influence, and the position it seems to mark out for him in India's religious history, we are to examine in our next chapter.

BY FAITH ALONE *

In God, in God—forget him not!—
  Do thou thy refuge find,
Let every other plan or plot
  Go with the wind!

Why toil for nought? Wake, wake from sleep
  By learning's load weighed down,
Thou in the world's abysses deep
  Art like to drown.

O, flee from thence. Only by faith
  Canst thou to God attain.
And all thy knowledge, Tukā saith,
  Will prove in vain.

A STEADFAST MIND *

Honour, dishonour that men may pay,
Bundle them up and throw them away.

Where there is ever a steadfast mind,
There thou the vision of God shalt find.

Whereso the fountains of peace abide,
Stayed is the passage of time and tide.

Calm thou the impulse that stirs thy breast;
Surely, says Tukā, a small request.

THE DEDICATED LIFE *

Ah, wherefore fast or wherefore go
  To solitude apart?
Whether thou joy or sorrow know
  Have God within thy heart.

If in his mother's arms he be
  The child knows nought amiss.
Cast out, yea, cast out utterly
  All other thought than this.

Love not the world nor yet forsake
  Its gifts in fear and hate.
Thy life to God an offering make
  And to him dedicate.

Nay, Tukā says, ask not again,
  Waking old doubts anew.
Whatever else is taught by men,
  None other word is true.

* Translated from Tukārām, *P. M. S.*, pp. 83–4.

Chapter VII

Tukaram's Permanent Place and Influence

I. His Influence Among his Countrymen

This obviously is a subject on which foreigners must express themselves with caution and what we offer here are personal impressions based on reading and observation.

1. His Popularity with Peasants

Tukārām is best known among the twenty million peasant people of Western India. His language, difficult even to a Deccan Hindū, would seldom be intelligible to readers from other parts of India. In the Deccan he is exceedingly well known to the peasantry. Almost all of them know a few sayings or lines from his *abhangs* and many know much more. There are some who commit many of them to memory. Amongst these classes the pilgrimage to Paṇḍharpūr is often undertaken, some devotees being such as retire from worldly life and spend a great part of their time in pilgrimage between the holy places associated with Tukārām and Vithobā—Dehū, Ālandī and Paṇḍharpūr. The influence of these devotees of Tukārām, who bear the name of *Wārkarī*, and who include both men and women, has probably been the chief factor in the popularizing of the Dehū *bhakti* poet. That a grocer, one of the despised Śudra caste, should have been accepted as a religious guide in the face of Brāhman pretensions, helps to explain his becoming literally the idol of the people's devotion and his being worshipped to-day all over the Deccan as an 'incarnation' of the divine. When we remember, too, that the cosmopolitanism of Viṭhobā's worship referred to in chapter 3, section 9,[1] which makes it so acceptable to the masses, finds remarkable expression in 'the *Wārkarī* preachings of equality', we have sufficient explanation of Tukārām's unique position in the religious life of Western India. That these *Wārkarī* teachings find willing hearers everywhere is in no way surprising, in view on the one hand of the history of Brāhmanism, and on the other of the fact that the Marāthās of the Deccan, ever since the golden age of Śivājī, have always manifested a hankering after equality with the highest of their countrymen. This democratizing enthusiasm

[1] See pp. 54–55 and chap. 6, sect. 8, pp. 163–5 for the sad exception of the 'untouchables'.

and disregard of caste,[1] partial and defective though it was, provided 'a valuable counterpoise to Brāhman domineering' after Śivājī's death, in the century of Brāhman rule (1714–1818) which was probably 'the only time during the last two thousand years when Brāhmans united political and religious power in the Deccan.'[2] No wonder then that the *bhakti* poets enjoy such popularity among the Deccan peasantry, especially Tukārām the greatest of them, who has been so devotedly preached by the sect of the *Wārkārīs.*

2. 'Warkaris' and the Religion of Maharashtra

Who are these *Wārkarīs*, the most devoted of Tukārām's followers? And what are the principles which have enabled them up to the present hour to provide Mahārāshtra with an effective offset to Brāhman exclusiveness? Their name *Wārkarī* means literally 'time-keepers' and indicates simply their habit of travelling regularly on pilgrimage between the places named in the preceding paragraph. A few of them know no less than four thousand of Tukārām's *abhangs* by heart, a statement which may stagger Western readers but which can be substantiated. The sect is said to have been founded by Dnyāneshwar in the 13th century and consolidated, either by Tukārām himself or by his immediate followers in the 17th,[3] but the whole subject calls for careful investigation. They are divided into several groups or schools, each of which has its acknowledged head. For an account of them in English which is reliable as far as it goes, though it needs supplementing in important particulars, *The Bombay Gazetteer* (vol. xx. pp. 471–3) should be read, while those able to read Marāthī should not fail to master chapter 5 given up to this sect in the Marāthī Life of Tukārām by Mr. L. R. Pāngārkar, himself a present-day Brāhman and a respected leader of the *Wārkarī* sect, a chapter let us add whose information needs confirming in some particulars by other authorities.[4]

So simple and catholic are the beliefs of the *Wārkarīs* or 'time-keeping pilgrims' that most of their number are drawn from the lower classes of the people, while some members are even Mohammedans. Each *Wārkarī* must travel to Paṇḍharpūr so as to be present on the great *ekādashī*[5] days, which are the 'elevenths' of *Āshādh* (June or July)[6] and *Kārtik* (October or November), and for such other *ekādashī* days or 'monthly elevenths' as are technically

1 See last three sections of chap. 1.

2 *B. G.*, vol. xx, p. 473.

3 *B. G.* vol. xx, p. 471

4 See Dr. P. R. Bhandarkar, *Navayuga*, March 1921, pp. 149, 168.

5 For definition of *ekādashī* see p. 56, sect. 10, last two lines.

6 See pp. 48–9, 62–3.

BĀBURAO HARI DEVAḌIKĀR OF PAṆDHARPŪR A BLIND 'HARIDĀS' (PREACHER) AND 'WĀRKARĪ' WHO KNOWS TUKĀRĀM'S THOUSANDS OF *abhangs* BY HEART

called *Vārīs* (periodical pilgrimages). From the known attendance of pilgrims at the annual festivals (see page 48), and from the fact that other followers of Tukārām go up to Paṇḍharpūr for this purpose, it may be inferred that the *Warkārīs* cannot exceed 100,000 even if they reach that number, but certainty is impossible. All the members are on an unusually equal footing and anyone, man or woman, anxious to become a *Wārkarī* may do so by merely indicating his or her wish to the head of the sect he or she desires to join. While *ekādashī* days are regarded as the luckiest, a person may join at any time by bringing a rosary or necklace of basil or *tuḷśī* beads and an ochre-coloured swallow-tailed banner. The leader then bids the candidate lay the rosary upon Dnyāneshwar's commentary on the *Bhagvadgītā* named the *Dnyāneshwarī* kept in a niche of every *Wārkarī* monastery. Taking back the rosary the candidate then puts it round his or her own neck and falls at the feet of the leader by way of salutation who returns the salutation in the same way whatever be the caste of either party—an unusual feature in Hinduism. The candidate is told regularly to visit Paṇḍharpūr on the *ekādashī* days, the rule is urged that no *Wārkarī* can serve two masters, since Viṭhobā cannot tolerate worldly rivalries, and the principle is enunciated that to serve Vithobā well a *Wārkarī* should remain poor, seeing Vithobā dwells chiefly with the poor and lowly. The only books a *Wārkarī* is expected to read besides the *Gītā* and *Bhāgawat* are the following ten, all being works of the four great Marāthā *bhaktas*: Dnyāneshwar's *Dnyāneshwarī*, his *Abhangs* and *Amritānubhav*; Eknāth's *Bhāgwat*, *Abhangs*, *Bhāvārth Rāmāyan*, *Rukmini Svāyamvar*, and *Hastāmalak*; Nāmdev's *Abhangs*; and Tukārām's *Abhangs*. Other 'saints' are regarded as less important and their writings are not quoted. Of the four great *bhaktas* a traditional interpretation is preserved among the *Wārkarīs* who will produce it if requested, but it is often uncritical and unsatisfactory in obscure passages. A step in advance was taken by the late Mr. Joga, head of one of the *Wārkarī* schools, when he produced a large commentary on Tukārām's *Gāthā*, and it was highly fitting that his remains were buried at Āḷandī near the *samādhi* of Dnyāneshwar.

If the chapter on the *Wārkarīs* by Mr. L. R. Pāngārkar may be trusted as free from the over-statement due to the special pleading of a case, then they are to be considered the chief repositaries of the Bhāgavata Religion of Mahārāshtra (on which see page 27). He sets forth their tenets under 15 separate heads:[1] (1) Their chief object of worship is Viṭhobā, though the formless Brahma and his manifestations under various forms are regarded as one and indivisible, all the *avatāras* of Vishṇu being accepted (see chap. 2, sects. 3–4), especially Rāma and Kṛiṣṇa. (2) Their

[1] See *S. T. C.*, pp. 113–5.

authoritative Sacred Books are the *Bhagavadgītā* and the *Bhāgwat*, the two chief scriptures of the Bhāgavata Religion, along with the others already indicated. (3) Their Ideal or Goal is that of becoming one with God, by deep devotion to a God regarded as Personal, thus ultimately realizing unity in diversity. (4) Their chief Methods for attaining the Goal are the nine forms of devotion—*sravaṇa* (hearing), *kīrtans* (praise), *smaraṇa* (meditation), *pādasevana* (worshipping the feet), *arcana* (worshipping an image), *wandana* (salutation), *dāsya* (attendance), *sakhya* (friendship), and *ātmanivedana* (communion), with special emphasis on *smaraṇa*, remembering or repeating the name of God, and on *kīrtans* performed disinterestedly. (5) Their chief Mantra being *Rāma-Kṛiṣṇa-Hari*, all the thousand names of Vishṇu are worthy of remembrance. (6) Their *Bhakta-Rāj* (exemplars for all devotees) are Pundalīka, Garud and Hanumant. (7) Their great Pioneer is Shankar, there being no distinction between Hari and Hara, i,e., Vishṇu and Śiva, a characteristic Doctrine of the Bhāgavata Religion (see pp. 27, 156–8). (8) Their chief 'Saints' are ancient ones like Nārad and Pralhād,[1] and modern ones like Dnyāneshwar, Sopān,[2] Muktābāī,[3] Eknāth, Nāmdev and Tukārām. (9) Their Doctrine is that by remembrance of the 'Saints' comes salvation just as it comes by remembering the names of gods, in line with the principle that 'the gods are saints and the saints are gods'. (10) Their objects of Veneration are 'Saints', Cows, Brāhmans, Guests and the *Tulśī* plant. (11) Their chief Observances are—*ekādashī* for Vishnu and each Monday for Śiva; pilgrimage to Paṇdharpūr during *Āshādh* and *Kārtīk* being essential save under exceptional circumstances, and even then at least one visit must be paid; the *Mahā-Śivrātra* (the great night in the Hindū year devoted to worship of Śiva) also being essential. (12) Their chief Holy Places are the river Chandrabhāgā and the town of Pandharpūr, Trimbakeshwar near Naśik, Ālandī, Paithan, Sāswaḍ, Dehū, these being viewed as sacred because of 'Saints' who lived there; the Ganges, Jumna and Godaveri as sacred rivers; and Benares, Dwārkā and Jagannāth as pilgrim centres. (13) Their Prohibitions are—another's wife, another's wealth, speaking ill of others, also the use of flesh and wine; *ahimsā* is obligatory under all circumstances, the taking of any life being utterly forbidden at all times and in all places. (14) Their Rules of Conduct are all caste, sub-caste and family observances, with performance of duty according to life's four stages,[4] all rites and duties to be performed with a view to pleasing the Unseen. (15) Their Vow is that of Benevolence, based on the principle that

[1] On these two see *F and M.*, vol. I p 408.

[2] Brother of Dnyāneshwar.

[3] Sister of Dnyāneshwar.

[4] *Bramhacarya* (unmarried life of a student), *grihasthāśrama* (life of a householder), *vānaprastha* (the life of meditation or of preparation for the ascetic stage), *sanyāsa* (abandonment of the world).

the Divine is present in all beings, that every man we meet is God Himself; therefore to help every man is to do the service of God.[1]

3. Popular Kirtans and Kathas

Acknowledged authorities on Tukārām and his views serve the cause by holding *kīrtans* at Pandharpūr and other places for the exposition of his principles, both to praise the god and to explain the poet's lines. Special *kīrtans* or *kathās*[2] are held on the famous shore of the Bhīmā and they may best be seen and their effect appreciated at this spot. The arrangements are simple. An awning is spread on bamboo poles sufficiently large to shelter perhaps a thousand people sitting closely together on the ground. A narrow circle is left empty for the *kīrtankār* or leader of the service who stands there waiting for the gathering to compose itself into a reverent attitude before he begins. As they enter, the more devout of the visitors make their way into his presence and fall down and embrace his feet—whatever be his caste, whatever be theirs—setting apart the recognized 'untouchables': this is permitted or even enjoined.

Round the *kīrtankār* stand a small group with little cymbals in their hands who are ready to support him by taking up the refrain when he quotes any well-known poem. Anyone who feels inclined may join their number. The performance may begin at any hour but as a rule it occupies the night, starting say about eight and going on sometimes till dawn. It begins with a few well known lines of invocation and then proceeds with exhortation to a devout life, interrupted by illustrations of God's dealing with men drawn from the well-known *purāṇic* stories which Tukārām sometimes introduces. As far as a foreigner can judge or conjecture these addresses appear to be always on well known lines. They contain no study of Tukārām's character, no discussion of doubtful points and no interpretation of obscurities. They are straightforward exhortations to praise and trust Vithobā whose incarnation on the brick stands before them as a proof of his unwavering goodwill to men.

Marāthī-knowing readers will do well to supplement this section and section 9 in chapter 1 (page 10) by reading Mr. L. R. Pāngārkar's pages (123–8) on the subject.

1 In view of the above tenets it is perhaps not surprising that the *Wārkarīs* are sometimes criticized for not helping on the nationalistic spirit of Mahārāshtra as the somewhat similar sect of the *Rāmadāsīs*—devotees of Rāmdās—are supposed to have done The *Wārkarīs*, nevertheless, are not without their modern defenders (see Dr. P. R. Bhandarkar, *Navayuga*, March 1921, p. 168k)

2 See sect 9, chap. 1.

4. Tukaram and Indian Pessimism

It is not unlikely that much stress is laid by *kīrtankārs* on those poems in which Tukārām speaks of the unreality of the world and the path of escape from it. Hindū sentiment always moves in this direction, just as clouds which appear stationary in the sky are nevertheless always falling. It by no means follows that Tukārām succumbed to this impulse himself but his followers seem to prefer the lines written under its influence. And some of his admirers are ready to place him among the thorough-going *advaita* philosophers, to whom the deep-seated unreality of the world is the most profound of spiritual truths. Enough is said elsewhere in this book—see chapter 8, Part II—to show that this may be an imperfect view of Tukārām's teaching, but it certainly is one which some of his admirers support.

These admirers are to be found among Brāhman pundits. It is somewhat of a mystery why men of this class are always such ardent friends of the pessimist view. Perhaps it is the view which comes nearest to suiting the requirements of the systematizing temper which seems to be the Hindū temper in things intellectual. Certainly many obscure questions of human nature and of Hindū psychology are involved. It is easy to understand why the country people of the Deccan like to listen to those poems of Tukārām that deal with the darker side of things. The Deccan as elsewhere stated has its pleasant aspects but as one goes into the interior it grows very dry, very stony and very unpropitious to the agriculturalist (see pages 1, 9). When bad seasons predominate as they have done sometimes for years together, though much less now than formerly owing to British irrigation, life is one long dreary struggle. Crops are sown that never yield return. Harvests are gathered that permit the maintenance of life to the next scanty harvest only with the most penurious management.[1] The water is scanty and bad, overhead there is always the scorching unpitying sun and on earth nothing to relieve the weary eye or take the thoughts pleasantly away from the struggle for existence. And it is easy to see that times of this kind are not good for human relations. They encourage parsimony, even dishonesty, in the bazar and check generous impulses. The whole round of life becomes in every way a trial to be borne and the pleasantest thing you can hear about it is that it will some day pass out of existence.

Such reflections will certainly rise on the mind at the sight of the crowds that assemble on the pebbly bank at Paṇḍharpūr, especially if they are seen at the close of a long period of hard years. The battered features of the people tell unmistakably of

[1] 'In the terrible *Durgā Devā* famine of 1396–1408, no rain at all fell for twelve whole years, and for two decades the land was a desert,' H. G. Rawlinson, *Shivājī the Marāṭhā*, p. 14.

want and toil. Clearly what they come to Paṇḍharī to enjoy—if you were to ask them—is the thought of a gracious Being whose love is not like the seasons, capricious and unaccountable, but eternal and inexhaustible, nor like the small measure of grain bought after long haggling in the bazar, scanty and grudgingly doled out, but free and abundant. As this assurance steals on their minds they pass into ecstasy, and the outpouring of song and joy that fills the night at a *Hari-kīrtan* provides a demonstration that only deep religious passion can evoke. Whether this is rightly or wrongly based is not just now before us. That the ecstasy is there is unquestionable, and the worshipper puts away from him, at least for the time, the throng of cares and duties, and the world recedes into the far distance. It is most likely, however, if only we could find out, that life as a whole for the Deccan millions is one of blank pessimism and that the incessant struggle with poverty and with other ills compels the vast majority to take the dark view of life just as some interpreters of Tukārām do. We cannot say how far this pessimistic impulse is influenced in saner, quieter hours by a truer estimate of Tukārām's teaching. That would require a knowledge of the Hindū people which foreigners do not possess. But we may surmise that Indian pessimism in Mahārāshtra as elsewhere is 'environmental, temperamental and speculative' and has become quite stereotyped and conventional.[1] It would be a service to the present generation to induce the Marāthā people to see that in this aspect their favourite is not seen at his truest and his best.[2]

5. Tukaram and the Prarthana Samaj

The poems of Tukārām have been largely used by the Prārthanā Samāj of Western India both for private reading and for public worship. The Samāj is a body whose views with certain essential differences resemble those of the Brāhmo Samāj in Bengal. Its members' list, however, is much smaller in number, though including a few distinguished men who may be said to possess wide influence on the political and religious life of India. The student of developments finds it interesting therefore to note that such a body has given prominent place to Tukārām in its religious literature. They hold that Tukārām's spiritual experience is genuine and that the same experience is accessible to each devout worshipper of God.[3] An informing lecture on the relation between Tukārām and the Prārthanā Samāj may be found in that 'unique Marāṭhī book,' *Religious Writings and Sermons*, (the latest edition

1 H. D. Griswold, *E. R. E.*, Art, 'Pessimism (Indian)', Vol. 9, p. 813.

2 For another 'antidote to Indian Pessimism' see *The Holy Spirit the Christian Dynamic*, p. 293.

3 *E. R. E.* Art, *Prārthanā Samāj*, Vol. 9, pp. 151-2.

of which was published in 1919) by Dr. Sir R. G. Bhandarkar, 'an attempt to purge the existing Hindu religion of its accumulated dross of superstitions and to impart to it its pristine purity'.[1] The following paragraph summarizes Sir Rāmkrishna's Marāṭhī narrative of facts on pages 506–513 of his book.

Founded in 1867, it was not until more than two years later that the Prārthanā Samāj began the devotional use of Tukārām, the first occasion being some annual festival when four or five of his *abhangs* were printed on a hymn-sheet to the great delight of those present. Thus far religion had been viewed by the Prārthanā Samājist as an intellectual and philosophical matter, but the influence of Tukārām meant the spiritualizing and individualizing of religion. The Samāj had had no hymn-book worthy of the name but now a hymn-book was produced largely of Tukārām's verse. In each succeeding edition more and more of Tukārām's aspirations have been embodied, until in the present edition, the ninth, there are no less than 550 of his *abhangs*. The monotheism of the Samāj[2] had strictly limited the number of Tukārām's *abhangs* in the first three or four editions, his usual terms of Viṭhobā, Pāṇḍurang, Keshav, etc., being inadmissible to *ekeśwarīs* (worshippers of one God). The difficulty has, however, been overcome by these names being changed to 'God', 'Hari', 'Nārāyana,' etc. Besides providing assemblies of the Samāj with material for their songs, Tukārām began to supply their preachers with themes for their sermons and a verse of his, as often as not, is given out as the text in much the same way as Christian preachers take a text out of the Bible. It has been Tukārām's insistence on faith in God, on heart-devotion, on the necessity of minute self-examination, and on prayer, that has won for him this exalted place, despite changing times and customs. That Tukārām has become so great a factor in the life of the Prārthanā Samāj, some of whose members are among the leading social reformers in India, illustrates the extent of Tukārām's influence in the India of the twentieth century.

If we remember, too, that many of his verses are household words among the twenty millions of the Marāthī-speaking population, the grocer who failed in business at Dehū may be said to occupy a unique position among his countrymen. Probably there is an element of truth in such criticisms as Father Nehemiah Goreh[3] a generation ago, and the Rev. G. R. Navalkar in more recent years (see page 179 below) expressed, that the Prārthanā Samāj has sometimes put Tukārām in too exalted a place, reading a lofty theism into *abhangs* which have either been interpolated or have been interpreted in light of later Christian knowledge. Against all such 'false scents' the honest expositor must ever be on his guard.

1 Prof. G. E. Bhate, *Indian Social Reformer*, Sept. 14, 1919
2 On the attitude of the Prārthanā Samāj to idols, see pp. 150, 153-4.
3 *The Tenets of Tukārām*, pp. 1-4.

6. Tukaram's Usefulness for Religious Exercises

It is of more than passing interest to note to what elements in Tukārām's poems his present-day followers attach most importance. We are enabled to do this by the seventy-six *abhaṅgs* translated by Dr. Macnicol in his *Psalms of Marāthā Saints*, for most of these were supplied by Dr. Sir R. G. Bhandarkar, as a list of those which he himself uses daily in his own personal religious exercises. 'To anyone who knows Sir Rāmkrishna Bhandarkar as not only a great oriental scholar, but the outstanding representative in India to-day of the ancient school of *bhakti*, the fact that these psalms minister nourishment to a spiritual life so beautiful and so sincere is in itself sufficient testimony to their religious value.'[1] A similar list of about forty *abhaṅgs* 'which the ideas of the Prārthanā Samāj would select as most valuable from a devotional point of view' was kindly supplied for the purposes of this present work by Sir Nārāyan Chandāvarkar whose letter[2] stated: 'I have selected these because ever since I joined the Samāj in 1882 I have heard them more often than any other *abhaṅgs* chosen for prayer and sermon.'

One of the most interesting features in recent years of the Marāṭhī portion of the weekly *Subodh Patrikā*, organ of the Bombay Prārthanā Samāj, has been a series of articles expounding the more devotional *abhaṅgs* appearing in the Prārthanā Samāj hymn-book referred to above. Some of these Marāthī expositions of Tukārām, as also a few by Sir Nārāyan Chandāvarkar in his published (English) *Speeches and Writings*, and particularly the Marāṭhī work containing Dr. Sir R. G. Bhandarkar's *Religious Writings and Sermons*, provide the student with some of the richest devotional reading we know. Doubtless a deeper meaning is imported into some of Tukārām's seventeenth century terms than they would then have yielded, possibly even theistic interpretations may be foisted on to language originally idolatrous. Nevertheless, though these expositions may occasionally reveal historical anachronisms, their value in purging the Hinduism of Mahārāshtra from its grosser and more debasing elements cannot be estimated, and it is such work as reformers of every religious creed should heartily encourage.

7. Tukaram's Claim on Christian Missions

Tukārām makes a special claim on the Christian missionary who is working among Tukārām's own people. The claim is that Tukārām's verse shall be carefully studied. Some careful students

[1] *P.M.S.*, Preface, p. 5.

[2] Found by me among the late J. Nelson Fraser's papers in March, 1918, Sir Nārāyan's letter being dated Jan. 21, 1916—J.F.E.

of India's religious literature hold that, along with Tulsidās, the saint of Dehū represents India's closest approximation to Christian truth and that a study of his poetry is the best possible introduction to the treasury of Indian religious devotion. Tukārām may therefore be regarded as a true index to the depth and nobility of those religious aspirations the satisfying of which is the acknowledged aim of Indian Christian missions. There are two reasons why the foreigner should utilize all the available treasures of Indian religious literature; first, as supplying a most excellent means of bringing about that union of the various races in India without which British rule cannot achieve its ideals; and second, because it is through the avenues of a people's own literature and through sympathetic study of its inner life that any people can best be understood. Happily this duty is recognised to-day in Indian missions more fully than ever. This was amply demonstrated by a questionnaire sent out in preparation for the World Missionary Conference of 1910. 'The replies, one and all, lay emphasis upon the necessity that the missionary to Hindūs should possess and not merely assume, a sympathetic attitude towards India's most ancient religion. They emphasize, too, the need of prolonged and patient study, in order that sympathy may be based upon knowledge and may not be the child of emotion or imagination. . . . Even when a missionary has got some hold on the intricacies of practical Hinduism, in its mixture of philosophy and ceremonialism, in its innumerable connections with almost every detail of human life, he may still be an outsider if he has not mastered the third and most essential part of his study, the religious life of the individual. Below the strange forms and hardly intelligible language, lies life, the spiritual life of human souls, needing God, seeking God, laying hold of God, so far as they have found Him. Until we have at least reached so far that under the ceremonies and doctrines we have found the religious life of the people, and at least to some extent have begun to understand this life, we do not know what Hinduism really is, and we are missing the essential connection with the people's religious life. . . . Nothing is more remarkable than the agreement that the true method is that of knowledge and charity, that the missionary should seek for the nobler elements in the non-Christian religions and use them as steps to higher things, that in fact all these religions without exception disclose elemental needs of the human soul which Christianity alone can satisfy, and that in their higher forms they plainly manifest the working of the Spirit of God'.[1] For missionaries and Indian Christian leaders there could be no better example of the 'religious life of the individual' within the pale of Hinduism than Tukārām affords. That his is also the religious life of one enshrined in the hearts of the people of Mahārāshtra

[1] *The Missionary Message*, (1910), Vol. iv, pp. 171–2, 267.

further enhances his claim to be carefully studied by missionaries and the Indian Church. On this subject Miss M. M. Underhill (Oxford), a Z B.M.M., missionary in Western India since 1904, reviewing the *Psalms of the Marāṭhā Saints* said: 'There is a wealth of love and faith and devotion in these poems which ought not to go unknown or disregarded by either the Indian Christian or the European missionary. . . . As a missionary from Western India the reviewer would like to see some of these hymns used in the worship of the Christian Church in India.'' Not all would approve of this last suggestion as readily as they would to the further observation that the following verse by Tukārām better expresses the feeling of an Indian Christian congregation than do some of the English and American hymns in use at present.

> The duty of the man of faith
> Is trust and loyalty,
> A purpose hid within his heart
> That cannot movèd be.[2]

II. Tukaram's Permanent Place in Religion

We shall attempt to indicate very briefly in this Part the type of student who may expect to learn from Tukārām or obtain through him religious edification. We do not here seek to evaluate his religion: that will be done in the last chapter.

1. Erroneous Attempts to Classify Tukaram

Sufficient has been said to demonstrate the erroneous character of most modern attempts to classify Tukārām. The commonly accepted biographical facts and the trend of his writings alike show that none of the resemblances fit his case. 'While the Prārthanā Samājists have transformed Tukārām into a deist, believing in nothing but in the unity and supremacy of a personal God that has not revealed Himself in human form or in a book-revelation; and the Vedantists represent him as a transcendentalist, to whom the deity was a vast abstraction, the Universe a dream, and moral duty the creation of a morbid imagination; some Christians would regard him as almost a Christian believer'.[3] We believe all three are in error, the two former for reasons which this book should already have made clear, the last for reasons which will appear.

Let us state at once that there are whole classes who from the personal religious standpoint have but little to gain by reading

[1] *I R.M.*, April 1920, pp. 299–300.

[2] *P. M. S.*, p. 72.

[3] Rev. G. R. Navalkar, *Tukārām the Mahārāshtrian Poet and Saint*, Introduction.

Tukārām, though they may learn something of value as to how best they may approach his type of religious experience. Such are all those who have attained a matured faith according to any systematic or widely-accepted form of religious belief. To all those living under the protection of any organized religious system no spiritual aid from an 'outsider' like the *bhakta* and poet of Dehū is necessary. What *is* needful on their part, if they are at all to understand and appreciate this 'gentile' of the seventeenth century who lighted on many aspects of truth, is to approach him with sympathy. In short, they must approach Tukārām with a mind freed from all dogmatic prepossessions. They must be willing to accept that striking principle laid down by the greatest Teacher of all, that He 'has other sheep which do not belong to this fold.'[1]

2. Tukaram and the Religious 'Outsider'

Tukārām is of most value as a religious teacher to that large number of human beings who follow no definitely organized religious system. A great English thinker once said he would give his right hand to be able to believe some things, and it may be that there is a type of temperament unable to accept systems. They see the blanks in all the systems, their assumptions, their fallacies. They realize the danger of accepting as solutions of problems what are really restatements of them, the possibility of the covert reintroduction of principles professedly rejected, in short the laxity which often lurks under the guise of theological definition.

It is a matter of regret that such men who revolt against organized system cannot all be brought into general accord under the guidance of some simple interpretation of the world. Often they drift through life undecided, wanting in impulse, neglectful of opportunities, sometimes melancholy at heart and mostly ineffective. Any definite appeal to men of this type is hardly likely to create a 'mass movement' among them. But more religious writing might with good results be directed to their case, and the testimony of religious experience outside stereotyped forms might be presented to them. Tukārām's writings may be regarded as a testimony of this kind, living as he did in contact with a gigantic religio-philosophical system but standing somewhat outside it, and attaining a religious experience far above its level.

3. Essential and Non-essentials In His Message

As we read Tukārām's poems we find that spiritual contact with God is almost the whole of what he means by religion. In a

[1] Moffatt's rendering of St. John x. 16, on which verse Dr Westcott has the significant comment. 'He (Christ) "knows" others as His whom we cannot recognize. . . He "has" other sheep, who even if they know Him not are truly His.'

casual way he holds certain traditional tenets of India. He does not reject the dogma of reincarnation. But with him it is so small an affair that you may reject it without altering the centre of gravity in his world of thought, while under the management of a skilled theosophist it becomes a monster of such prodigious dimensions that almost all one's energy is needed to comprehend, accept and live up to it. The embodiment of God in the stone image of Vithobā occupies a very different position, for he is very serious about that. If you take this away you do certainly dislocate his position, for the fact of the image standing there is what *proves* to Tukārām that God sympathises with man's needs. An atheistical reader may very well say: 'If you take away this proof what is there in Tukārām to turn anyone to religious faith?' But Tukārām has no message at all for such a reader. It is for those whose impulses bring them on the side of religion but find a difficulty in taking the definite step of faith. To these it may be pointed out that though Tukārām *thought* his faith was established by the fact of God standing there on the brick, sober psychology, not to mention any other factor, forbids us to suppose the contemplation of a stone image was the whole cause and explanation of his spiritual experiences. The truth is that he had these experiences because, though in his *thought* he apprehended Vithobā, in the real longing of his spirit he approached the living God. And what is reassuring to us is that even he could make this approach. He had his 'treasure in an earthen vessel' but it sufficed for him to carry it. Tukārām's example shows clearly how little the 'vessel' really matters, and we can see this the more easily because it is only Vithobā, a stone idol, dumb, lifeless and unattractive. And among his *abhangs* there are some which show that Tukārām could and did often take the view that the stone idol was a *mere* stone, neither embodying nor even symbolizing the divine presence, as we have seen in the section on 'idolatry' in chapter VI.

4. His Influence often Christian in Type

Even to sketch a view of Christian belief would be quite beyond the province of this book: we are only concerned to show what help a writer like Tukārām can give to the religious enquirer who is not built on organized lines. And so we place first his daily testimony to the fact of spiritual experience, to the fact of God's personality, and to the condescension of the divine nature to the needs of man, in whatever way these be manifested. Let us add that Tukārām's morality is often of a Christian type and those who accept this type will surely accept the aid of a writer who puts the call of morality into such emphatic and moving words. From him we learn the need of constant watchfulness and of resistance to temptation. We hear nothing of ingenious arguments of self-indulgence, of pleas for more enjoyment, though we may suppose sophistries of the kind were not unknown in his day. Tukārām stands as a great example of the austere type of moralist.

It is from this point of view that we may observe him with great admiration and pleasure. There is nothing much in his surroundings to produce him. Whatever the 'saints' may have taught him, the ordinary village life in the Deccan of his day assuredly did not contain much to encourage the life of a self-denying saint. It is not easy to say what does do so and perhaps we shall never get further than to remember that 'the wind blows where it lists', that 'there is a light that lighteth every man'. We may say, however, in a narrower sense that the encouragement of help and approbation was not specially bestowed on Tukārām and that what he accomplished was accomplished only by exertion. Perhaps it was his view of God as Mother which gave him most practical encouragement, a view which brings his religious thinking nearer to the Christian plane than does any other factor in his whole system. See chapter 8. II. 3, and Prof. Patwardhan on this idea in chapter 6, pp. 152–3.

5. Tukaram's Mystical Conflict

His spiritual struggles we may view variously. We should know better what to make of them if we knew something of the chronology of his writings. It is possible that they belong chiefly to his early years, but it is just as probable that his inward conflict was lifelong. There are so many *abhangs* speaking of spiritual desolation and they are so scattered throughout his other poems and so interwoven with them that it seems unlikely they were all produced at one epoch. We must suppose Tukārām had many oppressive hours even after he had seen all the final truths he ever saw. This is a saddening conclusion whichever way we look at it, though our chapter 9 will confirm our previous conclusion that he had glimpses, and let us hope more than glimpses, of something brighter. And in any case his inward conflict, so intensely personal and mystical in character, has stamped upon it throughout something of the true nobility of all spiritual struggle. To the very end, however, he appears to have been deeply sensible of the mysteries of the world, feeling acutely all the perplexities of the universe, the inscrutable ways of God, the unsounded depths of human nature. What sustained his soul, probably, was his favourite doctrine that man must somehow live in companionship with God, whatever the form of His manifestation. This is a deep mystical truth which knows no East nor West, for it is applicable to all people in all climes.

It is therefore by his mystical vein, found in so many of his poems, that Tukārām makes a religious contribution of enduring value, expressed though his mysticism was often in rough and uncouth phrases, and often again in terminology tinged with idolatry; but it was always religious passion none the less, and very often religious passion of the noblest kind. The mystical aspect of religion, being timeless in character, is independent of either time or place, and it is from this timeless element, which breathes in all his poems, that the saint of Dehū must be given a place in the rank of the world's teachers. Tukārām teaches his fellow-men not chiefly by what he says, though that is worthy of attention, but by what we realize him to have felt and experienced of aspiration, conflict and communion. As a poet he belongs to India; as a true mystic he belongs to humanity. Being a mystic, his worth is further enhanced when we remember that competent observers consider the mystical aspect of religion to have been invested with richer significance by the world-war and its aftermath. One scholar of world-repute,[1] speaking of 'the increasing sympathy with mystical types of religion', affirms that 'far more people than we should ever suspect, not recluses but ordinary citizens, have been drawn to the mystical view of life' and that many of the religious developments of our time are 'due to the interest we now take in religious experience, as distinguished from abstract doctrine'. By his repeated emphasis therefore on experimental religion as distinct from doctrine and dogma Tukārām may perform a ministry of lasting value not only for his modern countrymen but for men of other races who have similar aspirations.

Dr. T. R. Glover has suggested that Tukārām's mystical vein gives him deep affinities with Madame Guyon, the French Mystic and Quietist whose life was beginning—she was born in 1648—just as Tukārām's was closing. 'Some of Dr. Nicol Macnicol's verse renderings of Tukā,' says Dr. Glover, 'might be interpolated among Cowper's poems from Madame Guyon, and not be detected without reference to the French.'[2] Nor is the parallel inapt, for Madame Guyon's 'obscure night of the soul' in 1680, occasioned by successive bereavements and much personal suffering of her own, followed as it was by a new 'unitive' state in which the old 'self-me' was supplanted by a new 'God-me',[3] has some resemblance to the inward experience the saint of Dehū had gone through some fifty years before, as outlined in part iii of chapter 5 on the Autobiography. The heroism and solitude of Tukārām's 'obscure night of the soul', with but little in his immediate environment to help him, invest his deep and prolonged inward conflict with something of an epic character.

[1] Dr. Ernest F. Scott, *Union Theological Seminary Bulletin*, New York, Jan. 1921, vol. iv. No. 2, pp. 14–5.

[2] *Jesus in the Experience of Men*, Jan. 1921, p 40.

[3] *E. R. E.*, vol. x. p. 536, art. *Quietism*,

6. His Place in Theism

It is comforting to feel in reading Tukārām that his devotion, like that of all true men, was known to the same God and Father and was accepted by Him. This great truth is open to abuse and in no country more so than in India. But that need not prevent us from recognizing it and feeling grateful for it and making it a working principle in our dealing with those of other faiths. The conceptions which men have formed of God have varied, but in so far as they have been the fruit of reverence and of true devotion, the supplications of men have never failed to reach His ear. Tukārām teaches, especially his fellow-Hindūs, that it is a man's duty to seek still to purify his faith, and to accept light from whatever quarter it comes. This does not mean that any creed will do if only it saves us the trouble of reflection. It is still and always our duty to purify our faith, and even to bear patiently with error where it is not such as arises from spiritual pride or self-deception.

In the absence of a critical edition of Tukārām's writings and of any approximate chronology of his religious experience it is impossible to reach any accurate estimate of his place in Indian Theism, though praiseworthy efforts have been made with the available material.[1] Unless, however, interpolation has taken place in the poems on a far more extensive scale than in the present state of our information seems probable, the Prārthanā Samājists are likely to be correct in assigning him a high place in Indian Theism though we cannot call him a monotheist. This twofold position is largely owing to the fact that though he was unquestionably an idolator, and recognized Śiva, Gaṇpati, Mārutī and Ganga, etc., as deities—see our section 1, chap. 6—yet his worship was offered mainly to *one* idol only, and that one of the purest, Viṭhobā being an 'incarnation' of Kriṣṇa whose worship is not vitiated by erotic accompaniments as elsewhere, for as Dr. Sir R. G. Bhandarkar has pointed out, Vithobā is regarded not as the lover of a mistress, as Kriṣṇa so often is with lamentable results, but as a husband and consequently 'the Vaisbṇavism of the Marāṭhā country is more sober and is purer' (*V. S. M. R. S.*, p. 89). And as Viṭhobā is pure in comparison with most other Indian idols, so is Tukārām one of the purest and most high-minded of Hindū devotees. How closely, indeed, he approximates to the theistic position of many Western Theists, particularly those of the Unitarian type, may easily be seen by changing the name of his god, as the Prārthanā Samājists do so

[1] Dr Sir R. G. Bhandarkar in *V. S. M. R. S.*, pp. 92–101; Dr. Macnicol in *P. M. S.*, pp 18–33, *Indian Theism*, pp. 122–6, 217–9, and scattered articles in *I. I.*, *I R. M.*, and *Hibbert Journal*, also Dr. Sydney Cave in *Redemption, Hindu and Christian*, pp. 116–9.

freely, and substituting for it such divine appellations as obtain in the religious literature of the West. It then appears that on most of the fundamentals of Theism, such as a consciousness of indwelling sin, prayer, faith, sense of the Divine Presence, longing for union with God, personal experience as the essence of religion, etc., Tukārām makes a contribution of surpassing interest as we shall see in our next two chapters. What finer, for example, can Western teaching, merely Theistic, show than Tukārām's query, 'If the ears drink no nectar of God's glory, what use are they?' (151). Or than his affirmation, 'God is my bosom friend; the bosom friend of this helpless creature · according to His glorious might let Him adorn us with purity'? (771)

Finally, though the claim of novelty is to be admitted with care in an age which has so many cranks, yet in a reasonable way it may be admitted and even urged as a reason for the study of alien books of devotion. Old truths shine forth occasionally with greater force in unfamiliar language and the problem how we are to sanctify our daily life receives fresh light when considered in the light of human experience amid different surroundings. Tukārām's language and his *abhaṅgs* often illustrate this, and his rugged diction, his quaint examples, as well as his occasional beauties of expression and his command of the language of religious passion, make him an author for whom the Westerner may have a great regard. As Sir Alexander Grant, a former Vice-Chancellor of Bombay University, wrote in 1867: 'If intense personal religion can be found anywhere it can be found in Tukārām. It is impossible to avoid comparing his songs with the Psalms of David. They are the natural expression of a mind holding constant communion with God, poured out like the notes of a bird, in all the occasions and various moods of life.'

This chapter on Tukārām's place in religious thought may fittingly close with his description of 'the heart to which God makes Himself known'. The crowning-point of all Tukārām's teaching has an imperishable message for Occident and Orient alike: 'Where pardon, peace and purity dwell, there God abides' (706). 'Blessed are the pious, for their heart is pure' (894).

Having concluded that our Indian poet-saint of the early 17th century must be given a worthy place in man's agelong story of quest after peace, another conclusion is forced upon us, viz., that his Religious Ideas may be worthy of sympathetic investigation.

'I CANNOT UNDERSTAND, I LOVE'*

Thy greatness none can comprehend,
    All dumb the Vedas are.
Forspent the powers of mortal mind;
    They cannot climb so far.
How can I compass him whose light
    Illumes both sun and star?

The serpent of a thousand tongues[1]
    Cannot tell all thy praise;
Then how, poor I? Thy children we,
    Mother of loving ways!
Within the shadow of thy grace,
    Ah, hide me, Tukā says.

THE INWARD PURPOSE*

To keep the Holy Order pure,—
This ever is my purpose sure.

The Vedic statutes I proclaim,
To imitate the saints my aim.

For, with no firm resolve within,
To quit the world is deadly sin

Vile he who does so, Tukā says,—
Evil the worship that he pays.

'I LONG TO SEE THY FACE'*

I long to see thy face,
But ah, in me hath holiness no place

By thy strength succour me,
So only, only I thy feet may see!

Though Sādhu's robes I've worn,
Within I'm all unshaven and unshorn.

Lost, lost, O God, am I,
Unless thou help me, Tukā,—me who cry!

[1] *The serpent of a thousand tongues*, Sesa, the thousand-headed snake which is at once the couch and canopy of Visnu and which upholds the world.

* Translations from Tukārām, *P.M.S.*, pp. 67, 85, 64

Chapter VIII

Tukaram's leading Religious Ideas

This is to be a chapter on Tukārām's teaching, and his poems are our chief, almost our sole, authority. Our investigation cannot pretend to be anything like exhaustive, either as to range of subject or extent of treatment. As to the latter we shall let him, in the main, speak for himself; as to the former, the subjects will comprise his teaching about God, God's Worshippers, Sin, Salvation, the Religious Life, the Moral Ideal, the 'Saints', Animals, Reincarnation, Death and the Hereafter. It will be noted that nearly all these subjects are practical and experimental. We attempt no final synthesis of his teaching, this being impossible without a critical edition of his writings.

I. God and His Relation to the World

1. The Divine Existence: 'Lila'

Tukārām enters into no formal proof of the existence of God, nor does he contemplate the downright atheist among the enemies he has to face.

He seems in many passages to accept most of the orthodox answer of the Hindū system. God dwells apart from the world: He is formless and void of qualities. Personal, no doubt; we do not think that Tukārām ever inclines to the view that the supreme Spirit slips off personality along with other limitations, but he sometimes tends to think that God has no dealings with the world. But this does not always content him. Elsewhere he says that God at once pervades the world and is left outside it, and again that 'God makes and unmakes the world: it is He who makes all action visible' (406). How or why has this come about? The answer is that the world is a diversion (*līlā*) of the eternal Spirit: 'You have created amusing games to soothe your eyes with watching them; apart from that end we all know what the world is, a wooden tiger and a wooden cow' (221). Being void of qualities He had sought diversion in the drama of the world (1286).

This *līlā*, however, when it meets our eyes, becomes a veil that hides God from us. 'Take off the veil of illusion that thou hast spread between us and thee' (442). 'False is the world; Hari alone is real, apart from him all the senses are futile' (1665). ''Tis Thou, O Viṭṭhal, art real. Why then hast thou shown us this outward form of the world? Thou hast given a name to a thing that has truly no form' (3427). Tukārām here drifts towards the *advaita* view, yet he always seemed to be hovering near the discovery that the world which is a *līlā* of God's, may become the same thing to us as to God if we look at it in the same spirit. It will then be as permissible for us to enjoy it as for God to create it.

2. Was Tukaram a Pantheist?

What is Pantheism? We really do not know any meaning for the word except a loose and evasive way of talking as though the world was God and God was the world. This sort of talk is commoner in popular Hinduism than in other popular religions, just in proportion as Hinduism concerns itself more with cosmogony than other systems do. But it is paying it too much of a compliment to treat it seriously as a system of thought. When Tukārām says that God pervades the world he really means, though he does not quite say so, that God directs the world so that it all serves a divine purpose. God with him is always a Being, an overruling Being. If he had gone a little further we might say a Providence.

As to whether, therefore, Tukārām is to be regarded as an *advaitist* or Pantheist, opinions differ violently and it is well-nigh impossible to say more than that he sometimes seems to incline towards the *advaitist* position and sometimes towards its opposite, the dualist. We have on the one hand Mahīpati's story of Tukārām sitting under a blanket, with his fingers in his ears as a protest against the act of a Vendantist who was reading to him an *advaitist* treatise (see page 102); also Dr. P. R. Bhandarkar's suggestion that Mahīpati views the receiving of the *guru-mantra* in a dream as a Providential interposition saving Tukārām from the repugnant *advaitist* tenets which any *guru* of the time would have been certain to pour into his ear had Tukārām needed to obtain a *mantra* in that way (see pages 91–2); and lastly the note of triumph with which Tukārām himself dismisses the *advaita* philosophers: 'Away with knowledge of Bramha and intuitions of the self within the self' (518). See further pp. 194–5 below and also 218–9. On the other hand we have references in his poems which appear to show that it was only when the *advaitist* became 'void of devotion' that he raised any serious objection to his teaching: 'Listen not to such a one; the wisdom he discourses is like chaff, void of devotion. He extols the doctrine that seeks absolute union, he sets aside devotion . . . . Saying "I am Brahma", he nourishes his own person; we should not speak to such a disputant as he' (1177). For both sides, see on the one hand, the thirty *abhangs* in Fraser and Marāthe's translations under the heading, 'Distinction From God Necessary'; and on the other, see Mr. L. R. Pāngārkar's Marāṭhī *Life of Tukārām*, p. 114, etc, and Joga's *Commentary*, Vol. 1, p. 280.

Some students, however, would state Tukārām's inclination towards *advaita* far more strongly, adducing as evidence in their favour all the *abhaṅgs* in Fraser and Marāṭhe's translation bearing the headings, 'Union with God Necessary,'—54 in all—and 'The All-Pervading Character of God' numbering 36, in particular such *abhaṅgs* as: 'Pāṇḍuraṇg has truly shown us his grace by driving out of us all doubts, all sense of difference from him' (2866); 'I am melted, I am lost in Thee; when fire and camphor mingle, is blackness of any sort left behind? My flame and thy flame, says Tukā, are become one' (1679); 'God and his worshippers are bound together, they appear separate but they are really one' (201); 'God and devotee, Lord and servant—this duality had its birth in unity, there is no difference here, says Tukā; the devotee is God and God is devotee'[1]; and the pathetic cry in 200, an *abhaṅg* reminiscent of the *bhakta's* heavy bereavements: 'Many have died who were dear to me; how is it, O Hari, you have survived them? . . . Thus I conclude that all men, myself too, have to be placed in you as a deposit'. Those who believe Tukārām hold the *advaitist* position have in their favour the fact that the *Bhāgavata Purāna* is regarded by most an *advaitist* book, and the *Bhagavad-gītā* also, in spite of the *bhakti* dominating them, these two great works being the most sacred books of the Vaishnavism or *Bhāgavata* religion of Mahārāshtra.[2]

Modern scholars are equally divided on this subject. Dr. Farquhar concludes—though his dealing with questions of Marāthā religion is necessarily scanty—that 'so far as philosophical thinking may be traced, Tukārām tends to be a monist.'[3] Concerning the 24 *abhaṅgs* narrating the end of Tukārām the writer of the brief English sketch of the poet's life in the *Indu Prakāsh* edition says he 'was absorbed in contemplation and the actual realization of the Vedantic doctrine of Pantheism', though we need to add that these *abhaṅgs* can scarcely be regarded as other than spurious.[4] In his *Tenets of Tukārām* the converted Brāhmin, the late Rev. Nehemiah Goreh, strenuously argues for the *advaitist* character of all Tukārām's teaching, seeking to harmonize its many contradictions by his theory that from the worldly standpoint of practical everyday life the poet was certainly a dualist, while from the spiritual or 'other-worldly' point of view he was a pantheist, a view which, however tempting and convenient, cannot be accepted as solving the real difficulty. On the other side, among those who regard the saint of Dehū as a dualist, are to be reckoned the Prārthanā

[1] See *F. and M* 823 for another rendering.

[2] See pp 171–2 and Dr. Justin E. Abbott, *Dnyānodaya*, June 9, 1921.

[3] *O. R.L.I.*, p. 300

[4] See p 126 above.

Samājist thinkers whose authority concerning everything relating to Tukārām, their chief *guru*, is indisputably high, the Prārthanā Samāj position being represented by Dr. P. R. Bhandarkar[1] with whom agree Dr. Murray Mitchell who wrote about the middle of last century and Sir Alexander Grant who wrote in 1867. The last-mentioned regrets that Tukārām 'impairs his poetry by the use of the metaphysical terms of Vedantism' and that he is 'extremely wavering in his point of view', his apparent pantheism being merely an intense form of devotion.

Could we have asked Tukārām himself as to his true position he would probably have pointed to his words in *abhang* 1924: 'We will give up this dispute; let us go before the saints to settle this', meaning, 'Let us grant that the monist position is strictly correct, that God has not really created us as beings with individualities of our own. . . Still, why not leave it so? Why not let the attitude of worshipper and worshipped continue?'[2] He would probably have summed up the discussion in the words of the cradle-song sung over him by his mother: 'Monism and dualism are each half true'—see page 79. See also Dr. Macnicol's similar conclusion.[3]

II. God's Relation to His Worshippers

1. God's Way of realizing Himself

Tukārām is not greatly interested in cosmogony and he spends no time in speculating how the separation of the human soul from God became possible or was accomplished. But he has no doubt of the purpose in view when the development took place. It is only through this that God realizes Himself, that He becomes truly God. 'God becomes what we make Him' (586). 'It is our faith that makes thee a God' (1795). 'What is the head without the feet? We are the feet that suffer and bear thee' (1787). Without His worshippers God would not know the bliss of receiving devotion and sharing in mutual love: 'What does the lotus flower know of its own perfume?' (207) 'Water cannot taste itself nor trees their own fruit. At the sight of the child the milk comes into the mother's breast. What delight there is when they meet each other' (211). Accordingly, 'God calls Himself His worshippers' debtor: He is even grateful to them. He feels especial delight in the helpless, because He can do most for them' (282). 'In those who are helpless He feels His chief delight' (286). 'Had I not been a sinner how could there have been a Saviour?' (213). Much is said of the delight shared by the worshipper and the God who is worshipped: ''Tis like a father with his child, who feels and gives pleasure at once' (210).

[1] *Two Masters Jesus and Tukārām*, pp 35–45.
[2] See *F and M.* vol. 2, 'note' on p 444.
[3] *P. M S.*, pp. 21, 25–6.

2. Unity of the Divine and the Human

Tukārām strongly maintains the unity of the divine with the human spirit: 'That my soul is the soul of all things—who can rob me of this truth?' (1698). 'Nārāyana gives and himself enjoys the gift' (227). This means that it is the same spirit that is active in both the giver and receiver, the same thought being expressed in the lines, 'If we are burned or fall into fire it is Nārāyana that suffers in us' (1802). 'He pervades my frame, yet he keeps our two beings distinct' (1130). Tukārām does not feel called on to reconcile the opposing aspects of the divine nature, indeed he seems rather to rejoice in the thought that God is 'incomprehensible by mind or reason' (1657). And time after time he tells us that 'He exists and exists not in all things'; 'He is all and none of us;' 'not by knowledge or reflection canst thou be comprehended, nor can any system search thee out' (3213). But he looks with horror on a final emancipation or absorption into Brahman that will leave behind no sense of personality, because it will rob him of the joy of union, devotion and service. See further, all the *abhangs* in *F. and M.* in each volume under the heading 'Union with God Necessary'.

We may note other ideas of God's relation to His worshippers. He knows what they need without being told · 'Thou knowest our hearts though we tell thee nothing; thou dost pervade the world, there is no need to tell thee aught' (307).

3. Divine Accessibility and Condescension

God makes Himself accessible to the infirm apprehensions of the worshipper: 'He has embodied himself in forms to suit our pleasure: he has laid out paths such as we can discern and follow, while he himself, beyond our comprehension, surveys the circle of the skies' (1753). This refers partly to the embodiment in an image, partly to the willingness of God to receive humble devotion. Tukārām insists often on the feebleness of human devotion and hugs the thought that God is pleased with the stammering childish accents of humanity. Then again God accepts as evidence of devoted faith the mere utterance of His name--it is little, but if offered in the right spirit it is enough. Thus 'God meets every man in a shape fit for him' (1757); 'God conforms himself to every man's speech' (1756).

This leads to a very trustful relation between God and His worshippers. The image of the child and his parents may even seem to us somewhat overworked by our poet and his language of fond familiarity somewhat wanting in due gravity: 'We are God's companions, his old crazy frolicsome friends: he led us by the hand' (2164). Sayings such as this justify the observation that the relation between man and God as conceived by Tukārām may occasionally to a Christian seem wanting in dignity or reverence, and that he presses the image of a playful childhood too far. It is only a partial truth that 'men are but children of a larger growth' and Hegel with greater insight than Tukārām has observed that we are not to *be* little children but to *become* as little children. Let us not forget the pleasing simile in which he points out that 'the bee has no fear of being imprisoned in the flower that encloses it' (2601). At the same time the figure of Mother and child as applied to God and His worshippers is Tukārām's closest approximation to the Christian idea of God. See also quotation from Prof. Patwardhan on pp. 152-3.

4. Ancient Scriptures and 'Authority'

The general tone of Tukārām's writings shows he is not in the least a theologian. He seldom raises and still more seldom answers the thousand and one questions that delight theologians. The exact extent of Tukārām's learning we do not know. See pp. 127-128. It is possible that he picked up a little Sanskrit and read some of the *śāstras* in the original tongue and even drew some of his ideas from them, but he never admits anything of the kind. We must remember that the Vedas in the strict sense were quite unintelligible both to him and to anybody he ever met and even the great commentators were probably beyond him. It is not surprising therefore that he sometimes regards the written word—the word of tradition—as unimportant. Along with the place of the Scriptures we have to settle the place of authority and the extent to which an immediate revelation is vouched to the enquirer who seeks it.

Hinduism, one need hardly say, has no centre of dogmatic authority, that is to say, no living centre.[1] Hindū bodies look mostly to their scriptures, but even here there is no absolute agreement as to which scriptures are inspired. It appears however from Tukārām's example that a Hindū may almost throw off the authority of the scriptures altogether.[2] One must be careful however not to press this point too far, in view of *abhang* 2561: 'He who admits not the authority of Scripture—his face you should not see.'

1 For several centuries past Hinduism has recognized the authority of four Śankarāchāryas whose 'four spiritual seats are—Joshi *Maṭh* in the Himālayas, Northern India, in the district of Garwal, Sarada *Maṭh* in Dwāraka, Western India, in the State of Baroda; Sringeri *Math* in Sringeri, Southern India, within the Mysore State; and Govardhan *Math* in Puri, Eastern India . . . Two *Gādīs* in those of Sarada *Maṭh* and Joshi *Maṭh* are at present without their recognized Spiritual Heads. . . As regards the Sarada *Maṭh* various complications have arisen' (*Mahāmandaḷ Magazine*, May, 1921). Of interest to Marāthā students is the fact that there is also a Karvīr *Maṭh* in Kolhapūr State.

2 'I believe our present knowledge of the Hindū scriptures is in a most chaotic state,' said Mr. M. K, Gandhi in *Young India* of October 6, 1921.

An *abhang* like this shows he was not a rebel against the Vedas. He probably thought that Vedic authority if duly explored would be found on his side, that the Vedas were obscure, that many interpretations were against him, that many scriptures of less but much-vaunted authority supported views which he rejected, and that the study of all scriptures led to much wrangling. Simple devotion, on the other hand, was rewarded by peace and light and for him at least this was sufficient. What chiefly roused his anger was a merely formal devotion to external 'authority' without any corresponding inward religion of one's own: 'What have they achieved by committing texts to memory? They kept their self-sufficiency. They have a scrap of knowledge; they are puffed up with pride; they are scoundrels, says Tukā, batter in their faces' (2544); 'it is in vain you have studied the Vedas, unless you feel sobs of love rise when you hear God preached (2543).' See further pp. 159–60.

In the brief account which he gives of his spiritual life we learn that he met a *guru* who placed him in touch with his Vaishṇavite predecessors, and we may recall the importance he attaches to intercourse with the 'saints' (see section viii in this chapter). It is they who preserve doctrine in its purity, they who point the enquirer to the source of light. Thus tradition plays a great part in Tukārām's system, though he never asks in a critical spirit how tradition is related to personal experience; it is on practice that he lays the greatest weight.

III. Sin

The natural state of the human soul, Tukārām would say, if he knew what 'natural' meant, is union with God in mutual love. What is the state in which men's souls actually are? How has it arisen? It is a state of separation. The first beginning of this is a matter on which Tukārām offers no speculations—indeed the Hindū speculations concerning the origins of things, though in general more elaborate than Christian, do not much discuss the fall of man. At least they do not treat it from the human side; they consider more how the divine nature may be supposed to have thrown off emanations. That these emanations should be sinful is perhaps thought to follow without further explanation, as a matter of course. In Tukārām the sinful nature of man appears as a matter of common knowledge. Thus, sin consists in (i) breaking the appointed rules of caste; (ii) breaking the rules of morality in a narrower or wider sense as we may variously phrase it; and (iii) indulging the sense of *mīpaṇa*.

The first (i) and second (ii) we may leave aside for the present and examine the notion of *mīpaṇa* (self-centredness). This offence is often and strongly condemned by Tukārām, yet he never tells exactly what he means by it. Nor is it a thing easy to express in English. It is not selfishness nor self-indulgence nor even self-satisfaction or self-conceit, though these last come near to it. An exact equivalent would be the word 'egoism' if it were not so often used in conversation for boring other people by talking about oneself. *Mīpaṇa* means wilfully dissociating oneself from God, nourishing the feeling of independence instead of gratefully leaning upon Him. It may easily but not necessarily be associated with pride. A man may be guilty of it without taking any exaggerated view of his own merits.

Anyhow this fault separates man from God and is, one might say, a mortal sin in Tukārām's theology. God does not willingly see this separation. He perpetually offers all men the opportunity of reunion: 'All are empowered to approach Him, Brāhmans, *Kshatriyas*, *Vaiśyas*, *Śūdras* and low-caste men, children and all others' (247); 'Hari does not remember a man's origin' (228); 'here prince and peasant are alike' (532). On Tukārām's own sense of sin see pp. 135–7 and 225–7.

IV. The Means of Salvation

1. Tukaram's Attitude to 'Moksha' or 'Mukti'

It is necessary to remember what a Hindū means by 'salvation.' One of the many striking aspects of Tukārām's teaching is the energy with which he sometimes dissociates himself from the common Hindū desire for *moksha* or *mukti*, which terms he uses synonymously (see below). On this subject it is not sufficiently recognized that when the Hindū speaks of 'liberation', the usual translation of the Hindū terms *moksha* and *mukti*, and the Christian of 'redemption' or 'salvation', they are usually moving in different worlds of thought, the Hindū referring to liberation or release from rebirth, the bondage of *karma*, the Christian to deliverance from the guilt and power of sin.[1] In Tukārām, however, there would appear, as far as we can understand him, to be an approximation to the latter idea seldom found in Hinduism (see also pp. 196–7 below). We have already seen how ambiguous and uncertain the saint of Dehū was concerning the Vedāntist view of the Impersonality of God—see pp. 187–90, this chapter. Similarly he seems to waver between acceptance of and opposition to the Vedāntic idea of 'liberation' for which he uses *moksha* and *mukti* alternatingly. Again and again, however, he definitely disclaims the desire for such 'liberation' in the common Hindū sense of cessation from personal existence. See p. 211 below on Reincarnation, especially two striking *abhangs* there (3134 and 3325), in which he states positively that he 'desires not liberation' and 1692 where he prays, 'O Pāṇḍuraṅg, grant me not liberation';

[1] See *E. R. E.* vol. xi, pp. 132–7.

also 211: 'I am thoroughly resolved to desire liberation no more'—in all of which the word *mukti* is used; and note 208 and 209 where the twin word *moksha* is used: 'Liberation belongs to you, O God; keep to yourself that hard acquisition' (208); 'your worshippers do not seek liberation' (209). Another of Tukārām's strong disclaimers has been turned into English poetry by Dr. Macnicol, the *abhang* numbered 763 in Fraser and Marāṭhe and 1462 in the *Indu Prakāsh* edition, the word used being *mukti*

> Hear, O God, my supplication—
> Do not grant me liberation.
>
> 'Tis what men so much desire,
> Yet how much this joy is higher!
>
> But that name how strangely dear
> That in songs of praise we hear!
>
> Ah, says Tukā, it is this
> Makes our lives so full of bliss.[1]

Nothing short of a critical edition of Tukārām's poems, followed by an exhaustive investigation, can determine exactly how far Tukārām was either consistent or whole-hearted in his disclaimer of 'the great release' (*mukti* or *moksha*)—see further pp. 218–9 in chapter 9—but it is a disclaimer characteristic of *bhakti* which prefers to continue in the fellowship of the saints on earth, singing God's praises and doing His service. This follows on the rejection by *bhakti* of the view that the Supreme Spirit is impersonal.

2. Hindu Methods which Tukaram Rejects

What are the means of salvation? We shall begin with certain things that Tukārām rejects. He rejects (i) The complete fulfilment of the rules of caste. This is out of the question, no matter how much we strive after it: 'You may give up doing or undoing or looking into sacred texts' (273); 'this business of rules and prohibitions is heart-breaking' (540); 'not through the burden of rules and prohibitions mayest thou, O generous lord, be found' (1727).

(ii) Austerities. 'By sacrifice and austerity and union with the body or by recourse to contemplation thou canst not be found' (231); 'such men (i. e., those who practise austerities) cast rudely from them the rug they long have worn, this is an impediment to service, it is a craving too hastily conceived' (336).

(iii) Mystic intuition. 'We trust not to knowledge of Brahman or union with the supreme soul' (204). Doubtless Tukārām joined Kabīr in protesting against the immoral doctrine that reading

[1] See *P. M. S.* pp. 83–4 for the whole *abhang*.

and hearing *Purāṇas* destroys sin and that a man may be absolved from the guilt of murder if he hears scores of *Purāṇas*; though see *abhaṅg* 265 quoted in line 7, page 198 below.[1]

3. Tukaram's Way of Salvation

Then what is the right path? (i) Repentance. The necessity of repentance, though implicit in Tukārām's system, is not emphasized in the same clear language as we find in the New Testament and in Christian writings generally. He speaks often of the purifying effect of God's grace and of course there can be only one motive for seeking it, but the actual moment or mood of repentance is not prominent in his lines. This does not mean that he is silent on the subject: 'Through repentance, guilt vanishes in the twinkling of an eye and the transgressor remains at peace; this is the true ceremony of purification, to bathe the mind in repentance; sin cannot touch repentance' (486).

(ii) Following on repentance there must be goodwill towards all creatures: 'if he be merciful towards all living creatures, be he learned or ignorant, the infinite one loves him more than his own soul' (487); 'to lay aside hatred is the secret of attainment; other rules of renunciation are waste of words' (489). And to this we may add: 'If you would attain means of salvation you must be calm and silent' (549). You must also be humble: 'With the exalted he is exalted, with the lowly he is lowly; you cannot seize him by an effort of strength' (294). 'Conquer your senses, control your mind, lay aside pleasure; this is how to secure salvation. Some fast and break their fast, others persevere with texts; these practices will bear fruit only if they are quite void of error. You will find fruit where the root is. Make haste to seek shelter in God (2538).'

(iii) Most important of all is faith, the firm belief that God is able to save: 'you will reach God by faith (*bhāva*); by efforts to know him you will not understand him' (505). 'The joy of faith (*bhakti*) enlightens the ignorant through their own fond desire' (233). 'Faith (*bhāva*) controls God Himself' (2034). 'Faith (*bhāva*) is the all-sufficing principle of the saints' (889). One of Tukārām's richest *abhangs* on the futility of external rites reads: 'Why do they worship stone and brass and the eight metals? The wretches have no faith. 'Tis faith (*bhāva*) alone that moves us and is fitly called the means of salvation. What avails your rosary? 'Tis only pleasure of the senses you count on it. What will you do with your learned tongue? It will make you proud and conceited. What will you do with your skill in song, as long as your will is foul within you? If you serve God without faith

[1] See also *E. R. E.* vol. xi, p. 562 a.

(*bhāva*), says Tukā, how will you become fit for him?' (2597). Concerning the *object* of faith see chapter X, section 6.

As for the *content* of Tukārām's idea of salvation it is probably not incorrect to conclude that sometimes he looks towards the commonly accepted Hindū idea of *moksha* and sometimes towards the ethical deliverance connoted by our term 'salvation'. See p. 194 above on these terms.

4. The Question of Merit

The question may be raised whether the power to accept what God bestows in salvation is a reward of merit. This brings us to the troublesome question how merit is conceived by Tukārām. We doubt if any particular answer can be given to this question. That there is such a thing as merit he does not doubt; he is always talking about it but he never defines it.

As a rule Tukārām is quite clear that God's grace is not bestowed as a consequence of merit: 'He requires no store of merit' (304). But passages may be quoted in flat contradiction of this: 'If you have merit stored up from the past you may suddenly meet with perfect satisfaction' (524); 'my merit has bestowed it on me' (324); 'this immeasurable flood of nectar—it is due to our great merits that it runs along this path' (338); 'if merit is stored up grain by grain then this is the reward after many lives' (339); 'my store of merit has found its consummation' (1831). Every man's future thus corresponds to his store of merit.

The above passages, however, do not represent Tukārām's most habitual or profound conviction. What he really feels is that the whole problem of the place of merit is troublesome and insoluble, and it does not repay men to hunt after its solution. Arguments on the point belong to that verbal theology which he deprecates. He would say plainly that to suppose God saves us because we deserve salvation is a piece of presumption, and he would not countenance this. On the other hand he would have said just as plainly that if merits do not count then the action of God may be called capricious. He would have seen these issues had they been presented to him, but as a matter of fact they were not so presented, for Hinduism has not debated this point with the persevering interest of Christian theology. It faintly emerges in Tukārām's poems but the conclusion to which he hastens is that the man who seeks salvation should waste no time in argument but throw himself at the feet of God. And he consequently expresses his own joy that he is done with the tormenting question whether his merits are sufficient or not: 'The Vaishṇavas have brought down heaven to earth with Vittho the chief thereof; merits past, present and to come, are all buried deep; they are driven forth as feeble creatures into exile' (3476a); 'exertions will leave you nothing but exertions, if you embrace peace it will bestow joy upon you' (327). Various lines dwell on the ease with which this great acquisition may be made: 'Viṭṭhala stands forth easy to attain by songs of praise' (287); 'unexpectedly without an effort I have heard the secret, I have learned to know God' (573). Much is said of the power of God's name: 'Uttering his name it takes not one instant to burn up millions of the five great sins' (265).

V. The Obstacles to Salvation

Of the obstacles that hinder men from approaching God, from seeking and finding salvation, we can make a long and interesting list from Tukārām We might place at the head of it the habit of saying to oneself 'I', 'I' and 'Mine', 'Mine', for Tukārām often blames this, but strictly speaking this is not the cause of separation but the separation itself: 'If a man keeps within him his private purpose—were it as small as a sesamum seed—or his sense of self, Nārāyana will not draw near him' (3207).

Perhaps the same might be said of desire or the habit of indulging desires. The propensity of the mind to form desires is compared to the exuberance of a wild creeper just as the headlong impetuosity of the mind is compared to that of an unruly horse. All this we can understand, but there is one curious uncertainty about Tukārām's position; we do not learn whether he teaches that it is the pains or the pleasures of life that most keep us from God, though we are quite certain that it was life's pains that led *him* to God:[1] 'Wasted is labour on wife, son and wealth, where the fruit is sorrow the seed is sorrow' (1730); 'through the attractive power of life, the mind is filled with hopes' (3183); 'the world is an imposing uproar of pleasures' (1842). His thoughts often dwell on the misery of life, the disappointments that befall the votary of pleasure, and then again he observes that men are often swallowed up by worldy pleasures so that all serious thoughts escape them. Putting the difficulty another way we may say that if by a pessimist we mean one who holds that human life is usually or always wretched, by an optimist one who holds that it is or may be always enjoyable, Tukārām is neither an optimist nor a pessimist. He has not realized the question or analysed the case. Nor has he any firm hold on the difference between pleasure and happiness, though this is essential to a philosophic statement of his views. He really gets no further than a perception of the fact that a man who is busy with the pursuit of objects of desire cannot open his mind to the love of God.

He sees also that fear of ridicule keeps many men from God. Much as Indian sentiment has always respected the devotee, men

[1] See pp. 83–4, 137–8.

have never been wanting in India—any more than in other countries—who have been swayed by worldly sentiment and have laughed at religion or at least at any religion that calls for the sacrifice of comfort: 'Shame and prosperity stand in the path' (324).

Above all he is afraid of learning. The most hopeless of men in Tukārām's eyes is the theologian: 'God is hidden by arguments good and bad and by the reasoning of theologians' (556); 'knowledge of God sets us far from God' (551); 'search not the forest of philosophy' (509); 'discussions of thy nature are a maze of error, let me refuse to enter into them' (217); 'annihilate this separation, the fruit of learning, between us; save me, O Viṭṭhal, I am better off as an ignorant servant' (463). The source of separation is partly the pre-occupation with arguments, partly the pride which learning fosters. Nothing parts man and God more than pride, but to him who bends, God bends Himself; He is not found where pride rules.

How great a hindrance to salvation was encountered in philosophical disputation, as Tukārām saw and heard it, is clear from the following vigorous words: 'If you would attain to means of salvation, be calm and silent. Tukā says, Verbosity has ruined crowds of Brāhmans' (549); 'O ye pious, quit the company of reasoners' (2542). The love of disputation was certainly associated in Tukārām's mind with the champions of the *advaita* philosophy, though it must not be forgotten that this system has its practical side and a monist might rely on its central doctrine of *maya* and yet might protest against a disposition to dialectics as much as Tukārām. Actually, however, the *advaita* schools are more verbal and verbose than the other, though Chaitanya is fond of disquisition about the various sorts of love enjoyed between Kṛiṣṇa and Rādhā.

VI. The Religious Life

1. Renunciation and Trust

How will the believer treat the world? There are passages in which he is exhorted to leave it behind him, to thrust it away from him with violence: 'There is peril in worldly affairs: seek shelter in God' (2305); 'resign the world' (841); 'I am angry against the world; it is a poisonous snake gleaming before the eyes' (322); 'take not on your head at all the burden of the world; devotion itself compels you to cast everything aside' (846); 'if pleasure seeks me out I will renounce it forthwith' (850); 'the saints look on birth and death as a dream' (888); 'avoid the world, let no stain of affection come upon thee' (510). He who has conquered his senses and destroyed his desires, thereafter forms no designs: 'Tukā takes a stick and fiercely assaults his body; he has made it pay for all the luxuries it has enjoyed' (842); 'strip the trees of their foliage and eat it; pick up rags and sew them together with a thread and cover your loins therewith' (2329); 'reduce your speech to silence, keep it away from all objects of sense' (277); 'there was one who lived a life of fourteen ages, yet he took shelter under a bundle of straw' (2328).

We have quoted a number of these passages in order to present fairly what Tukārām actually does say, but they probably do not represent his final or most characteristic view. We may now turn to those in which a different opinion is expressed. In some moments Tukārām seems to think that the religious man will simply look on at the activities of his body in a detached sort of way like a spectator. This is summed up in many passages about the body 'A vigorous body is the instrument needed for your service' (480); 'let the body be treated with all respect, for thereby we attain to all happiness through the recitation of his name' (820); see also 825, 829 and 836. This idea, however, is only fugitive, and the same may be said of pain and pleasure: 'Pleasure and pain we should view as coming of themselves: our business is to store up merit' (2298); 'labour suffices your belly but never forget Rāma' (834).

His final principles appear to be these: (1) Mere renunciation leads to nothing: 'What avails to live in a glen of forest if peace be absent?' (828). The essential thing is that we should not place ourselves in the power of desires: 'If you are to become an ascetic do it in this spirit: renounce desires of the world—it matters not then whether you live in a town or a forest, sleep in a cot or on a rock' (2316).

(2) Let the satisfaction of desire be viewed as an offering to God: 'I go on eating and drinking but I keep the account in thy name' (1798): 'in eating or drinking alike say: It all passes on to Govinda' (1802); 'renunciation leaves room for pleasure; .... what keeps God away from us, *that* is sin' (822); see also 3414.

(3) Thus the right course is certainly to stay in the world and go on with our duties: 'Whatever I do, O God, I offer thee as a service' (193); 'your proper course is to ask nothing of God, but to do the work appointed you to do, provided it be not done through any sort of desire' (3199); 'let us return to our tasks but refuse to identify ourselves with them' (183); 'it is not murder when a soldier does his duty. for he seeks no personal gain from the action' (2400); 'entrust your body to God but employ its strength in due season yourself' (3189); see also 222. Such passages may be contrasted with those in opposition to them: 'God does not suffer His worshippers to follow any worldly vocation' (3188); 'worldly life and life with the highest—he who acts both parts together, in the end achieves neither' (3465); see also 494.

(4) There is thus no objection to pleasures that come in the course of our duties: 'Be ready to honour pleasure when it comes: do not moan over sorrows' (3477).

(5) Tukārām deprecated anxiety about our worldly lot. It is a common thought that God takes sufficient care of His own: 'God undertakes the care of acquiring and keeping for them' (286). Perhaps it is in this connection that we should take the lines: 'If God is friendly to you then all the world is kindly to you' (243); 'God is bound to feed all animals, we need not trouble ourselves what we shall get to eat' (1653). The result is the devotee enjoys true and perpetual peace, the passionless state, *vairāgya*: 'I enjoy peace because my thoughts are fixed on him' (2272). Resignation is mentioned, but it is hardly conspicuous: 'Silence now my foolish speeches, what the Giver resolves will come to pass' (1817). Those are condemned who approach God for wealth: 'The ignorant seek for wealth through devotion; how can there be any true perception in their souls? They perform rites with their thoughts set on gain' (3466). For himself he says: 'If I cannot fill my belly with food I will eat dust, but I will not lay a burden on thee' (3323). Words like these reveal the depth and disinterestedness of Tukārām's religious devotion.

2. Religion an Experience

Some of Tukārām's most valuable observations are concerning the necessity and value of personal experience in religion and the worthlessness of all else without it: 'If you have no experience do not assume the exterior of knowledge' (560); 'you must pass along the road if you mean to reach the spot; it is no use listening to mere tales of it' (554); 'if God ceases to speak to a man, he too ought to be silent; people act very differently—when God has ceased to speak to them they go on talking about Him' (561); 'if we do not meet him face to face, what is the use of dry talk about him? Listen to the evidence in your own hearts' (584). Apart from inward religious experience the 'holiest of holy places' will bring no blessing to men: 'What good will *Kaśī* and the Ganges do you if you are not pure within? A man who talks without love is merely barking' (543); 'without the sweetness of spiritual experience both teacher and taught increase their tribulation' (549). With these statements agrees the striking saying of Eknāth a generation earlier than Tukārām: 'You may visit one *tīrtha* (holy place) after another, but if you have not forgiveness in your heart your merit vanishes.' Without such heart-experience of religion all profession is mere words: 'Till a man has some experience of his own, who would honour mere words?' (2081). 'The man has a crooked perverse heart, let not him wear the garland; the man with no sense of religious duty, void of compassion and a

26

peaceful spirit, let not him put ashes on his person' (2089). A religious experience of one's own is all-sufficing: 'Look at my experience; I have made God my own. I need only speak what he puts into my mouth' (3230); 'experience will enlighten the mind in its own season' (3231); 'you must make experience your own, by putting up a prayer to God' (3233).

It goes without saying that Tukārām has many poems dealing with the ecstasy of communion: 'I feel an inward sweetness as I gaze upon my treasure of faith· God is my bosom friend' (771). The thought is many times expressed in general terms, but it is an intercourse marked by a special limitation. One characteristic of Tukārām is that he appears to know nothing of the prayer of petition or intercourse in the New Testament sense. Prayer in a *general* sense—prayer for grace, for spiritual help, for purification—is found on every page of Tukārām, but prayer in *detail* is not customary with him. We read nothing for example of prayer against a specific failing, *e.g.*, against falsehood or cowardice, or of prayer for material wants. 'Give us our daily bread' is a form of petition we have not met in Hinduism. It is replaced in practice by the vow. For instance a woman will not pray that she may have a son but she will vow a certain offering or pilgrimage if a son is born to her. Tukārām has nothing to say about such vows, though there are passages in which he deprecates asking God for worldly blessings. Some might say he held the view that God 'knoweth that we have need of such things.' Nor does he mention prayer on behalf of others, even for spiritual blessings. 'The fact that there is in it no impulse to intercession for men' would appear to argue a grave 'lack in Hindū mysticism even at its highest' as seen in Tukārām. 'The prayers of the Hindū saints are for their own needs', not 'for the sake of sinning, suffering men.'[1]

VII. The Moral Ideal

1. Tukaram's Picture of a Good Man

It will be understood that we leave out of account here the qualities of devotion that have been dealt with in connection with the religious life. We are counting up the common virtues that are needed in daily life. In a good man then we shall find:

(*a*) Humility. This means not simply the absence of *mīpaṇa* but the simple absence of a high opinion of one's merit: 'Possessing all accomplishments, the saints claim no knowledge; one who knows all, yet keeps as still as though he knew nothing—such a

[1] *I. R. M.*, Vol. 5, No. 18, April 1916, p. 220.

one the saints come to visit' (888); 'give me, O God, a humble condition, for grandeur brings sharp torments' (362); see also 702.

(*b*) A peaceable disposition: 'As we utter Kṛiṣṇa's name a peaceful love to all men is born within us' (3403). This will show itself for one thing in avoiding argument: 'We ought to answer yes to every argument, to show that we have no mind for disputation; we ought to pursue no controversy' (2536); 'hate none; be jealous of no being' (3346); 'much the best thing is meekness' (3362).

(*c*) Kindness: 'The saints cannot bear to see another hurt; it is a sort of pain to themselves; they feel the soul in all creatures is the same; this is the law of morality; this is what is meant by worship; it keeps the soul at peace' (3477).

(*d*) Truthfulness: 'When a man speaks the truth, pleasures come welling up' (364); 'a man whose spoken words take effect, who leaves no debts unpaid, who restores loans to those who lent them, such a man is esteemed' (2196).

(*e*) A cheerful contented disposition: 'Each should take refuge in his lot' (3370). Perhaps along with this we may put the lines —all too few—in which he recommends a brave heart: 'Why should we lead abject lives? Our past brings us into the world; the right thing then is a steady spirit of courage; whatever can betide us can be no great disaster' (3434); 'you should be ready for the lot that overtakes you; you should not throw your troubles on God' (2219). The Christian would have left out this last negative because of his different conception of God.

(*f*) Simplicity. Though this is not often mentioned expressly, no doubt it should receive a prominent place in Tukārām's moral ideal, as instances in the biographical chapter show. It means an absence of duplicity, of concealed motives, of a calculating disposition, even though the objects of the calculation may not be discreditable. Tukārām would in any case think that very little in the way of prudence goes far enough. Not that he is without an occasional trait of shrewdness, which is amusing, even refreshing, in so unworldly an author: 'If a man irritates us it is best to keep away from him' (3373); 'we should give food to all creatures, but money only after a due consideration of their fitness' (3354); 'speech brings its own evils but a silent man is like a dumb post; avoid too much and too little, this is the wise plan; let your speech and silence be both appropriate' (984).

2. Hindu Toleration: 'The same to All Men'

Perhaps the most generally received, the most often quoted, maxim of Hindū morality is that we should be the same to all men. It is usually enforced by some illustration, such as that of the tree which offers its shade to the man who waters it and to the man who cuts it down. Clearly, however, this elegant simile does not clear up the exact meaning of the maxim, concerning which one is generally left in doubt. There appear to be the following possible interpretations:—(1) We ought not to allow any feeling of displeasure or anger to arise in our minds over bad actions or of pleasure over good actions. (2) We ought not to seek to injure men guilty of bad actions, even though they cause us displeasure: we ought to seek only to make them better. (3) Identical with this is perhaps the doctrine that we ought not to feel any warmth of love towards the good nor any hatred towards the bad. It is possible to add either that we ought to love all men or that we ought not to love any, but remain wholly unmoved towards all men.

In its essential meaning, the maxim 'the same to all men' seems to hover between these various positions and those who use it seem reluctant to define it. In practice it has done good as a force against harsh judgements and malevolence; it has also done much harm as an excuse for the lazy toleration of other people's misconduct, or for compromise in matters of principle. It is certainly abused in India.

How far does this maxim appear in the writings of Tukārām? When we meet with it, it is never far from something that interprets it as a practical rule: 'God is bound to enquire into guilt and merit: to us all men alike are good' (1653). This sounds in strange contrast with Tukārām's wrathful denunciations not only of mankind and of whole classes of men but even of individuals, including those who went to sleep in his gatherings or interrupted him with objections. Possibly Tukārām, who freely confesses his own shortcomings, would have admitted that he broke his own precepts occasionally in rebuking evil-doers with such personal severity. But under no circumstances would he have maintained that we are not to distinguish between right and wrong conduct. Probably, however, if pressed he would have said that we have no right to decide the degree of guilt in any particular action; we can only say that in our opinion it is right or wrong. And probably, too, he would if pressed have told us that he saw the difference between the warm love which the saints feel towards each other and the benevolence which the good man feels towards all companions of his human lot. He would have seen too that punishment, involving pain, is often necessary to save offenders and is not in the least the same thing as vengeance.

All these positions seem to be implicit in his sayings, but he does not make any of them quite explicit. With this admission we quote a few passages, but to estimate their meaning it would be necessary to read all the poems—not very numerous—in which Tukārām discusses our attitude towards mankind: 'Let me not distinguish the guilty, the vicious, the holy, wise; they are all forms of thine, O God; let me bow with my whole heart and serve them' (2238); 'a cloud distinguishes not a dunghill and a field;

consider not what the result will be; devote yourself to the work in hand' (2242); 'God is our friend; through Him all are our friends' (2247); see also 2246 and 3372.

3. Vices, Despondency, Ecstasy

A very large number of the poems are devoted to censure of vice. If we enquire what are the faults chiefly rebuked our list will comprise—(*a*) lust, especially running after other men's wives; (*b*) slothfulness; (*c*) a fault-finding and quarrelsome disposition; this appears to have been the commonest fault that met Tukārām's eyes, at least it is the fault of which he speaks most; combined with it appears the love of gossip and ill-natured criticism of one's neighbours; (*d*) meanness and stinginess; (*e*) hypocrisy and false pretence of piety; (*f*) gambling, though we do not hear much of this; (*g*) lying, though this again is not very often mentioned, and rather curiously there is little about dishonesty in trade; though Tukārām must have seen a good deal of this and even suffered from it: 'he who swears falsely in court he is a sinner in the worst degree' (3592); 'doubtless the liar will fall into hell' (2495); (*h*) all faults are deepened when they are combined with hostility to the 'saints' and Tukārām does not spare those who disparage them or refuse to help and cherish them.

On the whole he takes a desponding view of humanity: 'I am sick of mankind; I cannot contain my disgust for them' (994). He is strongly impressed by the difficulty of reforming the wicked. Their obstinate self-conceit and love of error seem beyond the reach of instruction, for some men are just like animals; you can do nothing to help them: 'The heart of the wicked cannot be penetrated though you reason with him all his life long' (2455). He heaps simile upon simile to illustrate this melancholy truth.

Tukārām never turned his eyes to schools or to schooling as an instrument for elevating our race. Indeed he has hardly anything to say about the young except for the constant use he makes of the image of the child and the mother to illustrate our relation with God.

It will be seen that Tukārām really escapes from the perplexities of the problem of the state of mankind by dwelling on the duty to serve all men. His strong sense of this duty swallows up all minor difficulties as to how we should judge them or even how we should feel towards them. We shall return to this point when we speak of the 'saints'.

Notice too that Tukārām has no doubt about the duty of examining and judging oneself. We should sit down and examine ourselves, like a tradesman does: 'When his accounts will not fit, he lights a lamp and sits examining them' (2194). When we find anything wrong let us freely take all possible blame: 'Let the object of our irritation and resentment be ourselves, then the rest of the world we shall look on as Hari' (3380).

What is his view of the worship we should offer to God? Tukārām by no means rejects outward ceremonies, as we see in another place, but here we may notice what he requires as an attitude of mind. There are places where he says: 'To contemplate God is to serve Him' (106); 'blessed is the time that is spent in contemplation' (201). But mere contemplation is not enough for his ardent spirit. He longs to fling himself at God's feet—literally at his feet in the temple, to roll in the stone courtyard in ecstasy. He loves to find himself in the joyous gathering of saints, with his cymbals in his hand, lost in rhapsody. Whatever else the pious devotee will do he will find time for these seasons of ecstasy and rejoicing. (On the distinction between ecstasy and devotion see chapter x, sections 6, 8.)

But we must credit Tukārām with a more practical piety than that of the mere ecstatic or enthusiast. A man's daily life must prove his devotion: 'Work for the master, devotion to the teacher, obedience to parents, service to the husband, these are the solemn service of Vishṇu: it cannot otherwise be experienced' (2059); 'every action should be offered to God; this is the only worship that reaches Him' (1126).

VIII. The Saints

1. Their Calling and Character

Tukārām often refers to 'the saints', by whom he appears to denote the body of devotees who undertake no worldly duties, look to the faithful for support, and spend their days praising Vishṇu. Such people existed in the Deccan, as they do still, and it is certain that Tukārām looked on them with no unfavourable eye.[1] He probably thought that the world was at least none the worse for the example of these simple, trustful, harmless enthusiasts, but if we weigh all his utterances concerning the religious life we shall feel that he did not think this retirement from practical life either a positive duty or a plan to be deliberately encouraged. One wishes he had spoken more plainly on the point; we should at least be more certain what his opinion was, but Tukārām leaves many things doubtful and the nature of the saint's calling is one of them. He leaves us in no sort of doubt, however, as to their great helpfulness personally. On this see page 139 and section 12 in chapter 9.

Tukārām would not have denied the name of 'saint' to any man whose life was saintly. What this means may be gathered from

[1] See section on 'The Wārkaris' pp 170-3.

the passages already quoted concerning the religious life. Many others may be added from the pages given up to the subject of the 'saints' in the volumes of the poems. To take the first volume alone[1] Tukārām emphasizes (1) their humility and unselfishness: 'Possessing all accomplishments, they claim no knowledge; they cannot tell their own from what is other men's' (888); (2) their purity: 'Blessed are the pious, for their heart is pure. The saints worship the visible God, they testify that they have faith therein. They know nothing of rules and prohibitions; their hearts are filled with devoted love' (894); (3) their happiness: Here come Tukārām's priceless words on the peace of the saints: 'Wherever we be, our minds are at peace in themselves' (897): 'mercy, forgiveness, and peace—where these are, there is the dwelling place of God' (706); (4) their other-worldliness: 'We tell you we live in heaven, but we have no dwelling of our own place' (896); (5) their love: 'A Vaishnava is one who loves God alone, his caste may be anything at all' (942).

2. Their Service to Men

Tukārām dwells with special earnestness on the services of the saints to mankind. Time after time he says something like this: 'They wear out their bodies in serving others; forbearing love is their stock-in-trade; their happiness is in the happiness of others' (2375). Of what service is he thinking? He does not make this point clear, but evidently religious and moral instruction is part of it. From the saints men learn what devotion is; they practise it and preach it. But it is probable that Tukārām included in the service of men the most ordinary help in the recurring needs of daily life. His own practices described by Mahīpati would bear out this view and it is a little curious that he does not explain his meaning more clearly. His influence for good would probably have been larger if he had been more concrete in dealing with the practical aspect of his teaching, though he gives us suggestions that help us.

Note the part of the 'saints' in helping to save mankind. There is no idea that they intercede for men or that their merits are in any way imputed to others, but they remain always a channel through which the grace of God is poured forth and made accessible to the world. Perhaps this is only through their spiritual example but Tukārām does not consider this a trivial service. On the contrary he is always brimming over with gratitude to the great company of the saints and exhorting his fellow mortals to fall at their feet: 'Cling to the robe of the saints' (232). In particular,

[1] *F.* and *M.* vol. 1, pp. 288–304.

the saints help to save mankind by serving their fellows :—(i) by means of their own companionship and fellowship : 'In the society of good men we have the actual presence of God' (926) ; 'make me a servant of the servants of saints ; let all my thoughts be employed on service to the saints' (236) ; 'let me sacrifice my life to win the company of the saints' (917 ; 'let me keep company with the saints in any guise ; let me lie at their doors like a dog' (948) ; (ii) by the peace they impart : 'To converse with them is perfect peace ; . . . I ask not who or whence they are ; . . . true heroes, pure in spirit, every one of them' (930) ; 'it is a blessed season when you have met the saints and embraced their feet ; the knot of doubt is unravelled ; there is calm within the heart' (931) ; 'in the village of the saints there is a full harvest of love, there is no pain or disquietude' (911) ; (iii) by the message they give : 'When shall I hear the saints tell me, Pāṇdurang has accepted thee ? After that my spirit will be at rest ; I shall feel assured that I am saved' (937) ; (iv) by the way they ignore caste and give every man his true value : 'A Vaishṇava, his caste may be anything at all' (942) ; 'shame on a Brāhman who is void of devotion' (946) ; 'one who sells his daughter, his cow or his sermon, he is rightly called a low-caste wretch ; the standards of goodness are merits and demerits ; God considers not a man's caste' (944). (V). We have already seen (at the close of chapter 1) what the 'saints' or *bhaktas* did towards building an Indian Democracy.

There appears to have been no definite organization of the 'saints' but since Tukārām does not raise the point we are left largely to surmise. Those professed devotees of Viṭhobā who had left the world and who gave themselves wholly to religious exercise were not ascetics in the usual sense. They practised no austerities. But neither did they do any work or earn money in any way. They seem to have trusted for support to the less thorough-going votaries of the god, who entertained and fed them and in recompense for this received spiritual instruction. This life as we have said Tukārām does not in set words either encourage or forbid. We may suppose he thought it a noble life for those who felt called to it, but there is a vein of common sense running through his poems and he was no doubt quite able to see that without pious friends these teachers would perish and that such friends must help them whenever needed. There are passages where he clearly says that it is permissible for a man to live in the world and to be a faithful servant of God, and he probably remained satisfied that most men should take this line. His genius was remotely averse to any sort of organization and he seems to have done nothing in the way of organizing the saints in spite of the *Bombay Gazetteer* assertion that he organized the *Wārkarīs*.[1]

[1] B. G. xx. p. 471-3.

IX. Duty towards Animals

1. Tukaram and 'Ahimsa'

The doctrine of *ahimsā* is that it is wrong to take animal life. This doctrine has been stated to be a deduction from the doctrine of transmigration, the inference being that the slaughter of any animal interferes with the process by which a soul is working its slow way towards emancipation, but this is very doubtful. It is, however, certain that we have here a reflex influence of philosophy on life. The doctrine is by no means accepted by all Hindūs. In the Deccan for instance many Hindūs are flesh-eaters and are no more scrupulous about mutton than anybody else. Mahārāshtra Brāhmans, of whom there are twelve divisions, all abstain from it, save the Janals who are fish-eating Brāhmans.[1] The doctrine of *ahimsā* makes its appearance in Tukārām's pages. Strange to say, the caste to which he belonged, the Marāthās, do not hold it, the use of animal food being common amongst them, though Tukārām shakes his head over the taking of animal life: 'What have the water creatures done to the fishermen that he seeks to destroy them?' (2523). But his most devoted followers, those belonging to the *Wārkarī* school of thought, hold tenaciously to the principles of *ahimsā*. See their principle numbered 13, on page 172, in accordance with which all *Wārkarī* pilgrims to Āḷandī, Dehū and Paṇḍharpūr are vegetarian in their habits.

2. Affection for Animals, especially Dogs

He recognizes duties towards animals: 'Despise dogs and pigs for their bodies, but show them respect for their souls—embrace spiritually beasts and trees' (876). This vein of reflection is not much worked and Tukārām does not, for instance, offer any suggestion how the needless suffering of animals may be averted.

On the other hand his attitude towards animals is extremely sympathetic and he shows a degree of observation rare in his country. He makes use of images from animal ways to illustrate all sorts of spiritual truths. Some of the images are drawn from the quaint old beliefs about animals that abound in every unsophisticated land. As the flamingo can separate milk and water with the tip of his break so Tukārām can distinguish the true and false doctrine. It is believed that the *chātaka* bird will not drink water from the surface of the earth but waits for it to fall from the sky into his mouth (2144); in the hot weather therefore he has to exercise a good deal of patience; in the same way will Tukārām wait for God's blessing.

1 See R E. Enthoven, *Tribes and Castes of Bombay*, pp. 241-2, 246.

Other images again are drawn direct from nature. Some may be stereotyped. Tukaram cries for mercy like a nestling crying with open beak for food, like a fawn for its mother when it is wearied by hunger and thirst in the jungle: 'What messenger need go to the ants' house? At the sight of sugar they come running' (2422). So too, he thinks, it should be unnecessary to proclaim the mercy of God, or tell men it is offered them since they feel the need of it themselves and know their own instincts. And Tukārām recalls in beautiful language the *Purāṇic* stories of the birds and the hunter (318), the hunter and the deer (238), Gajendra (150), the birds on the battlefield of Kurukshetra (1782), to show how God protects His people when they call upon Him.

Finally one recalls, even with amusement, the similes that Tukārām produces from his own observation. On one occasion he remarks how people are deceived about the importance of their own affairs: 'A bedstead is a mountain fortress to a bug; how much he has to climb up and down'! (2572). This will only be appreciated by those who have climbed up and down the mountain fortresses of the Deccan. 'A false teacher is as greedy as a cat, he goes begging from door to door' (1187). 'We may beat a thievish dog on the head; he howls but he does not give up his tricks' (996).

This mention of the dog, however, reminds us that the most beautiful and interesting of all Tukārām's animal similes are to be found in the series on dogs. The dog is not a favourite in India, as he is generally a mere scavenger, a lean, mangy, cowardly brute who picks up a disgusting living on the heaps of filth that surround the village. His humble condition makes him to Tukārām an appropriate image for the devotee of God, and at the same time he shows a surprising sense of the affection of the dog for the human species and his capacity for being trained. We cannot say if this vein is quite peculiar to Tukārām, since our knowledge of Hindū literature is so small, but we do not know of anything like it elsewhere. The *abhangs* concerned are 2143 and 2708 to 2712: 'If a dog be encouraged he hovers round his master's feet; so it is with me—I keep close beside thee'; (2143); as dogs suspect strangers, so 'Tukā trusts nobody but God' (2710).

X. Reincarnation and the State After Death

1. Reincarnation

That reincarnation is accepted by Tukārām as by all Hindūs is a simple fact which needs no proof. The continuation of individual life through various stages appears to him no more difficult to comprehend than its continuation through waking days interrupted by nights of sleep. The soul may pass from a human body to an animal tenement and back again to a human: 'If you behave like an owl you will return to birth as a pig' (972).

Holding this view, most Hindūs hold that the final end of the spiritual life is to escape from this cycle of rebirth, from personality at the same time, and to enter the state of final 'liberation' concerning which the only statement you can make is 'not that, not that'; nothing you could say about it would be true. This idea of final beatitude is by no means shared by Tukārām. He seems to think that it is somehow possible for those who desire it, but for his part he would reject it with horror.

What is it then to which he aspires? We get contradictory answers to this question. Complete faith in Vithobā transports the votary after death to *swarga* or *vaikuntha*, (Paradise) where he enjoys the bliss of devotion: 'Men of low degree that might not hear the Vedas have found a place in *vaikuṇṭha*' (2394); 'utter this name which will save you from the cycle of rebirth' (1730), 'the worshippers of Hari have gained an everlasting gain; they will return to the womb no more; they will enjoy supreme bliss in the highest Brahman; there is one alone who passes not into the womb, it is the servant of Vishṇu' (2146); 'the name of Hari drives away death and incarnation' (248); 'supplicate Pāṇḍuraṅg, save yourself from the 84 lakhs of rebirths' (320).

At other times, however, Tukārām seems to reject the escape even into *vāikuṇṭha* and goes so far as to express a positive preference for mortal rebirth, as it will afford him an opportunity to praise Viṭhobā and glorify Viṭhobā: 'Make me servant of the servants of the saints, then I will gladly return to the womb till the end of time' (936); 'grant me future lives wherein I may serve thy feet; I shall rejoice to be born again; great is the gain if one goes time after time to Panḍharī' (2304); 'we desire not liberation nor a place in *Vaikuṇṭha*' (3325); 'I desire not liberation, I should rejoice to be born again into the world' (3134); 'O God, grant me this boon that I shall not forget thee; all my wealth is with love to sing thy praise; I desire neither *mukti*, wealth nor offspring; only give me the constant companionship of the saints; if not, *then* grant me rebirth' (Translated from *Indu Prakāsh* 2306).

We do not see that any reconciliation of these conflicting views is possible as a matter of strict system. But Tukārām leaves the question of rebirth to his master, provided he is not cut off from personal service and from the joy of praising him.

2. Penalty of Evil-Doers

So far, however, we have only considered the reward of the really good, but there is the question what becomes of those who do not reach this level but die like ordinary mortals with their imperfections on their head. With regard to these Tukārām adopts the usual Hindū view that they are allowed a period of reward or of punishment according to their merits, after which they return to the earth in a form appropriate to those merits. This period is spent in *Vaikuṇṭha* or in *Pātāḷa*, (a place of punishment corresponding to the Christian hell). Tukārām has, however, very few references to the good man's days of happiness in heaven: 'What shall I ask for? Should I ask for the joys of *Swarga*? When my merit is exhausted I must return here again' (3135). On the other hand he has many references to the pains of hell, of which vivid descriptions are given. The ruler of this realm is Yama who is the agent of eternal justice, but not like Satan a tempter of mankind: 'The stern servants of Yama beat and cut and thrash them in countless ways; they make them pass over the edges of swords, over glowing coals of *khaira* wood; they roll them on the burning ground; they make them clasp fiery pillars' (1033). Illustrations of these proceedings may be bought anywhere in India.

This sojourn in hell is part of a man's *karma*, though as we have seen, Tukārām does not solve the question how merit can be stored up and operate. He does not try to solve the question how *karma* operates, and for himself he prays only that his *karma* may be broken up and dispelled by the power of God's name. But when he is reasoning with the wicked he makes much use of the threats of hell; he considers it certain the wicked will eventually find wickedness does not pay. For this reason he often stands amazed at their folly. And having this certainty of punishment in view he feels acutely how urgent it is that men should reform while there is yet time. Western thinkers have sometimes considered that the Hindū system perhaps encourages a procrastinating attitude towards moral reformation, for if according to the *karma* philosophy we have endless ages to accomplish the reformation, it is easy to postpone this; especially if after all it is not oneself that will suffer but some other person theoretically identical. Whatever is true of Hinduism as a whole, there is one place in Tukārām's system for this comfortable quiescence: the evildoer will suffer in hell with a full recollection of himself and his offences. To learn what Tukārām says on this whole subject all the poems in Fraser and Marāthe should be studied under the headings: 'The impossibility of escaping our past', and 'Rebirth'.

Many are his vigorous appeals to men to be prompt and wise. Make the most, he says often, of what your merit has already brought you: 'After many lives you have at least been born a man; now make yourself a friend of God' (3537); 'after many a birth you have secured this gain, you have entered a human body' (958). But how fast the opportunity passes away: 'Measure in hand, Time sits measuring out your days and nights; as thieves follow short cuts, so must we run ahead of time' (2302); 'no one can avoid the end; I have seen hair cherished with scented oils yet in the end it turned grey' (2322). Men interest themselves in perishable things, acquiring them by questionable means: 'What will they do when Death with his adamantine chain seizes and binds them?' (1029); 'neither millions of wealth can follow us nor the rag upon our loins' (2326). Yet the lesson is lost upon men: 'You know you are to die, yet you look for foundations to build a house upon earth' (439); 'you watch the bodies of your fellow-men burned, how is it the sight does not awake you?' (2396). Such sentiments inspire the most powerful of Tukārām's poems.

3. The Future Life

Tukārām does not share the Christian interest in the Future Life. In this he resembles his countrymen who have given little thought to this matter. Hindū speculation is much more concerned with the question how the world began than with the question how it will end. It is perplexed as to why the Indivisible Eternal Spirit came to take the step—so unnecessary, so deplorable— of suffering portions of Himself to pass out of His control, but as to how this step in the end will be retraced they have much less to say. Tukārām follows their lead in directing his speculative interest to cosmogony rather than eschatology. He does not, however, debate matters much He finds it sufficient that God created man, created His own 'incarnation' in order that the bliss of mutual love might be enjoyed between them. As regards the end of the world he is quite obscure. Of one thing he is sure, that the wicked are punished after death. And he seems to regard 'liberation'—the end of personal feeling—as a possibility, for he often says he does not want it; he even paradoxically seems to think that a man might go to Paradise, but he does not want that; the only thing he cares for is that the true devotee may on earth experience the bliss of the spiritual union with God.

If you ask his followers where he is they will tell you that he is in *Vaikuṇṭha*, the Paradise of Vishnu—not devoid of personal feeling but a glorified spirit. You may suggest that it is curious that Tukārām does not say more about his hope of attaining this end and some will answer that his modesty prevented him from anticipating such a reward. On the other hand in Mahīpati's record it is said that whenever Tukārām was asked where he was going he used to say he was going to *Vaikuntha* (see pages 105, 115–6, 126), and such a belief may without difficulty be attributed to him. From all the above it follows that there is nothing in Tukārām's teaching corresponding to the Christian faith in the resurrection.

Our enquiry in this chapter has sufficed to demonstrate the impossibility of seeking to reduce Tukārām's religious ideas to anything like a system. A man's own religious experience, however, may both be deeper and more consistent than his terminology would indicate, particularly if as in this case the terminology is that of a religion dominated by a time-worn philosophy. In the two remaining chapters, therefore, we shall examine Tukārām's personal experience of *bhakti* religion and estimate the value of that religion for the life of to-day.

MAN'S EXTREMITY *

Ah, then, O God, the efforts all are vain
By which I've sought thy blessed feet to gain.
  First there was loving faith, but faith I've none;
Nowise my restless soul can I restrain.

Then pious deeds, but no good will have I
For these; nor wealth to help the poor thereby;
  I know not how to honour Brāhman guests;
Alas! the springs of love in me are dry.

I cannot serve the *guru* or the saint,
Not mine to chant the name, with toil to faint,
  Perform the sacred rites, renounce the world
I cannot hold my senses in restraint.

My heart has never trod the pilgrim's way,
The vows I make I know not how to pay.
  'Ah, God is here,' I cry. Not so, not so.
For me distinctions have not passed away

Therefore, I come, O God, to plead for grace,
I, worthy only of a servant's place.
  No store of merit such an one requires.
My firm resolve is taken, Tukā says.

THE SECRET OF PEACE *

Calm [1] is life's crown; all other joy beside
    Is only pain.

Hold thou it fast, thou shalt, whate'er betide,
    The further shore attain.

When passions rage and we are wrung with woe
    And sore distress,

Comes calm, and then—yea, Tukā knows it—lo!
    The fever vanishes

HE LEADETH ME *

Holding my hand thou leadest me,
  My comrade everywhere.
As I go on and lean on thee,
  My burden thou dost bear.

If, as I go, in my distress
  I frantic words should say,
Thou settest right my foolishness
  And tak'st my shame away

Thus thou to me new hope dost send,
  A new world bringest in;
Now know I every man a friend
  And all I meet my kin

So like a happy child I play
  In thy dear world, O God,
And everywhere— I, Tukā, say
  Thy bliss is spread abroad

[1] *Calm*, or Peace (*Śānti*) * Translated from Tukārām, *P. M. S.*, pp. 68 80, 71.

Chapter IX

Tukaram's Experience of Bhakti Religion

There is no need at this stage of our investigation either to argue the case for the inward character of Tukārām's *bhakti* religion or to seek to establish the real moral strain marking it throughout. Both points should be clear from the preceding pages. Our remaining task is twofold: to delineate, as far as the available materials will allow, Tukārām's own personal experience of the *bhakti* faith; and then to evaluate his *bhakti* as a religion for the India of the twentieth century. The former enquiry is the subject of our present chapter, the latter that of the concluding chapter of the book.

I. Importance of the Bhakti School

We fail to reach the heart of our Dehū saint until we seek to understand his experience of that Indian *bhakti* which transformed Hindū philosophy into a religion, effected in India a reformation and revival contemporaneous with Europe's religious awakening out of her long sleep of the Middle Ages, and introduced into Hindū thought a spiritual element which represents India's closest approximation to the Christian faith. We are not here called upon to trace the origin of this doctrine of *bhakti* 'professed by at least one hundred and fifty millions of the inhabitants of India'[1] nor to show how in *bhakti* 'India rediscovered faith and love'[2]. This has been done in the luminous article on the *Bhakti-Mārga* by Sir George Grierson in the *Encyclopædia of Religion and Ethics* and by Dr. Sir R. G. Bhandarkar in *Vaishṇavism, Śaivism and Minor Religious Systems.* Suffice to say that apart from *bhakti* we shall miss the deepest secret of Hinduism, its enduring past, its present trend and its probable future, for *bhakti* has been the watchword of that purer and more democratic type of Hinduism which has enabled the system to adapt itself to all conditions through the changing centuries. The secret of the enduring character of Indian *bhakti* lies in its aspiring after a personal relation to a deity conceived as personal, in its use of the people's own vernaculars as distinct from the Sanskrit of the Vedas, and in its predominantly emotional character. In contrast with that type of Hinduism concerning which Tulsi Dās complained that 'the worship

[1] *E R. E.*, Vol. 2, 539a.
[2] *Ibid* 550b.

of the impersonal laid no hold of my heart', the religion of *bhakti* may be defined in general as a 'clinging of the heart'[1] or a 'personal faith in a personal God, love for Him as for a human being, the dedication of everything to His service, and the attainment of *moksha* by this means, rather than by knowledge, or sacrifice, or works'.[2] Such a religion, after ages of barren Hindū philosophy, could not but make a moving appeal, besides which, *bhakti's* power of adaptation to differing environments is greatly assisted by the fact that 'the highest *bhakti* may be directed not only to the Adorable in His highest form, but also to any of His incarnations'.[3]

2. Moksha, Yoga, Bhakti in Indian Mysticism

We have already seen 'the attitude of disclaimer adopted by *bhakti*' and particularly by the *bhakta* of Dehū, towards the Vedantic conception of *moksha*.[4] How far Tukārām was consistent and whole-hearted in this attitude we cannot say, but it seems certain that some of the stages leading to *moksha* or *mukti* were regarded by him as both attainable and desirable. For *moksha* or *mukti*, the goal of an orthodox Hindū's religious quest, has four stages: *salokatā*, dwelling in the neighbourhood of the *Paramātman* or Supreme Spirit; *samīpatā*, nearness to God, 'as near as a nestling child to its mother'; *sarupatā*, likeness to God, reflecting His glory 'as the glory of the moon is reflected in a clear still lake'; and *sāyujyatā*, complete union with God, absorption in Him, 'as the river is lost in the sea, or as the nectar of a flower is merged in the sweetness of honey'.[5] There were blessings obtainable *en route* to this last goal of *moksha*—those of *salokatā*, *samīpatā* and *sarūpatā*—which Tukārām doubtless desired. But connected with the highest stage of all, *sāyujyatā* or absorption in the Supreme Spirit, there are two features which Tukārām often controverts: 'there is no persistence of personality'[6] and as a rule it is held that the highest stage of religion can only be gained by *Yoga*. Both these aspects are disliked and often rejected by the *bhakti* school and Tukārām. For the latter see chapter 8, IV. 2, 'Hindu Methods Rejected', and in the present chapter pp. 227, 230. How emphatic Tukārām can be against the notion that man must lose his personality in order to scale the summit of devotion, the

[1] A. S. Geden, *Studies in the Religions of the East*, p. 351.

[2] L. J. Sedgwick, I.C.S, *J. R. A. S. Bo.*, Vol XXIII, No. LXV, (1910), p. 109.

[3] *E. R. E.*, Vol. 2, p, 539 b.

[4] See chapter VIII. pp. 194–5

[5] Mrs. Sinclair Stevenson, *Rites of the Twice Born*, pp. 197–8.

[6] *Ibid*, p. 198.

following utterances indicate: 'This doctrine that God and I are one is false, I shall not let it interfere with me' (212); 'the servants of Vishṇu are separate from him' (1685); 'Thou art void both of guilt and merit: *we* carry them in our hearts, whether washed away or still clinging to us' (1686); 'had I not been a sinner, how could there have been a Saviour?'—a profound suggestion. See also 1695 with Fraser and Marāthe's note upon it, p. 443, vol. II. It follows therefore that of the three chief Hindū 'Ways' to salvation, Tukārām appears to have decisively rejected both the *Dnyān Mārga*, the Way of Knowledge, and the *Karma Mārga*, the Way of Works, while the *Bhakti Mārga*, the Way of Loving Devotion, has had few nobler devotees.

India's mystical tendency, of which Tukārām is so outstanding an example, has followed, generally speaking, two chief lines of development, one of *Yoga*, the other of *Bhakti*. Devotees both of *yoga* and of *bhakti* have experienced a mysticism of a unique kind, but in the case of the former it has been linked with an asceticism absent almost entirely from the latter. Eknāth, Tukārām's predecessor, well expressed the difference between *yoga* and *bhakti*: 'The senses that *yogīs* suppress, *bhaktas* devote to the worship of *Bhāgavat*. The things of sense that *yogīs* forsake, *bhaktas* offer to *Bhāgavat*. *Yogīs* forsake the things of sense, and forsaking them, they suffer in the flesh; the followers of *bhakti* offer them to *Bhāgavat*, and hence they become for ever emancipated'.[1] The two types have been further distinguished as follows: 'The *Yogīn* seeks the bliss of contact with the Absolute by rigour and self-discipline; the *bhakta* seeks it through the beauty of song, dance and hymn. The former tries to suppress his desires, the latter to express them. The watchword of the former is "concentration", mainly an intellectual effort; the watchword of the latter is "devotion," largely emotional "abandon". To the *Yogīn*, Peace is the goal of the mystic quest; to the *Bhakta*, Joy. The former tries to satisfy man's craving for the changeless by penetrating ever deeper into the spiritual profound; the latter is allured by exuberant vitality, expressed symbolically in movement and rhythm. The former is individualistic, preoccupied with solitary meditation; the latter is social, deriving joy and inspiration from the company of kindred souls. The *Yogīn* neglects the accompaniments of sacerdotal worship, and loves the seclusion of forest or cave. The *bhakta* makes full use of temple, idol, hymn. The former may adore Eternal Being whether personally or impersonally conceived; the latter's rich and full devotion is directed towards a Rāma or a Krișna who represents the supreme Divinity in human form.'[2]

[1] Dr. Macnicol, *Indian Theism*, p. 270.

[2] W. B. Streeter and A. G. Appasamy, *The Sadhu, a Study in Mysticism and Practical Religion*, pp. 238-242.

3. Bhakti—Pure and Impure

It is true that the *bhakti* faith has often grown in unpromising soil, that it is found linked with pantheism and idolatry, that in the words of Grierson the *karma* philosophy 'hangs like a pall over it', and that the blessing it has imparted has too often been as fugitive and fleeting as the emotionalism accompanying it. The divinities to which some forms of *bhakti* have offered their devotion have occasionally been somewhat 'misty', and the extravagances of some other forms have degenerated into gross sensuality, the female element being so idolized as to lead to disgusting corruptions. But these degrading elements have been the debasement of *bhakti* and from these grosser aspects Tukārām's experience of *bhakti* is well-nigh free, though *abhangs* like 539, 1301–5, 53, 2495 (and p. 667 *Indu Prakāsh*, vol. 2) cannot be overlooked.[1] 'There are *bhakti* sects which can justly claim a place among the higher religions of the world. There are others which countenance, some which even aim at, a religious exaltation which finds symbols of mystic union in rites of an immoral character.'[2]

Happily the *bhakti* experience of the saint of Dehū belongs to the former type, the erotic imagery familiar to some other forms of *bhakti* being rare in his poems, thus giving the student the pleasant task of studying *bhakti* at its best. Such a student, moreover, is driven to the conclusion that he is studying one to whom *bhakti* is the whole sum and substance of religion, of whom it might be said, what was said of Kabīr, that to him 'religion without *bhakti* was no religion at all.'

What Tukārām's experience of *bhakti* meant to him has already been partly set forth in chapter 5 on the 'Autobiography', while our eighth chapter sets forth much of his teaching gathering around the *bhakti* ideal. In the sections dealing with the Ideas of God, Sin, the Means of Salvation, the Obstacles to Salvation, the Religious Life, The Moral Ideal, The Saints—in all these sections the exposition of 'Tukārām's Religious Ideas' deals with most of the fundamental aspects of Tukārām's *bhakti*. It only remains therefore to bring together Tukārām's personal experience of *bhakti* and his teaching about it, seeking to trace the deep underlying idea of the whole—the soul's quest after God, its faith in God, its devotion to God.

4. Bhakti Poetry and Terminology

In all study of the experience of Marāthā *bhaktas* two or three preliminary cautions are necessary. The *first* is a repetition of something said more than once in the preceding pages, viz., that we

[1] On these see chap. X, sect. 5.
[2] Streeter and Appasamy, p. 238.

cannot be sure of the authenticity of our documents or of the chronology or correct sequence of the poems on which we have to rely in our study of Tukārām's experience and teaching. This makes impossible any deductions as to the stages of his inward progress.

The *second* reminder is that a poet has his moods and that the religion of every *bhakti* poet was largely a religion of emotion. Says Sir Nārāyan Chandāvarkar, one of the most enthusiastic of Tukārām's modern admirers: 'To understand the hymns of Tukārām aright we must. . . trace the different phases of transition through which his soul had passed. . . (1) exaltation, (2) humiliation, (3) self-abnegation or self-surrender. Of the experience of Tukārām while he passed through his mood of exaltation we know nothing with certainty.'[1]

The *third* reminder, perhaps the most important of all, is that it is impossible always to be certain regarding the exact content of the terms he employs in expressing the yearnings of his soul. It is probably as incorrect to read into these terms *all* the commonly-accepted orthodox Hindū connotation as it is to give them the Christian interpretation sometimes adopted. We know his environment was entirely Hindū and that the ancient Hindū heritage had been handed down to him from his fathers. We know too that he by no means succeeded in breaking loose from that heritage, even if he consciously attempted to do so. That much of his religious terminology bore the Hindū stamp is therefore quite certain. But when we ask how much and how far, our difficulties begin. And yet the question is of the utmost importance when we deal with fundamental terms such as 'Sin', 'Salvation', 'Faith' and many others. We are probably safe, however, in concluding on the one hand that such terms conveyed to him far more than the merely ceremonial or philosophical implications held by most Hindūs of the time, and on the other hand that they could not have for him that full ethical and spiritual significance with which they are invested in the New Testament documents and later Christian literature. For example, we cannot afford to forget the probable chasm between his view of God and that held by most of his modern readers, his own educated followers not excepted; for even his loftiest flights of religious communion were probably more or less connected in some way with the image of Viṭhobā at Paṇḍharpūr. Of course on a matter like this, no one can be dogmatic, but it would appear unsafe in light of his poems to rule out the possibility of his having held communion with God of a purely spiritual character, altogether unconnected with the idol. In many *abhaṅgs* there would appear to be a measure of approximation to the richer moral meanings of some of the fundamental terms of religion, such an approximation indeed as to justify present-day *bhaktas* and expositors of Tukārām like Sir Rāmkrishna

[1] *Speeches and Writings of Sir Nārāyan Chandāvarkar*, pp. 525, 557.

Bhandarkar in attaching *some* deeper significance to Tukārām's devotional phraseology, as we do in the following exposition. But so many keys to the understanding of Tukārām are yet missing, that it is well to premiss the possibility that there may be whole tracts of Tukārām's experience concerning which every modern interpreter has gone wrong, ourselves included.

5. Divine Presence and Guidance

Alternating rapture and despair have left a deep mark on all Tukārām's pages, but on one theme he is unvarying and consistent: 'Cling to God always; think of God always; make God part and parcel of your life.' This is the one steady beacon-light that shines through all his poems. 'If you place your hopes in anything but God you will surely be disappointed;. . . when God is made the settled goal, He bears the burden of that man's welfare and does not forsake him.'[1] 'No particular time is necessary for the contemplation of God, says he: it should be done always. That mouth is pure which always utters the name of God. . . So preaches Tukārām to all people'.'[2] 'Tukārām has his home in the Inconceivable' (1578). 'In the Stainless One I have established my home; in the Formless One I abide. In the unconscious I dwell serene' (2755). 'God is ours, certainly ours, and is the soul of all souls. God is near, certainly near, outside and inside. God is benignant, certainly benignant, and fulfils every longing even of a longing nature. God protects us, certainly protects us, and subdues strife and death. God is merciful, certainly merciful, and protects Tukā'.[3] 'When thou takest service from anyone, it is service beyond measure; when thou givest, O God, though givest without measure. . . . When thou leavest us, thou leavest us far from thee; when thou drawest near, thou dwellest in the very heart' (1663). 'My spirit is firmly lodged at thy feet; wherever I am I will keep my eye on them. Tukā says, I am able to speak of thee, because God is contained in my heart' (1670). 'Thy feet are lodged in my heart, they point me out thy secret, O God. Thy feet guide my blindness, in thy wisdom thou leadest me; my mind is at rest, my senses repose; this is no strength of mine, O God. The difference of guilt and merit—this darkness thou hast removed. . . . Tukā says, This is an act of thy valour, O Generous One, I know it who seek thy aid' (2147). There comes next to the last *abhang* in the order of the English translation, one which might well have been a Hebrew psalm: 'Wheresoever I go, thou art my companion; thou takest me by the hand and guidest

[1] I P. *abhang* 661. Translated by Dr. P. R. Bhandarkar, *Two Masters Jesus and Tukārām*, p 18

[2] Sir N. G Chandāvarkar's translation, *Speeches and Writings*, p. 527

[3] Sir R. G. Bhandarkar's trs, *V.S.M.R.S.*, p. 95.

me. As I walk along, I lean on thee, thou goest with me carrying my burden. If I speak wildly, thou orderest my words; thou hast taken away my shame, I am made bold. I look on all mankind as gods and protectors; they are kindred and dear to my soul. Now, says Tukā, I pray with childish delight; I feel thy bliss within and without me' (2149). Of this beautiful hymn Dr. Macnicol has given the charming translation, with the title 'He Leadeth Me', which we have quoted opposite the title page of the present chapter In a sermon on this *abhaṅg* Sir Nārāyan Chandāvarkar has the illuminating comment: 'Mark the successive changes of the relation. We start in life with God as our Master; we begin by obeying him; His will is our law; and soon the Master develops into our Friend as we go on serving Him; then the Master and the Servant begin to be familiar; and the Master stoops to serve the Servant. . . The nectar of Tukārām's hymns is shed for us when they are sung; and of this hymn it is especially true. It has no falls—line rises upon line, thought grows with thought, and the poet pictures to us our God changing from Master into Friend, Teacher, Lover until at last His companionship turns Him into our very being. . . And growth from within means walking with God, feeling His touch, realizing His presence and communing with Him, filling ourselves with the spirit of what the Bible speaks of as the Holy Ghost and the Upanishads term मातरिश्वन्.'[1]

6. The Non-plussed Bhakta

This 'pilgrim of eternity', however, had passed through many a 'slough of despond' ere he reached so exalted a summit. 'O God,' he cries in one place, 'how many days I have spent in meditation and in praise of Thee! To meet with Thee and to enquire of Thee I came, but Thou dost not even turn to look at me. Not one word dost Thou speak of concern for my condition. Thou art altogether silent. I am in distress. For some word of comfort from Thy lips I waited, but Thou art so unconcerned that it seems as if Thou hast covered Thyself with a cloak lest my very shadow should defile Thee. I am ashamed at being called Thy servant.'[2] Many passages of Tukārām's passionate pleading with his god remind us forcefully of that non-plussed prophet of the Hebrew Old Testament, Jeremiah, who in the paroxysms of his doubt and grief accused God of having 'played with him and made a fool of him', as well as having deceived His own people. 'Ah, Lord God!' the prophet cries, 'surely thou has greatly deceived this people and Jerusalem, saying, Ye shall have peace, whereas the sword reacheth unto the soul. . O Lord, thou hast deceived *me* and I was deceived; I am become a laughing stock' (Jer. iv. 10, xx. 7). 'No need to

[1] Sir N. G. Chandāvarkar's *Speeches and Writings*, pp 629-31.
[2] Translated from *M. W.* etc., pp. 177-8.

tone down the complaint of deception,' says Dr. A. B. Bruce,[1] 'let it stand there in its unmitigated bluntness. The Divine Spirit, Author of all noble impulses, judges men by the habitual bent of their will, not by the verbal escape of their dark doubting moments.' Nor must we judge the earnest *bhakti* pilgrim when he cries out to his god, 'Thou art jesting, thou art joking with me,'[2] or 'Thou hast begun to play with me'.[3] The Hebrew prophet had exclaimed: 'And if I say, I will not make mention of Him, nor speak any more in His name, then there is in my heart as it were a burning fire shut up in my bones, and I am weary with forbearing and I cannot contain' (Jer. xx. 9); and our Marāthā *bhakta* cries out: 'Effect my salvation or acknowledge defeat; stand fast, O God, by the words Thou hast spoken. . . . I have clung fast to Thee. . . . I am sorely cast down; I cry to Thee, O God, for mercy' (1938). And he waxed even bolder in remonstrance with his god: 'You are cruel and inconceivable, you are stern and heartless; you do what should not be done; what no other has done, you do. You took from Harishchandra his glory. . . You brought together Nala and Damayanti, and you parted them; this all the world knows. . . Those who worship you are brought to such straits as these. Tukā says, We know not what you will do in time to come' (426). But just as the prophet, despite the self-contradiction, resumed his mission in spite of his repugnance towards it, so Tukārām, in spite of the disappointing attitude of his god, will still cling to him in loving loyalty. Despite the utter unconcern in place of the desired response, the longsuffering Tukārām resolves he will persist in his devotion.

It must be faithfully recorded, however, that Tukārām sometimes expresses views that cannot be harmonized with any worthy conception of the divine. Along with our *bhakta's* earnest remonstrances with his god there are reproaches which go far beyond either reverent doubt or good-humoured raillery: 'God is a timid creature; when He sees violence coming He hides Himself' (1755). 'Why dost not Thou run to my cry? Thou art keeping thy own body secure; for all thy strength thou art turning a rogue' (1963); 'I have now-well learned the nature of God; . . . people know thee for a thief and vicious wretch. . . Many found thee false in days gone by; this has been my experience too; Tukā says, O hypocrite, thou hast moved me to anger; now I cannot restrain my mouth' (2138). Such abuse of his god, however interpreted—and there are various interpretations—must be regarded as a dark trail across the bright path of the noblest *bhakti*[4] as is also the strange idea of sin in *abhang* 1862: 'Fail not in thy duty, O Lord

[1] *The Providential Order*, p. 349
[2] Translated from *M W*. p. 180.
[3] *F.* and *M* 294–6.
[4] See further chap. x, sect. 5.

of Rakhumāī; it is appointed to us to sin; it is thine to save the fallen; our part we have carefully performed; thy share must be done as it will.' That Tukārām had other ideas about sin our next section will show.

7. Bhakti and the Sense of Sin

How grave an obstruction, in his great quest, was his sense of sin, Tukārām has made abundantly clear, as we have already seen on pages 135–137 of chapter 5. Since that section was prepared for the press there has appeared the eleventh volume of Dr. Hastings' monumental *Encyclopaedia of Religion and Ethics* with an exposition of the Hindū teaching on Sin by Dr. A. Berriedale Keith, Regius Professor of Sanskrit and Comparative Philology in the University of Edinburgh. It must be pronounced inadequate. Apart from the statement that 'the (*Gītā*) doctrine of grace in effect overthrows the whole rationale of the *karma* theory, without substituting for it any basis of a moral system', and the mention of Kabīr's 'indignant protest' against 'sin-destroying' ceremonies that are either non-moral or immoral, there is no recognition of the depth of moral feeling which characterizes the sense of sin in not a few *bhakti* devotees. 'The later Hinduism of the *Purāṇas* and the law digests,' says Prof. Keith, 'devote their energies to multiplying the number of sins, ceremonial, social and moral, between which they make no distinction, but at the same time regard all those offences, of whatever degree, as capable of expiation by *prāyaśchittas*, . . . or by the saving grace of a sectarian deity whose favour can be won by acts of pilgrimage or devotion of purely formal character—doctrines wholly incompatible with the development of any deep moral sense of the heinousness of wrong-doing in itself'.[1] This imperfect characterization entirely overlooks the deep-rooted sense of personal sin and of moral need which finds expression in South Indian Śaivite saints like Apparswāmi and Mānikka Vāsahar[2] as well as in our own Vaishṇavite Tukārām: 'The Endless is beyond, and between him and me there are the lofty mountains of desire and anger; I am not able to ascend them, nor do I find any pass.'[3] 'I know my faults, but I cannot control my mind; O Nārāyana, stand before me to shield me; prove thou art truly called a sea of mercy; I speak but I find it hard to act, I am a slave of the senses; I serve thee as best as I can, says Tukā, be not heedless of me, O Nārāyana!' (1369); 'call this sinful one to thee; do not rake up any memories; root out my sinful acts' (1503); 'I know not how to cleanse me of sin, so I have seized thy feet. . . . Tukā says, if thou dost take a thing in

[1] *E. R. E.*, vol. xi. p. 562a.

[2] See *Hymns of The Tamil Śaivite Saints*, Heritage of India Series, pp. 43–7, 97–9, 101.

[3] *V. S. M. R. S.*, p. 96.

hand, what is impossible?' (2035); 'thy title "Lord of the humble" is justified in the eyes of men, thou hast saved many a humble, many a guilty, many a sinful man; Tukā dwells at thy feet; preserve him, O God!' (248); 'my strength was wasted by the long drag of the senses' (768); 'what can I do now to this mind of mine? In spite of all my prayers it will not stand still; . . . it seeks to drag me down to hell; . . . it is full of eddies of sensual pleasure; . . . hopes and projects are full of sin; they have ruined me altogether' (3031); 'I heard thy name, thy established fame as Saviour of the Sinful, therefore I hoped on; now I have found thee pitiless; I have lost all hope, says Tukā' (3036). 'What prayer can I put up? Who will decide that what I say has found favour? O Store of Grace, I can form no inference concerning this; most piteous cries have I uttered; no answer have I heard; up till now, I felt sure that some of my service had been accepted; Tukā says, now nothing but the struggle is left me; I see no sign of assurance in him who stands hand on hip' (3010).

I am a mass of sin;
Thou art all purity;
Yet thou must take me as I am
And bear my load for me;[1]

'though I made myself ceremonially pure, some impurity would cling to me. . . In every ceremony, errors arise, a fruitful cause of sin' (2968).

So remorseless was his introspection that even in his *kīrtans* and in the popularity resulting therefrom he saw 'the snare of pride' within. *Abhang* 1858 in Fraser and Marāthe has been rendered by Dr. Macnicol:

None skilled as I in craft of subtle speech;
But, ah.... .. ..
.... Who knows my inward part?

I proud became from honour that men paid
To me, and thus my upward growth was stayed.

Alas! the way of truth I cannot see,
Held fast by self in dark captivity[2]

In a sermon on this *abhang* preached at the Golden Jubilee celebration of the Poona Prārthanā Samāj, the Hon'ble Dr. Sir Nārāyan Chandāvarkar said: 'In this *abhang*, Tukārām warns us against the danger of self or conceit, showing how every moment of our life we are apt to be victimized by it. . . He says, I started with the idea of conquering myself but in the very process people come and praise me which is apt to swell my head. . . . They call me saint, but they do not know how much of sinfulness there is in me. They do not know how I have to struggle with myself.'[3]

1 *P. M. S.*, p. 65.
2 *Ibid.*, p. 76.
3 *Subodh Patrikā*, May 22, 1921.

In view of the foregoing and of many other proofs of a 'deep moral sense' in Hindū *bhaktas*, Dr. Keith and other scholars need greatly to revise their estimates if they are rightly to understand India's agelong religious passion.

8. The Quest for Inward Purity

Inward purity thus becomes a prime necessity in order to achieve the quest for salvation. 'I heed not ascetics and preachers of Hari, their views are many and diverse; I may salute them out of courtesy, says Tukā, but what I delight in is purity of heart' (2632); 'let this be your renunciation, to expel the sense of self;. . . what you need, says Tukā, is a clean heart and a spirit at peace' (2309); 'blessed are the pious, for their heart is pure; the saints worship the visible God, they testify that they have faith therein; they know nothing of rules and prohibition; their hearts are filled with devoted love' (894).

How shall this needed purity be found? Not by ceremonies nor yet by pilgrimage. 'What hast thou done by going to a holy river? Thou hast only outwardly washed thy skin. In what way has the interior been purified? . . . If peace, forgiveness and sympathy do not come in, why should you take any trouble?'[1] 'Do not give up food; do not betake yourself to a forest-dwelling . . . Dedicate everything you do to God, and have done with it; nothing else is to be taught but this.'[2] Not by anything which this 'helpless sinner' can do will he win the haven of rest: 'We cannot reach this God by hypocritical words; He knows the smallest thing that keeps you from Him' (2187); 'when I look for some means of escape, I am caught in such a strait that my intellect and force are reft away, . . . I am held as in a cleft by rules and prohibitions, . . . I am tortured by the desires that pursue me; now set me free; I am altogether feeble, O God!' (334). For Tukārām has full confidence that God can satisfy His child's desire: 'Tukā says, When God assists, He makes the incomplete complete' (2218).

9. Where the Path of Blessing?

How then obtain the divine blessing? It is a great question and Tukārām has a great answer: 'It is faith (*bhāva*) that procures the grace of God' (812); 'my single-minded faith (*bhāva*) has put an end to pilgrimage to and fro' (2773); 'Tukā says, the chief thing needed is faith (*bhāva*); God comes quickly and stands where He finds faith' (3671); 'it is faith (*bhāva*) that moves us and is fitly called the means of salvation. . . . If you serve God

1 *V.S.M.R.S.*, p. 95.

2 *Ibid* p. 97.

without faith (*bhāva*), says Tukā, how will you become fit for Him?' (2597); 'says Tukā, without devotion (*bhakti*) and faith (*bhāva*) everything else is useless trouble;[1] 'lay reasoning or learning aside in a bundle, for here faith (*bhāva*) is the one great criterion;'[2] or as translated in Fraser and Marāthe: 'Wrap up and put away your knowledge; here faith is what you must trust to' (558). In Tukārām's own mind there appears to be no doubt that *bhāva*, translated as *faith* in all the above cases, is the path of blessing. But when we ask his modern interpreters what the word *bhāva* means they seem to speak with muffled sound. Sir R. G. Bhandarkar defines it as 'faith, love, or the pure heart' (*V.S.M.R.S.*, p. 109); and again he says it has different meanings in different contexts and it is necessary to examine each case;[3] in the last instance given above the word meaning simply that heart-religion whereby the knowledge and vision of God are attained without conscious effort; and he supplies a deeply instructive parallel from the *Śvetāśvatara* Upanishad referring to 'those who by the heart know the Supreme Spirit who dwells within'.[4] Without importing into the word too much it would certainly appear to be on one side of it a remarkable anticipation of that heart-trust in God's mercy which alone brings peace to the troubled conscience. On its more practical side, what we may call its ethical aspect, Sir Nārāyan Chandāvarkar well points out that 'this faith on which Tukārām insists' has for its 'basis' the 'three principles of *Dān*, *Daman*, *Dharma*—charity, self-restraint and self-reverence. . . . The cultivation of these three virtues constitutes faith and we say with the saint that it is practical for ordinary men to live the life described by Tukārām?'[5] It is, however, with the inward aspect that *bhakti* is most concerned, what Tukārām alludes to when he says: 'The great precept of religion is to hear God in the heart' (812).

10. Change of Heart necessary

Without this personal experience of religion, both purity and comfort will remain as strange to us as sorrow is to a Gujarāti woman who will readily feign grief and will mourn to order for a few annas a day.[6] 'Fortunate, indeed, are those persons in whose heart dwells forgiveness, . . . who both internally and externally are pure like the Gangā and whose heart is tender.'[7] The great problem resolves itself therefore into one of change of heart,

1 *V.S.M.R.S.*, p. 95.
2 Translated from *M.W.*, p. 223.
3 *M.W.*, p. 187.
4 Translated from *Ibid*, pp. 187–8
5 Sir N. G. Chandāvarkar's *Speeches*, pp. 577–9.
6 *M.W.*, p. 248–9.
7 R. G. Bhandarkar's tr. of *abhang* number 5383 in Tukārām Tātyā's edition, *V.S.M.R.S.*, p. 97.

as many *abhangs* quoted above have already shown. 'Whether I am indeed God's child, truly accepted by Him, how am I to know? How shall I know of a surety that my heart is purer, my mind less tainted with anger? For if love be not in my heart how has my heart been changed?'[1] This wonderful seeker, says his greatest interpreter, points out three ways aspired after in his own experience of *bhakti*: (1) personal meditation and worship, in which the whole powers of mind and heart are concentrated on God, His words and saints, the latter especially; (2) personal self-examination, so intense as to root out pride and self-esteem, and Tukārām's self-examination—an essential part of his *bhakti*—was of a most merciless type; and (3) personal self-surrender to God, taking refuge in Him, so that there is no need of man or of his approval, no voice being desired but the voice of God, for man is the child of God his Mother and in that experience he may find a peace affecting the whole range of conduct.[2] If Sir Rāmkrishna Bhandārkar's richly-laden Marāthī paraphrase of one cry of Tukārām has not read too much into the *bhakta's* simple words—a possibility against which we always need to guard—then in one *abhang* Tukārām has brought all the above three 'means' together. Sir Ramkrishna's Marāthī paraphrase we translate thus: 'How sinful my body was, O God! But by meditation, by self-inspection, and repentant prayer my sin is cleansed and now my mind is full of love'.[3] Fraser and Marāthe render as follows: 'My body was filthy, but it was cleansed by thy name; my heart was washed clean with love; penitence brushed off the dirt; the chain of my deserts was severed; Tukā says, I laid my body at thy feet and bought myself off' (2064). With this agrees the commentary of Mr. V. N. Joga,[4] the meaning of the phrase 'the chain of my deserts was severed' being that his '*karma* was broken', illustrating how orthodox Hindū ideas and deeply devotional aspirations are mingled throughout.

11. The Steep Road to Bhakti's Summit

It was a long, rough road this pilgrim had to travel in quest of peace of heart. He confesses that his mind by turns is fickle, dull and restless. Often have faith and devotion been preached to him but what they really are and how they are attained he does not know. Let God therefore do with him what He will; let Him save or let Him kill; let Him be near or far away; at His feet this seeker will persist in staying, tarrying there in the spirit of a deep humility, a simple faith in divine protection, and a despairing

1 Translated from *M. W.* p. 315.
2 See *V S M. R. S*, 40, 55; and *M. W.*, 315–21.
3 Translated from M. W. pp. 143–4.
4 See Joga's edition, vol II, p. 675 on *abhang* 3997.

abandonment of self and its whole powers.[1] Deeply moving is the *abhang* expressing this resolve, too long to quote in full: 'Now thou shalt do as seems fit to thee; . . . I have sought thee, all ignorant, . . . I cannot rule my wayward senses; I have exhausted every effort; peace and rest are far from me. I have offered thee perfect faith (*bhāva*); I have laid my life at thy feet; do now as thou wilt, I can only look to thee; O God, I trust in thee, I cling firmly to thy robe. Tukā says, It is for thee to deal with my efforts' (92). In reaching so noble a resolve, despite its note of half-despair, Tukārām reached *bhakti's* summit, though he knew it not. In making the steep ascent, he had been compelled to leave behind much that had encumbered him, for only by the *bhakti* path could the Eternal be discovered, and the path was narrow as well as steep. Not by *yoga* could union with the Supreme Spirit be attained, nor by *mantras*. 'The five fires'[2] brought much torture but not God. Utterly vain too were all other austerities, and all mere knowledge. Not by these could the assurance of the Divine Presence be imparted to the soul. 'So devotion has been invented to measure thee withal, . . . for verily there is no other way to do it. By sacrifice and austerity and union through the body, by recourse to contemplation, thou canst not be found' (231). Thus it is only by single-hearted devotion (*bhakti*) that God is realized. To such a heart He appears everywhere and creates therein penitence for all wrong, says Tukārām; losing himself in God, such a one is filled with joy and his life becomes entirely fruitful[3]. On *bhakti's* summit Tukārām discovered a trio of graces—pity, pardon, peace—of which he grew especially fond, for we find them again and again in the hymns he sings. The *Vishṇu-dās* or servant of Vishṇu he describes thus: 'He who gives to God simple-hearted devotion which manifests itself in manifold ways, within his soul there dwells that spirit of pity, pardon, peace which keeps pain far away;'[4] 'there is no Saviour of the needy save God alone; for in Him are pity, pardon, peace and those other eternal graces which are the secret of bliss;'[5] 'where pity, pardon, peace abide, there God dwells; thither He runs and makes His home, for spirit is the place of His abiding, and where these graces have free play He tarries;'[6] 'when I attain the bliss of him who sees Brahma in all mankind then shall the ocean of my life swell with billows of joy, my heart will be turned from lust and other sorrows and in their place pity, pardon, peace will have free play.'[7]

[1] Paraphrased from M. W pp. 461–2.
[2] See p. 45, last two lines.
[3] Paraphrased from *M. W.* 179–82
[4] Translated from *Ibid* 436, see also *F.* and *M.* 1707.
[5] Translated from *Ibid* 581.
[6] Translated from *Ibid* 535–36, see another translation, *F.* and *M.* 706.
[7] Translated from *I P.* 2467; See also *F.* and *M.* 2189.

TEMPLES ON THE RIVER BANK AT PANḌHARPŪR

12. The Fellowship of the Bhaktas

We noted above in passing that Tukārām attaches special importance to meditation in company with saints. 'One special characteristic of the *bhakti* school,' says Sir Rāmkrishna Bhandarkar,[1] 'is that all the devotees meet together, enlighten each other as to the nature of God and contribute by discourses on Him to each other's elevation and gratification. This is almost a characteristic mark of *bhaktas* as distinguished from the *Yogīns*, who have to go through their exercises singly and in solitude'. 'In the Marathi *bhakti* poets', says Mr. Sedgwick,[2] 'the saints, i.e., *bhaktas*, men whose spiritual life is already developed are treated with extraordinary honour. Their society is to be continually enjoyed'. According to Nāmdev, the true disciples of *bhakti* must 'abide ever near the saints'. We may be very sure therefore that Tukārām's eager spirit was not out of their company for long. For the place they occupy in his system see the section on 'The Saints' in the last chapter. Here we are concerned with their place in his own experience of *bhakti*: 'I learned by heart some speeches of the saints, being full of faith in them; when others sang first, I took up the refrain, purifying my mind by faith; I counted holy the water wherein the feet of the saints had been washed. . . I honoured the instruction my teacher gave me in a dream, I believed firmly in God's name. . . God never neglects his worshipper; I have learned that he is merciful' (101); 'O Lord, thou art impatient to serve thy devotees. . . Sages and saints without number have learned what thy great purpose is; imperishable is the bliss thou hast bestowed on those that have altogether ceased to heed the world' (747); 'there is unending peace with the saints' (749); 'they dance and clap the hands and roll on the earth in a transport of love; my friends are the saints, the simple and faithful people of Hari; they have no concern with the world' (895); 'the meal which the saints have partaken of is a plate of nectar'[3]. On the defective aspect of this ecstasy among the saints, see chapter 10, sections 6 and 8.

13. 'Unsatisfied Religious Anxiety'

Stimulated in his inward conflict by the examples of the saints, and buoyed up by personal faith, Tukārām would appear to have reached some kind of goal in his soul's great quest. What goal he did reach, and how intense a 'lover of God' Who had led him there he became, is hinted in hymns like the following: 'I feel an inward sweetness, as I gaze upon my treasure of faith; God

1 *V. S. M. R, S.* p 20
2 *J. R. A. S. Bo.*, vol. xxiii, no lxv, 1910, p 133.
3 L. J. Sedgwick,'s *J. R A. S Bo.*, vol xxiii, No. lxv, 1910, p. 133.

is my bosom-friend, the bosom-friend of this helpless creature: according to his glorious might let him adorn us with purity. Tukā says, God eats with us, to give us a share in his love' (771); 'If I praise any other than thee let my tongue rot away. If I care for any other, let my head be crushed. If I find pleasure in others, surely it is sinful that very instant. If the ears drink no nectar of God's glory, what use are they? Tukā says, If I forget thee for one moment, what purpose can life serve?' (151). How he solved that other problem of his haunting guilt the following stanzas show:

Guard me, O God, and O, control
The tumult of my restless soul.

Ah, do not, do not cast on me
The guilt of mine iniquity.

My countless sins, I, Tukā, say,
Upon thy loving heart I lay[1]

And again:

The self within me now is dead,
And thou enthronèd in its stead.[2]

Students of Tukārām find themselves longing that the above might be regarded as describing the final haven of rest reached by our 'wrestler with the troubled sea' but we cannot be quite sure that they express more than a passing phase of emotional ecstasy, not uncommon with devotees of *bhakti*. If so, we have to fall back upon Dr. Wilson's diagnosis of Tukārām's highest attainment as having been one of 'unsatisfied religious anxiety'[3].

That there is real ground for this view is shown by the following considerations regarding our preceding paragraph, illustrating the constant need of the watchfulness spoken of on page 221 above. First, the lofty *abhang* 151, just quoted, is addressed to his favourite Hari, that name of Vishṇu which characterises him as 'sin-remover'.[4] Second, the first three stanzas quoted above in poetical form are given in Fraser and Marāṭhe (347) as a bitter cry arising from a poignant sense of sin not yet wholy appeased; 'Still my agitated soul; cast no reproach on me; receive within Thyself O God, the million offences I have committed'. Third, the last poetical couplet on 'the self' belongs to a class concerning which there is a violent cleavage of opinion; in place of the triumphant note of self-surrender, one school of thought representing some of the best authorities interprets the whole clause as expressing the destruction of personality itself through its becoming absorbed in the Supreme Spirit.[5]

[1] *P.M.S.*, p. 76.
[2] *Ibid*, p 79.
[3] J. T. Molesworth's *Marathi-English Dictionary*, p. xxvii.
[4] See note in V N. Joga's edition, vol. I, p. 87 on *abhang* 260 there
[5] *Ibid*, vol. II. p. 153 on *abhang* 2611

Thus our *bhakta* had not discovered any sure inward stay, but advanced and receded by turns, suffering as a victim of *bhakti's* moods possibly to the end. All these possibilities are indicated in 1434: 'Such faith (*bhāva*) as once I had I have not now. . . I see a loss of my capital before me; I think of the faults of others whom I see around me, to exalt myself thereby; I am like a cock, says Tukā, who goes on scratching the dung-hill and knows not if he is gaining anything or not.' By the very honesty of his introspection Tukārām here enables us to draw three inferences: first, that his faith was no *abiding* refuge—probably because it had no sure basis (see section 6, in chap. 10); second, his inward life suffered from a corrupt environment, leading to self-comparison with imperfect standards; third, he was still far from the goal of final spiritual assurance, for he 'knows not if he is gaining anything'. As we leave him, his heart is all 'agitated' with deep dissatisfaction concerning his own inward life and concerning his god: what these meant 'once' to him they mean 'not now'.

One task remains to complete our inquiry, that of estimating the adequacy of Tukārām's religion for the needs of present-day India.

A TRUE DEVOTEE

A true devotee, says Tukārām, is one who not only takes delight in singing God's praises but holds fast by Him and implicitly relies on Him, one too who is holy; and humble in his dealings with others and for whom no distinction of 'mine' and 'thine' exists. How is such devotion to be attained? It is primarily a work of self-discipline to which grace may in time be added. To promote such self-discipline is the object of this and other Samajes. As such their work can never come to an end. Nor can they show quick results. Tukarām's *abhangs* are sufficient evidence of the long and laborious journey which spiritual progress involves and the ups and downs to which it is liable. None therefore need despair but all should faithfully and earnestly strive for their moral and spiritual uplift till death itself releases them from the perpetual effort and the never-ending strife in which they are placed in this world.

Part of a sermon preached by Mr. V G. Bhandarkar, B.A., LL.B. at the Opening Divine Service of a Prārthanā Samāj Anniversary.

Subodh Patrikā, May 4, 1919

THE DEVOTEE'S PERPLEXITY

What may I know? What may I not know?
To turn to Thee for light is the thing.

What may I do? What may I not do?
To turn to Thee for light is the thing.

What may I speak? What may I not speak?
To turn to Thee for light is the thing.

Where may I go? Where may I not go?
It is well now to remember Thee

Says Tukā, What thou doest is easy.
Righteous acts become sins in our eyes.

Translated from Tukārām in *Subodh Patrikā*, Aug. 21, 1921.

THE DEVOTEE'S IDEAL

'Blessed are they who in their sojourn in this world carry mercy in their hearts, who came hither for doing good unto others, but whose abode is in Heaven; whose words never come untrue and who are indifferent to their own bodies; who have sweet words on their lips and big hearts within: so says Tukā.'

Translated from Tukārām, Dr. P. R. Bhandarkar, *Two Masters; Jesus and Tukārām*, Foreword.

INDIA'S DESTINY

With a liberal manhood, with buoyant hope, with a faith that never shirks duty, with a sense of justice that deals fairly to all, with unclouded intellect and powers fully cultivated, and lastly, with a love that overleaps all bounds, renovated India will take her proper rank among the nations of the world, and be the master of the situation and her own destiny. This is the goal to be reached, this is the promised land.

M. G. RANADE,

Chapter X

Is Tukaram's Religion adequate for To-day?

1. Conclusions reached: Remaining Problem

Our studies thus far have established the unworldliness and other-worldliness of Tukārām's character, the nobility of his long inward struggle, and the fact that while he largely acquiesced in the Hindū formalism of his day there was yet burning in his heart the lamp of a fervent faith whose light is reflected in his verse. We have heard his poignant cries for inward peace and through the three intervening centuries have felt something of his travail of spirit with his aching heart unsatisfied. His life-story represents the revolt against the ceremonialism and intellectualism of the contemporary Hinduism and illustrates once more the truth of Augustine's prayer, 'Thou hast made us for Thyself, and our hearts are restless till they rest in Thee'. Tukārām's religion was essentially personal and experimental, surrounded though it was by a desert of pantheism and a wilderness of polytheism. He supplies an instance of that epic struggle for a living religion that must have gone on in many another heart during the long milleniums of Hindū history. In him we see Hindū *bhakti* as a religion of spirit with marks of the flesh still clinging to it. That *bhakti* should have blossomed at all in the soil of medieval Hinduism is proof of some seeds of a divine life within it, and the combination in Tukārām of religious fervour and practical kindness establishes in a measure the ethical value of his *bhakti* though it often took quixotic forms e. g., his attitude to wife and home. His religious life was thus full of antinomies and incongruities and part of our task in this remaining chapter is to discover whether these arise from merely temperamental defects or whether they are the warp and woof of his *bhakti* faith. In short, we are to try and get behind his heredity and environment, his emotions and his moods, and see if his religion can hope fully to satisfy the heart and reason of modern India.

We shall more fully appreciate the wonder of Tukāram's *bhakti* religion if we frankly recognize the dark setting of its background. His *bhakti* was never entirely free from coarse and gross elements, for polytheism and pantheism were never far away. It was still a *bhakti* devoted to an idol and in tracing out the path he trod we have to pass through many a jungle of popular mythology. Nor did his fellow *bhaktas* always worship the same God, Rāmdās the contemporary of Tukārām being as devoted to Rāma as our poet is to Viṭhobā, and in the surrounding society the superstitions of animism were all-too manifest. Oftentimes, indeed, our *bhakta* himself is found worshipping more idols than one,[1] and it has to be admitted that irreconcilable inconsistencies concerning the nature of true religion meet us in almost every one of Tukārām's hymns. It is not surprising therefore that rapture and despair are strangely mingled and that to the very end he appears to experience far more yearnings than satisfactions. These and many other defective elements pointed out in the preceding pages must be faithfully recorded and they may appear of themselves to answer in the negative the question at the head of this chapter. Despite, however, the inevitable influence upon him of the conventional Hinduism of the 17th century, what we see in Tukārām of Dehū is a living religion asserting itself in face of the lifeless formalism or world-illusion of his day. The cry of his heart reveals a deep and real hunger of the soul. We believe every unbiassed student of Tukārām will be driven to conclude that in the religion of *bhakti* he was treading the highest 'way of salvation' of which he knew, that amid a superstitious environment he somehow communed with the Supreme Spirit Who as a Personal Being had won his heart's devotion, and that he possessed that element of true *bhakti* which consists in 'surrendering all actions to God', in 'feeling the greatest misery in forgetting God', and in experiencing 'the enjoyment of bliss which the soul finds in God'.[2]

In seeking to evaluate, in this last chapter, the contents of Tukārām's *bhakti*, and to measure its adequacy for the life of present-day India, there is great advantage in concentrating our attention upon an individual Hindū instead of roaming over a system, for Hinduism is not one religion but many, and its amorphous and encyclopedic character, which successfully defies analysis in any single treatise, is not sufficiently recognized by Western authorities. Seeing the term Hindū covers so great a variety of religious beliefs and practices as to make it impossible to point out any single one as all-essential, it is beneficial in every way to limit our study to a single individual. Moreover, in Tukārām we have an example of introspective piety of the very highest type Hinduism can show, one to which increasing prominence is being given in the writings of modern Hindūs, a type indeed in which the ideals of Christ and of a 'Christianized Hinduism' are more and more claimed as being found reflected. In our poet-

[1] Hindū students of Tukārām surmount this difficulty by pointing to such *abhangs* as 176 on p. 158 which teach the oneness of Vishṇu and Śiva and by taking a similar view to that of Sir R. G. Bhandārkar on p. 151 (4th and 5th lines from bottom of page) to the effect that all idols symbolize one God. Rām Mohun Roy's view quoted on p. 148 and our views set forth in section 5 below are a sufficient reply to these contentions.

[2] *Bhakti Sutras of Nārada.*

saint we thus see Hindū *bhakti* at its highest, and as with persons so with religions, we do not know them thoroughly until we see them at their best. Moreover, in Tukārām we are able to judge Hinduism by its aspirations, for all his ideals and longings are claimed as having been thoroughly Hindū. And in our final investigation we need to remind ourselves once more that Indian *bhakti* is largely emotional and liable to fluctuations, now exalted in ecstasy, now following the philosophical path to impersonality and uncertainty. This will help to save us from misunderstanding and censoriousness. Tukārām is a rebel spirit inside Hinduism, but, whether from want of conviction or of inspiration, he lacks the courage to become a reformer, a consideration that will help us to understand his instability, his ambiguities, his hesitations, help us also to sympathize with his sense of desolation and weariness. An additional attraction in favour of this individual method of studying the chief religion of India is that in hundreds of Deccan villages the beliefs of Tukārām matter ten thousand times more than do the tenets of the Sanskrit Scriptures. For the problem is exactly this: Are these beliefs adequate as a moral and religious force to-day for the millions in the Deccan, educated or illiterate?

2. W. B. Patwardhan's Verdict: Tukaram 'One-Sided'

Indian scholars have faced the problem and, despite their veneration for Tukārām and his principles, have not been unwilling to indicate what they feel to be his deficiencies. Perhaps the best instance is supplied by a discriminating essay of Principal W. B. Patwardhan's in *The Indian Interpreter* on 'Tukārām's Doctrine of Bhakti'. The whole essay of twelve pages is worthy of the closest study and though compelled to abbreviate it, we give its substance as nearly as possible in his own words.

First comes the important reminder that 'it is very difficult to say what exactly Tukārām preached on any particular activity of the human mind', chiefly because his poems 'often present a conglomeration of contrary and contradictory statements, and there is hardly any clue to lead to a decision'. Even the order of his verses 'in the various editions varies in every case; nor do the manuscripts that have been preserved agree in the order of *abhangs*.' Moreover, there is 'no standard edition available', and with 'hardly any men among us who have made a close study of our literary masters' and the needed research on 'the individual works of Tukārām' still awaiting those who may undertake it, 'it is very difficult to say what exactly Tukārām was, what he felt and thought.' Therefore the 'tentative character' of all conclusions must never be forgotten.

Secondly, we have an excellent sketch of Tukārām's *bhakti* experience, and of the conflict within when in 'disgust and despair' he turned away from the world. 'Where was he to go? He did not know, he only felt he was a blind man groping in the dark.' Suddenly he falls in with the *Wārkarīs* (on whom see pp. 170–2) and following their advice he 'adored with his whole heart the idol' at Paṇḍharpūr. 'Sing the name of Vitthal and you will be blessed', said they, and 'this counsel was like a straw at which the drowning man clutched'. But 'soon the first fervour was over' and 'recitation of the name lost its novelty', so that 'he felt he was as far from his destination as ever'. To make matters worse, 'he discovered he had lacked the very first principle of *bhakti*' which was '*bhāva* (faith)'. Nothing could make up for this. 'All my days, O God, have been wasted.'[1] The question suggests itself: 'Was he an atheist? The fact remains that he often castigates himself for want of *bhāva*'. He soon discovered 'it was not enough to believe in God, but that he must also believe in the power of God'. And after all, 'was not Viṭhobā—called *Kṛpāsāgara* (ocean of grace)—as full of pity as the ocean is of water?' Moreover, 'the Lord of the distressed is my Father'.[2] And 'He was also the Mother. Ah! the Divine Mother', and in this 'profound conception' Patwardhan sees 'an explanation of the ardour and enthusiasm that has gathered round Mary the Virgin Mother of Christ', for 'the conception of the Motherhood of God is perhaps the greatest, the most inspiring contribution that the Hindū theology, or rather the Vaishṇava school of *bhakti*, has made to the religious thought of the world'.[3] Nevertheless, Tukārām 'experienced a conflict between his faith and the tendencies of his flesh . . . Anger and rage and cupidity—all these passions were still tumultuous'. He therefore tried 'rigorous discipline', looking upon 'wife and children as entire strangers with whom he had nothing to do' and he sought 'to lose his being in the service of Vitthal'. He resolved to 'attain to this standard of *bhakti*—would, and perhaps did, live in God will in will, thought in thought and heart in heart'. But 'the blessings that result from *bhakti*. . . I do not propose to dwell upon, for the fact is that *bhakti*. . . . became perhaps an end in itself. . . . What does life in this world signify when man can go through the round of its routine without conscious participation therein, when he can remain in entire aloofness therefrom'?

Thirdly, W. B. Patwardhan proceeds to 'examine Tukā's doctrine of *bhakti*'. He willingly grants that 'it has been able to superinduce in Tukā the most ecstatic flight of devotional imagination' and continues: 'But while admitting that, I cannot bring

[1] *F.* and *M.* 1872.

[2] *I.P.*, 3839.

[3] At this point come a few lines quoted in our section on 'Tukārām's Idolatry', pp. 152–3.

myself to be oblivious of the fact that all this is a superstructure upon a view of life that was at best one-sided. The first turn of feeling came on the heels of a series of severe afflictions and bereavements. . . . Tukā's soul naturally under the severe conditions was almost crushed, and unfortunately for us it received a bent and bias that left much to be desired. His outlook upon human life and its conditions was warped permanently. . . . He was driven to despair. It was the sense of his own utter helplessness and a desire to get rid of this besetting evil that turned him to *bhakti*. His end was individual, the peace and solace and beatific rest of his own restless soul. . . . Such a view of life appears to ignore more than half of our life. A view of life to be a sound basis of our philosophy of life—to be the guiding force of our life—needs to be many-sided. Our outlook on life in these days has immensely changed. Life with us is infinitely fuller. The fulness of life and its all-sidedness, as some of the gifted among us can view it, leave no room for the one-sidedness of pessimism . . . Tukārām was far in advance of his own time perhaps, but he was withal a creature of his time. He just moved in the direction in which his Vaishṇava predecessors had gone before him. In fact, he walked in their footsteps. If, therefore, his view of life was in a way narrow, he could not help it. Any view of life that looks at only one side of it is narrow, be that side the pain or pleasure side. . . The *bhakti* of the future, therefore, ought to be broader based, fuller veined and larger souled. . . It ought to learn to reconcile the apparent discord, and value both as two halves of one whole. The diversity of life is perhaps as real as its unity. The *bhakti* of the past, as we have seen, would have very little to do with what appeared to it of this earth earthy. The *bhakti* of the future ought to blend earth and heaven. It ought to be able to live this life as a whole, wherein every power and faculty has full scope to grow to its fullest stature, and is employed in an endless process of development and adjustment of present ends to that vast infinitely distant end. That is to me the sanest *bhakti*.'[1]

We have quoted Principal Patwardhan's view fairly fully because it is not only the view of an Indian scholar of accepted repute but as preparing the reader for our own conclusions in subsequent sections.

3. N. V. Tilak's 'Bridge to Christ'

With the above verdict agrees that of another great Indian, one who was 'in the true succession of the Marāthā *bhaktas*' and who on the occasion of his public break with Hinduism showed in a

[1] *I. I.* April 1912, Vol. vii, pp. 19–30.

hymn he composed that he was in no sense breaking with India but was rededicating himself to her service:

> My wealth, my thoughts, ay, verily,
> My life itself I give to thee,
> My Hindistan so dear to me! [1]

We refer to the late Christian poet Nārāyan Vāman Tilak 'whose glory,' says Sir Nārāyan Chandāvarkar, 'rests in the fact that he reminds us of the poets of the great Marāṭhī *bhakti* school, . . . not a poet lost to other-worldliness,' but one who 'speaks to the heart of India because he has upon him the stamp of Dnyāneshwar' and who 'wished to dedicate himself to the service of his mother-land by poetry, politics and social service.'[2] How this patriotic poet of modern Marāṭhās estimated Tukārām's religious value we have already seen (pp. 165–6), the Christian *bhakta* pronouncing those void of appreciation who do not find in Tukārām the very soul of religious devotion. Tukārām's chief defect, in the eyes of his Christian critic, is that he makes God conform to his own changing ideas, thus making religion a sport of the human intelligence, instead of allowing the conception of God to shape his ideas. So changeful and inconsistent indeed is he that today's opinion is just as true as tomorrow's opposite will be. Is it possible, asks the Christian poet, to accept as final guide and helper one so fickle and with a mind tossed to and fro so much by pros and cons? Among *seekers* he must be esteemed the prince, seekers after the true God, seeking always, seeking to the end, but among those who have 'attained' he may not be numbered. Such is N. V. Tilak's verdict. By the *bhakti-mārga* was God's blessing sought by this prince of *bhaktas* whose personal character must shame many of the great, the most signal service he has rendered being that in his own land he has spread religion from house to house, bringing spiritual vision to the despised, leading them to aspire after knowledge and salvation. Then comes the most striking tribute of all from the once Chitpāvan Brāhman: 'As for myself, it was over the bridge of Tukārām's verse that I came to Christ.'[3]

It is a great testimony, witnessing on the one hand to Tukārām's enriching ministry and on the other to his inadequacy as a modern religious guide, testifying also to the fact that since Tukārām's day another name has begun to send forth its perfume through the Deccan country. N. V. Tilak's words, our translation of which fails to convey anything like the rich fullness of his vigorous Marāṭhī, are invested with the authority of one intimately acquainted with Vedic and Hindū philosophical literature, of

[1] *I. I.* July, 1919.
[2] *Dnyānodaya*, Sep. 11, 1913.
[3] Trs. from N. V. Tilak's Marāṭhī *Abhangs* numbered 44–51 in *Dnyānodaya*, May 24, 1917.

whom a Calcutta weekly said 'it was of no account to him whether God sent His light *via* Benāres or Jerusalem or Medīna'. His heart and mind having been captivated by a copy of the New Testament handed to him by a courteous European on a railway journey, on three successive nights he had the same dream in which he heard a voice, 'Follow Him and fear nothing,' and in his introductory 'apologia' to his poem, the *Christāyan*, singing of his new *Guru* to Whom he had been 'led across the Tukārām bridge', this loyal-hearted Nationalist dedicates his motherland to that *Guru* in the assurance that between serving Christ and serving India there is no distinction.

Patwardhan and Tilak by different routes thus reach the same conclusion, that Tukārām's *bhakti* faith is inadequate for modern India, Tilak the poet adding a supplementary conclusion that Tukārām nevertheless supplies an ideal preparation for something higher. See further his balanced view quoted towards the close of the next section, pp. 244–5.

4. Indian Comparisons between Tukaram and Jesus

In 1903 an English essay of 55 pages entitled *Two Masters: Jesus and Tukārām*, was published by Dr. P. R. Bhandārkar, while on June 8, 1921, the Hon'ble Dr. Sir Nārāyan Chandāvarkar, President of the Bombay Legislative Council, stated in *The Times of India*, that 'the best minds of India' were 'striving to diffuse among the masses the best that is in the Indian religions and to show that the best is not different from but is the same as Christ's teachings'. Since, therefore, on the one hand, our query regarding the adequacy of Tukārām's religion has presented itself in this comparative form to Indian thinkers of our time, and since on the other hand there are students of Tukārām who for one reason or another may feel the incongruity of such comparisons, the suggested parallels and contrasts between the Marāṭhā and the Nazarene call for consideration. Moreover, since this opens up the question of the 'comparative study of religion' we may as well here state our attitude to the 'comparative' principle in its relation to Tukārām's case. We regard it as an advantage every way to have a definite criterion whereby to measure Tukārām's ideals, and that Indian scholars have themselves adopted Jesus as their standard of comparison is matter for thankfulness, for it is against such a background that we are able more surely to discover the deficiencies of Tukārām's position. We have striven throughout this work to present Tukārām sympathetically and appreciatively, at each point giving him the benefit of every doubt, and we believe him to be one of the worthiest representatives of that Indian *bhakti* which is 'the nearest approach to Christianity among India's many cults.'[1] So

1 *I.I.*, October 1915, p. 131.

many, indeed, are the points of contact between Tukārām's writings and the devotional terminology of the New Testament that the question has been raised whether the Marāthā *bhakta* may not in some way have been indebted to Christian influence. *See Appendices II. III.* Happily, educated Indians of all classes more and more manifest a disposition to investigate the respective claims of the great complex called Hinduism and of its greatest 'organized rival'. As Nārāyan Vāman Tilak observed as far back as 1903, 'all modern thought has been touched by Jesus with penetrating energy, and Hinduism is by no means an exception.'[1] If only we can ensure that there is no mixing up of Christ and Kṛiṣṇa as by the Isāmoshipanthis in South Behar, and no such unscholarly syncretism as that of a Sanskrit pundit who told his class that the mystic syllable *Om* was the equivalent of the Three Persons in the Christian Trinity, then we may hope that the Indianizing of Christian theology, the naturalizing of Christianity in India and the Christianizing of India's *bhakti* poetry by the Indian Church will enable India to make a contribution to world-religion of unique and enduring value. While there can be no tampering with historic facts in the praiseworthy effort to Indianize Christ's message, yet it is a great gain that leaders in the Indian Church are seeking to produce a true Indian *bhakti* with Indian methods of expression and a heart wholly Christian.

It is in the spirit indicated above that we apply the aims and methods of the comparative study of religion to Dr. P. R. Bhandārkar's detailed comparison between Tukārām and Jesus in his English essay of 1903 and—in a later section of this chapter—to his remarkable Marāṭhī article of about 40 pages in the monthly magazine *Nava Yuga* for March 1921, when he administered a public and, as we believe, a well-merited rebuke to Mr. L. R. Pāngārkar for his uncritical and fulsome panegyric of everything pertaining to Tukārām in his *Śrī Tukārāmāce Caritra* (Life of Tukārām in Marāṭhī). Dr. Prabhākarrao[2] is deeply impressed, in *Two Masters*, by the great number of coincidences of teaching in Tukārām's *Gāthā* and the four Gospels, particularly by the 'great resemblance between the strictures' hurled against Pharisees on the one hand and Brāhman pundits on the other. 'Woe to you, you impious scribes and Pharisees,' says Jesus[3]; 'a Pundit by his fault-finding leads others to ruin,' says Tukārām. 'They talk but do not act,' says Jesus[4]; 'the Brāhmans have worked their ruin by disputation,' says Tukārām. 'They make their phylacteries broad, they wear large tassels,' says Jesus[5]; 'how can Hari be reached by rosaries and

[1] *Dnyānodaya*, July 9, 1903.

[2] He is thus referred to by Marāthī writers, partly to avoid confusion with his honoured father, Dr. Sir R. G. Bhandarkar.

[3] Moffatt's translation St. Matthew xxiii. 13.

[4] *Ibid*, xxiii. 3.

[5] *Ibid*, xxiii. 5.

markings and such shams ?' asks Tukārām. 'Irreligious Scribes and Pharisees are like tombs whitewashed,' says Jesus[1]; '*Gosāvīs*[2] profess that they beg no alms; they bring disgrace on their garb, though they try to play the part,' says Tukārām.[3] Other parallels in expression between the Prophet of Nazareth and the poet of Dehū will be found in Appendix II, the poet on occasion also displaying remarkable similarity of disposition, so that the bitterest of foes became the most ardent disciples, e.g., the case of Rāmeshwar Bhatt in sections 29–30 and that of Mumbājī in section 31 of our chapter 4. Calling attention to the invectives employed both by Jesus and Tukārām against religious formalism Dr. Prabhākarrao notes the price both had to pay. Not only did both denounce 'those people whose sole religion consisted in strict religious observances, in not eating or touching what in their view was unclean, in avoiding contact with people whom they considered to be low, etc., while great moral laxity prevailed below these appearances', but 'we know the outcome of this war with prevalent religion. One Master was crucified by the hard Jews and the other was persecuted by the mild Hindūs'.[4] The enquiry is concluded thus: 'Who is the greater of the two Masters ? The question is no sooner asked than answered. One is the Master of almost the whole of the civilized world, . . . the other is hardly known outside Mahārāshtra . . . We plainly see that it has pleased God to glorify Jesus, and let no man attempt to take away from the glory. But who was the better of the two Masters? It is not possible for us to answer this question. . . There is no room for such rivalry. And I have at times pictured to myself the pair, Tukārām calling Jesus, "Rabbi, Rabbi", and Jesus declaring to the world, "I am in Tukā and Tukā is in Me" . . . But if this essay of mine leads one Hindū to read the Gospels with reverence, and one Christian to read Tukārām with the same reverence I shall consider myself to be amply compensated'.[5] As, however, Dr. Prabhākarrao takes up some curious and untenable positions before reaching his indeterminate conclusion it is obvious the matter cannot rest here.

Discussing the 'historical values' of Gospels and *Gāthā*, our author takes up an attitude which would be sustained in no reliable quarter concerning either set of documents. If Dr. Prabhākarrao still believes that the Gospels are 'mixed up with legend' we can only refer him to a host of works disproving the contention, the Roman historians themselves not being higher authorities concerning the life of the first century A. D. than, for example,

1 *Ibid.* xxiii. 27.
2 See footnote 2, p. 6 for definition.
3 *F. and M.* 1205.
4 *Two Masters*; *Jesus and Tukārām*, p. 8.
5 *Ibid.*, pp. 52–5.

St. Luke's writings.[1] Still more unfortunate is the Doctor's characterization of the *Gāthā* as being 'with very few exceptions a faithful collection of the Tukārām's own sayings', for the answer to which uncritical assertion we will simply refer to Patwardhan's view in section 2 above (pp. 235–7) and to our discussion on pp. 119–26 in chapter 5.

There can be no doubt what would have been the attitude of our broken-hearted *bhakta* to any comparison between him and the Man concerning whom even a Roman judge declared after full investigation, 'I can find no fault in Him'[2] and who on one occasion confronted hostile critics with the question, 'Which of you convicteth Me of sin?'[3]. Contrast with this consciousness of sinlessness, a consciousness unshakable to the end and accepted by the world's thinkers as in no way inconsistent with matchless humility—contrast this with what Tukārām says of himself. We have already quoted on pages 50, 135–7 many *abhangs* indicating his desolating sense of sin. Here is one of Dr. Prabhākarrao's own renderings: 'Hear these words of mine, oh saints! I am a great sinner; why do you love me with such tenderness? My heart is witness unto me that really I am not redeemed. People take outward appearances for realities (*F. and M.*, 126, translate: Men look upon me with honour, because I follow a track that others have laid down). Much was I vexed with family affairs. . . I cut off connection with wife, sons and brother, and thus necessarily became a dull, unlucky wretch. I could not show my face to the public, and (therefore) sneaked into a corner. By the (cravings of the) belly I was extremely tormented. My forefathers served God[4] and hence I naturally worship Him; let none take it for (my own) faith, says Tukā.'[5] Is there a single living thinker, either in East or West, who could for one moment imagine words coming from the lips of Jesus expressive of such moral distress as the above? Can it therefore be a matter for surprise that many people in 1903 felt 'the incongruity of the comparison'[6] Dr. Prabhākarrao had drawn between sin-stricken Tukārām and One accepted by millions as their Sinless Redeemer? This matter merits closer attention. 'Is there anything in Tukārām's *Gāthā*', asks our author, 'which supplies a want not satisfied by the Gospels? Most assuredly yes . . . Tukārām has left us for our guidance an invaluable record of his doings—of *his* double *strife with* the world outside and *his own mind inside.* He has shown us by his own example "that *of our vices*

1 See the works of Sir W. M. Ramsay, Dr. Hastings' *Bible Dictionary*, etc., where full bibliographies will be found

2 St. Luke xxiii. 14, St. John xviii. 38

3 St. John viii. 46.

4 'This God'—*F. and M.*, 126.

5 *Two Masters*, p 5.

6 *Dnyānodaya*, Oct 8, 1903.

we can frame a ladder" . . . as a pattern after which to construct our own and scale the heights.'[1] There is, however, in all this not a word regarding the conviction of millions of people all over the world that in the Jesus here made the standard of comparison there were *no* 'vices' of any kind, nor *any* 'strife with His own mind inside'. Possibly Dr. Prabhākarrao would say that this claim is part of the 'distorted image of Jesus presented by the Gospels'.[2] But such an evasion does not explain the fact that millions of sin-laden souls affirm they have 'really been redeemed' by this sinless Jesus. Since, however, the 'ladder' of Tukārām's lifelong conflict with 'his own mind inside' is actually set forth as the one point of superiority to Jesus and as 'a want not satisfied by the Gospels', the question presses for an answer, which of the 'Two Masters' is more likely to be of help, the Sinless One who says, 'I voluntarily lay down my life for my lost sheep', or the despairing *bhakta* who cries, 'I have sought thee because I am fallen' (1860); 'I am vicious, guilty, how guilty, how can I tell?' (1881); 'what shall I do with this mind of mine? If I restrain it, it chafes the more and leaps down into a wrong place . . . It likes not to worship God or to hear about Him, and runs at the sight of sensual objects'.[3]

When we examine the Tukārām 'pattern after which' we are 'to construct our own' we find in it several aspects for which Dr. Prabhākarrao honestly feels he must apologize, affecting both Tukārām's life and teaching. We shall have to note in a later section (see section 8), how he apologizes for Tukārām's 'far from dignified' way of speaking of women, and indeed on this question he knocks away the Tukārām 'ladder' altogether, for in his Marāthī article in the *Nava Yuga* he states quite plainly that Tukārām cannot be regarded as a 'pattern' in any of the problems affecting India's women. He further apologizes for Tukārām's coquetting with the pantheism of his country, for his inability completely to understand it, and for the inconsistencies that mar his teachings at every stage. And, gravest necessity of all, he has to apologize for Tukārām's idolatry, though he minimizes its gravity by bringing forward the Prārthanā Samāj theory that it was only '*at an early stage* (our italics) of his religious life he was a pure idolator and a polytheist', on which theory see our second paragraph, p. 150 above. It seems tragic that there should be any need to ask the obvious question whether Jesus was *ever* an idolator? Dr. Prabhākarrao has unfortunately defaced the pages of his book by the five words we italicize at the end of the following sentence! 'It is true that Tukārām never looked upon idolatry as an absolute sin—no Hindū would, *and perhaps no man should.*' There is no need to answer this

[1] Ibid., pp. 50–2, our italics.
[2] Ibid., Foreword page.
[3] Ibid., p. 19.

conclusion, unpardonable as coming from a Prārthanā Samājist, for its author himself in his later article in the *Nava Yuga* wrote burning words on idolatry, words which leave little to be desired.[1] But we press one question arising: If Tukārām's *bhakti* tolerated idolatry, one of India's most degrading forces, is it possible for such *bhakti* to purify and uplift India's millions? See further in our next section, pp. 246–50; also our 'Additional Notes' in Appendix IV, where we reply to Dr. Prabhākarrao; criticism (of the above position) published in the *Subodh Patrikā* of Oct. 30, 1921.

Two other Indian scholars of deserved repute rejected Tukārām as a religious guide largely on account of his attitude to idols. Ganpatrao R. Navalkar, famous as grammarian of the Marāthī language, at the end of a dispassionate investigation concludes that Tukārām 'was not repelled by the gross immoralities of the *Avatāras*,'[2] while the Rev. Nehemiah Goreh, formerly known as the Brāhman Nilakanth Shāstri Gore, in a treatise extremely, perhaps unduly, unfavourable to our poet throughout, affirms that Tukārām 'believes like other Hindūs in Kṛiṣṇa's immoral acts'.[3]

Where such extremes meet, with Pāngārkar and Prabhākarrao Bhandārkar on one side and Navalkar and Goreh on the other, something has clearly gone wrong with the principles of interpretation. These conflicting views appear to be reconciled in the reasoned conclusion of the late Nārāyan Vāman Tilak, in an unpublished paper he handed to us when it seemed probable he would be a collaborator in publishing this book. Of the poet whose verse had been a 'bridge over which he came to Christ' (see page, 238 in this chapter), he observes: 'You can find much in Tukārām's poetry that runs parallel with the teachings of Christ, save its principles and spirit. These latter, eclectics such as the Prārthanā Samājists easily read into his words, and when they cannot do so they put them there. Tukārām's poetry is based on his own experience of life, which makes his poetry like a picture gallery where his own life is exhibited in pictures, and since the lives of Christ and Tukārām differ, their teachings must necessarily differ. As a religious enquirer, I made a careful comparative study of Jesus and Tukāram, because I first tried to follow Jesus without being His, and I found out that, since merely ethical maxims and sentiments are not enough to make a religion, Tukārām has nothing in common with Jesus. But he was a saint. Of these Hindū saints I have said in my *Christāyan*:[4] "They are far from Thee, and yet they are Thy devotees—none need doubt this; they are genuine saints who live for Thee." Tukārām was one of the

[1] See our p. 150.

[2] *Tukārām, Mahārāshtrian Poet and Saint, p. 33.*

[3] *Tenets of Tukārām*, pp. 11–2.

[4] N. V Tilak's posthumous Marathi poem of the Life of Christ in which the poet had nearly completed the Incarnation section when he passed away, May 8, 1919.

greatest saints of India, and as such he has influenced and is still influencing the devotional trend of his people. In the case of us Christians, he is one of the most powerful of sidelights. Only a a few weeks ago he threw me into the very arms of my Lord.'

Our own study of Tukārām's experience and autobiography has convinced us that could the message of Christ have fallen upon his ears it would have met with a favourable reception by the Marāthā saint. His heart was so utterly broken by his sense of sin and of moral inability, his yearning after God was so insatiable, his inward despair seemed so far from final satisfaction, his rapture so ecstatic whenever he seemed to have a glimpse of the distant goal, that we believe he would have felt every problem of his soul had found solution had he heard of Him whom the New Testament proclaims as the living Christ, God's Revealer to men, man's Saviour from sin's guilt and power, and the Sender of the indwelling Comforter as man's 'Friend-in-Need'. Could the poet-saint of Dehū only have heard Christ presented as the manifestation of God's redeeming love to a world of sinners, we believe his despairing heart would have leaped for very joy. In addition to what is stated in Appendix III regarding the improbability of Tukārām's ever having directly heard of Christ or of his ever having come under definite Christian influence, we would point out certain Christian fundamentals which are missing from his pages, truths which would so completely have harmonized with his deepest aspirations. The Resurrection has already been alluded to in passing (see p. 213) a truth which we believe would have assured Tukārām of the Living Divine Companion he so often longed for in seasons of disappointment with his god. To this may be added that other fundamental truth of the redemptive sacrifice, which would have answered his haunting sense of guilt. The all-enriching conception of the indwelling Spirit of God would have satisfied his yearnings for union with the Unseen, supplying him with a reforming, dynamical energy in place of the static, traditional system of the surrounding Hinduism. And lastly the *avatāra* on the brick at Paṇḍharpūr meant so much to him that could he have known of the wondrous Incarnation 'beneath the Syrian blue' we can easily believe it would have satisfied every longing of his aching heart. As Ganpatrao Navalkar observes: 'The times in which Tukārām lived and preached were characterized by an intense nationalism, just as the present, and at such times what is new and foreign does not command serious attention. Still we may believe that one who had known so much of higher truth and expressed it with extraordinary power might have been attracted by the glorious embodiment of it in a living person and that he would have offered Him his heartfelt homage. . . Tukārām would not have approved a narrow patriotism, . . . for he enjoins the universal acceptance of the supreme claims of truth', uninfluenced 'by considerations of the source from which it is derived', teaching that 'when one stands in need of sugar, he should not enquire into the caste and family of the grocer who sells it.'[1] See further our paragraph in Appendix IV, 'Additional Notes,' relating to Dr. P. R. Bhandārkar's attack on the 'child-like faith' of the *Dnyanodaya*.

5. Has Tukaram a Soul-Sustaining View of God?

True religion, such as shall sustain the soul in all life's crises, must be rooted and grounded in a worthy conception of God. As an English thinker has put it: 'In religion we should take care of the great things, and the trifles of life will take care of themselves.' Probably all will agree that the greatest thing religion has to 'take care of' is its doctrine of God. We have already noted our saint's profound religious aspiration, into what transports of ecstasy his soul can soar, and as an American preacher states, 'in regard to all religious feeling we must ask of its parentage and its offspring'. Of what divine 'parentage' is Tukārām's *bhakti* the offspring? When a man spends so much time in the company of his god as does our *bhakti* devotee it means that that god is leaving an ineffaceable impress for either good or evil. What then is the character of Tukaram's deity?

Religion, if it is to quicken conscience and sustain the soul, must be unshakably founded on the Holiness of God, and Tukārām has but a varying conception of this cardinal doctrine; he certainly does not realize that this truth *is* cardinal. Many sections in this book have pointed to this conclusion, especially such a section as that on 'Tukaram's idolatry' at the beginning of chapter 6, but to see his experience of *bhakti* in its true perspective and to estimate its religious value for to day we need always to bear the matter in mind. We may safely pass over unessential details marring Tukārām's conception of the divine—for many such elements India's educational advance will of itself sweep away—and concentrate on the fundamental aspects. That God is eternal, true, illimitable, ultimate is clear from Tukaram's verse. But what of the all-essential Holiness? Here is an element on which we must always insist. What sordid aspirations sometimes mar the earnest longings of our *bhakta* is clear from an *abhaṅg* like 539 in Fraser and Marāṭhe on the unchastity of the cowherdesses: 'The wives of the cowherds became immoral and unchaste and committed adultery with God: but what he gave to them he gave to none other, for he became entirely one with them. Unholy deeds we should commit, if they bring the possession of God.' Such words as these, however interpreted, mean at least two things: first, that the idea of God inspiring Tukārām's *bhakti*

[1] *Tukārām, Mahārāshtrian Poet and Saint*, pp. 22, 33.

needs much purifying before it can regulate man's wayward conscience; second, the *bhakti* itself needs to be ethicized if it is not to degenerate into moral turpitude. Both needs are clear also from Tukārām's lines numbered 25–30 on page 667, vol. 2 of the *Indu-Prakāsh* edition, lines not translated by Fraser and Marāṭhe: 'By the touch of Hari they became Hari themselves and were unable to express their joy. While following the traditions of their families they enjoyed the Endless One by adultery. Hari enters their hearts, refusing his presence to all others, and blessed are they who live in him. He never permits them to lack anything and he keeps them safe everywhere. The ways of God are mysterious even to Brahma and others. Such a God the *Gopīs* made their own (or, God is what His devotees make Him, i.e., He does things to satisfy His devotees). Blessed is their adultery, says Tukā, for they have secured unbounded bliss.' We have already explained on pages 31–33 why the allegorical interpretation of such things cannot be accepted as worthy of religion and we will only add that even if such a line of interpretation were eventually established it would still remain true that such expressions are the wrong way of conveying truth. Similar deflections concerning the divine character are found in the 'complaints' of Rādhā, Satyabhāmā and Sītā in Fraser and Marāthe (1301–5), while *abhaṅg* 53 has the pernicious notion that the utterance of a mere *mantra* with the name of God in it will palliate sin, and 2495 encourages the dangerous doctrine that God may sin through human agency: 'Nārāyan compelled Dharmarājā to utter a falsehood'. Since our enquiry in this section is entirely concerned with the doctrine of God in its bearing on Tukārām's adequacy as a religious guide to-day, it would not be allowable, in extenuation, to trace these things back to his ancient teachers or recognized scriptures, for that would necessitate an enquiry into the teaching of the two foundation scriptures of Mahārāshtra, one of which, the *Bhāgwat Purāṇa*, among other grave aberrations on the part of the gods, in X. 33, 30–35 says: 'The transgression of virtue and the daring acts which are witnessed in gods (*Īśvaranām*) must not be charged as faults to these glorious persons . . . Let no one *other than a god* even in thought practice the same . . . The word of gods is true, and so also their conduct is *sometimes* correct.'[1] Where there are such aberrations in conceptions of the divine character itself, it means that the polestar of true religion has become a shifting factor, for what is not good can never be divine, and where 'adultery with God' is pronounced 'blessed', even though it be by way of allegory, the inevitable result will be that man must 'relax into an adultery of the soul', which is exactly what we find in the idolatrous conditions of Tukārām's land.

1 Our italics, ref. from *Crown of Hinduism*; see also pp. 398–99 for similar teaching by Rāmānuja, the greatest of *bhakti* theologians, by Tulsī Dās (pp, 395–434) and by Govindāchārya (p, 320).

Multiplicity, as well as immorality, has deformed the idea of God in Tukārām's pages, and this robs God of His supremacy, just as the other factor robs Him of His purity. But the Living God must not only be pure, He must be One and Alone. Wherever there is a host of gods and demons, as there is in well-nigh every village in the Deccan, wild confusion is introduced into man's conceptions of the Universal Ruler. The bewilderment of polytheism is always closely linked with the absence of a supreme Holiness, as the bewildering and immoral stories of the *Purāṇas* show. Let men go wrong in their view either of the divine unity or of the divine purity, they will go wrong on all else besides. Tolerance of evil or of disunity in God will mean confusion in the whole of man's religious ideas. Hence the belief that the agelong proximity of Muhammadanism, with its stern view of the oneness of God, to polytheistic Hinduism may be part of India's Providential preparation for a purer faith. Tukārām it is true sometimes condemns the gods in the village pantheon, as for example,

> A stone with red lead painted o'er,
> Brats and women bow before,[1]

but it is mere denunciation and is only occasional, for in other places he can say that where 'village gods' are neglected it is a sure sign of the *Kali Yuga* or dark age. It is therefore quite gratuitous for Dr P. R. Bhandārkar to pronounce as 'perverse' those who cannot agree with him when he affirms that 'even a cursory reading of Tukārām's works will show that he uses these words (Pāṇdurang, Keśav, Vithobā, etc,) merely as synonyms for God'.[2] The mass of evidence, some of which we have given in the section on 'Tukārām's idolatry' in chapter 6, cannot be so evaded. Dr. P. R. Bhandārkar must surely know that these and many other deities are so consistently viewed by the people as living beings that the god Vithobā is regarded as going and staying permanently in several places at the same time, a place like *Viṭṭhalwaḍā*, 20 miles from Poona, for instance, to receive the worship of a particular *bhakta*. Are such deities to be viewed 'merely as synonyms for God.' If so, then the unity of God is reduced to a mere phrase, and confusion of a perilous kind is introduced into man's whole conception of the Divine Being. Not by such ambiguous methods did the monotheistic prophets of Israel overcome the idolatrous tendencies of their people. Neither is it in this way that Deccan idolatry will be extirpated. 'In every age,' says a Basel commentator, Dr. C. Von Orelli, 'ambiguous language has helped to distort religion.' Hence the uncompromisingly clear message through the prophet: 'I will take away the names of the Baalim out of her (Israel's) mouth' (Hosea. ii. 18–9). By 'the Baalim'

[1] *P.M S* p 23.
[2] *Two Masters*, p. 34.

were meant the different varieties of the one national deity worshipped in different places, and as Dr. Cheyne says on the passage, the danger to the religious purity of Israel is viewed as being so grave that, 'tenacious as the popular memory is, the unholy names shall be expunged from it'. A later prophet declares on Jehovah's behalf: 'I will cut off the (very) names of the idols out of the land' (Zechariah. xiii. 2). And as with the Israel of the 8th century B. C., so with the Deccan of the 20th century A. D., the only possible antidote to idolatry is its utter abolition and the complete removal of all possibility of such compromise and ambiguity as may arise from identifying idols with the Living God.

When an educated Hindū brushes aside this question of idolatry with the remark that an idol is a mere symbol reminding the worshipper of the Living God, he is able to refer to some of Tukārām's *abhangs* which look in this direction. See p. 152. But this attractive theory is completely negatived by the 'life-implanting' ceremony called *prāṇapratiṣṭhā*—see p. 148; it concedes a great deal too much to the 'spiritually lame' who thereby become 'confirmed invalids' (see p. 150), for the masses of the people can hardly be expected to draw the fine distinction between a symbol which is not to be worshipped and the Living God said to be symbolized; besides which, it overlooks the terrible results of religious ambiguity as seen in the widespread character of Deccan idolatry—see p. 153. Behind the first and second commandments given to Israel on Sinai there lies a religious philosophy infinitely wise and far-seeing. Just as the first commandment, 'Thou shalt have no other gods in front of Me'[1], has in view the sin against God's unique Personality, so the second commandment, 'Thou shalt not make unto thee a graven image', has in view the grave offence of sinning against the spirituality of God's Nature, seeing it is impossible to represent His spiritual Being by *any* material likeness. When Israel 'heard the Voice' of God they 'saw no form', and therefore to 'no form' or image must they yield homage, 'lest they corrupt themselves' (see Deuteronomy iv. 12–6). Hence the sternness of the second commandment against image-worship with its terrible words about the 'jealousy' of God lest any image, even of Himself, should be worshipped. In its last resort, the sin of worshipping idols as mere symbols of God—were such worship possible, which is doubtful—is the sin of misrepresenting the Supreme Being, for *God is Spirit*, and no symbol or idealization or personification can ever 'photograph' Him to the human mind, since the loveliest of external images is inferior to the lowest of spiritual ideas. Therefore, to seek to satisfy our conception of God by localizing Him is to limit and fetter our thought of Deity, so that the 'great fathomless, shoreless Ocean of the Divine

[1] The rendering of the Hebrew in Exodus xx. 3 by Dr. Driver, whose note on the phrase 'in front of Me' is, 'obliging Me (unwillingly) to behold them.'

Nature' becomes a 'closed sea'. To change the figure, idols or images inevitably mean a petrifying of those spiritual ideas which should ever be expanding, and substitute a visible fellowship for spiritual communion with the 'Father of our spirits' (Hebrews xii. 9). Nor does it mean only limitation and petrifying of our ideas about God, for degradation soon sets in. The Brahmo Pandit Sitanāth Tattvabhushan has shown that the degradation of Vaishṇava worship 'from spiritual contemplation resulting in exalted feeling, to the worship of images with material offerings' is to be clearly traced to the fact that 'the Supreme Being was represented as of the human form with a female consort, both having human passions and appetites', as set forth in the *Brahma-vaivarta-Purāṇa.*[1] All these implications lay behind St. Paul's argument against idolatry before Athenian philosophers (see especially Acts xvii. 29) and behind his scathing exposure of idolatrous conditions in the Roman world when he denounced 'the folly of misrepresenting the majesty of the immortal God by making images of mortal men . . . and calling them representations of Him' (Romans i. 23, A. S. Way's translation). On this matter of such fundamental importance Tukaram must therefore be pronounced an unsafe guide and our conclusion is that, if Tukārām's people are to receive the needed conception of God as far as His unchallengeable Superiority and Holiness are concerned, then Tukārām as a teacher for to-day must be deemed insufficient.

This is not a treatise on Hinduism in general, but it must be pointed out that Tukārām's view of God is further hampered by the presuppositions of all Hindū thought, such as Pantheism, Karma and Transmigration, by his coquetting with them much too often, and by his halting between two opinions regarding them. We only need refer to the relevant sections in our previous chapters, and point out the bearing of his ambiguities and contradictions upon his working conception of God. 'India is radically pantheistic from its cradle onward' says Barth, and Tukārām dallies with the idea sufficient to make impossible a religion of assurance and trustful certainty—hence his many cries of despair. The Pantheistic idea of God is a total denial of divine freedom, robs life of the comfort arising from Providential control, and takes from prayer its nerve and soul. Not for ever will educated India be put off with this time-worn philosophy—for it cannot be called religion —which holds no comfort for life's lonely crises. 'Can't you tell me *something* which will comfort me'? was the touching appeal of a Bombay Indian lady who had lost her only daughter. As sure as the stars move in their courses, India will refuse to be comforted by a philosophy which robs God of all power to help the broken-hearted or to heal the sin-stricken spirit. Pantheism, Karma and Transmigration are a poor substitute for the Living Father. They

[1] *Indian Messenger*, October 23, 1921.

crush hope out of man's soul, so that the music of God's forgiving love cannot be heard within. We would not deny to our lonely *bhakta* the one crumb of comfort which according to W. B. Patwardhan he enjoyed: 'The infinite round of reincarnation itself loses all its terrors before the prospect of the continuance of the privilege of association with God in *bhakti*. If Tukā could keep on serving his Lord, if he could practise *bhakti* as he finally came to conceive it, he would not mind, yea, he would even pray for, a return again and again into this world'.[1] Of this morsel of comfort we would not rob the despairing saint, though W. B. Patwardhan himself admits it was but an anodyne, deadening the effect of the fanciful reincarnation 'terrors' and the *bhakti* which could do no more than this was indeed 'an end in itself', much too 'individual' in its goal, with no assurance of immortality for Tukārām's many friends snatched from him by death's cruel hand (see pages 83–4, 138–9) or for himself when his own turn came. As one thinks of the oft-bereaved *bhakta* in the quiet town of Dehū he finds himself longing that the sorrowing man might have been supported by the soul-sustaining truth set forth in St. John's Gospel, chapter xi, and in chapter xv of St. Paul's first letter to the Corinthians.

6. Can Tukaram's 'Avataras' Assure Salvation?

Tukārām's religious life, or the greater part of it, is wrapped up with Vithobā's 'incarnation' (*avatāra*) of Vishṇu, the latter being regarded as existing in five forms—as absolute, by emanations, 'incarnations', saints, and images. We have already seen on pages 26–33 how great a place the whole idea of 'incarnation' (*avatāra*) has in India, one of the strongest possible testimonies to India's innate religiousness and its agelong passion for salvation, the latter term in this section meaning not release from rebirth but deliverance from sin. Incarnation, if it is to assure salvation to men, must be supported by two kinds of evidence, the first historical, the second ethical and spiritual. There must be historical certainty, and there must be the moral and religious assurance of lives transformed and of hearts and consciences set at rest.

Does the 'incarnation' worshipped by Tukārām, and implored by him for salvation, stand the historic test? Is there historical certainty regarding the Kṛiṣṇa 'incarnation' who stands on the brick at Paṇḍharpūr? Since God is separated from man and must choose some means of spanning the dark ocean that lies between Himself and man's despairing heart, what kind of historical proof is there that He has spoken to man in Kṛiṣṇa? Since Tukārām's intense *bhakti* must be regarded as that cry of the human heart for communion with God which He *must* answer, have we reasonable

[1] *I. I.*, April. 1912, p. 28.

assurance, nay unbreakable certainty, that He has manifested Himself through Kṛiṣṇa—the Kriṣṇa about whom we have some thirty pages of poems from Tukārām in *F. and M's* translations? And since the comparison with Christ has been brought in by Indian thinkers (see section 4 above), and since for *His* Incarnation there *is* the twofold assurance required (see below), can it be said that Kṛiṣṇa's claims as an 'incarnation' are in any sense comparable with His? The historic spirit is so much at work to-day in India, producing innumerable modifications in the whole idea of incarnation, a process intensified by Christian influence, that many thoughtful minds are asking the question: What if, after all, the *avatāras* are shown to be mythical? A sample of this process is given on pages 30–3 and in view of the considerations there set forth it is surprising to read in a journal like *The Indian Social Reformer* for August 28, 1921 that, although, as is admitted, 'there is no reference to Kriṣṇa in contemporary foreign literature,' yet 'to the Hindū there can be no doubt about' his historicity, no grounds of any kind being assigned for this wholesale swallowing of a difficulty which constitutes to-day probably one of the most haunting problems in thousands of Indian minds. Such haunting doubt is in accord with the protestantism of Kabīr who plainly declares the ten *avatāras* to be 'dead', a point our Tukārām never seems to reach. The *bhakti* theory being that God's manifestation and man's salvation are both to be accomplished through the medium of *avatāras*, it becomes a matter of the highest importance that each *avatāra* must bear the closest possible historical scrutiny, for if it appears that the *avatāra* is but 'a cosmic legend,' then the solid usefulness of *bhakti* as satisfying either heart or intellect will be gravely diminished. For the very essence of Tukārām's *bhakti* is in its being lavished on the idol supposed to embody the 'incarnation', and if this latter will not bear the searchlight of ordinary historical investigation, it means the *bhakti* is misplaced and misdirected. Hence the ever-recurring unsatisfiedness of heart and mind in our earnest *bhakta*, such as none but the Living God, manifested in a Supreme Person, can ever appease. The great initial advantage yielded by the historicity of the Incarnation of God in Christ does not depend on the 'few and vague references' to Him 'by contemporary Roman writers,'[1] but on the fact that the historic reality of Jesus has withstood the most searching investigation in the history of mankind, and on the further *fact* that the purifying power of His personality has become a historic *factor* testified to by millions of witnesses representing every race.

But what of the actuality and personality of those 'incarnations' (*avatāras*) of Vishṇu to which Tukārām pinned his faith? The Brahmo Pundit Sitanāth Tattvabhushan of Calcutta affirms: 'The Vishṇu of the *Purāṇas* is the universe conceived as a person. . .

[1]*The Indian Social Reformer*, August 28, 1921.

The *Purāṇas* represent what is only a figure of speech as a person in flesh and blood moving about and conversing with his creatures. The ignorant and thoughtless reader of the *Purāṇas* does not see that their authors are indulging in poetic fancy and takes them as stating facts. . . But the writers of the *Purāṇas* can hardly be blamed for this. They make no secret of the fact that the representation of Vishṇu as an embodied person with limbs and organs like those of a man is purely metaphorical.'[1] In face of these withering words, can the historic reality of Vishṇu's 'incarnation' at Paṇdharpur be regarded as tenable?

If, then, the historic test fails when applied to Vishṇu's 'incarnation' worshipped by Tukārām, what of the ethical and spiritual test? Is there evidence that man's insatiable craving is satisfied by the *avatāras* of Tukārām's belief, a craving for communion with the Unseen, all barriers of sin removed? Since Deity transcends human apprehension, the *bhakti* theologians hold that only by a mediating 'incarnation' can God speak with man or act on him, or man worship God and be saved from sin, hence Tukārām's astonishing devotion to what he deems such a manifestation. Is there convincing evidence that by the particular 'manifestation' in Vithobā the sickness has been cured which another Hindū *bhakta* diagnoses as 'the pain of separation from God'? For though, says this same *bhakta*, 'a man should have thousands of devices, even one would not assist him in obtaining God.'[2] Does the device of *avatāras* avail to 'obtain God'? Here we are confronted with the perplexing paradox that while the *avatāras* and their images are in theory supposed to 'symbolize' the divine presence, hey have in point of fact been the most degrading force in India's history, leading to religious confusion, barrenness and formalism as anyone may discover by trying to count and characterize the deities in nearly every Deccan village. When we ask why these 'incarnations' have exercized a degrading, rather than a saving, influence we find the Vaishṇavite *bhakta*, despite his longing for purity, has either to allegorize, or apologize for, the impurities attributed to the god he worships, and stamped on the scriptures he reads. Fraser and Marāṭhe's thirty pages in volume 2 of their Tukārām translations quite suffice for the purpose, though the matter is made much more luminous when reference is made to some of the scriptures on which Tukārām sought to nurture his soul. Not only is 'incarnate' Kṛiṣṇa viewed in Tukārām's favourite *Bhāgwat Purāṇa* merely 'as a partial incarnation of God' but the same scripture sets forth Kṛiṣṇa as bearing grave 'moral stigma,' his character being sorely marred by 'illicit love'. When we go to others of the eighteen *Purāṇas* at whose sullied fount Tukārām drank, some of them are

[1] *Indian Messenger*, June 26, 1921.

[2] Nānak, Japi I quoted in *Indian Theism* from Macauliffe's *Sikh Religion*, I, p. 196.

popular only because of their 'outrageously indecent descriptions of the *Rasalīla* and the loose ideas of morals permeating'[1] them. This is sorry stuff on which to build a hope of salvation, for it brings in moral confusion of all kinds instead of assurance of pardon for man's soul. It would have been a surprising thing if assurance of salvation from sin *could* have reached Tukārām through such channels.

Disillusionment and bitterness of soul were thus often the lot of our *bhakti* poet, as of one Akho in Gujerat who 'compared his *guru* to an old bullock yoked to a cart he could not draw, a useless expense to his owner, and to a stone in the embrace of a drowning man which sinks where it is expected to save.'[2] Tukārām's unsystematic utterances on the one hand reveal his many disappointments with the god whom he roundly abuses. On the other hand they represent a religious revival in Maharashtra which expressed the deep cry of men's hearts for true salvation and a revolt from pantheistic formalism. It was, however, a revival with but little ethical content, consisting as it did so largely of ecstasy in the idolatrous atmosphere of the *avatāras*; and as Nārāyan Vāman Tilak has told us, ecstasy is not devotion, still less is it salvation from moral despair as Tukārām's dark moods too plainly show. N. V. Tilak tells of an acquaintance really devoted to God, but who thought he had not felt such devotion as Hindūs feel, the reason being that 'he mistook the Hindū idea of ecstasy for devotion; Hindūs,' continues the Christian *bhakta*, 'whether followers of the knowledge theory or the devotion theory, whether holding the pantheistic idea of liberation, or the dualistic principle of assimilation, aspire to lose the very consciousness of self, and there to stand still in a state of ecstasy,' this being regarded as 'the *summum bonum* of all knowledge, of all devotion.'[3] Hence we read that Gora the potter, not a *Bramhavādīn* but a *bhakta*, i.e., a believer in a personal God, one day forgot himself and the world around him so much as to tread on his own child and crush it while singing and dancing in the ecstasy of what he and others called devotion. Similarily, Tukārām's *bhakti* is too deeply rooted in the emotions to set at rest a troubled conscience, or soothe a broken heart or satisfy an enquiring intellect. That this is still the case with *bhakti* inspired by Viṭhobā we have already seen on page 62 where a Bombay Prārthanā Samājist says of his visit to Paṇḍharpūr's chief religious season in 1920: 'People do not get true spiritual benefit'. From all this it is clear that Origen's point in the third century still holds good for India in the twentieth, that transfigured lives are far superior to images for setting forth God's love and purity and spirituality.

1 Pundit Sitanāth Tattvabhushan, *Indian Messenger*, Sept. 11 1921.
2 *Indian Theism*, p. 129.
3 *Dnyānodaya*, July 9, 1903.

Still the longing for salvation by Tukārām's modern devotees must somehow be met. 'Had I not been a sinner, how could there have been a Saviour? So my name is the source, and hence, O Sea of mercy, comes thy purifying power. . . Tukā says, through the petitioner's faith comes the honour of the tree of wishes.'[1] The very despair in Tukārām's sin-laden soul assures him there must be relief somehow, somewhere—some Saviour, some way of true salvation. The Christian position is that his yearning hope has been filled with historic content by means of the Cross and Resurrection of Christ and by the resultant Pentecost when the Incarnate One sent the Incarnating Spirit of His Own Personality to apply redeeming love to men's hearts and assure them of their place in it. Tukārām's way of salvation is much too subjective either to give solid assurance or to be 'ethically enduring'. 'Where faith is, there is God' is the fundamental principle of his *bhakti*, which means that faith has to create its own object, shaping that object according to the *bhakta's* own imperfect longings and shifting ideas. This is to rob inward religion of all guarantee of steadfastness, besides being unsatisfying to the mind. For the object of such faith being self-created, the whole tenor of the religion must suffer in consequence. In place of this subjectivism and emotionalism the Christian message substitutes an ever-present Supreme Person as faith's object, One Whose actual example quickens conscience, and Whose tender love provides a personal motive for daily conduct—'for My sake'. Only on such definite concrete lines can the soul hope to receive an answer to its prayer:

> Dwell further in that doubt than go,
> And make 'I hope' become 'I know'.

Who can listen to Tukārām's oft-repeated cry for full satisfaction without being deeply moved? His uncertainties and ambiguities on well-nigh every subject are an index to his mental and spiritual conflict. His disillusionments with his god, his deep and constant discontent, drove him to the anodyne of quietism to deaden the effect of his wearisome struggle. Despite occasional ecstasy, the note of sustained joy is conspicuous by its absence, and his experience is mostly that of 'the dark night of the soul'.[2] If he did obtain any blessing he certainly shows but little concern that others should get it, and intercession or prayer for others is entirely absent from his pages.

If 'the universe *conceived* as a person' be the highest position modern Indian thought can yield to Vishṇu, the source of India's 'incarnations', if one in the great Triad thus fails to minister salvation, if 'erotic' Vaishṇavas are 'evidently conscious' of 'narrating deeds worthy of condemnation'[3], what shall be said of the

[1] *F.* and *M.* 213.
[2] See sect. 3 above, also pp. 135–8.
[3] Paṇḍit Sītanāth Tattvabhushan, *Indian Messenger*, August 28, 1921.

particular 'incarnation' on which Tukārām lavished his love? The narrative in section 14 of chapter III on the calamity to Vithoba in 1873 is left to make its own impression, but nearly thirty years later, in 1902, a serious quarrel between the *Badvas* (or Brāhman trustees of Viṭhobā's temple) and the *pujarīs* who perform the menial offices of bathing and dressing the idol, regarding certain gifts offered by worshippers, went to such lengths that for eight days the god Viṭhobā had no bath, no offerings, no flowers, no food. From the statements made in the Bombay High Court it appeared that many of Vithobā's worshippers were unable to take their own food or bath in consequence, with possible risks to health, besides which, the public peace was in risk of being endangered owing to the irritation of disappointed pilgrims at the approaching festival.[1] The whole story illustrates a truth driven home by the monotheistic prophets of Israel—the contrast between idols which have themselves to be 'carried' and the Living God Who is the Burden-bearer of His children. Instead of being a help to his devotees, Viṭhobā had been to them the occasion of trouble, loss and anxiety, a contrast similar to that between 'the dead-weight of the idols' in Isaiah's day and 'the living and lifting God' Who in the Person of His Incarnate Son 'bears our griefs and carries our sorrow'.[2]

Indian *bhakti's* dream has, however, been more than realized. 'He, the jewel from eternal ages incorrupt, has come' and every longing *bhakta* may pray: 'Grant grace to me to find the path that leads unto Thy feet.'[3] 'God is love' and He '*so* loved that He gave His Son', the true 'image of God', the one and only 'image' it is safe for man to worship, for in worshipping Him they 'will be like Him'. Worthy indeed is the Incarnation seen in Him, for He is veritably 'the image of the invisible God', being 'stamped with God's own charcter', 'the image that bodies out for us the essential Being of God', 'the expression of His Essence', 'the outflashing of God's glory, the perfect expression of His Personality'.[4] Any other 'image' leaves room for the bewildering multiplicity of polytheism, but *this* true 'Image of God' is unique and apart. This Incarnation, Who offered Himself for man's sin, meets the aspirations alike of those noble Samājists who long for a true Theism and of the illiterate mutitudes given up to idols. *Bhakti* of any other type than that must be pronounced inadequate for India's needs.

Assurance of salvation is the topic of this section, for India's quest has ever been after certitude in the things of religion, and despite much that is excellent in Tukārām's poems, there is no abiding certitude. 'I see no sign of assurance in him who stands hand on hip' (3010) is one of his most characteristic lines. So

[1] *Dnyānodaya*, September 11, 1902.
[2] See Isāiah 46, 3–7 and 53. 4.
[3] Mānikka Vāsahar in *Hymns of the Tamil Śaivaite Saints*, pp. 97, 107.
Colossians i. 15 and Hebrews i. 3 trs. by Moffatt, Way, Westcott, Weymouth.

often do we seem to hear from his lips the 'orphaned cry' of the Psalmist: 'My soul crieth out for God, for the *living* God', and so often do we find him unsatisfied, 'leaning on a wreath of mist'. Hence his constant wavering between *Yes* and *No* on almost every fundamental of religion. But the conception referred to in our preceding paragraph, that Christ is 'the visible Representation of the invisible God,'[1] 'the exact Representation of His Being,'[2] conveys the heart-assurance that every such 'orphaned cry' has been answered, for 'in Christ' the unknowable God becomes knowable and 'in Him' men gain spiritual vision of 'the King Invisible and go on unflinching' (Hebrews xi. 27). Dwelling for ever in the 'glorious privacy of light' with the Eternal, Christ Jesus 'shines within the heart to illumine men with the knowledge of God's glory' (2 Cor. iv. 6). Invincible certainty is the hall-mark of *this* Image, for the ambiguity, uncertainty and hesitation which so often tantalize the reader of Tukārām have no place here. St. Paul has a fine passage where he affirms that 'Jesus Christ, the Son of God, did not show Himself a waverer between *Yes* and *No*, but it was and always is *Yes* with Him; the Divine *Yes* has at last sounded in Him, for in Him is the *Yes* that affirms all the promises of God; in the proclamation of God's Son Jesus there was never any wavering affirmation and negation; no! by the inspiration of God it was ever one consistent affirmative.'[3] In Christ Jesus, Revealer of God and Saviour of men, 'an Eternal *Yea* has come into being', a sure antidote to the doubtfulness and vacillation of Tukārām and to the waywardness of Hindū speculation.

7. Does Tukaram's Religion Supply Dynamic Power?

Any true pathological analysis of India's condition—her society petrified by caste, her very air vitiated by idolatry and its infamies—leads to the conclusion that the only remedy is a 'divine energy, exhaustless vigour, and resistless power' such as never meet us in Tukārām's pages. Our *bhakti* poet has a lofty ideal of character before him, but nowhere does he indicate by what power his readers may achieve it. What could be nobler than the following *abhaṅg*, a 'song of songs which has passed into the mouth of every man in the street in Mahārāshtra,' and which Sir Nārāyan Chandāvarkar paraphrases as follows? 'I bow down before him who lives up to what he utters in words; I bow down to him whose life is a continuous movement forward to the goal he sees; I would, like a menial, sweep clean the courtyard of his house; so low

[1] Lightfoot and Weymouth's rendering in Colossians i. 15.
[2] Weymouth in Hebrews i. 3.
[3] 2 Cor. i. 19 as rendered by Weymouth, Moffatt and A. S. Way.

would I humble myself before him. I would be his loyal disciple, entirely at his service in thought, word and deed. Whosoever has God truly enshrined in his heart, him will I implicitly obey. To him I offer my faith, my allegiance.'[1] Nothing could be more beautiful as an ideal and Tukārām shows that the only secret of its achievement is inward. But all depends on what is truly 'enshrined in his heart', seeing it is not impossible for the two Marāthī words that yield this fine phrase to mean that the man is mentally occupied with the Paṇḍharpūr deity, though this interpretation Sir Nārāyan and every other Samājist would probably repudiate. Even assuming that the term refers to the True and Living God, still the question remains: How shall man attain the experience of that Indwelling Presence—a question to which Tukārām gives no satisfactory answer. Could he have known of the 'radical supernaturalism' assured by that other *Guru* Who always 'acted as he spoke', we believe Tukārām would indeed have offered Him his 'faith' and 'allegiance'. That he often sinks into wild despair, becoming a victim to the pessimism of the Deccan,[2] means that he knows nothing of that divine dynamic which assures 'not only inward deliverance from the power of sin, but ultimate deliverance from everything that cripples and depresses the entire life of man.'[3] That the *bhakti* of Tukārām fails to stand the test laid down by the anthropologist who says that 'the function of religion is to restore men's confidence when it is shaken by a crisis', is clear from our biographical and autobiographical chapters.

By way of contrast, turn to one of the most fascinating figures in the Christian history of the early first century, one called Hermas, just such another man as our own poet. He followed the same trade of shopkeeper, was unhappy at home, lost all his property, occasionally gave himself up to fasting and trances, and had the same temperamental weakness, 'the hesitating, wavering spirit of timidity that destroys faith and depresses the spiritual life.' He wrote a book called *The Shepherd of Hermas* whose message shows that Hermas had discovered the antidote to both doubt and gloom: 'The Spirit of God endureth not sadness, neither constraint; therefore clothe thyself in cheerfulness'.[4] Another book which serves as a window through which we can clearly see Christian *bhakti* at work in men's hearts, sustaining them in those dark days, is one called *The Odes of Solomon*, probably several decades earlier than *The Shepherd*. Every sentence ends with a *Hallelujah*, with 'never a trace of that pathetic occasional reaction from faith to uncertainty, from ecstasy to despair' so familiar to

[1] *Subodh Patrika*, Jan. 23, 1921 . see *F. and M.* 3339 for another rendering.

[2] See sect. on 'Tukārām and Indian Pessimism', pp. 174–5 above.

[3] *The Missionary Message in Relation to Non-Christian Religions*, Vol. iv World Missionary Conference, 1910 Report, p. 250.

[4] *The Ancient Church and Modern India*, pp. 90–1.

the student of Tukārām. How that 'reaction' was prevented is indicated by such words as these: 'As the wings of doves over their nestlings, and the mouth of their nestlings towards their mouths, so also are the wings of the Spirit over my heart; my heart is delighted and exults; . . . for faithful is He in whom I believed . . . Thou hast given us Thy followship; it was not that Thou wast in need of us, but that we are in need of Thee.'[1] This last phrase shows how different is the spirit of true Christian *bhakti* from that of Tukārām who can say: 'How happy we are that such a God makes himself our debtor.'[2]

Doubtless many of Tukārām's present-day followers are ready to admit into their secret pantheon the true Source of this dynamic energy, just as Tukārām was willing to let other gods into Vithobā's shrine, and as Vishṇu and Siva are side by side in almost every Deccan village. But we believe the dynamic Spirit of God is narrowing down the solemn issue in many Indian hearts to that confronting a modern poet: 'the light hath flashed from heaven and I must follow it.'[3] India's cardinal religious defect is clearly her lack of a moral dynamic. Her aching heart, at the end of her long history of renunciation, sacrifices and pilgrimages, argues the absence of a satisfying power. 'Disputation has turned to waste the places of Brāhmindom' says Tukārām. But let religion be viewed as a matter of dynamics, let it be experienced as an enabling force, then there must be an effectual closing up of India's 'great gulf between assent and conviction, and of the still greater gulf between conviction and action'. Let the whole religious issue in India be regarded as a dynamical one—and any other is a mockery of needy men—then teachers of religion everywhere will realize their chief responsibility to be one of giving to India such a dynamical faith as transforms and uplifts. For such a task the enunciation of mere ethics will be utterly inadequate; the ethic must be *endynamited*. The one Divine Spirit in place of popular idolatry, the Personal Spirit of God in place of the impersonal essence of the Vedanta, the rich dynamic or motive power of the indwelling, all-enabling Spirit of Christ instead of the mere ideals, however lofty, of the *bhakti* movement—this is surely the message to meet India's needs. Upon the leaders of the *bhakti* movement a heavy weight of responsibility devolves, for if India is to advance to the light of the truest *bhakti*, that centred in Christ, it will be as the devotees of the purer *bhakti* of Tukārām and Tulsidās lead the way.

In the constancy of that indwelling presence of God's Spirit set forth by Christian *bhakti* there is more than compensation

[1] *Ibid*, pp 84–5.
[2] See *F. and M.* 1389, also *P.M.S.*, pp. 27, 82.
[3] From this point to the end of this section 7, we slightly modify one or two paragraphs from our chap 1 in *The Holy Spirit, The Christian Dynamic*, on 'India's Need of the Dynamic of the Spirit.'

for 'the innumerable incarnations' of Hindū *bhakti*, for there is thereby assured a power not ourselves, working in us and through us for righteousness, always present and always within, which is surely more satisfactory than innumerable interventions on our behalf. This is the power Tukārām needed, though he knew it not, and must be regarded as his *bhakti's* missing link, a driving force enabling every *bhakta* to realize *bhakti's* highest ideals. One branch of the *bhakti* school does indeed conceive God as pervading all things as their '*antaryāmin*' or inward Restrainer, but man needs a mighty Constrainer also. Duty is a great word in the *bhakti* movement, but 'duty is a grievous burden and a hard yoke unless there is the sense of power abundant to discharge it'. Here is the grand question by which every system must be tested. How is the power to be appropriated? Christian *bhakti's* answer is that 'in the communion of the Holy Spirit is an exhaustless source of abundant power'. Such religion is dynamical, while every other religion is static. With all its excellencies, and it has many, Hindū *bhakti* is utterly unable to rid itself of its intimate connexion with a static religion, hence its inadequacy for this age of progress. Only by Divine Power dwelling *in* man may the *bhakti* ideal be realized. This indwelling Energizer alone can empower the soul to a daily realization of that still loftier ideal of *bhakti*, namely, love. For, inevitably, the question arises—How is this loving and dutiful devotion to be inspired in man's unresting soul? To this question of questions in religion Tukārām gives no satisfactory reply. 'Where pity, pardon, peace abide, there God dwells', says our poet, but *how* man's sin-stained soul shall receive that Holy Guest we are not told. Tukārām's *bhakti* here, as often, sets up an ideal without showing what will empower men to achieve it. But the clear answer of New Testament *bhakti* is that 'the harvest of the Spirit's sowing is love, joy, peace'.[1]

8. Will Tukaram's Bhakti Build an Enduring Social Order

A religion that has to satisfy the needs of modern India will need to be intensly democratic, meeting the desperate case alike of India's sixty million out-castes and its down-trodden women. How does Tukārām's *bhakti* stand this test? On both subjects he halts and wobbles, for, though the 'social' principles of his *bhakti* were far superior to the orthodox Hinduism of his time, Tukaram was never able to say with the much earlier Christian leader Tertullian: 'Here I stand, this truth I will never forsake; you

[1] Gal. V. 22 A. S. Way's translation.

may disgrace me, make me poor, kill me, but you cannot make me conceal my faith'. There is no subject on which Tukārām's ambiguities and compromises are so fatal as in this matter of a healthy social order for his country. In order to be concrete, we confine ourselves to three questions: caste, woman and world-outlook.

(1) Caste

Tukārām's social ideals as represented by his position on the caste question have already been left far behind by Indian thought. India's educational aspirations, its growing passion for nationalism, along with widespread Christian influence, have combined to initiate one of the most tremendous social reform movements ever seen in any land, a campaign for the abolition of 'untouchability'. This campaign is in the very teeth of Tukārām's own easy-going tolerance. We have already seen on pp. 54–55 and 162–5 that three centuries before his day a poor Mahār was thrown out of Viṭhobā's temple at Paṇḍharpūr simply because he was an 'untouchable' and that at his monument on the other side of the street to that leading into the great temple, the 'out-castes' of the Deccan, excluded from Viṭhobā's presence, have worshipped ever since. It was a wrong against which Tukārām should have protested with all his might, but since his *bhakti* tolerated it, the wrong has been perpetuated to this hour. Shortly after the High Court case reported on page 256 when the idol was neglected for days together on account of squabbles over temple dues, a Chāmbhār woman went regularly into the Paṇḍharpūr temple for a fortnight giving out that she was a pure Marāthā. When it was discovered that she was a despised Chāmbhār, there was a great hue and cry that Vithobā had been defiled. She was arrested and placed before the magistrate who very properly, according to the laws in British India, dismissed the case. It was not stated whether the cause of offence was that the idol, or his worshippers, observed caste nor why anyone must worship at a side shrine. It is not surprising therefore that Dr. Rabindranāth Tagore declares 'the regeneration of the Indian people, to my mind, directly and solely depends upon the removal of this condition of caste'. Probably Mahārāshtra is freer from caste-prejudice than any other part of India (see close of first chapter), but the struggle going on all over the Deccan, as we write, between Brāhmin and Non-Brāhmin, throws a lurid light on the caste question even in our comparatively 'cosmopolitan' Mahārāshtra.

How deeply Tukāram's modern disciples are concerned over this problem and yet with what 'distressing timidity' they approach it have often been illustrated at Social Reform conferences in recent years. We have more than once in this book referred to Dr. Sir Rāmkrishna Gopāl Bhandārkar as being one of the greatest of Tukārām's followers both in point of learning and of true *bhakti* spirit. Yet in his presidential address at the Provincial Social Conference held at Sholapur in 1902, after stating that to eradicate the germs of caste was 'perhaps as hopeless as drying up the Indian Ocean', and that Europe had 'destroyed those germs in their infancy by using the antidote of the spirit of nationality', Sir Rāmkrishna went on to say that his view of his people was that 'the great *Shastra* or spiritual adviser whom they obey is custom', and that 'the only efficacious way is to devise a radical course of reform based upon the reform of the Hindū religion', though, he concluded, 'for obvious reasons I must not go into the question further.'[1] In both their nobility and their insufficiency those words were characteristic of a great disciple of Tukārām, and we believe Indian reformers are increasingly realizing that they *must* 'go into the question further', that Sir Rāmkrishna's remedy of a mere 'reform of the Hindū religion' will not suffice, and that caste and orthodox Hinduism are largely synonymous. That the doubt he expressed on that occasion concerning 'forming a nation with caste' was well-grounded has since then been conclusively shown all too often. During a debate in the Bombay Legislative Council, July 1919, the Hon. Sir George Curtis showed how caste defies even the force of nationality and obstructs the benign process of self-government. Sir George told of a Mahār whose bravery had been recognized by the title of Sirdār Bahadūr but whose presence had been objected to as a representative on a Municipality, his fellow-members sending in 'a representation to the Collector that all the business should be conducted by correspondence so that members might be saved the disgrace of sitting with a Mahār.'[2] In the same debate, the Director of Public Instruction had to report concerning the Deccan that 'many of the Primary Schools in villages were held in temples, which prevented the depressed classes from availing themselves of these schools'. In the same session a simple proposal to make wells available for 'the untouchable classes' was lost by vote, the Hon. Mr. Paranjpe plainly telling the high caste members that 'it was inconsistent to ask for rights from Government' when they themselves were refusing to their own lower classes the 'most up-to-date democratic right' of drinking-water. Such plain speaking by Indian statesmen is a welcome sign of progress, for several years ago a Mahār at Jāmkhed in the Deccan was convicted by a Brāhman magistrate and fined eight rupees or in default a fortnight's imprisonment for having gone to a public spring built with public money, on the ostensible ground of having polluted the water thereby. The British Magistrate of Ahmednagar referring this decision to the Bombay High Court, the conviction was quashed and the fine ordered to be refunded.

[1] *Dnyānodaya*, Nov 13. 1902.
[2] *Bombay Government Gazette*, July, 1919.

Indian leaders are openly acknowledging that India will never attain to any true nationhood apart from the emancipation of the 'untouchables' and that this emancipation can be affected only by religious reform. Take the following, which illustrates the force of Mr. Gandhi's public statement that the New Testament has been one of the greatest influences on his life and ideals. Speaking at Ghātkopar near Bombay on June 15, 1921 he stated, with reference to 'several threatening letters he had received from Vaishṇavas because of' his campaign for the recognition of 'untouchables' as common citizens, that 'if Vaishṇavas did not want to have anything to do with the untouchables, then they were not real Vaishṇavas but only godless and sinful people . . . If Vaishṇavism taught them to despise their fellow-creatures, then he for one could not call it a religion but a monstrous perversion of religion. . . For what was religion without love for the oppressed and the depressed?'[1] There is true Christian teaching in this, but a campaign for 'untouchables' is certainly not Vaishṇavism, else that greatest of all Marāthā Vaishnavas, our own Tukārām, would have passionately denounced the necessity for 'untouchables' in Paṇḍharpūr and every other place having to worship across the street.

To the same effect, the words carrying us a stage nearer our goal, are the words, spoken the very same day as the above, by Mr. K. Natarajan, editor of *The Indian Social Reformer*, that most fearless of journals. Presiding over the Mysore Economic Conference, Mr. Natarajan said: 'So far as I know there is no word in our vernaculars conveying the precise idea of what is connoted by "neighbourliness". There is plenty of the thing itself but that is mostly in places where neighbours are generally also people of the same caste . . . "Love thy neighbour as thyself". To the extent that we succeed in inculcating this idea in the minds of the people . . . to that extent we shall lay truly and firmly the foundation of the quality on which alone can be raised a superstructure of high public spirit and patriotism.'[2] This is clearly stated and our one criticism is that it does not take us far enough. *How* is the 'neighbourliness' to be acquired? What power is to breathe within India's millions of hearts the spirit of 'love to one's neighbour' though that neighbour be of a different caste? Is there any power other than the Spirit of Christ, that divine dynamic power which alone can overcome all such obstacles? This is the Christian message to such noble movements as the Depressed Classes Mission and a hundred others all over the land, which, against the agelong prejudice of two hundred millions of Hindūs, are working in a truly Christian spirit for India's uplift.

1 *Bombay Chronicle*, June 16, 1921.
2 *Times of India*, June 17, 1921.

Unprejudiced observers of India's progress are more and more ready to admit that Christ has proved to be the greatest solvent of caste prejudice not only in Tukārām's country but all over India and that the only principle on which any lasting social fabric can be built in India is that expressed by Lactantius in the fourth century: 'Slaves are not slaves to us; we deem and term them brothers after the spirit'. The essential principles on this matter were fought out once for all in the early Church on the basis of complete equality in Christ[1] and in so far as the Indian Church, be it Roman Catholic or Protestant, departs from those essential principles, the Church will lose her power and will discover what one of her truest leaders means when he warns her of the grave danger of 'elephantiasis' in the Church's feet, this elephantiasis being the spirit of caste.[2] Exclusiveness in the Church, be it in India, Europe or America, is utterly un-Christian.

(2) Woman

That no society can ever rise above the level of its women is axiomatic, and Tukārām writes about woman as if she must for ever occupy the narrow and confined sphere allotted to her in the Hinduism of his day. His poems have no recognition of her true place in society and of her needed restoration to her proper position in the world. In view of the fact that women are numbered among *bhakti* saints and poets before Tukārām's day it is all the more surprising that 'Tukārām speaks of women in a manner that is far from dignified'. Dr. P. R. Bhandārkar, who makes this last statement, urges in palliation: 'We must make special allowance in Tukārām's case, seeing how unfortunate he was in having a wife who could not understand him or give him sympathy. When all this is taken into consideration we can hardly wonder at Tukārām's attitude towards women'.[3] He urges the still more extenuating circumstance that in the Hinduism of Tukārām's environment the relation between men and women was so narrow and constrained. Such were the considerations advanced in 1903.

In this connection it is well to remember that everywhere in the Roman Empire of the first century woman was equally despised. 'The radical disease, of which, more than of anything else, ancient civilization perished' was 'an imperfect ideal of woman' says one historian. A different method of treatment, however, inspired by a worthier ideal, has enabled woman to fulfil her mission as the ministering angel of the race.

1 See a helpful discussion on 'the caste question' by G. E. Phillips, *The Ancient Church and Modern India*, pp. 28–31.

2 Sādhu Sundar Singh in *The Sadhu*, chap on 'Indian Christianity' pp. 230–1. . . .

3 *Two Masters. Jesus and Tukārām*, p. 14

Students urge as a further palliative that Tukārām was concerned only with his own religious life, but in his much later *Nava Yuga* article of March, 1921, Dr. P. R. Bhandārkar frankly confessed Tukārām's attitude towards women to be one of his chief defects. Quoting the poet's prayer in *abhaṅg* 121 to be saved from 'the fellowship of women', following on the incident referred to on page 98 (last paragraph), and his resolve in 122 now 'to look on other women like Rakhumāī', two conclusions are drawn: first, that his minute self-introspection revealed a self-honesty and self-triumph rare among men; and second, that his withdrawal from feminine society was a course impossible to-day and thus the example of Tukārām could not be followed by his modern disciples in this important matter. The same article forcibly set forth that since Tukārām believed a man should treat his wife with no more affection than his maidservant, the women of modern India will never attain to self-realization or to their destined ministry for mankind on the lines indicated by the saint of Dehū.[1]

If there is any Indian question to-day requiring the 'inherent vital energies' of the gospel of woman's greatest *Guru*, it is this. Whether as seed or as leaven, Christian principle is prevailing in India to such an extent that thousands of India's best men and women are seeking to extirpate some of the most blazing wrongs against women that ever spoiled the fair fame of any country—enforced widowhood, child-marriage, the sale of girls for infamous purposes in temples, and other crimes. The same Christian dynamic, working unconsciously in many places but no less surely, is transforming woman's position to-day in India as it did in the Roman Empire of the first century. 'Woman never did have a Vedic value' says Cornelia Sorabji; she certainly never has such value in Tukārām's eyes. Contrast with this the view of Augustine who says: 'The Saviour gives abundant proof of the dignity of woman in being born of a woman'; and that of Chrysostom: 'They surpass us in love to the Saviour, in chastity, in compassion for the miserable'. How noble woman can be is shown by her place in 'the noble army of martyrs'; how truly wonderful Indian women can be is shown by such Indian Christian women as Pundita Rāmabāī, rescuer of thousands of helpless widows among Tukārām's own people.

(3) World-Outlook

In the new era upon which mankind has entered since the world-war, no race of people can expect to build an enduring social order save as part of an international society enriched by the ideals of other lands. We have already seen that no true nationality

[1] *Nava Yuga*, March 1921, pp 164–5

can be created unless every class is included, be it the despised out-caste or despised woman. Similarily, so absorbingly 'individual' is Tukārām's whole idea of God in all his poems, so entirely is his *bhakti* 'an end in itself', that he is utterly unconscious of the big throbbing world outside his own little Dehū or Paṇḍharpūr, save as once and again he thinks of bathing in the distant Ganges or other holy rivers. It is no fault of Tukārām that he cannot help us here, for he was the child of his age and of a faith in no sense universal in its scope or sweep. His limitation of outlook so much affects him that he never appears to consider the case even of the Muhammadans of his day whom he knew so well. It did not strike him that his teaching might interest, or possibly help, them. If he gave the matter a thought he no doubt rested vaguely content with the idea that Islām was sufficient for the Moslem, just as for the Hindū there was the worship of Viṭhobā. He has none of the broad horizons of the prophets in Old Testament page who address their message of righteousness to surrounding nations, nor of the New Testament apostles whose hearts are so moved with pity that they are equally concerned for the needs of far-off races as for their own kith and kin. It required the sovereign conceptions of God's impartial righteousness and universal love to give to these inspired teachers, though they lived millenniums before Tukārām's day, such national and international ideals that the world is still striving after their attainment. If we would realize the full force of this factor, then, over against Tukārām's religious exclusiveness whereby India's sixty million 'untouchables' are denied their rights, should be set the universal outlook of Biblical prophets and apostles whose large-heartedness leads them to see the whole world as a unit under One Control and to treat humanity as one vast whole, subject to the same imperial laws of righteousness and love. That Tukārām's moral world is bounded by the confines of Mahārāshtra is due to the fact that his god Viṭhobā is limited to the same territory, authority over which is shared by a multitude of deities of doubtful character. Not on such an unstable foundation can a successful theodicy be worked out or an enduring social order be constructed. What is needed is a God, supreme in righteousness, belief in whose over-ruling Providence is the inspiring factor towards world-unity and world-progress, a Providence in whose hands nations are employed as divinely appointed agents for the overthrow of the tyrants of mankind. Such a faith is the only possible basis for a stable nationalism as it is the only guarantee for that world-democracy which means liberty, equality, fraternity for all classes and conditions. To 'make the world safe for democracy' something far superior to Tukārām's *bhakti* is required, for he did not ensure true democracy even for his own Mahārāshtra. This can be secured only by faith in the One Supreme God, who as 'infinitely High' treats all men with equal justice and as 'infinitely Near' helps the very lowest of the low in all life's detailed needs.

A *kīrtan* BAND SUCH AS TUKĀRĀM LED (AS AVAILABLE IN ORIGINAL)

By whatever test, then, it is measured, whether by the caste problem, or the needs of woman, or by its limited world-outlook, Tukārām's *bhakti* is found to be insufficient to build up a stable India. *Bhakti* principles are far and away the loftiest in Indian religion, but they fail to follow out their implications, probably because *bhakti* has seen no Supreme Person embodying them in sinless form and because it is without the dynamic energy to carry its ideals into practice. But whatever the reason, we have such a *bhakta* as Tulsidas offending every ethical and democratic principle by affirming that 'a Brahmin must be honoured though devoid of every virtue', a sentiment like that of our own *bhakta* when he says 'a Brāhman is superior in the three worlds though he fail in duty'.[1] On such lines no true democracy can ever be founded. For an increasing number of Indian reformers the two regnant principles are the Fatherhood of God and the Brotherhood of Man, and on these two bedrock Christian principles a new India is being built. Reformers of every school, those who call themselves Christians included, must now go on to recognize that apart from daily imitation of the burden-bearing Saviour, of the example of social service in the Pentecostal Church, and of the social service of Spirit-filled men and women in every age, India's problem will remain unsolved. None but the indwelling Spirit of Christ can supply the supernatural motive of benevolence or inspire a worthy cosmopolitan benignity. It is by the welding together of dynamical religion and social reform that India will enter upon her greatest era

There is a final lesson for every Christian student of Tukārām's *bhakti*. One of its chief methods is that of song, and one of Tukārām's greatest contributions to the Indian Church may prove to be that of *Kīrtans*. At the same time, the Christian Church may well take warning from the fact that Tukārām must often have spent himself on *Kīrtans* when he should have been exerting himself on behalf of his out-caste brethren and sisters, kept outside Vithobā's temple while he inside was singing and dancing to his god. This is still one of the perils of the Vaishṇavism of Paṇḍharpūr. It was an unforgettable sight when in October 1920 we gazed down from the famous roof of Vithobā's temple on the singers below who for full three hours had been shouting and dancing in their rapture, at the close the leader reverently flinging himself prostrate before the idol. It was a moving spectacle as we gazed upon it, though as N. V Tilak reminds us, 'ecstasy is not devotion'. In this connection we may add that it is not service. For as we went back through the alleys of Paṇḍharpūr—not before we had visited the Prārthanā Samāj Orphanage there and had seen the Mission Dispensary workers—and as we came back through the needy Deccan we wondered what value to the struggling millions in Tukārām's land was that rapturous bliss. It

[1] *F. and M.*, 3352b.

is a lesson we all need to learn, that to sing ourselves away, whether in Christian Church or Hindū temple, is not enough. India's poverty is almost unparalleled on earth, and the economic condition of the Indian Christian community itself is probably lower than that of any other Christian community in the world. India's supreme need therefore is a practical religion, for economists tell us India's resources are quite sufficient to maintain her mighty millions if only those resources are distributed on Christian principles. Happily Tukārām's modern disciples are taking a worthy lead in Indian reform of every kind, and the benevolent activities alike of the Prārthanā Samāj and of the Poona and Indian Village Mission in Tukārām's sacred city are an illustration of that work of social uplift which is uniting all races and creeds in India.

Appendix I

Hindu *Avatāras* and The Christian Incarnation

The fundamental distinction between the Hindū theory of *avatāras* and the Christian doctrine of the Incarnation, which has not always been sufficiently recognized, is worthy of exhaustive treatment based on such an investigation of the two religious systems as cannot possibly be attempted here. All we can do is to call attention to a few scattered articles on what is a vast subject, illustrating the wide distinction between the Hindū and Christian conceptions.

India's yearning after *avatāras* or 'incarnations' which shall bring God near to man must be regarded as a God-given instinct. In the famous text of the *Bhagvadgītā*, expounded in the repeated teachings of Tukārām himself, the aim of an *avatāra* is thus defined: 'Whenever, O descendant of Bhārata, there is a decay of righteousness and an ascendancy of unrighteousness, then I create myself; for the protection of the good, for the destruction of evil-doers and for the establishment of righteousness, I am born in every age.' Hence the innumerable *avatāras* in Hinduism (see pp. 27–30 of this book). As the *Bhaktakalpadruma* states: 'When He seeth His servants in sorrow He tarrieth not but Himself cometh as an incarnate Deity to save them.' The loftiness of this conception has been universally recognized by Christians and Hindūs alike. In *The Catholic Herald of India* for April 7, 1920, the Hindū standpoint was sympathetically expressed by the Rev. W. Wallace, S. J., M. A., in his article entitled 'From Evangelical to Catholic by Way of the East': 'The Hindū doctrine of numerous incarnations seemed in some way superior to our doctrine of a unique descent of the supreme. Their God had come down time after time, when *dharma* was neglected, when the good needed support, and the wicked repression. Our God had only spent thirty-three years on earth, and then had left mankind to its fate without voice to speak from on high, without divine presence in its midst, without guide, without consoler.'

Under the title of *Vaishṇava and Christian Doctrines of Incarnation* there appeared in the *Indian Messenger* for March 20, 1921, organ of the Sādhāran Brāhmo Samāj in Calcutta, the substance of a deeply interesting lecture in Bengal by the Brahmo Pundit Sitanāth Tattvabhushan. 'The popular Vaishṇava theory of Incarnation,' said the learned pundit, 'is a theory of special, occasional incarnation.' Since 'the immanence of God, in man and nature, which seems to be ignored' in the above oft-quoted *Gītā* text, is a prominent feature of the philosophy of the *Gītā*, this text is given more in concession to popular opinion than as a part of its serious teaching. The basis of the philosophical doctrine of incarnation taught in the *Gītā*, the *Bhāgavata Purāṇa* and other later sacred books of the country, is to be found in a text of the *Kaushitaki Upanishad* where Indra teaches Pratardana that man's highest good is to know him, 'the Infinite One who is manifest in every person as his true self'. The Vaishnava *Purāṇas* 'pander ever and anon to the popular view that particular persons are incarnations of God in a special sense'. Careful examination leads to the conclusion that 'neither the old nor the new exponents of Vaishṇavism have any definite theory of the distinction of God and man on which alone a true doctrine of *bhakti* can be based', it being clear that to the author of the *Bhāgavata Purāṇa* more than anyone else, the personality of God is 'purely imaginary but nevertheless necessary for cultivating *bhakti* religion.' On June 26, 1921 the abovementioned journal had a paper on 'The *Bhāgavata Dharma*' by the same Brāhmo scholar who observed that what the *Purāṇas* set forth 'as a person in flesh and blood' is really 'only a figure of speech', their authors merely 'indulging in poetic fancy', for their 'representation of Vishṇu as an embodied person is purely metaphorical', (see p. 252 for fuller quotation). On August 28, 1921, writing on 'the Old and New Schools of Vaishnavism,' he pointed out that the 'manifestation of God' which constitutes an 'incarnation' is seen to be 'conscious only in rare individuals' and even in these it comes only 'in rare moments and disappears', Kriṣṇa being made to say in the *Anugītā* in reply to Arjuna's request to repeat his teachings that he had 'lost the state of *Yoga* in which he had given out those utterances and therefore could not repeat them', while the old *Purāṇas*, including the *Bhāgavata*, speak of Kṛiṣṇa 'as a partial incarnation of God', and 'only a particle of the Supreme Being', an idea which 'must have humbled all thoughtful Vaishṇavas' as must also the 'new erotic Vaishṇavism' of *Purāṇas* like the *Brahmavaivarta* where, in the *Kṛiṣṇajanma Khanda* even Rādhā says to Kṛiṣṇa, 'O licentious person, your conduct is always like that of men; so be born as a man. . . and go to India.' We have seen no reply to this series of expositions.

Pundit Tattvabhushan then turns to 'the Christian theory of incarnation' which he characterizes as one which is 'even more dualistic than the popular Vaishṇava theory, and totally ignores the immanence of God in man and nature.' We are not concerned here to rebut the charge of 'dualism', for Christian teaching has always insisted on the reality and distinctness of Divine and human personality and so has rejected the opposite of 'dualism' which is pantheism. The Christian view is that the 'immanence of God in man and nature' is fully upheld in the Christian doctrine of the Holy Spirit, a truth which is held to ensure in actual experience the fullest possible realization of the Divine Immanence and of the untold riches which such a truth brings to men. The Pundit goes on to observe that the Christian 'recognition of the presence of divine power in man is based on the doctrine of miracles—occasional interferences with the established order of nature.' With the first part of this sentence Christians would have no quarrel, for the elimination of the miraculous is held to be tantamount to eliminating God. Similarly, when the Pundit defines 'miracle' as he does he would appear to be assuming that man knows what that 'established order of nature' is which meets with the 'occasional interferences'. After all, may not God have under His control a 'law of miracles' just as He has many other laws? Then comes an irradiating expression of the Christian doctrine of Incarnation in both its 'popular' and 'philosophical' aspects, both of which, in general, Christians would accept, despite the Pundit's statement that 'we in this country never or scarcely ever hear anything about the latter, 'either because the generality of Christian missionaries sent to this country do not know it or choose to hide it from us,' the said view being that Christ's unity with the Father 'could be communicated to other men if they observed the eternal laws of the spiritual world'. Then comes the observation that 'philosophical' Christianity teaches a more exact method than is taught in 'the higher Hindū Scriptures', and the 'popular' is distinguished from 'philosophical' Christian teaching on the Incarnation as follows: 'The prophets prove themselves as agents of God by their power over nature and by the foretelling of events in human history. But these manifestations of divine power are not instances of incarnation. Christianity recognizes only one incarnation of God, and that is Jesus Christ, the evidences of whose divinity are both in his supernatural power and his moral perfection. His unity with the Father as His "only begotten Son" is unique, and cannot be shared in by any other man. . . . Side by side with this popular view there has always been in Christian history a philosophical theory of divine incarnation which has commended itself to the greatest Christian intellects. . . . This philosophical view cites several passages of the New Testament in its support, for instance, the prologue to the fourth gospel and the long prayer of Jesus in chapter xvii. of the same gospel. . . . Our ethical experience—our sense of sin, our moral struggles, our aspirations after perfection—all reveal the presence of the perfectly Good and Holy in us as our Higher Self. The whole of Reality, comprehending everything and every self, is the Father. The manifestation of God as the finite self of man is the Son. The Son's consciousness—awakened through the grace of God—of his unity with the Father is the Holy Spirit. The last is the highest and most concrete manifestation of God. . . The everlasting existence of the Son in conscious unity-in-difference with the Father is the most important lesson taught by philosophical Christianity.' Pundit Tattvabhushan has succeeded in making a clear philosophical statement of a profound Christian truth.

A Marāṭhī Note by the late Narayan Vaman Tilak in the *Dnyānodaya*, April 8, 1915, may be summarized in English as follows: The differing conceptions of Hindūs and Christians concerning 'incarnation' affect the form it may assume, the number possible, and its mission. Hindūs are believers in the idea that an *avatāra* or 'incarnation' may be in part only, in the sense that any particular 'incarnation' may be described as a portion of God Himself. Christians hold that an 'incarnation' of only a part of the Almighty must be regarded as an impossibility, for if God incarnates Himself at all, His Incarnation must be in itself complete and perfect. Hindūs cling to the belief that by their faith they can bring gods into being, so that they are able to accept and worship any number of gods which their faith may create. 'It is our faith that makes thee a God' says Tukārām (1795 *F.* and *M.*). All else naturally follows. This being a mark of the Hindū religion, it comes to pass that in case of need, besides the *avatāras* or 'incarnations' made famous in the *Purāṇas*, even King Śivājī can be made an *avatāra* or 'incarnation' of Shankar. Christianity holds tenaciously the opposite view, viz., that none but God creates or inspires faith, that just as the mother necessarily precedes the mother's love, so God comes first, faith second (reversing the Hindū order), and, therefore, that to forsake the One Living God by conceiving other gods must be held to be sin. Of necessity therefore Christians hold the very idea of a multitude of 'incarnations' to be an impossible one. Moreover, the work of the numberless *avatāras* or 'incarnations' in Hinduism is usually the same: entering the family line of someone who has acquired the fruit of some penance or merit, their work is that of slaying demons, acting in defence of gods, cows and Brāhmans, or, in the language of the *Bhagvadgītā*, to protect those esteemed as saints and destroy those believed to be sinners. The mission of the Incarnation of God in Christ, on the other hand, is solely to seek the lost, welcome the despised, save the fallen, and establish the kingdom of God among men. In short, the fundamental differences concerning the ideas of 'incarnation' arise entirely from fundamentally different conceptions regarding God.

In addition to the foregoing the Christian answer usually takes the following line. The difference between the Hindū and Christian conceptions is indicated by the different terms employed, '*avatāra*' and 'incarnation' not only being different words but connoting different ideas. By *avatāra* is meant 'descent', but it is a descent which may be followed, and is followed, by a withdrawal, this being again followed by other descents. But incarnation means humanity being laid hold of by God, and entered by God, who thus manifests Himself in and through man. This divine act effects such wonders that no repetition of it is required. 'Once done it is done forever.'[1] A new power is poured into the very

[1] Dr. Macnicol, *Dnyānodaya*, March 4, 1915.

heart of the race and a wholly new relation between man and God is thereby manifested, mediated and assured. On this account the Incarnation of Christ is viewed not as a mere incident in history but as initiating a new moral and spiritual development in the human race of which Jesus Christ is the most distinguished member, while He is at the same time God Incarnate in human form. As Mr. Manilal Parekh stated the case in the letter referred to on page 29: 'The Christian conception of *avatāra* is altogether qualitative. The Christian can say, however, that God, though He incarnates Himself in Jesus Christ alone, did speak "by divers portions and divers manners" not only in the Jewish prophets, but in the teachers of other nations as well.' The true Christian view therefore[1] is that the Incarnation in Christ is unique as the grand climacteric manifestation of God in human history, a manifestation that creates a new humanity and leaves behind as a moral dynamic for the whole race the Incarnating Spirit of God who effected the manifestation. According to this view, the lack of the innumerable 'incarnations' of Vaishṇava Hinduism is more than compensated for by the constant indwelling Presence of God's Spirit, imparted to the soul as the result of the work of the Incarnate Saviour; that is to say, a Power not ourselves, making for righteousness in us and through us, always present and always within us—this is the distinctive Christian conception and it is held to be worth incomparably more to feeble humanity than innumerable interventions on man's behalf.

Contrast this lofty conception of the supremacy and sufficiency of the Divine Spirit in the life of man, with the deifying of the lover of Radha, the displacing of the spiritual by the sensuous, and the degrading of the whole idea of 'incarnation' (see also p. 250) as seen in the Rādhā-Krisṇa cult, with whose 'promulgation', said Pundit Sitanāth Tattvabhushan in *The Indian Messenger* for November 20, 1921, 'the worship of God, the Absolute Spirit, practically ceased in Vaishnavism, and the imaginative and sensuous worship of Krishna, conceived as a hero, specially as the lover of Radha, became the predominant, almost the sole, element in the spiritual excercises, if they can be so called, of the new schools. Krishna indeed was believed to be the incarnation of the Supreme Being, or else he would not be worshipped, but his attributes as the upholding and guiding Spirit of nature and immanent in it and as the Inner Self of man, ceased to have any attraction for the Krishna-worshipper, and his whole attention was absorbed by Krishna's Brindaban-lila, specially his amorous dealing with the *Gopis*. In short, it is not as God, but as a man, in his bodily form and human dealings, that Krishna now began to receive worship. To those unfamiliar with latterday Vaishnava literature this may seem an over-statement, but a close study of Vaishnava works on devotions following the writing of the *Brahmavaivarta* Purana leaves no doubt of the truth of our statement.'

[1] We here adapt a sentence or two from our book, *The Holy Spirit the Christian Dynamic*, p. 115.

Appendix II

Verbal Parallels Between Tukaram and The New Testament

No one can read Tukārām without being struck by the many turns of thought and speech which recall the New Testament In the following list will be found a number of the closer parallels; we refrain, however, from drawing any specific inferences. For one thing, there is no authoritative text and it is not impossible that some passages are the result of interpolation. In each parallel the reference to Tukārām in this list comes first, the numbers referring to Fraser and Marāṭhe's three-volume translation of Tukārām's poems.

1656: We know the fact, O God, that thy illusive ways cannot be fathomed.

Romans xi. 33: How unsearchable are his judgments and his ways past finding out.

17: It is worship that Nārāyan desires: God is a spirit.

John iv. 14: God is a Spirit and they that worship Him must worship Him in spirit and in truth.

545: It is something the spirit finds in itself.

Luke xvii. 21: The Kingdom of God is within you.

1713: He gave his life as sacrifice: he saved all feeble folk.

John x. 15: I have laid down my life for my sheep.

2041: The soul has first to perish and then to live.

Matthew x. 39: He that loseth his life for my sake shall find it.

355: Thou knowest the inward parts.

Acts i. 24: Thou, Lord, knowest the inward parts of men.

1755: God is a timid creature.

James iv. 6: God giveth grace to the humble.

1769: Who shall slay the man whom God protects?

Romans viii. throughout, ending: Who shall separate us from the love of Christ?

496: Though you perform the austerities carefully yet one mistake annuls them: you must observe your duties strictly or all your labour will be wasted.

James ii. 10: Whosoever shall keep the whole law and yet offend in one point he is guilty of all.

3465: Worldly life and life with the highest—he who acts both parts together, in the end he achieves neither. If a man seeks to lay his hands on two grain-pits at once, he will end by destroying himself.

Matthew vi. 24: No man can serve two masters: for either he will hate the one, and love the other; or else he will hold to one, and despise the other. Ye cannot serve God and mammon.

2588: Where now shall I set my foot? What stone shall I trust to? My spirit is at peace, because I see thee in every quarry. There is nothing that I need; thou art all to me everywhere.

Psalm cxxxix. 7: Whither shall I go from thy Spirit? Or whither shall I flee from thy presence?

1187 and 1189: When the preacher is fond of money, the listeners are alarmed. They say, he knows not what he sings, he opens his mouth to get something given him. If the preacher is fettered by desire of money and the listeners fearful of expense, the worship is all in vain.

1 Peter v. 2: Tend the flock of God which is among you, exercizing the oversight, not of constraint, but willingly, according unto God; nor yet for filthy lucre, but of a ready mind.

1042: A hypocrite is smooth-tongued, but his inner purpose is different.

Romans iii. 13: Their throat is an open sepulchre; with their tongues they have used deceit.

812: The great precept of religion is to hear God in the heart.

Romans ii. 29. But he is a Jew, which is one inwardly; and circumcision is that of the heart.

1417: Who cares for a letter? What men respect is the seal on it, and that is what makes the bearer respected.

2 Tim. ii. 19: Howbeit the firm foundation of God standeth sure, having this seal: The Lord knoweth them that are His.

1866: Why should I enquire into the virtues and faults of others—what lack of faith is there in me?

Matthew v. 3: Why beholdest thou the mote that is in thy brother's eye?

933: Amid a pile of pots one is used for cooking, another to hold filth: such are the different lots of men.

Romans ix. 21: Hath not the potter power over the same clay to make one vessel to honour and another to dishonour?

3369: If a blind man grasps a blind man's stick both leader and follower will come to grief at once.

Luke vi. 39: Can the blind lead the blind?

2507: You may wear rosaries and *maduras*, but how can you reach God by appearances?

Matthew xxiii. 5: But all their works they do for to be seen of men: for they make broad their phylacteries, and enlarge the borders of their garments.

1093: He who is void of moral conduct and of faith; who brings evil on others or cavils at them with superior wit; he, like a dog, pollutes sweet food when he touches it.

Matthew xxiii. 13: But woe unto you, scribes and pharisees, hypocrites! because ye shut the kingdom of heaven against men: for ye enter not in yourselves, neither suffer ye them that are entering in to enter.

1205: Our Gosavis profess that they beg no alms; they set their disciples to preach. They bring disgrace on their garb, though they try to play the part.

Matthew xv. 14: Let them alone: they are blind guides. And if the blind guide the blind, both shall fall into a pit.

976: Listen to this easy secret. 966: Receive God without price.

Matthew xi. 30: My yoke is easy and my burden is light.

1813: Every drop that is saved from the thief (time and death) must be accounted gain.

Eph. v. 16: Redeeming the time.

501: Whatever keeps you from God, be it your father or mother, give it up.

Matthew x. 37: He that loveth father or mother more than me is not worthy of me.

Blessed are they who came hither for doing good, but whose abode is in heaven. Also 713: their true home is Vaikuntha.[1]

Phil. iii. 21: Our citizenship is in heaven.

3530: The birds and wild creatures that live on the earth, Hari never forgets them. 909: Birds and beasts gather up no store yet the Infinite One protects them. 1653: God is bound to feed all animals; we need not trouble ourselves what we shall get to eat; the tall trees throw out shoots in the hot weather, who supplies them with water? 1777: My poor weak mind, why are you always dejected? Your only solicitude is about your food; better than you are the blessed birds. Mark certain animals in flood and field: what food do they find?

Matthew vi. 26–28: Behold the fowls of the air; . . . your heavenly Father feedeth them. . . . Consider the lilies of the field.

2052: He dearly loves the ignorant if they have simple-minded faith in him.

[1] P. R. Bhandarkar. *Two Masters.*

1 Cor. i. 27: God hath chosen the foolish things of the world to confound the wise.

894. Blessed are the pious for their heart is pure.
Matthew v. 8: Blessed are the pure in heart.

I am a depraved sinner, O God, and I have come to seek thy mercy: put me not to shame. I do not know how many men thou hast saved, but this I know that I am the worst of them all. Tukā says, I am a supplicant for Thy mercy: cleanse thou me completely from my sin, O God.[1]

1 Tim. i. 15: Faithful is the saying, and worthy of all acceptation, that Christ Jesus came into the world to save sinners; of whom I am chief.

It is essential to have a spiritual guide; we must submit to him. He at once changes men into his character; none need wait for experiencing the transformation.[2]

2 Cor. iii. 18: But we all, with unveiled face reflecting as a mirror the glory of the Lord, are transformed into the same image from glory to glory, even as from the Lord the Spirit.

Tukā says, he who will lay his burden on the Friend of the poor, will not fail to experience His mercy.[3]

1 Peter v. 7: Casting all your anxiety upon Him, because He careth for you.

Faith is the source of everything; it is the realization of salvation; it accomplishes the final complete redemption. It is impossible, says Tukā, to obtain grace by works that are destitute of faith.[1]

Romans iii. 28: We reckon therefore that a man is justified by faith apart from the works of the law.

See many passages in the sections on The Saints' in *F.* and *M*; also on pp. 206–8.

Romans xii. 13: Communicating to the necessities of the saints.

See the stories of Rāmeshwar Bhatt and Mumbājī (pp. 95–9).

Romans xii. 21: Overcome evil with good.

706: Mercy, forgiveness, and peace—where these are, there is the dwelling-place of God.

Romans xiv. 17: The Kingdom of God is righteousness and peace and joy in the Holy Ghost.

In many places the much-vaunted knowledge of the Vedas, according to Tukārām's view, is superfluous as compared with the practical experience of religion.

1 Cor. viii. 1: Knowledge puffeth up, but charity edifieth.

[1] G. R. Navalkar, *Tukārām, the Mahārāshtrian Poet and Saint*, p. 23.
[2] *Ibid.*, p. 24. [3] *Ibid.*, p. 25. [4] *Ibid.*, p. 72.

Tukārām: The antithesis of the letter and the spirit is implicit in Tukārām but not explicit.

2 Cor. iii. 6: The letter killeth but the spirit giveth life.

Tukārām: The idea of man's weakness and God's power is very characteristic of Tukārām.

2 Cor. iv. 7. We have this treasure in earthen vessels that the excellency of the power may be of God.

549. Verbosity has ruined crowds of Brāhmans; or as Sir Nārāyan Chandāvarkar translates this, 'Disputation has turned to waste the place of Brāhmindom.' (*Speeches and Writings*, p. 598)

Col. ii. 8: Beware lest any man spoil you through philosophy and vain deceit. Also Rom. xiv. 1: Not to doubtful disputations. Also 1 Tim. i. and vi., about strifes of words.

67: To each has been shown a path according to his own capacity; he will learn to know it as he follows it.

John vii 17: If any man willeth to do His will he shall know of the teaching.

This list might be extended if we sought parallels from the Old Testament, e.g.,

What hast thou done by bathing in the sacred river? Thou hast only washed clean thy skin. Thou hast not cleansed thy heart.[1]

Micah vi. 7: Will the Lord be pleased with thousands of rams, or with ten thousands of rivers of oil? Shall I give my firstborn for my transgression, the fruit of my body for the sin of my soul?

Tuka says, God's treasury is full; it is never exhausted.[2]

Psalm lxv. 9: The river of God is full of water.

952: A meal is delightful if it be eaten in peace, be the food rich or poor.

Prov. xvi. 1: Better is a dry morsel with quietness than a house full of sacrifices with strife.

1805: In thee I am placed on a firm base.

Ps. lxi. 2: Lead me to the rock that is higher than I.

[1] *Ibid.*, p. 25. [2] *Ibid.*, p. 26.

Appendix III

Tukaram's Alleged Indebtedness to Christianity.

As explained on pp. 240–1 the striking analogy between Tukārām and the New Testament has attracted the attention of widely divergent schools of thought. We may at once dismiss from our present consideration 'the wonderful acts ascribed to Tukārām' and considered by Dr. J. Murray Mitchell[1] to be 'coincidences' with scriptural miracles which 'appear too numerous and too marked to be merely accidental'. We may dismiss them for three reasons: first, because these miraculous 'acts' are presumed to have been the invention of Tukārām's biographer Mahīpati: 'tradition has credited Tukārām with having performed many miracles,' says Prof. P. R. Bhandarkar,[2] 'but he personally does not lay claim to any:' second, because Mahīpati invented them, so Dr. Murray Mitchell suggests, 'to glorify his Vaishṇavite hero by investing him with attributes and honour rivalling in Hindū estimation those of Jesus Christ Himself'; although, thirdly, it is not proved that Mahīpatī himself had ever heard of Jesus Christ (see below). Moreover, the crowning 'miracle' of Tukārām's career was that which Marāṭhī legend gives as the manner of its close, that 'Tukārām ascended to heaven without dying,' but this supposed 'coincidence' with the ascension of Jesus disappears, Dr Murray Mitchell himself pointing out that the story 'approximates rather to the ascent of Elijah than to that of Christ.' For these and other reasons therefore all supposedly miraculous 'coincidences' may be left out of our reckoning.

When we come to consider the 'verbal parallels' given in Appendix II, it is to be borne in mind that 'many of Tukārām's ideas are certainly not Brāhmanical', that much of his 'moral tone differs from that of genuine Hinduism' and 'frequently approximates to that of the Christian system'. The question comes to be therefore whether the cumulative weight of these and other facts make the conclusion tenable that in Tukārām's writings we see Christian ideas leavening' a non-Christian system, as Dr. Murray Mitchell suggested in 1849. It is evident that the whole subject demands close investigation, based upon an amassing of facts not yet available. When that investigation is entered upon, Dr Murray Mitchell's essay will have to be carefully considered. That the investigation remains practically where it was over seventy years ago shows how much lee-way has to be made up in the study of

1 *J. R. A. S. Bo*, vol. III, part I, 1849. pp. 1–29.
2 *Two Masters: Jesus and Tukārām* p, 29.

comparative religion in the Marāthā country–a challenge to Indian and foreign scholars alike. The following points merit attention.

Are we to pre-suppose such an 'intermixture of Christian ideas with the Marāthī legends' as Dr. Murray Mitchell suggests, and if there be such 'intermixture', can it be 'easily explained' by the facts he sets forth ? From the early part of the sixteenth century, Portuguese missionaries were actively, even fanatically, endeavouring to extend the Christian faith, particularly in Western India. In the Marāthā country Portuguese settlements sprang up at Goa, Bassein, Revadanda and Bombay, numbers of 'conversions' taking place. Looked at in the dry light of history there are some shameful aspects to the religious part of the story. 'The Portuguese dominion,' says an Oxford scholar in *The Cambridge Modern History*[1] 'was at once impecunious and corrupt, and was rendered intolerable to the native mind by its close connexion with the aggressive methods of the Catholic Church. . . The ruthless propagation of the Gospel by means of the power of the State was in the long run as much against the spiritual interest of the Church as it was against the political interests of the Portuguese.' Such is the historian's verdict concerning 'the first western nation to appear in Hindustan,' a verdict covering the first half of the seventeenth century, the period covered by Tukārām's own life. 'From 1650', the period of Tukārām's death, 'Portuguese annals form a dreary record of degeneration. The Portuguese were absorbed and degraded by the conquered, for the Portuguese. . . intermarried with native races' (*Cambridge Modern History*, vol. v, p, 695). In the absence of all evidence up to the present, can we at all regard it as possible or probable that Tukārām came in contact with either the Portuguese or any of their 'converts'? From the last of the settlements mentioned above, Bombay, Tukārām's birth place was about 100 miles distant and he is said to have descended the Ghāts for business in the Konkan (see page 81).

The very violence of the Portuguese in propagating their religious views must have 'conspired', says Dr. Murray Mitchell, 'to direct the attention of the Marāthās to the Christian religion. It is hardly conceivable that Tukārām should not have heard of the religion of the war-like, energetic and proselytizing foreigners who had been in the neighbourhood for 150 years. The biographer of Tukārām, who wrote 125 years later still, cannot surely with any shadow of reason be imagined ignorant of an event so vitally affecting the destinies of his own nation and religion, as the extension of the Portuguese dominion and the Christian faith.'[2] Should the objection be raised that over against the suggested approximation of some of Tukārām's ideas to Christian teaching there is yet too great and essential a difference to allow the

[1] Vol. IV, chap. XXV. (p.743), by Hugh E. Egerton, M.A., Beit Professor of Colonial History, Oxford, 1906.

[2] *J. R. A. S. Bo.*, vol. III, part I (1849), pp. 9–10.

theory of 'Christian leavening' to stand, Dr. Murray Mitchell replies: 'Every day's experience proves that when Christian ideas are inculcated on those who are familiar only with Hinduism, they are seldom at first rightly apprehended; the shape, the colour they assume are so far changed that a careful scrutiny is required before the parentage is detected . . . It may be observed that if the view now supported . . . be correct, one might expect that the influence of Romanism . . . might be pretty distinctly marked . . . and such would seem in fact to be the case. The reader who is acquainted with the *Acta Sanctorum* or books of a similar character will occasionally fancy he hears in the history of Tukārām the echo of monkish legends and the achievements of "saints" of the middle ages.'[1]

Skilful as is the above reasoning, we are bound to say the case for Christian influence on Tukārām must be regarded as non-proven. The 100 miles that separated Bombay and the area of Roman Catholic influence from Tukārām's country region included a range of hills two thousand feet high, a barrier quite sufficient in those days to prevent much intercourse. History is not without parallels of peoples equally near to one another yet with equal dissimilarity in religious faith and practice, the nations that surrounded ancient Israel being an example. Moreover, the Portuguese incursion and intolerance were a part of 'the medieval struggle between Christendom and Islám', affecting the fortunes of the Muhammadan faith more than the Hindū and there is little or no evidence in Tukārām's life and writings of any contact between him and the Moslems. Our own view is rather of the nature of an *argumentum silentio*, perilous in some circumstances we know, but Tukārām's seemingly complete ignorance of the name of Jesus Christ and of the fundamental facts and doctrines of the Christian faith (see page 245) is to us an insuperable difficulty in the present state of information. We would prefer to say that any supposed 'coincidences' are illustrations of the principle, so happily phrased by Dr. Murray Mitchell, that 'the human mind amid endless variety of outward circumstances, remains true to certain grand original laws impressed upon it by the Author of our being.'[2] Professor W. B. Patwardhan, who admits the coincidences but no more, states: 'That there is something in common between the love as preached by Christ and that inspired by the saints of Mahārāshtra is beyond question. It is, however, equally beyond question that the Mahārāstra school of devotion owed nothing to Christianity.'[3] Dr. Macnicol's conclusion is that 'either Tukārām was actually in contact with Christian teaching, which is by no means improbable, or he was a remarkable

1 *J. R. A. S. Bo.*, vol. III, part I (1849), pp. 10–13. 2 *Ibid.*, p. 11.
3 *I. I.* October 1910, pp. 113–4.

instance of a *mens naturaliter Christiana*.'[1] Our conclusion inclines in the latter direction, Tukārām thus affording a remarkable illustration of the striking saying of the second century Tertullian, the *Vakil* (lawyer) who became a Christian apologist and who speaks of the *testimonium Animae naturaliter Christianae* (the testimony of the soul naturally Christian). In the same class are probably to be placed Guru Nānak, Tulsi Dās and Kabir.

Our conclusion is in no way invalidated by any considerations arising from the Marāthī 'Christian *Purāṇa*', brought to light again in the first decade of the present century, 'the only song of Christ written in Marāthī by an Englishman'. 'Father Estevam,' or Thomas Stephens, was a Jesuit father who died in 1619 (Tukārām being perhaps 11 years old) after forty strenuous years of Christian activity among 'Brāhman Roman Catholics' of the Goa territory, at least 250 miles from Dehū and 150 from Paṇḍharpūr. He is chiefly known by his Marāṭhī Christian poem, published in Goa, probably in 1616, intended to become 'to the Christians what their *Purāṇas* were to the Hindus', a work containing Old Testament history and the life of Jesus Christ with which much legendary matter was mixed up. Written for the middle and lower classes, its Marathī, given in the manuscript in a Roman transliteration, is that spoken south of Ratnāgiri, modified by the Konkani dialect and a sprinkling of Kanarese words. Its teaching is suffused with Roman Catholic theories and 'converted' Hindus have left on it their stamp. 'In the two centuries that preceded the arrival of Protestant missionaries and before the Bible came into the hands of the people, this "*Purāṇa*" was in Western India a light that burnt brilliantly,' says Canon D. L. Joshi, who adds a sentence we may adopt as our own: 'How far its contents affected the thoughts of some of the Marāthā poets like Tukārām we have no evidence.'[2]

Possibly the partial resemblances between Tukārām's reformed Hinduism and the Romish Christianity of Western India in the seventeenth century is capable of another explanation, these particular elements in his teaching not impossibly being the result of a probable Christian influence on that Vaishṇava Hinduism which he had received as a heritage from the past. How far this might carry us in a scientific enquiry of Tukārām's teaching it is impossible to say. The *Gītā*, a product of Vaishṇava Hinduism, is held by some to 'betray Christian influence, but it seems rather more probable that the poem is purely of Indian origin.'[3] Other passages there are in Vaishnava theology in which 'a number of scholars have believed they detected distinct traces of Christianity,'

[1] *Indian Theism*, p. 279.

[2] Canon Joshi's paper, 'The Christian *Purana*', in *I. I.*, vol. VI, part 4, pp 166–75, and that by Dr. J. E. Abbott in the *Dnyānodaya*, May 1[illegible], 1921, are both worthy of careful study.

[3] Dr. Farquhar, *O. R. L. I.*, p. 92.

but the discussion so far has yielded 'rather doubtful results.'[1] The Christian reader, however, so often finds the New Testament recalled by Tukārām as to make easily believable a theory that Christianity, or an imperfect form of it, may have entered India in certain indirect ways extremely early. It is sometimes overlooked that among the many facts of Indian history which we cannot explain is that of an early Indian Christian Church in Malabar whose existence and hoary antiquity historians such as Mr. Vincent A. Smith accept as undeniable. Even if the legend of the Indian activity of St. Thomas must be given up, as scholars like Garbe and Keith affirm it must,[2] there still remain the following facts: the well-attested visit to India, probably Malabar, about A.D. 185, of Pantaenus, head of the catechetical school at Alexandria, who is said to have been invited by 'an Indian Christian embassy' sent from an already existing Indian Christian community; that John the Persian was present at the Church Council of Nicea in A.D. 325 as 'Bishop of Great India'; that the great Śankaráchārya and the chief (Vaishnavite) Alvārs (see p. 36) of Malabar were born and brought up amid these Syrian Christians, resulting as some believe in a Christian substratum to Tamil philosophy; that there were other early Christian communities in Mylapore near Madras, Ceylon and the Konkan, the first-named being near the birthplace of that great *bhakti* theologian, Rāmānuja (see pp. 36–7) who initiated what is called 'the first great theistic movement of India', leading not a few scholars to the conclusion that Christian influence on Indian *bhakti* is 'possible and even probable' (A. B. Keith, *J.R.A.S.* Oct. 1915); and that the vigorous Graeco-Roman commercial intercourse with India, *via* Alexandria, as far back as three centuries before Christ and up to A.D. 215, may have resulted in India receiving certain Christian ideas of an Alexandrian stamp.[3] *The Catholic Herald of India* during August and September, 1921 had a thoughtful series of papers on 'St. Thomas and San Thomè, Mylapore', showing that Alexandria gave to India St. Pantaenus in A.D. 185 and St. Frumentius in A.D. 327, the latter being identified by Mgr. Zaleski in his *Saints of India* (1915) with a certain Thomas of Cana to whom Portuguese historians and Malabar ballads at times attribute things 'which, it would seem, happened to St. Thomas the Apostle and *vice versa*,' a confusion which may have had serious consequences both for 'Malabar Traditions' and historians of the Indian Church.

Pointing in the same direction are some curious coincidences in the birth stories of Kriṣṇa and of Christ regarding which Dr. Sir R. G. Bhandarkar makes an interesting suggestion not accepted by all, that the Ābhīras, who according to his theory conveyed the

[1] *O. R. L. I.*, p. 99

[2] See *J.R.A.S.* October 1915.

[3] 'Christian influence in Indian Culture,' *The Madras Christian College Magazine, 1920*, pp. 168–77.

Kṛiṣṇa legend, 'possibly brought with them the name of Christ also. . . The Goanese and the Bengalis often pronounce the name Kriṣṇa as Kusto or Kristo, and so the Christ of the Ābhīras was recognized as the Sanskrit Kṛiṣṇa.'[1] Dr. Grierson goes so far as to say that it is 'perhaps probable that the worship of the infant Kriṣṇa was a local adaptation of the worship of the infant Christ introduced to India from the North-West, and the ritual of Kriṣṇa's birth-festival has certainly borrowed from Christian authorities. But it was in Southern India that Christianity, as a doctrine, exercised the greatest influence on Hinduism generally . . . In this reformation India rediscovered faith and love.' Grierson even quotes Hopkins statement with approval: 'In all probability the Hindus of this cult . . . have in reality, though unwittingly, been worshipping the Christ-child for fully a thousand years.'[2] Dr. Sir R. G. Bhandarkar agrees that 'some of the finer points' in *bhakti* 'may be traced to the influence of Christianity.'[3] If this partial Christianizing of Indian *bhakti* can be fully established it may solve many problems affecting Vaishṇava Hinduism, Tukārām included. Historial investigation[4] would appear to have demonstrated on the one hand that the *bhakti* professed by 150 million Indians is 'native to India' and on the other hand that Christianity has left a deep mark on the later development of the idea. That the threefold conception of a God of Grace, of personal faith in Him, and of belief in the soul's immortality is indigenous to India, being directly traceable to the *Bhagvadgītā*, certain sections of the *Mahabhārata*, the *Bhagavata Purāṇa*, the *Bhakti Māla*, and other works constituting 'the New Testament of the Bhāgavata religion,' is fairly well established by that trio of scholars, Dr. Bhandarkar, Dr. Garbe, and Dr. Grierson—an Indian, a German and a Briton. The Indian origin of *bhakti* and the partial Christianizing of its later stages appear thus to be equally indubitable conclusions. We can therefore adopt the following statement on this subject: 'With both these creeds (Christianity and Buddhism) Hinduism in the days of its greatest plasticity and receptiveness was in long and intimate contact; . . . but sufficient evidence is not available to indicate with certainty the doctrines or elements of belief derived from a foreign source. The fundamental thought of *bhakti*, . . . is certainly of Indian origin, and served as a religious motive in India long before Christianity entered the country. In its development and progress it may have owed much to Christian teaching and example. From the first, however, salvation through *bhakti* has laid greater stress upon

[1] *V.S.M.R.S*, p. 38.

[2] *E.R.E.*, vol. II, Art. *Bhakti Marga*, pp. 548–50.

[3] *V.S.M.R.S*, p. 57.

[4] The next three sentences are from our own book *The Holy Spirit the* Christian *Dynamic*, p. 19–20.

emotion, upon feeling, and the play of the affections, than Christianity. . . has done.'[1]

No more can probably be said at present than this: *If* 'Christian elements have been incorporated with the story of Tukaram' then they have probably come through the indirect channels indicated in the last paragraph. In that case, Principal Patwardhans' phrase about Tukārām's *bhakti* 'owing nothing to Christianity' is too sweeping.

It would take us beyond the scope of our present note to enquire how far Christian teaching has influenced the *interpretation* of Tukārām. It is our conviction, however, that just as all modern reform movements in India—Brāhmo Samāj, Sādhāran Samāj, Prārthanā Samāj and others—have come under Christian influence,[2] so most if not all of Tukārām's modern interpreters have come so definitely under the influence of the New Testament that many of their expositions of Tukārām are 'hardly distinguishable from Christian formulas'. This may be said of many of the weekly sermons preached in the Bombay Prārthanā Samāj Mandīr and published in the *Subodh Patrikā*, and of the published writings of Sir Rāmkrishna Bhandārkar and Sir Nārāyan Chandāvarkar.

[1] Dr. Geden *E. R. E.*, vol XI p. 136.

[2] See Dr. Farquhar's *Modern Religious Movements in India*, *passim*, and Dr. Geden, *E. R. E.*, vol. xi p. 136.

Appendix IV

Additional Notes

(*The figures in brackets refer to the pages of the present work*)

Mahārāshtrian or Marāṭhās (pp. 2–3)

While this book was in the press there appeared a discussion on 'The Origin of the Marāthās' by Mr S. M. Edwardes, C.S.I., C.V.O. in the 'Introduction' to his new edition of Grant Duff's *History of the Mahrattas* (1921) pp.xlii–lix, embodying a valuable ethnographical note from Mr. R. E. Enthoven, C.I.E., for many years in charge of the Ethnographical Survey of the Bombay Presidency. In addition to the considerations we have set forth on p. 2, and in development of our line of argument, it is pointed out that a cave inscription of the first century A.D. at Bodsa, Poona District, applies the term 'Mahārāthini to a princess, while the term 'Mahāraṭhi' has been found in a cave at Nanāghāt, Poona District, 'Mahā' probably being an honorific affix. This would negative the suggestion made in the *Census of India*, 1911, *vol. vii*, *Bombay, Part I, Report*, p. 289, that the word 'Marātha' comes from *maha* meaning 'great' and *rathī*, warrior'. In A.D. 610 the Chinese pilgrim Hiuen Tsiang referred to the Deccan as *Mo-ho-lo-cha*, the Chinese equivalent of *Ma-hā-rā-tha*. From A.D. 753 Rāshtrakutas or Rattas ruled for two and a half centuries and again from the eleventh to the thirteenth century. Whether, however, the Marāthā people derive their name from the country *Mahārāshtra* or whether the latter geographical name springs from the tribes inhabiting the land, is still matter for conjecture. There is much to show that the term 'Marāthā' has been loosely used and that it may have 'meant originally nothing more than a person dwelling in Mahārāshtra or using Marāthī as his home-tongue,' the term being found with such varying meanings, sometimes as describing 'a member of the superior Marātha land-owning or fighting class,' sometimes as 'a member of the ordinary cultivating caste' or Kunbī, the latter term signifying a 'cultivator' of 'inferior social status', while it appears 'a Kunbī may, if successful, rise to the superior Marāṭhā status', the facts even showing that 'there is by no means an insuperable barrier between Kuṇbīs and the tribe of Kolīs, an undoubtedly aboriginal tribe'. We have therefore Marāthā *Sutars* (carpenters), Marātha *Kumbhārs* (potters), Marāthā *Lohārs* (blacksmiths), Marāṭhā *Parits* (washermen or *dhobīs*). Higher class Marāṭhās are held to be of identical origin with the agricultural Kuṇbī tribe, these two being differentiated only by social status, and 'in both the Marāthā and the Kuṇbī there is a distinct aboriginal strain', from which it is to be inferred that Marāthās are descendants of Deccan primeval tribes The 'spurious distinction drawn between the upper-class Marāthā and the lowly Kuṇbī cultivator' was protested against by the All-India Marāthā League in its Memorandum of July 31, 1919, submitted to the Parliamentary Joint Committee on Indian Constitutional Reforms Bill of 1919 when they stated: 'There is no difference whatsoever between a Mahrāttā and a Kuṇbī . . . Since long days ago in the antiquarian history of this country they are related by blood to each other. . . . The terms "Mahrāttā" and "Kuṇbī" are synonymous; the educated and well-to-do portion of the community styles itself (as) Mahrāttās, while the ignorant and the rural passes under the name Kunbī, though the former is akin to the latter as members of the same caste.' This was also the weighty verdict of Mountstuart Elphinstone, statesman and historian, a century ago, the 'Mahrāttā chiefs,' he says, being 'all Śudras, of the same caste with their people, though some tried to raise their consequence by claiming an infusion of Rājput blood.'

The Marāṭhī Language (pp. 3–4)

Almost simultaneously with the above 'Introduction' by S. M. Edwardes which contained 16 useful pages on 'Marāṭhī Literature' prefaced by a brief note on the language, there appeared an able Marāthī essay by Rao Bahadur P B. Joshi, F. R. G. S., in the second volume (pp. 241–258) of the *Vividha Dnyāna Vistār* Jubilee Memorial publication (1921). Both these support the considerations set forth in our first chapter (pp. 3–4) and help forward the discussion. The *Mahārāshtrī* language from which Marāthī has sprung was a Prākrit, meaning a vernacular dialect, natural and unartificial, in contrast with the purified and literary Sanskrit language. As a dialect under the name of Saurāshtrī it was connected with another Prākrit, Magadhi, and as Mahārāshtrī it was the language of 'charming lyrics' and 'epic poetry,' while 'the popular vernaculars which formed the original basis of these polished literary dialects were styled *Apabhramsa*, i.e., corrupt, decayed; these *Apabhramsas*, used by the lowest classes of the people, in time, like the Prākrits, receiving polish and being put to literary use. Marāthī, the home language of the Marāṭhā people, is the direct descendant of the *Apabhramsa* of Mahārāshtrī'. (*Imperial Gazetteer*, 1908.) Exactly when Marāṭhī took its present form is an unsolved problem, but it is known that literature flourished from the sixth to the tenth century, that at the beginning of the eleventh century the country suffered frightfully from invasion during which thousands of libraries and temples were destroyed, and that intellectual darkness settled on the people until the thirteenth century when literature revived under the Yādava dynasty, one of whose kings, Rāmachandra or Rāmdev (A.D. 1271–1309), appears at the end of the *Dnyāneshwarī* as a sort of royal patron of Dnyāneshwar, 'the father of Marāthī poetry', whose moving story and that of his successors is referred to in our second chapter (pp. 38–40).

The Āndhra Kings (pp. 3–5)

See further an article, 'On the Home of the So-called Āndhra Kings' in the *Annals of the Bhandārkar Institute*, vol. i, part 1, pp. 20–42.

Gosāvī (p. 6, footnote 2).

The 1911 census reported 678 *Gosāvīs* in Bombay Presidency. A corruption of the Sanskrit *Gosvāmī*, the term means one who has mastered his passions. *Gosāvīs* are Śaivites, just as *Bāvās* are Vaishnavas, both terms describing religious mendicants who as vagrants go about in the name of religion. Most *Gosāvīs* are celibates, but have mistresses whose children they recognise as their own, some being rich money-lenders, traders, husbandmen and even writers. See above-mentioned *Census of India*, 1911 vol. p. 260.

Importance of Deccan Villages (pp. 7–8).

Eighty-two per cent of the population in Bombay Presidency resides in villages of less than 5,000 inhabitants (*Census* report p. 15.)

Domestic Religious Rites (pp. 8–9).

The Census volume for 1911 has an interesting section on 'daily worship' (p. 61), pointing out that 'Marāthās, Rājputs, Kuṇbīs and the artisan castes are expected to worship the house gods after the morning bath before eating, or to visit temples. . . . The worship of the house gods should be performed by the head or other elder of the family; but it is generally entrusted to the drone of the family, if there be one. It is often delegated to boys, and even to women as a last resort. . . . Castes below the Kunbīs and the impure castes have generally no house gods.'

See also illuminating paragraphs on 'ceremonies connected with agriculture', setting forth 'the field rites of the Marāṭhā Kuṇbīs' (p. 64 of 1911 Census Report).

Bhajans and Kīrtans (p. 10).

In recent years a well-organized school has been formed in Bombay for giving a systematic training to would-be *Kīrtankārs*, and a monthly periodical bearing the title of *Kīrtan* has also been started for their training. There are now professional *Kīrtankārs* who charge fees for their services, their fees varying in proportion to their attainments and popularity.

Power of the Brāhmans (pp. 14, 35).

'Brahmans are not always the priests of the important temples in the Deccan. . . Some of the officiating priests at Paṇḍharpūr are *Bhāgvats*, that is, worshippers of both Vishṇu and Śiva.' (*Census of India* vol. above-mentioned, p. 68). See further the paragraph below on '*Bhāgvata Devotion*.'

Democratising Influence of the Bhakti Poets (pp. 19–22).

In his 'Introduction' to the new edition of Grant Duff's *History of the Mahrattas*, (pp. lxxiii. iv.) S. M. Edwardes calls into question the democratizing influence of the *bhakti* poets. He observes: 'There is a tendency among some writers to over-estimate the influence upon the public mind of Mahārāshtra of the message of the Marāthī poets of the *bhakti* school. They would have us believe that these poets welded the different and often mutually hostile groups composing the population of Mahārāshtra into one people, that they made the Marāthās a nation . . . It cannot be gainsaid that the remarkable literary movement which centres so largely about the god Vithobā and Paṇḍharpūr. . . . embraced persons of various castes, and elevated to sainthood representatives of even the lowest classes in Mahārāshtra. . . Yet it is doubtful whether the poetry of the saints and writers of the *bhakti* school ever reached, or made such impression upon, the general mass of the people. . . Far more efficacious than the devotional teaching of the poets in suppressing caste-exclusiveness, and fostering a sense of "nationhood" was the rise to power of the Śudra, Sivājī, and his constant association with himself in the task of political and military administration of men, who, in many instances, were not Brāhmans'. Unfortunately for the objection raised, no explanation is offered as to *why* Mahārāshtra accepted the leadership and even kingship of a Śudra, and *why* the 'administration of men who were not Brahmans' was tolerated. But surely such a remarkable phenomenon calls for some explanation and until an alternative one is forthcoming it is safe to hold the view that 'the devotional teaching of the poets in suppressing caste-exclusiveness' exercized a sufficiently democratizing influence to weld the people into one under a Śudra king with his non-Brāhman ministers. That this democratizing influence was but partial we have shown on pp. 55, 163–5, 261–4, and we can therefore agree with the observation that 'when Śivājī's descendants degenerated into a line of royal phantoms and the Peshwas usurped all power, the ancient spirit of caste-exclusiveness reasserted itself with redoubled force, and the passionate cry of the Marāṭhī poet, "Find, O find, some means or other, To bring God and man together," was forgotten amid the caste disputes and the class-intrigues of that era of Chitpāvan predominance.'

Indian Scholars (pp. 25–6).

In his Inaugural Address at the opening of the Bhandārkar Institute, (see *Annals of the Bhandārkar Institute*, July 1919, pp. 2–5), Dr. Sir R. G. Bhandārkar remarked that 'the peculiar temptation of an Indian scholar' is that 'he is prone to see good in everything old'.

The 'Historicity' of Krisṇa, (pp. 30–2).

In the same Inaugural Address (p. 5) Sir R. G. Bhandarkar referring to the *Mahābhāratā* (and *Rāmāyaṇa*), the fountain-head of information concerning Krisṇa, said: 'The occurrences reported in them cannot be regarded as strictly historical'. See also our pp. 252–3.

After pointing out that various names of Ābhīras 'are all synonyms of the god Śiva', *Tribes and Castes of Bombay*, pp. 17–34, goes on to say: 'Hence the conclusion may be safely drawn that the Ābhīras were by no means connected with Kṛiṣṇa and his cowherds . . . . Only one conclusion is possible, viz., that the Abhiras did not originally represent the *gopas* of Kriṣṇa. . . . The traditions which are now current among the Āhirs and which connect them with Kṛiṣṇa, Mathura and the *gopas* are only later inventions . . . The influence of fiction on the disintegration of a formerly uniform conmmunity or on the amalgamation of different tribes need not be dwelt upon.'

Dnyāneshwar's Prayer (p. 38).

For a translation of this wonderful prayer a little more in detail than we have given in chapter II, and based on a critical text, see an article by Dr. J. E. Abbott, 'Dnyāneshwar's Prayer', in the *Dnyānodaya*, May 5, 1921.

Modern Hindūs and the Kṛiṣṇa Legend (pp. 31–3).

In the last of the series of articles on *The Bhāgavat Dharma* to which we have already referred, Pandit Sitanāth Tattvabhushan in *The Indian Messenger* for Nov. 27, 1921, quotes a passage on Chaitanya's *bhakti*, giving asterisks in place of 'a passage which would offend not only the taste, but even the moral sense of the reader', and he asks: 'Can such an "idea of God" . . . ever save any church from moral corruption?' In working up to this, the final conclusion of sixteen articles, extending over nearly eighteen months, he points out. 'The Kriṣṇa legend continually grew at the hands of successive Vaishṇava poets, the later ones making fresh additions to what they had received from their predecessors. Poets know what poetry is and evenwhat it is not. Minute details of sayings and doings ascribed to individuals, such as we find in the *Purāṇas* belong not to history, but to poetry and fiction. But the age which followed that of the creative Vaishṇava poets seems to have been singularly credulous and unimaginative. It took all poetry as history. It regarded every detail of the epic and *Purāṇic* account of Kriṣṇa as true and based its religious life on them as on a system of theology. Half a century of liberal education, largely scientific, teaching at any rate how to distinguish between dogma and reasoned truth, between fact and fancy, between history and poetry, has effected a revolution in the religious attitude of those who have received the blessings of such an education. They see that they must reject the old theology as based on mere poetry, or if they are to retain it in any shape, they must interpret the legends invented by the poets as allegorical representations of spiritual truths. Gravely questioning whether the story of an unholy love can be thus interpreted with any show of reason and without serious injury to the moral life of those who would accept such an interpretation, . . , one thing we are most anxious to emphasise, and that is that neither the authors of the *Purāṇas* nor their latter-day exponents and followers, including Chaitanya and his disciples, *offer even the slightest clue to such an interpretation.*'

Vithoba's Name (pp. 42–3).

In a critical review of Mr. L. R. Pāngārkar's *Śri Tukārāmāce Caritra* Dr. Prabhakar R. Bhandarkar, in the *Nava Yuga* for March, 1921, affirmed that the reading *Vicā kelā ṭhobā* given by Tukārām himself suggests a derivation that is imaginary (see our pp. 42–3), and he himself would suggest a different meaning for the words, so as to yield the sense—'rebirth was stopped'. No reason, however, is assigned for so attractive an interpretation.

Impossibility of defining the Term 'Hindū' (p. 25).

The *Census of* 1911 (pp. 55–6) shows that 91 per cent of the people in the Konkan and Deccan are Hindūs. Referring to 'the impossibility of framing a comprehensive definition of Hinduism intelligible to the average enumerator and of drawing a hard and fast line between Hinduism and other religions, Jainism, Islām, Animism and Sikhism', there being in Bombay Presidency '35,000 Hindu-Mohamedans whose creed and customs partake of both religions', the Report states: 'Various tests have been suggested to fix what constitutes a Hindū, but finally it was decided to treat all who call themselves Hindū as Hindūs.'

The God Khaṇḍobā (pp. 47, 132).

In his 'Introduction' to the new edition of Grant Duff's *History of the Mahrattas*, published while the present volume was in the press, S. M. Edwardes gathers together much useful information concerning Khaṇḍobā, 'the tutelary deity of the Deccan' as well as a popular household god, whose name is derived from *Khande-aba*, 'sword-father'. Besides its chief temples at Jejurī, Poona District and Pāl, Satara District, it has many other temples, the officiating priests often being non-Brāhmans, the officiants in Khaṇḍobā's three Bombay temples being a Brāhman a *Kamāthi* and a *Muraḷī* (on which word see pp. 47, 132) respectively. Besides being 'absorbed into the neo-Brāhmanic pantheon' as an *avatāra* of Śiva under the names Malhāri or Mārtand, Khaṇḍobā is a vegetable deity, turmeric powder being applied to his devotees and carried in tiger-skin bags by the males (*Wāghyās*) dedicated to him. He is also an animal god, always accompanied by a black dog, and is the god of the *Ramoshī* (watchman) caste and of *Dhangars* (shepherds), robbers often making vows to Khaṇḍobā when starting on robbing expeditions, their war-cry of old being *El-kot*, *El-kot*, referring to the '70 million' demons slain by him in conflict. It is, however, in his connection with 'religious prostitution or sanctified harlotry' that Khaṇḍobā exercizes his most widespread influence, even married women becoming *Muraḷīs* sometimes, forsaking husbands and children. As the result largely of missionary effort it has become an offence under the Indian Penal Code to dedicate a girl to Khaṇḍobā, though there are still women who 'serve as the brides of Khaṇḍobā and the mistresses of men'.

In view, however, of the fact that the *Bombay Gazetteer* (vol. xviii, part i, pp. 476–7) in 1885 reported only five *Wāghyās* and sixteen *Muraḷīs* in Poona District, within whose boundaries Jejurī, their centre, is situated, the question calls for further investigation, though missionaries at work among the people would probably doubt the accuracy of the *Gazetteer* figures in this particular.

Caste and Untouchables (pp. 54–5, 162–5).

'The touch of the Bhangī, Chamār, Dhed, Holiya, Mhār, Māng and Mochī is unclean, and none of these castes are allowed within the interior of the ordinary Hindū temples' (*Census* vol. referred to above, p. 66. See also the excellent note on 'Mahārs', p. 287).

'In Bombay Presidency alone,' said *The Times of India* December 1, 1921, 'there are somewhere about a million people who by the rest of the population are regarded on religious grounds as pariahs and outcastes, whose touch is regarded as a defilement, who are not allowed to draw water from the village well, whose children are not allowed even to enter the ordinary schools. These disabilities are in force altogether apart from the personal cleanliness or position of the individual and are solely based upon caste.'

Idolators and Monotheists in the Deccan (p. 153).

'The bulk of the people are polytheist, not many are monotheists pure and simple.' (*Census 1911 Report*, p. 67).

Bhāgavata Devotion to Vishṇu and Śiva (pp. 156–8, and 27).

'If a coolie or a cartman were asked if he were a Vaishṇava or a Śaiva he would not understand the question. . . . The inhabitants contribute to the local festivals of both religions alike, there is no conception of the idea that the two religions are mutually exclusive. The Brāhman recognizes differences of sect and would be able to say whether he was a follower of Vishṇu or Śiva, but the ordinary villager . . . is content to worship the village godlings to whom he looks for rain, etc. . . . There are, as it were, two religions; a work-a-day religion to meet the requirements of everyday existence and a higher religion, known only to the Brāhman who is called in to officiate on great occasions, which the average man does not attempt to understand. . . . Their death-bed *mantras* would be invocations to Śiva and Vishnu respectively. A curious instance of a death-bed *mantra* which combines the names of both deities is to be found among the *Bhāgvat* sub-sect of the Shenvī Brāhmans, who say "Śiva, Śiva, Nārāyan" when they are about to die. . . . Some of the officiating priests at Paṇḍharpūr are *Bhāgvatas* that is, worshippers of both Vishnu and Śiva. They may owe their standing in a Vaishṇava temple to the legend that the founder of the Viṭhobā shrine housed his idol in a disused temple of Mahādev' (*Ibid*. pp. 66–8).

On the problem of how Vishnu and Śiva became one in worship, S. M. Edwardes believes that foreign invaders led to 'a reconciliation between the two warring sects of Śaivas and Vaishnavas, which is symbolized in the installation of an image of Vithobā (Vishṇu) in the temple of Paṇḍharī . . . and its association with the *liṅga* of Śiva' ('Introduction' to new edition of Grant Duff's *History of the Mahrattas*, p. lxv).

Tukārām No Reformer (pp. 160–5.)

S. M. Edwardes (*Ibid*, p. 68) has fallen into the error of M. M. Kunte when the latter described Tukārām as a 'revolutionist', the former speaking of Tukārām's 'crusade' against Brāhman ritual, ceremonial and priestcraft, but if our argument holds good Tukārām was no 'crusader'.

N. V. Tilak as a poet (pp. 165, 238)

In his Presidential address to the Conference of Marāthi writers held at Baroda, November 26, 1921, Mr. N. C. Kelkar, editor of the *Kesarī*, said that among present-day Marāṭhī poets Nārāyan Vāman Tilak, 'received and deserved the honour of elder.' See *Kesarī*, Nov. 29, 1921.

The Upanishads on Inward Religion (p. 226)

In his *Thirteen Principal Upanishads* (*p.* 405, Dr. R. E. Hume of Union Theological Seminary, New York, gives the subject-title 'The Saving Knowledge of One, Kind, Immanent Supreme God of the Universe' to the stanzas IV. 11–20 of the *Śvetāśvatara* Upanishad, translating stanza 20 thus:

His form is not to be beheld.
No one soever sees Him with the eye,
They who thus know Him with heart and mind.
As abiding in the heart, become immortal.

Similarly, on p. 396, he gives the subject-title 'The All-Pervading Soul', to stanzas I. 15–16 of the same Upanishad, and translates 15:

As oil in the sesame seeds, as butter in cream,
As water in river-beds, and as fire in the friction-sticks
So is the Soul (*Ātman*) apprehended in one's own soul,
If one looks for Him with true austerity (*tapas*).

To stanzas IV 22–13 in the *Katha* Upanishad he gives the title, 'The Eternal Lord Abiding in one's self', with the twelfth stanza thus translated:

A Person of the measure of a thumb
Stands in the midst of one's self (*ātman*),
Lord of what has been and of what is to be.
One does not shrink away from Him.'

See also his translations of *Śvetāśvatara* Upanishad, III. 13 and *Katha* Upanishad, VI. 18, on his pp. 401, 361, Dr. P. R. Bhandarkar and the present writer p. 246.

'As for the argument with Dr. Prabhākarrao, who in the *Subodh Patrika* had observed that the present writer was 'child-like (I had almost used an allied word) in his faith,' and 'blinded by gross prejudice,' we assured him of two things, first, that our faith was every bit as 'child-like' as he had suggested, and secondly, we pointed out that in repudiating the distinction we had drawn between sin-stricken Tukārām and the sinless Redeemer he had taken up an attitude to Jesus which no school of Christian thought would support and which our accepted principles of scientific interpretation could only pronounce as untenable. . . . . Our position, in conversation with our critic, was that the lifelong miracle of Christ's character was of far deeper significance *as a miracle* than either the miraculous birth or the miraculous resurrection: grant the sinlessness, then *every other* miracle was possible. The striking fact, as we pointed out, is that all schools of Christian interpretation accept whole-heartedly the sinlessness of Jesus, so that our friend Dr. Prabhākarrao could not pit any liberal or modernist school against the orthodox editor who had so disturbed his peace. . . . . . We concluded by urging that the record in the four Gospels themselves be carefully studied to see if a view so universally accepted by millions of thinking people the world over could be so wide of the mark as our learned friend had suggested. And this is our plea with every thinking Indian who has difficulty about the Lord Jesus Christ. Study methodically the record of His life with an open mind, pray (in your own way) for light as you read, and resolve by God's help to follow whatever light comes.'

(*Dnyānodaya* Nov. 24, 1921, from an account of an interview between Dr. P. R. Bhandārkar and the present writer).

Appendix V

Bibliography

A selection of the relevant literature on the subject is indicated in the footnotes throughout this book and the aim of the present bibliography is merely to bring together the chief authorities and so guide the student of Tukārām as to what are likely to be the most helpful aids to further study. In the following list, which in no way claims to be exhaustive, the bracketed letters (E) and (M) signify that the book or article is in English or Marāthī respectively. See page of 'abbreviations' for explanation of those letters not given in full.

I. Historical and Philological

Bombay Gazetteer (1885) vol. xx. (E), the section on Paṇḍharpur; full of information unobtainable elsewhere.

V. L. Bhāve's (M) *History of Marāṭhī Literature* up to 1819 (1919) is far and away the best work dealing with the wonderful literature of the Marāthās.

Grant Duff's (E) *History of the Mahrattas* in 2 vols. newly edited by Mr. S. M. Edwardes, G.S.I., G.V.O., with an 'introduction' (1921) on Marāthā 'origins' and 'literature' etc., and annotations throughout. The only authoritative complete work covering the whole Marāṭhā period, though some of the author's views are contested by Indian scholars.

'C. A. Kincaid and D. B. Parasnis' (E) *History of the Marāthā People* (1918). Only vol. I is thus far published, dealing with the period to the death of Śivaji; the forthcoming second volume is to bring the story up to A.D. 1750, and the 3rd to A.D. 1818, with short appendices on the Marāthā States between 1818 and now. Comparisons with Grant Duff's work impossible until completed.

C. A. Kincaid's (E) *Tales of the Saints of Paṇḍharpūr* (1919). Traditions of Marāthā Saints translated into English.

Molesworth's *Marāthī and English* Dictionary (1857). Must be reckoned one of the finest dictionaries in India, but needs bringing up to date in certain parts.

W. B. Patwardhan's (E) *Wilson Philological Lectures* (1917) on 'The influence of the Saints of the *Bhakti* School in the Formation and Growth of Prākṛit Literature', published in the *F. C. M.*, Dec. 1917 to July 1919. The most useful account, from the popular standpoint, of the history and influence of the Marāthā saints and their books.

M. G. Ranade's (E) *Rise of the Marāthā Power* (1900). A brilliant fragment.

N. B. Ranade's *Twentieth Century English Marāthī* Dictionary (1916). Embodies conclusions as to Marāthī renderings of modern English words up to 1916.

II Biographical

Mahīpati's (M) *Bhakta Līlāmrita* (1774), chaps. 25–40, and *Bhakta Vijāya* (1762–3), chaps. 48–52, are the foundation of everything both in Marāthī and English. See our pp. 69–77 and 20–21 for estimates of the value of Mahīpati's works.

Dr. Murray Mitchell's (E) translation of part of the *Bhakta Līlāmrita* in *J R.A.S Bo.*, Jan 1849, is the only one we know and has supplied three or four pages in our chapter IV (see p. 109, footnote 3; p 114, footnote 3; p. 117, footnote. See further Appendix III)

Several Marāthī 'Lives' have been published, the latest by Mr. L. R. Pāngārkar (M), *Śrī Tukārāmāce Caritra* (1920) probably being the best, though the work must be pronounced deficient, first from the standpoint of the inadequate biographical material included and second because Mr. Pāngārkar has unfortunately accepted all the traditions regarding Tukārām without any critical examination of any kind. There are other useful Marāthī 'Lives,' among them being those by K. A. Keluskar and V. Mādgaokar.

III Editions of Tukaram's Poems

See the list given on page 120 with the discussion on their respective merits.

The (M) *Indu Prakāsh* (1869) still retains the premier position and it has also a brief biography both in English and Marāṭhi.

On Mr. V. N. Joga's edition with its commentary, see under 'interpretation.'

V. L. Bhave's (M) *Tukārāmācī Assal Gāthā* (1920) embodies the latest findings. See our pp. 121–2 and since then an article by B. A. Bhide in *Vividha Dnyāna Vistāra*.

Fraser and Marāthe's (E) *The Poems of Tukārām* in 3 vols. Prose translations (1909–15) of 3721 of Tukārām's *abhangs*, arranged under order of topics with notes and appendices. Though not a 'complete English translation' as erroneously stated by Dr. Farquhar (*O. R. L I.* p. 374) and though some renderings are disputed by Marāthī scholars this still remains the only English work giving anything like an adequate idea of the number and variety of Tukārām's verses.

IV Interpretation of Tukaram

Dr. Sir R G. Bhandārkar's (E) *V.S.M.R.S.* (1913), chapters xxv–vi, pp. 92–101. An authoritative statement of Tukārām's place in the *Bhakti* School of Vaishṇavism. The same author's (M) *Writings and Lectures* (1919) on religious subjects, with 100 pages of a (M) biography of this great *bhakti* scholar by Sir N. G. Chandāvarkar. A unique volume of expositions of Marāṭhī *bhakti*.

Dr. Prabhakar R. Bhandārkar's (E) *Two Masters: Jesus and Tukārām* (1903). See chapter x, section 4. The same author's (M) article in *Nava Yuga*, March, 1921, ably criticizing Mr. Pāngārkar's book referred to above. This criticism has since been been reprinted in pamphlet form.

Rev. Nehemiah Goreh's (M) *Tenets of Tukārām* (1892). Too unsympathetic, though correct on some points.

For a systematic study of Tukārām's poems, the 2 vols (M) by the late Mr. Vishṇuboa N. Joga, an edition of 4149 *abhangs* (1909), is far the best. See p. 121 in our chapter v. A running paraphrase unravels many hard knots, though a line of interpretation is often adopted which other schools reject.

Dr. Hastings' *E. R. E.* English articles on *Bombay*, vol. 2 (Crooke), *Bhakti Mārga*, vol. 2 (Grierson), *Mysticism (Indian)*, vol. 9 (Macnicol), *Prārthanā Samāj*, vol. 9 (Farquhar), *Tukārām*, vol. 12 (Edwards).

Dr. Macnicol's (E) *Psalms of the Marāṭhā Saints* (1919). The best presentation by a missionary, from the appreciative standpoint, of the whole spirit of Marāṭhī *bhakti*, and showing its approximation to Christian truth, with 75 of Tukārām's *abhangs* translated into felicitous English poetry, though some Marāṭhī interpreters would not accept all the renderings given.

Dr. Macnicol's (E) *Indian Theism* (1915). An illuminating book, pp. 120–8 particularly useful on present subject. See also its index *under* Tukārām.

Rev. G. R. Navalkar's (E) *Tukārām, Mahārāshtrian Poet and Saint* (1908). A treatise full of true discernment and embodying the Christian point of view.

Periodicals:

Subodh Patrikā (E & M), weekly organ of the Bombay Prārthanā Samāj: *Dnyānodaya* (E & M), weekly organ of seven Missions; *Vividh-Dnyāna-Vistāra*, (M), monthly; *Indian Interpreter*, (E) quarterly; all four have occasional articles on subjects related to Tukārām.

The quarterly publication of the *Bhārata Itihāsa Sanshodhak Mandaḷa*, an institution of which every student of Tukārām should be a member; office; 314, Sadashiv Peth, Poona. Also *The Annals of the Bhandārkar Oriental Research Institute*, Poona.

The *J. R. A. S. Bo.*, especially an article (1910, vol. 23, No 65) by L. J. Sedgwick, I. C. S. A notable exposition of Marāṭhī *bhakti*.

INDEX OF 'ABHANGS'

Since this book has mainly English readers in view the following list of Tukārām's *abhangs* has reference to the only English edition approximating to anything like completeness, viz , Fraser and Marāthe's prose translations of 3721 *abhangs* out of the 4621 in the—so far—standard Marāthī edition published by the *Indu Prakāsh* press As the corresponding numbers in the latter edition are given at the end of vols II and III of *F and M* there is no need to repeat them here, save in a few cases where special reference has been made, which cases are dealt with by the letter 'I' Similarly with Dr Macnicol's poetical translations of 76 of Tukaram's *abhangs* in his *Psalms of Marāthā Saints* (numbered xxxiii to cviii), out of these the present work has referred to 27, which will be found indexed in the following columns by the letter 'S' after the number referring to *F and M's* prose numbers To summarize, left-hand figures in the columns below refer to the order of *abhangs* in Fraser and Marāthe's *Poems of Tukārām*, referred to throughout the present work under the abbreviation *F and M* , right-hand figures refer to the pages of the present book, the letter 'I' to the *Indu Prakāsh* edition; and the letter 'S' to Dr Macnicol's *Psalms of Marāthā Saints*. A separate list is added of a few *abhangs* not translated by *F and M*.

'Abhangs' not translated in F. and M.

From *Indu Prakāsh* Edition	Page
(1) 8–11	116
28	116
1579	157
2306	211
2488	164
	236
4297	162
4420	118
Lines 25–30, p. 667 vol. II, 218,	218, 247
(2) From *Psalms of Marāthā Saints*	
LIV (p. 67)	118
(3) From V. N. Joga	
1728	164
(4) From Tukārām Tātya's Edition	
4733 (vol. I, p. 684)	154 f

INDEX OF AUTHORS

INDEX OF SUBJECTS

C

D

E

I

N

O

P

W